XENOGRAFFITI

ESSAYS ON FANTASTIC LITERATURE AND OTHER DIVERS TOPICS

SECOND EDITION
REVISED AND EXPANDED

by

Robert Reginald

THE BORGO PRESS
An Imprint of Wildside Press
MMV

*I.O. Evans Studies in the Philosophy
and Criticism of Literature*
ISSN 0271-9061
Number Thirty-Three

Copyright © 1996, 2005 by Robert Reginald
All rights reserved. No part of this book may be
reproduced in any form without the expressed
written consent of the publisher.

Published in the United States of America by
The Borgo Press, an imprint of Wildside Press
www.wildsidepress.com

Library of Congress Cataloging-in-Publication Data:
Reginald, R.
   Xenograffiti : essays on fantastic literature / by Robert Reginald.
    p. cm. — (I.O. Evans studies in the philosophy and criticism of literature, ISSN 0271-9061 ; no. 33)
   Includes bibliographical references and index.
   ISBN 0-8095-0900-8 (cloth). — ISBN 0-8095-1900-3 (paper)
   1. Fantastic fiction—History and criticism. I. Title. II. Series: I.O. Evans studies in the philosophy & criticism of literature ; no. 33.
PN3435.R44 2005   96-35246
809.3'8766—dc20   CIP

SECOND EDITION

CONTENTS

Introduction: Ooze from the Muse (2003) 7

1. Anatomy of a Phenomenon (1968) 9
2. Languid Dreams: Andrew Lang and *The Book of Dreams and Ghosts* (1972) 19
3. "They" Live! The Parodies of H. Rider Haggard (1978) 23
4. Dance of the Spheres: Keith Roberts and the *Pavane of History* (1979) 28
5. A Stitch in Time: Free Will in Ward Moore's *Bring the Jubilee* (1979) 34
6. Once Upon a Time: An Introduction to *The Holy Grail Revealed: The Real Secret of Rennes-le-Château*, by Patricia and Lionel Fanthorpe (1982) 40
7. Neb (1983) 50
8. Beware of the House: The Nature of Reality in Daphne du Maurier's Fantasy (1983) 54
9. Comeau's *Magic* (1983) 58
10. Curious Things: The Horror Fiction of Eleanor M. Ingram (1983) 62
11. The Devil Took Her!: Charlotte Haldane's *Melusine* (1983) 66
12. Gory Interludes: John Norman and the Ennui of Sexual Fantasy (1983) 70
13. Jewels of Fantasy: The Dunsanian Pastiches of Vernon Knowles (1983) 76
14. The Life of Death: Robert Nathan and the Necessity of Love (1983) 80
15. Merovingian Dreams: The Neustrian Fantasies of Leslie Barringer (1983) 84

16. One Is One and All Alone: Fritz Leiber's
    Solipsistic Fantasy (1983)..91
17. Paladorean Idylls: Sir Henry Newbolt's *Aladore*
    (1983)...95
18. Prospero Updated: The Fantasy of John Bellairs
    (1983)...99
19. Strange Lessons: Edward Heron-Allen's
    Cosmopoli Tales (1983)..103
20. Styx Tryx: The Humorous Fantasies of John Kendrick
    Bangs (1983)..107
21. A Thousand Nights in Serendip: Piers
    Anthony's *Hasan* (1983)..113
22. Vivo, Ergo Sum: The Problem of Immortality in
    Edwin Lester Arnold's *Phra the Phoenician*
    (1983)...117
23. Between Order and Chaos: The Fiction of Bruce
    McAllister (1986)..121
24. Moral/Immoral: The Fictional Universe of
    Michael Reaves (1986)...125
25. Teacher-Preacher: R. Lionel Fanthorpe and the
    Literature of Abundance (1986)...128
26. The Stafford Connection: An Introduction to *Stafford
    County, Virginia Tithables, 1723-1790*, by John Vogt
    and T. William Kethley, Jr. (1990)....................................131
27. The Brush of Æons: George Zebrowski's Fictional
    Universe (1991) 140
28. Derynian Dreams: The Fantasy Worlds of
    Katherine Kurtz (1991)...145
29. The Fat Man, the Consulting Detective, and the Seller
    of Speculations: The Curious World of Arthur Byron
    Cover (1991) 150
30. Slicing Away at Suburbia: The Fantastic Fiction of
    William F. Nolan (1991)...154
31. A Modest Proposal (1991)..158
32. Pilgrim Award Acceptance Speech (1993).......................162
33. A Requiem for Starmont House and FAX
    Collector's Editions, 1972-1993: A
    History and Bibliography (1993).......................................167
34. Laughing Like Hell: Brian Stableford's
    World of Agony (1995) 202

35. Margaret Atwood: The Young Woman in
    Agony (1996)..206
36. A Turbot at a Time: The Mystery Novels of
    Lindsey Davis (1996)..212
37. Thirty Years, 1965/66-1995/96: An Introduction to
    T Tauri (1996)...215
38. Measuring the Marigolds: The Fall and Rise of
    Borgo Press (2003)..217
39. On Be(com)ing a Librarian (2003).........................221
40. KO'd at the OK Corral; or, The Perils of Pullulating
    Pseudonymity (2003)...228
41. A Few Words, a Very Few Words, on Writing
    (2003)...231
42. Double Your Pleasure, Double Your Fun, Schizoid
    Living for Everyone! On Being a Pseudonym
    (2003)...235
43. Selected Reviews (1971-1993)..............................239
44. Selected Obituaries (1983-2003)...........................275
45. Amen for Now (2003)...296

Bibliography...299
Index..306

DEDICATION

For My Favorite People- and Dog-Sitter,

ΣΤΑΥΡΟΥΛΑ Η ΒΙΒΛΙΟΘΗΚΑΡΙΑ

and, as always, for

ΜΑΡΙΑ Η ΑΓΑΠΗΤΗ

Lifesavers in Every Sense of the Word

ABOUT THE AUTHOR

ROBERT REGINALD (Professor Michael Burgess) lives in San Bernardino, California, with Mary (his lifelong companion) and two old dogs, Easy and Mellie. He's a bit of an old dog himself, by all accounts. He played chess with the Grim Reaper during the summer of '03, but came away with a temporary draw (no more). He hopes he has yet a few more years to write and edit and kvetch about stuff in general.

Xenograffiti, by ROBERT REGINALD

INTRODUCTION

OOZE FROM THE MUSE

I am not the same person that I was when *Xenograffiti* first appeared in November of 1996. The intervening years have dealt harshly with me and mine, leaving me wondering, at times, what awful things could possible happen to us next. I will not try to enumerate the tragedies or occasional joys that Mary and I encountered during the recent past. Sufficient unto the day is the evil thereof, as Brother Theophilus (and my early Jesuit teachers) might say, and it is better not to dwell overmuch on such matters.

These random reflections of my writing existence, these miscellaneous essays penned over an authorial career that has now spanned some thirty-five years, were written mostly for cold hard cash, on assignment, to specifications provided by the respective publishers of the original pieces. Some have been modified here (a few rather severely), both to update them and to correct misstatements or misapprehensions on my part; but I have generally resisted the temptation to rework them in their entirety. I've tried to preserve the flavor of what I wrote back then, in that previous life, when I was young and full of vim and willing to tackle any exercise that might come my way.

The essays lack (for the most part) any philosophical underpinnings or academic jargon, first because they were not penned for such purposes or for such publications, and also because I have always preferred to adopt the tone of the delighted reader who wants to share his discoveries and excavations in literature with his interested friends (*viz.*, all of you). To me, "academese" only gets in the way of such

Xenograffiti, by ROBERT REGINALD

communication, and should therefore be discarded by any intelligent soul; and I make the presumption that anyone reading these words *per se* falls within the latter category!

I have added a few new autobiographical pieces written especially for this new edition, reflecting certain of the travails of the past few years, and perhaps providing the reader with some insight into my life and work. The contrast with the less personal essays reprinted elsewhere in the volume is deliberate: I can write both ways, when and if I choose.

Throughout my career, I have mostly worked at lengths longer than the accumulation of these short pieces might suggest to the casual reader. This is merely a reflection of where and when I was then receiving contracts for writing projects. Sometimes circumstances do change: in the past five years, Mary and I penned some 13,000 literary obituaries for various reference works published by the Gale Group, again, because that's just where our major assignments made their appearance during that half-decade. Hidden almost entirely from view is the extensive editorial service that I've performed over the past three decades for a half dozen publishers, editing (and sometimes rewriting) at least 650 books *in toto*.

My frequent collaborator and chief editor and dearest friend in all these matters, Mary A. Burgess, has also been my partner in life these past twenty-eight years; she deserves much credit for whatever quality is present here, for she has always been my first and most critical reader, in the kindest sense of that word. She saw most of this work in its infancy, and made innumerable suggestions to improve it, some of which I actually had the good sense to heed. What I would have done without her constant kindness, advice, and comfort, particularly during the horrific events of the past year, I just don't know.

Grazie, cara mia, grazie.

—Robert Reginald
(Prof. Michael Burgess)
San Bernardino, California
22 November 2003-3 August 2004

Xenograffiti, by ROBERT REGINALD

I.

ANATOMY OF A PHENOMENON

(1968)

NOTE: *I have added to this Second Edition my first professionally published essay, released just after my twentieth birthday, both to provide contrast with my later, more polished work, and to show my thinking at this early date. The history of science fiction related here is much oversimplified and even erroneous in parts, and I have removed several paragraphs of obvious anachronisms discussing then-current editorial policies of then-current editors near the end of the piece, as well as the now obsolete bibliography. Although the essay as a whole is somewhat turgid, I was still amused to find my earlier self predicting virtual reality.*

This essay was written to provide information concerning a phenomenon unique to our times—science fiction. Science fiction is literature, and as such is universal in patronage and scope. Since its inception some forty years ago, the genre has also been universally maligned, and only now is the field receiving the critical attention it deserves. There yet exists, however, an abysmal ignorance of what science fiction is, and, more importantly, of what it attempts to do. The best answer to this problem would be wide reading in the field; unfortunately, this is not often practical—hence this partial and abridged solution. Since it attempts to relate a definition and history of this genre, this paper necessarily contains much oversimplification. The best and most read-

Xenograffiti, by ROBERT REGINALD

able sections have been boiled down from excellent science fiction critics and historians, especially Judith Merril, Sam Moskowitz, Kingsley Amis, and Algis Budrys; the author must lay claim to the obscure and difficult. The author also regrets that space was insufficient to provide the examples and clarifications he felt necessary.

True science fiction possesses five readily observable qualities:

1. Science fiction is postulational, speculating on any person or thing under any conceivable (or inconceivable) conditions. Early science fiction wondered about strange places and occurrences, and man's reactions to their challenges. Later, the physical sciences and future technology were minutely explored, especially as those fields affected human society. The 1950s saw the examination of how the social sciences altered social structures when applied to and through the individual. The modern sub-genre, The New Wave, critically probes man the individual, and those disciplines closest to him, the fine arts. During all four periods of science fiction development, man was the proper subject for speculation.

2. Speculation is found in all literature; yet a peculiarity of the genre facilitates the easy interweaving of speculative themes. Science fiction possesses what I call a "foreign atmosphere," a certain strangeness in background which sets off the genre from mainstream literature. Wherever or whenever the plot takes place, it is pervaded with an eerie quality, a distinguishing air of the weird: perhaps an exotic setting in otherwhen or on a far-off world, or an alien culture or the aliens themselves, a man with unusual powers, a strange intervention produced by or producing unearthly effects, a catastrophe with freakish overtones, or simply an odd and unexplained occurrence in nature.

3. Science fiction stories must have, at the very least, a framework of science and technology, pseudo or otherwise. The importance of technology in the individual story varies from total emphasis (as in much of the science fiction of the 1940s) to almost no emphasis (in much of modern SF tech-

Xenograffiti, by ROBERT REGINALD

nology forms a shadowy background setting for a story which could occur at any place or time, including our own).

4. In four decades of science fiction literature, a standard set of rules, plots, devices, and vocabulary have cloaked the field in a shroud of cliquishness, obscurity, and isolationism. Readers are expected to understand such devices as time travel, interstellar travel (whether faster-than-light, inter-dimensional, or sub-light), the three laws of robotics, and so on. Science fiction authors, most of them one-time fans, have long since digested these plots, and spew them back at random throughout their own works. A basic background knowledge of the field is required for intelligent reading of science fiction.

5. Science fiction is logical in its speculations. Here the line is drawn between it and fantasy, which flouts logic. A science fiction world is based on reasonable extrapolations of the current situation; a fantasy world is derived solely from the imagination.

The definition which best incorporates the majority of these five elements is that of Sam Moskowitz, who states that:

> Science fiction is that branch of fantasy identifiable by the fact that it eases the "willing suspension of disbelief" on the part of its readers by utilizing an atmosphere of scientific credibility for its imaginative speculations in physical science, space, time, social science, and philosophy

I distinguish six other genres in imaginative literature: gothic horror, science fiction, weird fiction, heroic fantasy, and high fantasy. Before proceeding further, it is necessary to define and separate them so that no confusion may arise when they are later referred to.

Heroic fantasy: that branch of imaginative literature in which a hero of superhuman or at least superior qualities moves through a created, ordered, earth-like, and primitive

Xenograffiti, by ROBERT REGINALD

world to conquer totally and alone the major challenge (often evil) of that world.

Science fantasy: identical with heroic fantasy, except that the world is unearthly in culture and fauna, decadent, and usually contains elements of scientific instruments and powers intermingled with barbaric rites and weapons.

Weird fiction: that branch whose major theme is to produce by means of background a horrifying impact on our innermost instincts, and to touch our basic human reactions with revulsion.

Gothic horror: that branch of imaginative literature in which a heroine, trapped by evil within a medieval, legendary, Poe-like house or castle, is rescued after almost losing her life or soul, and then lives happily ever after with her rescuer. This is the soap opera of imaginative literature.

High fantasy: there are several types. One is that in which a hero or set of heroes overcomes the evil staining an otherwise idyllic created world. A second type is similar to science fiction except in not attempting to make its speculations credible. A third, postulated type, eternal fantasy, would occur if the cosmos became an eternal unreality, totally unlimited in time and space; such a story would become pure unending escape, whether the story emphasis is on character (where the reader himself becomes the story in an everlasting fantasy, to the exclusion of all reality), or on scenery (where the reader becomes an infinite set of characters in an unchanging world, a world which sweeps away the real world).

To give the reader a better idea of the differences and relationships between these fields, I have postulated a framework on which one may place these tags. Imagine a line on which every type of prose fiction has a point. Bisect the line: the top half is realistic or biographical literature, the lower imaginative literature. Each genre is distinguished and hung on this pole according to the time-nature of the implied world of its type of ideal story. This requires some explanation.

Every story is an implicit part of a great cycle or *kosmos* of stories. If the emphasis of a particular tale is on the hero, then the implied *kosmos* or framework for further such tales is that character's life. If on the other hand the story is built around the background (minimizing the importance of the characters), then the implied world is the setting. In many cases the main character and background are evenly balanced; here one must consider the implicit whole to be a combination of the two.

I place the genres on the line of literature according to the time sense of their respective *kosmoi*. The world of the autobiography, the top terminus of the line, is the life of its author; the ideal life-story would start with the author's birth and end with his death. This genre thus has a definite *kosmotic* beginning and end, and is limited in time. All biographical literature is defined in this way.

The ideal genre of imaginative literature would be the projected, non-existent field of eternal fantasy, with its pure, unending escape. Genres are placed into the category of imaginative literature if the time-senses of the *kosmoi* are infinite in some way, lacking beginning, middle, or end.

Between biographical literature and imaginative literature is a shadowy area possessing a *kosmotic* time-sense of uncertain length. Much of the science fiction of the 1940s and '50s falls into this category. Each genre is ranked by story type according to how closely it approximates the ideal genres (autobiography and eternal fantasy) of each half of the line.

The history of modern science fiction begins with the founding of the first science fiction magazine, *Amazing Stories*, in 1926. It was only then that writers found an outlet for their work, and science fiction gained a general circulation among the public. Three forerunners appeared in the fifty years preceding this date, and they had an overwhelming influence on the later course of the field. Jules Verne, H. G. Wells, and H. Rider Haggard all left groups of writers, almost schools, who followed their styles of writing.

Haggard, although not a science fiction writer, wrote adventures set in strange locales far from civilization. His works are permeated with lost races and cultures, strange people and devices, and reincarnation. Pulp science fiction followed his lead. Verne attempted to predict and postulate

Xenograffiti, by ROBERT REGINALD

the wonders of tomorrow through analysis and projection of today's science into the future. He stressed the scientific accuracy of his inventions, laying emphasis on the logical development of the machine and technology. Technological science fiction carries on his work in this area. Wells concentrated on society rather than the machine. To him technology and marvelous inventions were movable backgrounds for his main interest, development and change in human groups. His work is the prototype for sociological science fiction.

Early issues of *Amazing* consisted mainly of reprints of semi-science fictional works originally published in scattered magazines and book collections during the first two decades of the century. Hugo Gernsback, its founder and publisher, was forced to develop an entirely new kind of writer; professionals of the time, regarding the field as juvenile, refused to submit material. Consequently, the first decade of science fiction history was filled with a succession of hack amateurs, most of whom fell before the onslaught of quality writing in the late 1930s.

The major form of the first quarter century of science fiction history (to about 1950) was the short story. Science fiction writers had but one publishing outlet, the magazines, and these tended to concentrate on shorter subjects. Novels, when published, were serialized. Both short stories and longer works were simple in plot and Victorian in outlook. Indeed, writing standards in general were on a par with those of the 1890s. Following the lead of Haggard (who was a Victorian writer), nearly all of these stories were fabulous adventures set in strange locales, whether on an unexplored region of the earth, another planet, or another world via time or inter-dimensional travel. Explanations for scientific devices used in these tales were almost always glossed over; few pulp writers had scientific backgrounds. All of the stories were imbued with a childish "sense of wonder." For this reason, the SF of this period is often looked upon with nostalgia, but sheer lack of readability prevents much of it from ever being reprinted.

A late and curious development of the pulp period was the space opera, consisting of novel and multi-novel

Xenograffiti, by ROBERT REGINALD

length melodramas on a truly cosmic level. This form bombards the reader with such a rapidly expanding scale of distances and forces that, having no time to readjust himself to any one frame of reference, he is left stunned and numb from its creative impact. As in many other Victorian works, this sub-genre makes an extremely sharp distinction between good and evil. The hero, totally good, always encounters totally evil aliens seeking to destroy or enslave the human race; in the end, these creatures, being unreformable by nature, are wiped out to the last individual. The "it's us or them" attitude always prevails. Human villains exist for character conflict; women occur only to provide a simple love interest for the hero. A curious trait of the space opera is that, while a hero is always present, he is rarely the most notable character—the show is often stolen by the villain. The most successful writer of space operas was the founder of the sub-genre, E. E. "Doc" Smith. His famous tetralogy, *The Skylark Series*, opens with an invention of a means of space travel, and closes playing with universes and forces infinitesimal in magnitude.

Stanley G. Weinbaum inaugurated the modern period of science fiction with a series of stories published in the pulps in 1934-1935. His innovations merely followed the professional mainstream guides for literature in the 1930s: slick writing, a light, jaunty style, good characterizations, an excellent scientific background for his stories, and a treatment of alien life as wholly ahuman creatures.

Weinbaum's writing practices were sustained and enlarged upon by John W. Campbell, Jr., whose appointment to the editorial chair of *Astounding Stories* in 1937 signaled the founding of the second magazine school. Campbell demanded a high degree of sophistication for even the average story, in both style and idea. Science fiction became characterized by indirection is presentation of scientific material. To carry out his ideas, Campbell raised a new crop of young, professional authors with scientific educations; and in the following decade these writers (the best were Robert A. Heinlein, Isaac Asimov, A. E. van Vogt, and Theodore Sturgeon) examined virtually every conceivable aspect of future technology and science. During these ten years Campbell

Xenograffiti, by ROBERT REGINALD

alone dictated the course of the field, publishing every major science fiction work of the 1940s (with the exception of the stories of Ray Bradbury, who evolved separately from mainstream science fiction). He lost this sphere of influence when H. L. Gold founded *Galaxy* in 1950.

Gold shifted the emphasis to the social sciences, and like his predecessors Gernsback and Campbell, cultivated a new group of authors to write science fiction as he saw it (Poul Anderson, Philip K. Dick, Philip José Farmer, John Brunner, and Robert Silverberg all date from this period). Psychology was an integral part of these stories; Gold's school asked such questions as: How would societies of tomorrow be affected by ensuing technological and sociological changes? What kind of philosophy would future and alien societies be founded on? Individual man's inner, conjectured powers and mutations (ESP, telepathy, etc.) were carefully probed and measured, especially as they affected the society in which man dwelt. Farmer, James Rush, and others criticized current mores of religion and sex, formerly taboo subjects, and now touched upon for the first time with any intelligence. By 1960 this type of modern science fiction had almost completely displaced earlier forms. A major factor in the rise of its popularity was perhaps the upswing of the SF novel which began in the late 1940s. At first specialty houses, and then larger firms and paperback lines, began active programs in publishing hardcover and paperbound SF books. The magazines began to die.

By the early 1960s it was evident that a new wave in science fiction was about to break over the field, washing away the sense of stagnation. Fritz Leiber's *The Big Time* (Hugo Award for Best Science Fiction Novel, 1958), Heinlein's *Stranger in a Strange Land* (Best Novel, 1962) and *Starship Troopers* (Best Novel, 1960), and works by Philip K. Dick and Harlan Ellison all pointed to the advent of new styles and new ideas. The climactic turning point in 1962 saw the first publication of the works of J. G. Ballard in America, and the first stories by Roger Zelazny and the first novel of Samuel R. Delany. The New Wave, as it has been termed, has been defined by Judith Merril as:

Xenograffiti, by ROBERT REGINALD

...nothing more than the application of contemporary and sometimes (though mostly not very) experimental literary techniques to the kind of contemporary/experimental speculation which is the essence of science fiction.

In another context she states:

Inside science fiction the best people are reaching toward poetry, metaphysics, religion, psychology, symbolism, and myth as systems through which to explore the nature of man; and reaching too for the new techniques of expression being explored in the experimental and avant-garde fringes of the "mainstream."

The New Wave, then, consists of innovations in both style and content. Each New Wave writer varies widely in his own application of the different modes, some stressing expression, some content, and a few balancing the two. One finds that in expression these works contain poetic phrasing, fragmentary plots, loosely connected episodes, and in general mainstream avant-garde forms. Tone is personal and very much subjection.

Content forces the greatest gap between these writers and their predecessors. The New Wave explores man's inner nature and those disciplines closest to him: the fine arts. Thus, one may find fragments of poetry, artists as heroes (something which never occurred previously), problems without resolutions, a sense of great promise never attained, and much more, both exalting and detrimental. The stress has turned to what Ballard calls "inner space: that area where the outer world of reality and the inner world of the psyche meet and fuse." Science and technology become mere props, backgrounds for a story universal in scope and time, a tale which can occur anyplace or anytime.

As a result, science fiction today is in a state of great confusion, upheaval, controversy, and argumentation. The best of the new authors are writing New Wave stories; many

Xenograffiti, by ROBERT REGINALD

of the finest older writers have followed their lead in changing style and outlook. But while it is generally recognized in the field that the New Wave is the wave of the future, there remains an Old Guard who is resisting strenuously its inevitable takeover. Campbell, Asimov, and others bitterly resent the New Wave's hold on science fiction critics and the new generation of writers, regarding it as not sufficiently oriented towards science and technology. Their definition of science fiction closely follows that of Kingsley Amis:

> Science fiction is that class of prose literature treating of a situation that could not arise in the world we know, but which is hypothesized on the basis of some innovation in science and technology, or pseudo-science or pseudo-technology, whether human or extraterrestrial in origin.

Stories in which technology is only a stage setting are regarded by such critics as fantasy.

[several paragraphs cut]

Looking back, it seems that progress in science fiction has been made in extremely swift spurts followed by a decade or fifteen years of consolidation and even stagnation (it is hoped that events will proceed somewhat more rapidly with the New Wave). The future now looks bright: the New Wave was a necessary step for the field if science fiction was ever to rejoin the mainstream, if it was ever to produce quality literature, as it is now doing. This final jump six years ago left the genre quivering in shock, but it also seems to have pushed it abreast and even ahead of modern fiction. Where today can one find imagination, new ideas, different and changing modes of expression, and the most human and finest writing of our time? The New Wave, which is, I am proud to state, a part of science fiction. There is no doubt in my mind that science fiction is where the best literature is being written today.

Xenograffiti, by ROBERT REGINALD

II.

LANGUID DREAMS

ANDREW LANG AND
THE BOOK OF DREAMS AND GHOSTS

(1972)

It's a curious phenomenon of the writing world that so many of its better-known practitioners should find, at death, not only the demise of their earthly lives, but also a relatively rapid waning of their respective literary reputations. Perhaps it's just natural to strike out at the man who can no longer defend himself, or maybe it's the idea that since no further works will derive from the author's pen, whatever promise he showed earlier in his career was never quite realized; whatever the reason, it happens with astonishing regularity. Some authors never manage to recover from these critical postmortems, and spend the rest of literary eternity neither condemned nor praised, but merely dumped together with 3000 other hacks into some odd writers' limbo, or footnoted in one of an unending plague of literary histories. Others may eventually recoup a semblance of their former glory when it is discovered, quite by accident, that their books are somehow still in print, and much to everyone's surprise, still apparently being read with both enthusiasm and relish. Andrew Lang is one of these select few, for we are now witnessing a broad revival of Lang materials that augurs well for the ultimate literary judgment on this romantic Scotsman.

Xenograffiti, by ROBERT REGINALD

Lang was born at Selkirk, Scotland on March 31, 1844, at the family estate of Viewfield. The Langs were locally prominent, having settled in Selkirk some seven generations previous, and having held various town offices during much of that period. Andrew's father, John Lang, was Sheriff/Clerk of Selkirk at the time of Andrew's birth; like most of the Langs a businessman by profession, John Lang (a name later used by Austin Tappan Wright for the hero of his utopian novel, *Islandia*) had married Jan Sellar, daughter of a steward to the Duke of Sutherland, in 1843. Andrew (a common name in the Lang family) was their first child. He was a precocious youth, and taught himself to read by the age of four. Even then he possessed a remarkable memory for trivia, and by the age of seven or eight had searched out every available romantic tale and novel. He preferred short adventure fantasies, or the much longer histories of Sir Walter Scott and James Fenimore Cooper, to the stodgier classics of accepted literature. A trip to boarding school at Edinburgh at age ten sent him further into his bookish world, until he spent so much time devouring novels that all prose fiction was forbidden him by the schoolmasters. When he was then found reading Lord Byron's long romantic poem, *Don Juan*, his teachers gave up hope of restraining the boy's inclinations, and lifted the ban.

It was during these years that Lang's basic character was determined: raised in the Scottish countryside on Highland ballads and tales, and entertained thereafter largely through his own excursions into the literary world, he developed a lifelong devotion to romances and myths of every kind, and spent his most productive years collecting such tales, authoring them himself, and writing literary essays about them. Even at Edinburgh Academy, where he was force-fed Latin and Greek, he suddenly encountered the *Odyssey* of Homer, and found himself swept up in the grandeur of its epic story, not only reading it in the original Greek, but devouring the *Iliad* as well.

Lang transferred to St. Andrews University in 1861, and it was about this time that his readings broadened to include the old occult and alchemistic masters. Legend has it that he even tested some of the ancient formularies himself,

Xenograffiti, by ROBERT REGINALD

practicing the olden rites in the "haunted tower" of St. Andrews; hearsay has not, alas, provided the results of these experiments. His reactions towards the occult were somewhat mixed: while his nature inclined him towards belief in the transcendent and romantic (he was proud, for instance, of a family tradition assigning the Langs Gypsy blood, despite its probable untruthfulness); he could still parody the Latin original of magician Cornelius Agrippa with a phrase of his own: "*Hoc opus diligenter perlexi, et dico ut in amplissimo verbi sensu Bosh vel Rot vel Bolly sit*" ("This book has surveyed [its field] accurately, and I say in the fullest sense of the word that it's bosh, rot, and bolly"). In later years he tried to remain open-minded on the subject, and succeeded to the extent that his opinions then are difficult to judge from today's perspective; even the introduction to his major work on the subject, *The Book of Dreams and Ghosts*, is curiously noncommittal.

Lang entered Balliol College at Oxford in 1864. His talents as a writer were just beginning to shine forth, and one of his schoolmates noted that he could "knock off" an essay on any subject whatever in half an hour's time. By the time he went to Merton College, Oxford, in 1868, he was writing poetry, and his first book appeared during his stay there in 1872. He left Oxford in 1875, partly because of an impending marriage to Leonora Alleyne (school rules at the time forbade extension of a fellowship to married students), but primarily because of an expanding and rapidly developing career as an essayist and reviewer, a following to which he devoted thirty-seven years.

Lang was a scholar, poet, essayist, romantic novelist, and anthologist of the fairy tale; his first collection of poems was followed by more than sixty other books scattered throughout a dozen areas of knowledge. As a literary historian, he is best known for three studies of Homer which refuted the then-popular theory of collective authorship for the *Odyssey* and *Iliad*. He authored a history of Joan of Arc, and solved an historical puzzle with his novel, *Pickle the Spy*. His poetry, although published early in his career and never truly popular, had, nevertheless, a profound effect on its time, and certainly influenced British poetry of the first dec-

Xenograffiti, by ROBERT REGINALD

ades of the twentieth century. He knew well both Robert Louis Stevenson and H. Rider Haggard, and collaborated with the latter on *The World's Desire*, a fantasy sequel to the adventures of Odysseus. His own love for the romantic novel caused him to write a triad of fantasies set in the imaginary lands of Pantouflia and Fairnilee.

He is chiefly known today, and was best known in his own lifetime, for a series of twelve anthologies of fairy tales. His theme, as exemplified in the first of the series, *The Blue Fairy Book* (1889), was to present the best myths and tales of all times and civilizations in popular and readable form, packaged to attract children, and translated or rewritten to suit the language of his time. Called the "Rainbow" series for the distinctive color featured in each title, the books were an enormous commercial success, and remain in print to this day from Dover Publications.

The Book of Dreams and Ghosts first appeared in 1897, and was the first serious attempt to relate and retell the best-attested stories of psychical phenomena and ghosts with any kind of critical sense. Lang researched sources reaching back to classical times, and covering all civilizations, to discover what he believed to be the most authentic encounters of humanity with the unknown. Although he took no public stand on the material's veracity, he himself claimed to have seen three specters in his lifetime, one in 1869 of a deceased professor, another of a dark girl in 1894, and a third, the death omen of a cat, shortly before he died in 1912. His attitude is best summarized in his own words: "I do firmly believe that there are human faculties as yet unexplained, as yet inconsistent with popular scientific 'materialism.' I do believe, with all students of human nature, in hallucinations of one, or of several, or even of all the senses. But as to whether such hallucinations, among the sane, are ever caused by psychical influences from the minds of others, alive or dead, not communicated through the ordinary channels of sense, my mind is in a balance of doubt." There is no doubt, however, of the value of *The Book of Dreams and Ghosts* in preserving these accounts, and in the contribution to literature of its author, Andrew Lang.

Xenograffiti, by ROBERT REGINALD

III.

"THEY" LIVE!

THE PARODIES OF H. RIDER HAGGARD

(1978)

Sir Henry Rider Haggard (1856-1925) achieved almost instant fame with *King Solomon's Mines,* published in 1885. The book had been written in just six weeks, after his brother had challenged him to produce a better story than a recent adventure novel by Robert Louis Stevenson. Haggard followed his bestseller (it has never been out-of-print since its initial publication) with *She* (1887), which rapidly became even more popular than the earlier book. Although Haggard lived another thirty-eight years and wrote many more novels, including three others featuring Ayesha, She-Who-Must-Be-Obeyed, and another fifteen or so with Allan Quatermain, hero of *King Solomon's Mines,* as principal character, he was never again to achieve the recognition he garnered for these two early romances. His later novels have generally been forgotten and are nearly all OP at this writing.

The popularity of *She* and *King Solomon's Mines* prompted a host of imitations, as publishers tried to take advantage of Haggard's success. Indeed, the author can be said almost to have founded the "lost race" category single-handedly, for although books of this type had been published prior to 1885, it was only after that date that the genre truly began to flourish. Haggard's fictions established all the conventions of the genre: white European or American explorers are led by mysterious messages or documents or the need

Xenograffiti, by ROBERT REGINALD

to rescue other explorers into a non-surveyed part of the world, where they discover the remnants of long-lost civilizations, races, aliens, or peoples. Often these groups are bastardized descendants of such ancient groups as the Incas, Greeks, Egyptians, or Sumerians, now reduced to savagery by centuries of inbreeding. Inevitably, the explorers escape back to the modern world where "real" civilization still rules, despite the best efforts of their captors, and often the lost races are destroyed in the process. There are, of course, many different variations on this basic theme, but the pattern is the same in almost all.

The lost race genre flourished for about forty years, from the year *King Solomon's Mines* popularized the genre to to about the time of Rider Haggard's death, when the last unmapped areas of the world—the Polar Regions—were finally explored and filled in with aerial surveys. Other common settings for lost race books were Africa, central Asia, the jungles of the Amazon basin, the deserts of Australia, or the uncharted islands in little-traveled parts of the Ocean, often the Pacific. Most of the later stories were set in Antarctica. After 1930 fantasy writers began moving their settings into space or other dimensions, and the lost race category virtually vanished from the scene. Only a handful has been published since World War II.

Haggard's popularity in the mid-1880s is also reflected in the large number of parodies of his work published at that time. Haggard was not the only writer of the Victorian era to get a huge public response to his work. Sir George Chesney's future war pamphlet, *The Battle of Dorking*, had been followed by fifteen or more sequels, replies, arguments, and denials during the year it was published (1871); indeed, sequels were still being issued thirty years later. Edward Bellamy's *Looking Backward, 2000-1887* was similarly rewarded with a spate of imitations when it appeared in 1888, and the author was prompted to write his own sequel in response, *Equality* (1897), which produced its own group of imitations. Novels written to comment on Bellamy's ideas were appearing as late as the 1980s, when the late Mack Reynolds produced a set of pastiches featuring Julian West, Bellamy's protagonist.

Xenograffiti, by ROBERT REGINALD

But the response to Haggard was very different: instead of sequels, we have satires and parodies. Altogether, nine of these books were published in 1887, when the author reached the peak of his popularity. The true number of these works, and the correct information concerning the editions and authors, has long been confused by their relative scarcity and unavailability. No library or private collection appears to have a complete set. And although they received wide circulation at the time they were published, most were printed in cheap paperback form and printed on very poor quality paper; copies of the American editions which survive are generally brittle, yellowed, and crumbling.

The confusion is compounded by similarities in titles between the American and British books, and by the erroneous assumptions of scholars and bibliographers that the British and American volumes are the same. Everett F. Bleiler, writing in his *The Checklist of Fantastic Literature*, states:

> The authorship of the parodies is debatable. The Library of Congress attributes all five parodies [*He, It, Bess, King Solomon's Wives,* and *King Solomon's Treasures*] to John De Morgan (born 1848), an American writer of historical romances and juveniles, who was later to write many paperbacks for Street and Smith. The British Museum lists only *He*, in the large-paper edition, and attributes it to Andrew Lang and Walter H. Pollock.... J. E. Scott, in his bibliography of H. Rider Haggard, on the basis of a letter from E. Vizetelly, the British publisher of *King Solomon's Wives*, to the British periodical *Sketch*, attributes *King Solomon's Wives* to Sir Henry Charles [actually Chartres] Biron, a British jurist.... It seems obvious from the sources quoted above that the Library of Congress attribution of these two titles [*He* and *King Solomon's Wives*] to De Morgan is erroneous;

Xenograffiti, by ROBERT REGINALD

and that Lang, Pollock, and Biron were the true authors.

But this is not obvious at all, and is, in fact, an unjustified assumption. Actually, *all* of the attributions cited by Bleiler are correct, for there are two different books with the title *He*, and two different versions of *King Solomon's Wives*. This becomes obvious when one compares the bibliographical data for the books.

The British edition of *He*, by the Author of *It, King Solomon's Wives, Bess, Much Darker Days, Mr. Morton's Subtler, and Other Romances*, was published by Longmans, Green early in 1887; it consists of 119 pages of very large type. The American version, *He: A Companion to She, Being a History of the Adventures of J. Theodosius Aristophano on the Island of Rapa Nui in Search of His Immortal Ancestor* (no attribution of authorship), was issued in April of 1887 by Norman L. Munro, three months later than the Longmans edition, in 213 pages of very small type; both of these books are included in *They: Three Parodies of H. Rider Haggard's She*, edited by R. Reginald and Douglas Menville (New York: Arno Press, 1978).

King Solomon's Wives; or, The Phantom Mines, by Hyder Ragged [*i.e.*, Biron], was published by Vizetelly & Co. of London in 1887 in 125 pages of large type. *King Solomon's Wives*, by the Author of *He, It, Ma, Pa*, etc. [issued anonymously], was released by Norman L. Munro in 1887 in 239 pages of small type. The Munro edition was written by John De Morgan. The issue is confused further by the fact that the Munros later reprinted the Vizetelly book in one of their other series, the Seaside Library, in 100 pages of small type, complete with original pseudonym and subtitle. The Biron version has been reprinted in the anthology *King Solomon's Children: Some Parodies of H. Rider Haggard*, edited by R. Reginald and Douglas Menville (New York: Arno Press, 1978).

In addition to the two Munro books cited above, De Morgan also penned three other parodies for this paperback line: *It: A Wild, Weird History of Marvelous, Miraculous, Phantasmagorical Adventures in Search of He, She, and*

Jess, and Leading to the Finding of "IT": A Haggard Conclusion, a direct sequel to *He: A Companion to She*, and also featuring Aristophano as protagonist; *King Solomon's Treasures*; and *Bess: A Companion to Jess*. The latter two books were also reprinted in *King Solomon's Children*, and *It* was included in the anthology, *They*. The two remaining parodies, *Ma* and *Pa*, are not fantastic; both were written anonymously for Norman L. Munro in the spring of 1887 by Jacob Ralph Abarbanell, another hack writer for the line.

It is not recorded what Rider Haggard himself thought of these efforts. But if parody is the sincerest form of flattery, surely he must have been amused.

IV.

DANCE OF THE SPHERES

KEITH ROBERTS AND THE *PAVANE* OF HISTORY

(1979)

One of the more interesting and peculiar subgenres of science fiction is the alternate history, in which the known facts of past human existence are changed just enough to bring about a different result in the modern world. Hence, we have worlds in which the South won the Civil War (Ward Moore's *Bring the Jubilee* and MacKinlay Kantor's *If the South Had Won the Civil War*); in which the Nazis won World War II (Eric Norden's *The Ultimate Solution* and Philip K. Dick's *The Man in the High Castle*); in which the atom bomb never worked and the United States actually invaded the Japanese mainland (David Westheimer's *Lighter Than a Feather*); and even a novel in which the Arabs defeated the Israelis (*If Israel Lost the War*, by Richard Z. Chesnoff, Edward Klein, and Robert Littell). But perhaps the best-conceived and most human of these enterprises in destiny is Keith Roberts's masterpiece, *Pavane*.

In 1588 Queen Elizabeth I is shot and killed by a Catholic fanatic. As a result the Spanish Armada successfully invades England, Spain's Philip II becomes King, and the Catholic Church is restored to a position of pre-eminence. With the power of the English people now behind them, the Popes are able to subdue the forces of Protestant resistance throughout Europe, and once again make themselves political masters of the civilized world. The inquisi-

Xenograffiti, by ROBERT REGINALD

tion is introduced into England and the other ex-Protestant states. The American colonists remain permanently under Spanish rule.

Roberts choreographs his stately dance into six "Measures," each originally published separately, loosely connecting them to form a picture of a society in transition. The first story, "The Lady Margaret," is set in 1968, but this is a time that bears little resemblance to the year in which Martin Luther King and Robert F. Kennedy were assassinated. The Church has retarded technological progress: electricity is outlawed, and the internal combustion engine is banned. Society is restricted and controlled through a series of closed guilds and family enterprises.

Strange and Sons is one such business, a shipping firm which hauls its goods over the English countryside in six- or ten-car rail-less steam-powered trains. *The Lady Margaret* is the magnificent engine being driven by Jesse Strange, owner of the company, on the last run to the coast for the winter season. Jesse's father, Eli Strange, has recently died, and with the death of one driver, the firm is shorthanded; Jesse himself must make the final trip. The hauler's twin enemies are the cold and the *Routiers*, Norman bandits who roam the countryside looking for easy prey. But Jesse is intensely loyal to the ideals of hard work, tradition, and responsibility to his company, and he pushes on in spite of the danger and harsh conditions. Near the end of his journey he is attacked by the brigands, led by one of his old school chums; Jesse lets them have the last carriage in line, thereby saving the rest of his train. As he drives off through the night, the darkness is lit by a flash of light and a loud explosion: the bandits have been destroyed through their own greed.

The second measure, "The Signaller," is the tale of Rafe Big-land, a poor boy who has always been fascinated by the semaphore station located near his town. With electronic communication devices banned by the Church, the Popes and the state maintain chains of semaphore stations running throughout all of Europe. The Guild governing the signallers is one of the strongest in England; only twelve commoners are allowed admittance annually into the Guild's

Xenograffiti, by ROBERT REGINALD

training school. Rafe is determined to become one of the twelve, and with the help of the friendly sergeant at his local station, he obtains the proper forms, studies diligently, and wins a place in the school through a nationwide exam. The College is located in Londinium (the Latin name for London), and there Rafe learns all of the basic languages spoken in the realm—Norman French for the upper classes, Latin for the Church, modern English for commerce and trade, middle English, Celtic, Welsh, Gaelic, and Cornish for the peasant classes—in addition to signal codes and techniques, mechanics, and composition.

After several years of work, Rafe passes his exams, and is posted to a training station, a major switching center called St. Adhelm's. The final test is a daylong ordeal in which two trainees must transmit from one to the other an entire book of the Bible, signing on and off at the end of each verse. Rafe has finally become a Signaller, and is posted to his first assignment, a small personal station located in one of the great family estates. After a year's service there, he receives his first independent command, a small station located in the hills of Dorset, a lonely outpost isolated from the next nearest station by two rugged miles. The winters are harsh in the uplands, but the Signallers must still maintain vigilance. On one of his daily walks during an off-duty period, Rafe is suddenly attacked by a wildcat, and badly clawed. He crawls back to his station, falling into his bed. There he is comforted by the Fairies, a race older than mankind, before succumbing to his wounds and the bitter cold. His body is found in the spring by his replacement.

The third tale, "Brother John," examines more closely the workings of the Church. John is an engraver in the monastery of St. Adhelm in Dorset. One day he is summoned by his Abbot, and told to report to the head of the Court of Spiritual Welfare, as the Inquisition is now called in England. The Church wants a record made of the torture sessions used to extract "truth" from heretics, criminals, and political dissidents. But the sessions with the Court destroy John's artistic sense, and nearly drive him mad. When he leaves the city, John heads for the hills, plagued by visions, noises, and memories of the screams and pleadings of the victims whose sufferings he so faithfully recorded for the Pope. There he starts a revolution aimed at Church and state alike, and quickly gathers a following among the peasant class. Soldiers are assaulted and insurrections spring up around the countryside. The Cardinal Archbishop of England excommunicates the monk and puts a price upon his head in a letter dated June 21, 1985. But John escapes his pursuers when the commoners hide him from the searching soldiers, and the bounty on his body quickly escalates to two thousand pounds. John gathers a huge peasant army and marches to the coast, where he addresses the people, telling them of the great new age approaching when the Catholic Church will ease its grip upon the land, and when progress will ease the lot of the people. He turns to the sea, steps into a boat, and sails into the storm-tossed waves, on his way, he says, to see the Pope. The boat's keel is found washed upon the shore the next morning.

"Lords and Ladies" features Margaret Strange, niece to Jesse Strange, and the heir to the firm after her own father. Jesse is dying, and Margaret remembers her own adventurous life as she waits for the old man to expire. As a young woman, she had helped a poor fisher boy whose hand had been mangled in a winch. Her erstwhile companion, Robert Purbeck, son of Lord Purbeck, had then driven her home to his castle, which dominated the pass called Corfe Gate. After a brief courtship, Margaret found herself in Robert's bed, but when she awoke, Robert had been called away on the King's business. As she rode away from the massive walls, she spied an old man sitting amid the ruing pillars. This representative of the Old Ones, the Fairies, told her that the Church has a purpose and a place in this world that must be fulfilled, and it should not therefore be despised: "The great Dance finishes, another will begin." And then he vanished. She returned home to find her uncle dying. Now she sits reminiscing. After Jesse's death, Lord Robert comes for her, flogging his horse to a frenzy. One life ends, another begins.

"The White Boat," the fifth measure, was published a year after the main sequence of stories, and was not included in the British edition of *Pavane*, perhaps because its tone and

Xenograffiti, by ROBERT REGINALD

texture differs markedly from its five companion pieces. Becky, a young peasant girl, lives on the coast not far from the point where Brother John had met his untimely end. One day she sees a white boat sneak into the harbor, unload some cargo, and then move off. This pattern continues for several weeks, off and on. Finally the girl, driven away by her father's brutality at home, sneaks aboard the craft, and is taken by it to France, where a cargo is loaded and the men paid. They are obviously smuggling some secret goods into England. When she pries open a case, she finds a heretic device, a manufactured object not sanctioned by the Church; she hides one under her clothing, and takes it with her when she leaves. She shows it to her priest; he calls in the government troops to intercept the boat on its next pass. But Becky has second thoughts, and grabs the lanyard of a waiting cannon, setting it off prematurely. The white boat, now warned, turns away from the coast, laughing at the hapless guns of the enemy.

The sixth and final tale, "Corfe Gate," was actually the first written. Eleanor Purbeck, daughter and heir of Lord Robert Purbeck and Lady Margaret Strange, both now deceased, and granddaughter and sole heir of Timothy Strange, Jesse's sole remaining brother and head of Strange and Sons, has succeeded temporarily to Lordship of Corfe Gate on her father's accidental death; pending her marriage, when she will lose her independence, she rules the great castle standing astride the pass into Dorset. Shortly after her accession, Pope John XL levies new taxes on an already strained economy, and Eleanor declines to pay: her people, she says, will starve if she hands over the grain. A rakish knight is sent against her, but she meets him at the portcullis, and when he threatens Eleanor and her people, she herself ignites the cannon that kills a score of Papal soldiers. Soon the castle is invested, and the countryside is in arms. Sir John Falconer, Seneschal to Eleanor and her late father, is one of the Old Ones, the Fairies, a nonhuman race which has been helping man from before recorded history.

In the end King Charles returns to his lands and appears before the Castle, and Eleanor surrenders it to her Lord; Corfe Gate is dismantled, and Eleanor retires to ob-

Xenograffiti, by ROBERT REGINALD

scurity, later being assassinated in her old age by the King's agents. In a brief "Coda," Sir John Falconer ties together the loose ends of the story: the Church deliberately slowed technological progress until man's racial maturity had advanced to the point where atomic power would not result in mass destruction. There had been an earlier rise of mankind, an earlier Renaissance, an earlier Armada, and a civilization which had ended in flames. Only the Popes and the Old Ones knew the whole story. The siege of Purbeck had been the Church's last gasp: within ten years, Charles had gained sufficient independence to throw off his chains, and much of Europe had followed. A new Utopian Age had dawned.

Roberts's lyrical story cycle is intensely British in theme and outlook. Much of the story derives directly from the real-life history of the Isle of Purbeck, which is still dominated by the enormous ruin of Corfe Castle. During the English Civil War, Lord Bankes had placed the defense of Corfe in the hands of his wife, Lady Mary; her courage and resourcefulness were such that she was allowed to retain her lands at the end of the struggle. The castle itself was destroyed. Roberts imbues his tale with the best qualities of the English people, a curious blend of honesty, loyalty, love of tradition, and ironic dourness. Throughout the cycle we continually experience the loyalty of major characters to strongly-felt beliefs: Jesse Strange follows his ideals, even when they result in the death of his friend; Rafe Bigland is loyal unto death to the Guild of Signallers; Brother John follows his vision into the sea; Margaret Strange returns to her uncle's deathbed; and Robert Purbeck follows his love as far as he must; Eleanor surrenders her castle only to her liege lord, the King.

Indeed, the very title of the book suggests its theme: the stately dance between Church and state holds together an artificially retarded society that would otherwise disintegrate. In six clearly delineated snapshots, Roberts combines his love for the Dorset people with the grand theme of societal and cultural regeneration. "The great Dance finishes, another will begin." And so it has always been.

33

V.

A STITCH IN TIME

FREE WILL IN WARD MOORE'S *BRING THE JUBILEE*

(1979)

The philosophical debate between determinism and free will has been argued in science fiction stories and novels from the very beginning of the genre, and never more fiercely than in stories dealing with time. Can man affect the course of history? Or will the tide of events smother the most potent attempts of individuals to alter the nature of recorded reality?

Ward Moore answers these questions in *Bring the Jubilee* (1953) by having his hero, Hodge Backmaker, accidentally alter his world's history into one we recognize as our own. In Hodge's time track, the course of the Civil War was changed when Southern troops occupied Cemetery Hill and Round Top prior to the Battle of Gettysburg, thereby gaining a strategic advantage that won the battle for the Confederacy and altered the course of the war. The North was forced to surrender on July 4, 1863, leaving the nation permanently divided into two rival states. But the South, as victor, exacted a heavy price from the Federal government, forcing it to pay war indemnities that crippled its economy for decades and left it permanently impoverished, demoralized, and embittered. The South generously allowed the North to keep all the states above the old Mason-Dixon Line, but occupied Kansas, Missouri, and California, and also an-

Xenograffiti, by ROBERT REGINALD

nexed Mexico at a later date. The political rearrangement of North America affected other parts of the globe as well: France remained an Empire under the Bonaparte dynasty, and Germany became the German Union (not Empire). World War I was called the Emperors' War of 1914-1916. Still, the key event for Hodge and his fellow Northerners was always the "War of Southern Independence," as it came to be called.

Moore delineates the plight of the Northern states through the tale of Hodge's upbringing. Backmaker's family is poor, rural, ignorant, and penny-pinching. Hodge's only prospects are more of the same, or selling himself into indentured bondage to one of the small manufacturers or great landowners. Neither of these prospects is particularly appealing, so Hodge leaves home in 1938 at the age of seventeen, seeking his fortune in the great metropolis of New York. The United States has no public transportation except an expensive and inefficient railway system, and the roads are virtually impassible to anything but horse and carriage (minibiles—steam cars—do exist, but are confined to the wealthiest classes), so Hodge must walk the eighty miles to town. New York is the largest city in the United States, nearly a million strong, filled with second-rate technological marvels: cable cars, horse-cars, express steam trains, bicycles, gas lights on every corner, an intricate network of telegraph wires to every office and large household (providing instant Morse code communication from and to all central points), pneumatic lifts, and balloon airships running overhead. It also has its share of impoverished slums, tenement houses, and crime. Hodge has no sooner arrived in the Big City than he is robbed of his three dollars—a fortune in an era when 50¢ is the normal day's wage for a grown man—and left for dead. He is rescued and left with a bookseller named Roger Tyss, and Hodge's real education begins.

Tyss is a strange man, widely read, self-educated, but misanthropic, with a fatalistic philosophy of life. He takes the boy in and gives him a home, but also engages his mind in a running series of debates, queries, dialogues, and discussions. In one of the most interesting of these encounters, Tyss propounds his philosophy, a Calvinistic creed which

Xenograffiti, by ROBERT REGINALD

denies the possibility of free will. "The whole thing is an illusion," he says. "We do what we do because someone else has done what he did; he did it because still another someone did what he did. Every action is the rigid result of another action." This is a key passage in Moore's novel, the setting of the problem which Hodge will ultimately resolve. For Backmaker (and Moore) clearly believe the antithesis, that if "choice exists once, it can exist again."

One of the visitors to Tyss's shop is the Black consul for the Republic of Haiti, the sole remaining independent state south of the Mason-Dixon Line. African-Americans were ostracized from the North after the defeat of the United States, either being sent back to Africa or lynched outright—Monsieur Enfandin's position, even with diplomatic status, is not an easy one. But Enfandin is a cultured man, and makes an effort to read widely; in Hodge's life he becomes the counterbalance to the bookseller's bitter philosophy, a positive factor in Hodge's coming-of-age. Hodge decides to devote his life to history, and Enfandin is the first to hear of his decision. In the discussion which follows, the Haitian expounds his own theory of life, saying that free will is man's greatest gift. He later tells the boy that one cannot escape the responsibility of decisions merely because one fears the consequences: "Not acting is also action." Enfandin, in keeping with his philosophy, offers to help the boy gain admission to one of the few Northern colleges; when Hodge gives Tyss two weeks' notice, the bookseller points out that Backmaker has once again proved that nothing is left to chance. Hodge is a spectator type: "The part written for you does not call for you to be a participant." These words will later come back to haunt the boy with their irony.

Unfortunately, Enfandin is assaulted and returns to Haiti before fulfilling his promise; Hodge writes to the universities on his own, and receives a strange reply from Thomas Haggerwells of Haggershaven, York, Pennsylvania. Decades before, Haggerwells's grandfather had established a refuge for itinerant scholars on his farm, and over the years a center of learning and study for scientists, teachers, and researchers had developed. Haggerwells's daughter Barbara travels to the city to meet Hodge (now twenty-three), and

Xenograffiti, by ROBERT REGINALD

soon Backmaker is making the tedious train journey to rural Pennsylvania. Haggershaven proves to be the refuge he has been seeking all his life, a genial commune whose members work for the common good, contributing their financial earnings to the group in return for a secure place to pursue their researches. The farm had originally been settled by Major Herbert Haggerwells, a Confederate officer in the invading army of Robert E. Lee, who had so liked the country that he had never returned to his Southern home.

Barbara is a high-strung girl, an emotional tyrant to her men, but simultaneously the world's leading theoretical physicist, a scientist whose primary interest is the nature of time, energy, and space, and their interrelationship. They are, she says, interchangeable elements; theoretically, it should be possible to translate matter-energy into space-time. Once resolved into its component parts, anything, including man himself, could be reassembled at another point of the space-time continuum.

During the next eight years Hodge and Barbara each pursue their research independently, little realizing how their findings will ultimately converge. Backmaker begins publishing scholarly articles on the War of Southern Independence (his chosen field of study) in respected Southern and European journals (there are no such publications in the United States). The culmination of his studies is the publication of the first volume of his monumental history, *Chancellorsville to the End*. He receives a curious letter from the leading historian of his day, Polk, praising the book but questioning one of its conclusions. Hodge had mentioned in his work the key Battle of Gettysburg, the beginning of the end for the Northern forces, and how fortuitous it was that the Southern troops had occupied the Round Tops overlooking the battle site on July 1, 1863. Polk puts forth his own theory, ascribing the move to Lee's military genius, "regarding the factors of time and space not as forces in themselves but as opportunities for the display of his talents." Polk's letter so disturbs Hodge that he temporarily abandons the second volume of his work, suddenly beset with doubts. Has he indeed missed some key factor in his assemblage of the facts?

Xenograffiti, by ROBERT REGINALD

Meanwhile, Barbara has gone from theory to demonstration, persuading the community to support her efforts to build a machine that will travel through time. And now the drama comes together: when she hears Hodge is having difficulties completing his work, she offers him the chance of verifying each detail personally, by watching the battle unfold as it happens. He will be able to write history as no man has done before, from the perspective of the impartial observer actually present at the event. Initial tests confirm that the machine works within a range of one hundred years. Man can go back in time and return. Convinced by Barbara's arguments, Hodge agrees to the experiment, in which he will be sent back to midnight on June 30, 1863, the night before the battle began, and will return on midnight, July 4th.

York is about thirty miles from the battle site, and Hodge walks the distance during the night. He takes his position near the road where the Southern troops, pursuing the fleeing Federals, will push on to occupy the Round Tops, the key strategic positions on the battlefield. Before he realizes what is happening, the Rebel soldiers spot this unlikely civilian lurking in the brush, and start questioning him. Their captain rides up, and attempts to interrogate Hodge. But Backmaker is stunned by these events, because he *knows* from his research that no such pause in the Southern advance is recorded anywhere. When he fails to respond to the officer's questions, the soldiers panic and attempt to flee; the captain, whose face looks familiar to Hodge, tries to stop the turncoats, but is shot and killed by one of his own men. Hodge is left lying in the sun, alive but shaken. The battle which ensues is nothing like the one he knows: the Southern soldiers never gain a decisive advantage, and are eventually decimated in Pickett's crucial charge. The South loses the Civil War as a result. Somehow Hodge makes his way back to the barn in York by midnight of the 4th, but nothing happens. And as the sun of a new day dawns, he suddenly realizes who the captain was: Herbert Haggerwells.

Hodge's life is in direct counterpoint to the state of the Union. In the backward wreck of the twenty-six *dis*-United States, Hodge thrives and grows and becomes a man, in every sense of the word. He finds love, peace, a haven for

Xenograffiti, by ROBERT REGINALD

his studies, and companionship. But he, like all men, must take responsibility for his actions, and in attempting to learn more about the battle than he really needs to know, in attempting to become greater than history, the supremely impartial observer, he unwittingly becomes the key element in changing it. He destroys *his* history, and in the process restores the Union. The remainder of his life is spent, like most of the inhabitants of his old world, in wondering why. He lives as a ward and worker on the farm that would have been Haggershaven, and leaves these memoirs to be found by a skeptical farmer. Enfandin was right, after all: man may choose, or choose not to choose, but even that is a choice, and the consequences of man's abdication of his free will can be far more disastrous than an action purposely taken.

Moore's novel is a powerful philosophical discussion of man's place in the universe, and without a doubt the best fiction he ever penned. In posing the question of time and man's relation to it, he probes the nature of life itself. The man who waits for changes to happen to him, says the author, deserves no more than he gets. And what is true for one man is also true for the race as a whole.

Xenograffiti, by ROBERT REGINALD

VI.

ONCE UPON A TIME

AN INTRODUCTION TO
THE HOLY GRAIL REVEALED:
THE REAL SECRET OF RENNES-LE-CHÂTEAU,
BY PATRICIA AND LIONEL FANTHORPE

(1982)

"'Once upon a time...'"
The traditional words for the beginning of a fairy tale. The abracadabra that opens the magic door to a world where dreams come true, where men and women suddenly find lost treasure, become rich beyond their wildest imaginings, and live happily ever after. It can't happen in real life, of course. We all know, as we trudge our dreary ways back and forth to work each day that nothing of this sort will ever happen to us. But just suppose, just imagine what you might do with such a fortune. Because, you see, it actually happened, not so long ago, and the truth behind the story is stranger than most of the novels you've ever read or will read.
 Once upon a time, not quite a hundred years ago, there lived in southeastern France a poor priest named Bérenger Saunière, an odd name for a man with a still odder destiny. He was born and bred in a rural area rich in history, ruins, and historical artifacts. When he came of age, Saunière became a priest in the Roman Catholic faith, and upon completing his studies, was assigned to the impoverished parish church at the decaying French village of

Xenograffiti, by ROBERT REGINALD

Rennes-le-Château. The money he received, his "pay," if you will, was barely enough to feed him; the church was in bad repair, but he wasn't able to have it fixed until one of the local gentry offered a small sum to restore the altar to its original style. Rennes is an ancient place; parts of the church go back hundreds, maybe even a thousand, years; no one knows for sure. In the course of renovations, the priest uncovered a hiding place; within the alcove were some rolled scrolls and other artifacts—all this confirmed by the two men doing the construction work.

Within a few months, Saunière was lavishly spending money to improve his church, his home, and the surrounding area—he had a permanent road laid from the village to the church, for example. The priest is known to have made several trips abroad; even stranger, he was visited on several occasions by Austrian nobility, members of the imperial ruling House of Hapsburg. For more than twenty-five years, he maintained an enormously extravagant lifestyle by the standards of his community, defying all inquiries from his superiors in the Roman Catholic Church as to the origins of his sudden wealth. There is no doubt whatsoever that Saunière found a treasure of some sort, that he sold it or converted parts of it into cash, and that, within the period from the early 1890s to his death in 1917, he spent the equivalent of hundreds of thousands of dollars in modern American currency. Saunière himself was poor, his parish was poor, the surrounding community was poor, even the local gentry was poor for their class; none of these people, none of Saunière's equally impoverished relatives, no one in the community could have given him this wealth, even if he had had the means to pry it from them. And yet he died as he began, completely without resources, without ever having revealed the secret of his treasure.

For many decades, Saunière was the subject of local gossip only; he died unheralded by the world around him, although beloved by his parishioners. He was not particularly interested in the larger world in any case; he used his money to help the community and to build for himself a manor in which he never lived. It has only been within the last ten years that investigators from France and Britain have

Xenograffiti, by ROBERT REGINALD

begun looking into the mystery of Rennes-le-Château, trying to find possible explanations for the source of the treasure, trying to determine what the cache included, trying to probe for the reasons behind it all, if there are any. Several books have been published in French; three documentaries have been televised in England; and this is the second book on the subject published in English, the first, published just a month ago, having been written by the same group of British researchers who put together the television series.

Holy Blood, Holy Grail, by Michael Baigent, Richard Leigh, and Henry Lincoln, is a thoroughly enjoyable exploration of the Rennes mystery—readable, well illustrated, obviously well researched, well written. As presented, the speculations seem to fit together fairly closely with historical reality, until one actually begins thinking about them: then there are problems. All of it looks plausible enough on paper, with detailed genealogical charts fleshing out the arguments, and supposedly secret documents filling in gaps that can be bridged in no other way. The essential question remains: does it work? My gut response, having read the Baigent book, Fanthorpes' book, and other historical documents, is a fairly strong "No!"

As a professional genealogist, and one who has done an immense amount of original historical and literary research on such diverse topics as the chronology of world rulers from the beginnings of recorded history to date, a chronological checklist of Greek Orthodox patriarchs, complete genealogies of two American families dating back before the American Revolution, bibliographies of the mass market paperback and of fantastic literature, with twenty-odd published books and over a hundred articles in a wide variety of popular and professional publications, and as a person who is, moreover, a fairly well-read and -educated skeptic, I find several flaws in Baigent's theories, flaws serious enough, in my estimation, to prove fatal to his elaborate house of cards.

Let's backtrack a moment, though, and see just why Baigent's book has proved so controversial. In essence, these three British journalists claim that Christ either staged or escaped his crucifixion, had a family by Mary Magdalene, and either fled to France himself, or arranged for his wife and

Xenograffiti, by ROBERT REGINALD

children to do so. He then died at some later date, perhaps at the siege of Masada in 73 A.D. His descendants in France were the ancestors of the Merovingians, say Baigent and company, who ruled France and parts of France for several hundred years; they were then displaced by the powers behind the throne, the Carolingian "Mayors of the Palace," who proclaimed themselves kings in the eighth century A.D. But, Baigent says, some of the Merovingians survived in another part of France, and their line continued down through the middle ages to modern times, supported and nurtured by various political and social groups, who kept their faith in the "Holy Blood" of the Merovingians, and sought to restore their line as Emperors of Europe or the world, believing them to be the salvation of mankind. Some of these groups were the Knights Templar, the Cathars (Catholic heretics), and the Priory of Sion, the secret inner group of the Knights Templar, a cabal which survives to this day, according to Baigent. All of these groups used secret codes and messages to maintain their integrity; but some of the Priory's documents have been leaked by members of this group, and they confirm the Merovingian theory. This, in brief, summarizes the arguments of *Holy Blood, Holy Grail.*

Of course, such contentions, if true, would destroy the basis of the Christian faith, however it is practiced and by whatever sect or church, since they directly contradict the words of the Bible, traditions dating back two thousand years, and much established church dogma. Leaving aside religious arguments, however, there are still great difficulties with Baigent's book, difficulties which cannot be lightly passed over.

First, there is the problem of genealogy. One of the first things that a budding genealogist learns is to trust no one and no document; or, rather, to trust them with varying levels of skepticism, relying only upon well-verified documentation that, together with other proofs, establishes a pattern that can finally be accepted as "reasonably certain." For the common people—farmers, tradesmen, servants, slaves, anyone not wealthy or ennobled—it is difficult to prove lines older than about the year 1800, very difficult before the year 1700, and almost impossible prior to the year 1600—the re-

43

cords simply do not exist. For minor nobility and the very wealthy, it is difficult to establish lines before the year 1300, very difficult before the year 1200, and virtually impossible before the year 1000. For reigning royalty, there are no verifiable provable lines prior to the advent of the Merovingians circa 450 A.D.; there are various families who *claim* ancestry prior to this period, but can only provide oral documentation that has been recorded at a later date. In general, genealogies established prior to the year 1000 are based on the most fragmentary of records, and are often not provable for even major noble families holding major fiefs from the crown. One is often forced to rely on such statements as "such and such may be the son of so and so," or "it's possible that Count X was the son of Count Y mentioned in year Z," and so forth. (For a more detailed essay on the problems of establishing lines of descent, see *Genealogical Evidence,* by Noel C. Stevenson, a professional genealogist and practicing attorney.)

Baigent's theories make fascinating and entertaining reading, but the genealogical evidence is no more (and can be no more) than speculation, completely undocumented and completely without foundation. We are therefore left with the question: is it reasonable to assume that the Merovingians could have left descendants in the male line, offshoots who later proved to be the founders of several major noble families of Europe? Again I must respond negatively. We must not make the mistake of assuming that men who lived hundreds or thousands of years ago were less intelligent than ourselves; indeed, science has demonstrated that the intelligence levels of mankind have not altered appreciably in at least ten thousand years and probably for much longer. The names that we see in the history books, these olden kings, were just as bright as anyone who attains key positions of power today; they also had many of the same problems experienced by rulers throughout history. The Carolingians were self-made men, strong men, intelligent men, politically savvy men, hard men. The early members of their line shine out from the historical chronicles: such rulers as Charles Martel, Pépin III, Charlemagne ("Charles the Great") were neither fools nor ciphers. These three men had one enor-

Xenograffiti, by ROBERT REGINALD

mous political problem: although they held all the power of the state through their (now) hereditary position as Mayors of the Palace, they had absolutely no right whatever to the throne of France, under any law then in force. Pépin solved this problem temporarily by getting the pope to sanction his assumption of the crown. However, his claim was still very shaky, and one must assume that he only made his move when he felt absolutely certain that he could control the possible reaction of the people, and could remove any possible Merovingian pretenders permanently from the scene, therefore eliminating a major rallying point against his regime. Charlemagne would have been faced with exactly the same political realities.

The last Merovingian king, Childéric III, was childless, so Pépin did not need worry about his progeny; the king himself was locked away in a monastery under close guard, just to make certain that he could not escape or have children. Childéric died or was killed four years later. The historian must ask the obvious question: why was Childéric not killed immediately? The only possible response is this: his death was not necessary. Why was his death not necessary? Because all other possible pretenders were dead, leaving Childéric as the last of his line; with Childéric's death, the heir to the Merovingian line became any one of the surviving Merovingian princesses, several of whom had already been married off to the Carolingians to establish the latter's legitimacy after the fact. With Childéric under firm control (and perhaps not in the best of health), and especially with Childéric childless, there was no need to upset the natural order of things any further than they had been already, with Pépin's usurpation of the throne; there were undoubtedly old supporters of the Merovingians among the nobility, men who would have been offended with Childéric's execution without cause; and since there was no other obvious threat to his position, Pépin clearly was content to control the ex-King until his belated demise.

At that point, Pépin and his son became the genuine heirs to the crown. Had any other Merovingian males survived, they would automatically have become the rightful kings at Childéric's death. One must remember that the

45

Xenograffiti, by ROBERT REGINALD

Merovingian succession was not always from father to son, but often from father to *sons,* or cousin to cousin; every male heir had an equal right to the throne. The Carolingian kings could not have allowed even one Merovingian to survive for any length of time; their own necks were at stake. The price for political failure would have been torture and execution; there was no retirement to the Western White House in medieval times. Those who played at politics played either for complete power or complete oblivion; there was very little in between. Since Charles Martel, Pépin III, and Charlemagne are among the strongest rulers recorded in French history, they surely would have been eminently aware of this potential threat to their necks, and would have made absolutely certain that every Merovingian descendant had been accounted for. We must remember also that they had every means of the state at their disposal: these were absolute rulers in almost every sense of the word, men who knew how to use their power: they would have had agents everywhere throughout the land, officers beholden only to the new kings; it is virtually impossible that a Merovingian could have survived in a titled position of power anywhere in the French realm. History teaches us that even female members of deposed royal houses (and their offshoots) do not survive long under the new regime, be it another dynasty or a republic.

A similar argument can be applied to Baigent's contention that Christ staged and survived his supposed execution. We must again recall existing testimony on this subject, and the political realities of the time, irrespective of any religious considerations. Jesus was a major threat to the political and religious establishment, which were intertwined under the Roman procurators. Although the Romans had a large occupying force in Judea, and a Roman governor made (or carried out) all the major decisions for the province, the Jews were actually allowed a considerable amount of freedom in running their own affairs; the High Priest and the Sanhedrin (in effect his religious synod) also had political and judicial authority over the Jews in their area. If a Jew committed a crime, the religious bodies were allowed to deal with it, with exceptions; they were even allowed to invoke the death penalty, although the sentence had to be approved

Xenograffiti, by ROBERT REGINALD

by the Roman procurator. Christ threatened the hegemony of the Jewish High Priest, and therefore he had to be removed from the scene permanently. The Romans wet relatively indifferent to his death, but approved it to avoid unnecessary trouble. All of this rings true politically. As the Fanthorpes point out Jesus would not have abandoned his religious career prematurely this would have been completely out of character with the man depicted in the New Testament. Had he survived his supposed crucifixion for any length of time (beyond the fleeting glimpses we see of him during the forty days of his resurrection), the Sanhedrin would certainly have pointed to the fraud, arrested him again, and made certain of his execution the second time. They would have been doubly outraged at his first escape, and would have publicized it extensively as a sign of his duplicity.

There is no evidence in the Bible that states directly whether Jesus was ever married; the fact that others, including Simon Peter, are cited as having families would lead one to think, however, that such a fact would have been recorded if indeed he had a wife, and that such a person, given his character, would have played a major role in his ministry. In fact, celibacy is consistent with the person portrayed in the surviving gospels; here is a man devoted only to his mission in life, a mission that, in my estimation, precludes other preoccupations. I should mention here that I have no religious axe to grind, being an agnostic myself, as is Baigent; as a researcher, though, I must look at the New Testament in the same way I would examine any other historical document—and as a document, it stands up very well. The inconsistencies cited by Baigent are minor compared to the major consistencies between the four surviving accounts of Christ's life. The apocrypha mentioned by Baigent do exist, but tend, on the whole, to be much less consistent, either with themselves or the gospels or other apocrypha; obviously, this is one reason they have not been accepted by Christians as true accounts. Church authorities could not have suppressed documents that had widespread popular appeal.

One must apply in both cases the old philosophical rule, Occam's Razor, which holds that the simplest explanation for a particular problem is usually the best. The simplest explanation for the mysterious treasure of Rennes-le-Château is that Saunière found gold, jewels, or other precious artifacts in his church, which he then sold off at the highest price he could get; some of these artifacts may have had political or religious significance to his Church or to the Habsburgs, for whatever reason, and these he may have pawned directly to those most interested in them. The simplest explanation for the supposed later lineage of the Merovingians is that it did not exist, or at least cannot be demonstrated historically. The simplest explanation for Christ's existence is given by himself, presumably in his own (remembered) words, in the gospels; one may believe them or not, as one chooses, but one cannot easily deny their power, consistency, *and* simplicity. As for the Priory of Sion, if it exists, one can say very little about it, since it has deliberately chosen to remain hidden from us; we have no verification that the documents mentioned by Baigent really do exist, or, if they exist, that they derive from the Priory, or, if they derive from the Priory, that they fully represent that organization's beliefs, or, if they do represent the Priory's credo, that they are in fact true. The Priory may well believe in the descent of the Merovingians from Christ, or in the descent of modern royal houses from the Merovingians; the fact that they claim these things as historical facts, and have produced written documents from their own files supporting their claims, does not make them so.

In the end, one must say that Baigent and his colleagues have piled too many inconsistencies and unsupported suppositions one upon another; it is one thing to examine the problem from many different angles, as the Fanthorpes have done; it is quite another to proceed from a conviction that the evidence must support one particular theory. Having reached such a conclusion, for whatever reasons, a person tends to orient the supporting documentation and its presentation in such a way as to best demonstrate the conclusion one wishes to reach. The entire business becomes a perpetual motion machine.

The Fanthorpes are much less pretentious in their examination of the mystery surrounding Rennes. They have

Xenograffiti, by Robert Reginald

attempted here to comb the evidence for every possible clue, to examine the man, his place of origin, and each facet of the puzzle in order, like detectives scanning the scene of the crime. They have allowed their imaginations to consider every angle, every theory, every fact that might apply. Some of their suppositions are outlandish, as they readily admit; some of their speculations are as wild as any science fiction story; some of their hypotheses will stand your hair on end. But they never pretend to *know* what the answer is absolutely, although they have their own ideas, and are not hesitant to present them. I do not agree with everything they say; I did find their six-year adventure as much fun as they clearly found it themselves. This love of a mystery, this enjoyment in pursuit of the unknown, shines through every page of their account. In the end, when they sum up what is known and what remains speculation, one is forced to agree with them; when they itemize the possible theories, one must applaud their thoroughness; when they finally present *their* answer, but decline to shove it down the reader's throat, one must approve their evenhandedness.

Once upon a time, an impoverished parish priest in a little town of southeastern France stumbled upon a treasure, and suddenly found himself rich overnight. I wonder what he would think of all the commotion he has caused. I wonder if, somewhere in another space, time, or dimension, Bérenger Saunière is lying in his bed, laughing so hard that the tears are streaming down his cheeks. They do say in Rennes-le-Château that Saunière had a wicked sense of humor.

Xenograffiti, by ROBERT REGINALD

VII.

NEB

(6 February 1983)

I murdered my friend today. I didn't have the courage to do it myself, so I paid someone else to handle the dirty work. I put him in the car, and took him to a place that smelled of death and fear and hurt. He submitted to all of this without balking, without any doubt whatever that I, his oldest and closest and only friend in this world, would save him from this awful place and from the terrible things that were destroying him inside. I did neither. I had him killed.

It began just over ten years ago, in March of 1973. I was a lonely bachelor living in a duplex on a hill overlooking San Bernardino, three years out of graduate school, working at my first professional position, and finishing my second book. My work was my life, and vice versa—I had few friends, little furniture, minimal social life. I was still enjoying the exhilaration of being away from home for the first time, but beginning to realize that there are more things in heaven and on earth than I had dreamed of.

Into this rather austere life came an interloper, a thin, somewhat dirty, adolescent bluetick hound that I had noticed wandering the neighborhood during the previous few months. He barked at me in my driveway one night; for no reason I've ever been able to fathom, I went into the house, poured some milk into a saucer, and set it in the open doorway. He accepted my offering, despite some initial shyness, and returned the following evening for more, barking at my front door. Soon he was spending the night. Nothing las-

Xenograffiti, by ROBERT REGINALD

civious, of course—ours was purely a platonic relationship—but we did seem to fill a need in each other. He was black on top, with white patches shadowed with auburn highlights; the end half of his long tail was pure white, and he carried it curled over his back like a personal banner. Young, strong, arrogant, intelligent, self-assured, but never mean, with a bad habit of chasing cars, motorcycles, postal jeeps, and jackrabbits (and the scars to prove it), he was a good companion, particularly on the long walks we took together in the evenings.

I named him Nebuchadnezzar, after the Babylonian king of the sixth century B.C., but never called him anything but Neb.

Then one day he disappeared for three days, and I discovered that Neb had had a previous master, a man who had bought the dog for his boy a year before, but had then set him loose when he and his wife had gone their separate ways. The son was visiting then, so Neb had been kept in his first master's house. I managed to persuade them to let me take care of him permanently, with appropriate visiting rights.

In 1975 came a second crisis, when I met the woman who later agreed to share her life with me. Neb made his feelings on the subject perfectly clear the first time Mary stayed the night, when he crawled up on top of the bed between us. Thereafter, he tolerated her, since I did, but never failed to emphasize his own idea of the household pecking order, in which she fell somewhere between him and her own dogs (the hoi polloi of the canine world). I did notice, however, that he tolerated her much better on those occasions when she divvied out the food.

As the years passed, Neb gradually went blind from cataracts in both eyes at about the age of six or seven; by the time he lost his sight, he had memorized his way around the house and yard, and seemed to enjoy life as much as ever. Like many dogs who have scavenged on their own for a while, he would eat anything even vaguely edible, vegetable, fruit, or animal, in any quantity served, with great gusto and speed and much slurping and burping. No gourmet this. How ironic, then, that in the end he could eat nothing, that he

Xenograffiti, by Robert Reginald

would have starved himself to death if death hadn't visited him first, that his greatest pleasure in life was finally denied him.

Neb turned eleven in December, old for a middle-sized dog. He had grown somewhat cranky and solemn, as many beasts and pundits do in old age, but otherwise seemed in good health. His primary sport in his last years was "dog baiting," barking at the dog in the yard behind us (who of course barked back); he also had two or three personal "things" that were his alone, including an old bone, and a rubber ball with a bell in its middle. This he would toss with a turn of his head, and then pounce on it as it rolled, chewing vigorously for five or ten minutes. In the evenings, he'd curl up in an old chair, or stretch out on the couch on his back, with his feet pointing out at several curious angles. He also barked loudly when anyone came to the door. By his own standards, he more than earned his keep.

In early January, he cut the pad of his paw, giving him a noticeable limp, and making difficult the act of bending over a dog dish. For the first time in his life, he began leaving various portions of his dinner uneaten. His foot healed, but his appetite didn't, and so he made the trip to the dreaded veterinarian. The verdict came back the next day: advanced cirrhosis of the liver, a condition which also produces nausea and vomiting, among other symptoms. The injury to his paw had been merely coincidental. It was a death sentence, for, despite the inducement of special diets, meats, dairy products, and other tidbits that would previously have put him in dog heaven, Neb ate less and less, noticeably declining day by day, growing progressively thinner, until he finally resembled the homeless mutt I had first met almost ten years earlier. Nothing I tried worked: he was always a stubborn dog, with a mind of his own, and he had decided in his own mind that he would eat no more. In despair, I tried forcing food down his throat, with vitamin supplements; but he hated these violations of his body, and they weren't enough, in any case, to halt his decline. Finally, all he could do was slurp a few teaspoons of milk from a saucer. We had at last come full circle.

Xenograffiti, by ROBERT REGINALD

And so, old dog, I killed you. I took you to that place you feared and hated so much, with the men in white and blue coats, and I left you there. They put some foreign substance in your veins, and finally stilled the beating of that loyal heart. Your body they threw into a freezer, later to be collected by the fertilizer man, and ground into plant food. And the sentence I must serve for this premeditated act of murder is the memory of all the good times we had together, and the certain knowledge that never again will we share an evening stroll, or the comforts of the couch, with your head lying gently on my knee, or the joys of a man with his dog.

Xenograffiti, by ROBERT REGINALD

VIII.

BEWARE OF THE HOUSE

THE NATURE OF REALITY IN DAPHNE DU MAURIER'S FANTASY

with Mary A. Burgess

(1983)

  Daphne du Maurier is perhaps best known for her haunting tale of romantic suspense, *Rebecca* (1938), which has served as the classic prototype for that modern publishing phenomenon, the revival of the Gothic novel. That she is equally proficient in the field of fantasy is evident in such stories as "Don't Look Now," "The Blue Lenses," *Rule Britannia* (1972), and particularly in her tragic tale of time travel, *The House on the Strand* (1969).
  Richard Young has recently resigned his lucrative but boring position with a London publishing house, and is awaiting with no great pleasure the arrival of his American-born wife, Vita, and her two young sons. Vita, a strong-willed, unsympathetic woman, is determined that Richard will accept a "suitable" post with her brother in New York, thereby accomplishing his removal from England (which she dislikes intensely as being too parochial), and severing the ties which Richard has maintained with his childhood friend and mentor, the scientist Magnus Lane.
  Magnus, in the meantime, offers the Youngs the use of his family estate in Cornwall (Kilmarth) for their summer

Xenograffiti, by ROBERT REGINALD

holiday. In return, Richard will serve as a human "guinea pig" for a new drug developed by Lane. Richard agrees, and as the story opens, he is experiencing his first "trip," which, to his astonishment, has transported him back six hundred years into the Cornwall of the fourteenth century. At first skeptical, Richard experiences a new feeling of awareness and freedom—colors seem brighter, senses sharper than before; and, almost in spite of himself, he is drawn deeper into the ancient landscape, which seems, ironically, more vital than the insipid vistas of the twentieth century.

Richard's "guide" is the fourteenth century manorial steward, Roger Kylmarth; whenever he uses the drug, Richard gradually becomes conscious of Roger's presence nearby and is compelled to follow him effortlessly across hill and dale in the course of his travels. The people of this early time live out their lives completely unaware of Richard's presence. The uniqueness of his position as observer, and the fascination he develops for monitoring the lives of the people he observes, soon transform his interest into an addiction. Each session seems to last for several hours, after which the time traveler returns to his normal state. If, however, he attempts to touch one of the medieval persons, he is jolted back to reality with unpleasant nausea and vertigo. Chillingly, after several such "trips," Richard finds it more and more difficult to distinguish between past and present, between the reality of his modern existence and the real (to him) world of his guide, Roger, who has in a sense become Richard's alter-ego. Complicating the situation is the sudden arrival of Vita, who disrupts Richard's privacy, thereby also interrupting his now obsessive experiments. Vita's lack of sympathy with and disapproval of Richard's altered and unexplained behavior and appearance further impair his sense of reality and lead predictably to his falling hopelessly (in every sense of the word) in love with Isolde Carminowe, whom Roger also loves from afar. As the tragic lives of Roger and Isolde unfold before his eyes, Richard is drawn inexorably into the vortex which seals his own fate.

Lane finally decides to take a "trip" with Richard, having proven with historical research that the persons mentioned by Richard really existed in the fourteenth century.

Xenograffiti, by ROBERT REGINALD

Richard is elated; however, Magnus stumbles onto a railroad track and is killed by a passing car. With no mentor to guide him, Richard is devastated and grows increasingly disoriented, finally attempting to strangle his wife, whom he has mistakenly identified with the evil Joanna Champernoune from his other world. A local doctor befriends him and persuades him to leave England with Vita.

The couple reaches the airport, but Richard cleverly eludes Vita and misses the flight; driving back through the countryside without her, he feels freer than he ever has before. He takes the last dose of the drug (it had been hidden in Magnus's walking-stick) and enters his old world to discover that Isolde has died, Cornwall is suffering from the Black Death, and Roger himself has contracted the disease. In a moving final speech, Roger asks forgiveness for his sins, although it remains uncertain whether he actually senses Richard's presence at the end. Richard, a lapsed Catholic, gives extreme unction, feeling that this deed is the real reason for his involvement with the past, since it serves ultimately as a reaffirmation of his own faith. Richard returns to the present, where he confronts the doctor in Magnus's basement laboratory. The story ends with the doctor's unspoken but obvious conviction that Richard's use of the untested drug will ultimately prove fatal. Richard's enchantment, hubris, and eventual downfall are reminiscent of the hero's fate in Richard Matheson's *Bid Time Return* (1975), a comparable tale of love trapped in time, and in Jack Finney's *Time and Again* (1970); there are also resonances of the work of Robert Nathan, particularly *Portrait of Jennie* (1940) and *So Love Returns* (1958).

This moving and skillful portrait of the destruction of a person through obsession also demonstrates simultaneously the difficulty of separating fact from fiction, and, more important, the *validity* of doing so. This is the crux of du Maurier's message. *The House on the Strand* depicts a failed hero whose failing, in retrospect, is perhaps his greatest triumph. The author appears to be saying that the reality of Richard's fantasy world is more rewarding to him than his mediocre and unfulfilled existence in the twentieth century.

Xenograffiti, by ROBERT REGINALD

For some persons, perhaps, dreams are the only possible solace for the terminal disease of everyday living.

Xenograffiti, by ROBERT REGINALD

IX.

COMEAU'S *MAGIC*

(1983)

Nothing is known today of Alexander de Comeau; no biography survives, no obituary, no pictures. His nationality may be either French or English. He wrote only two books, the first, *Fires of Isis*, published in 1927 by a London vanity press (Arthur H. Stockwell), the second, *Monk's Magic*, issued simultaneously in London and America in 1931 by Methuen and E. P. Dutton, respectively. Letters sent to his publishers proved equally negative: the American publisher referred the matter to the English house, and Methuen reported all correspondence and records destroyed during the London Blitz. What survives of the man, for all practical purposes, is encompassed within the 250 pages of his only readily available novel.

And this is a marvelous piece of writing: witty, sparkling, filled with life and *joie de vivre*. Brother Dismas is a lay brother in an unspecified order of monks during the early Tudor period of English history. He has never taken the priestly vows, with good reason: his abbot has given him a dispensation to pursue the magical arts and alchemy in the hope that he can find an elixir of life to restore the abbot to youth and good health. Dismas's final attempt with dragon's blood merely produces an explosion, and he determines, with his abbot's blessing, to locate those magi who claimed in their writings to have found the elixir and to ask their help in supplying the missing ingredient.

The nearest of these men, Lucius Germanicus, was last known to be living in Germany; Brother Dismas's way there lies through London, where he gains two companions: Gabriel, a lad of about twenty, and Thomas Brackenridge, an English physician and healer. Gabriel seeks his father, Ralph Terven, who went abroad several years before and has never returned; Thomas must flee England at once, having offended a powerful nobleman with a cure that was more painful than the illness. Gabriel leads Dismas to Ibrahim bin Judah, a Jewish magician who helps the trio escape across the Channel. From Rotterdam on the coast, they voyage up the Rhine to Dachsenberg, where Germanicus is said to have lived. They take rest in a tavern below the castle.

During the night, the local Baron's men, having spotted "Gabriel" while drinking in the tavern, spirit "him" away to their lord; for, as Thomas explains to Dismas the next morning, Ralph Terven had but one child, a daughter called Radegonde, and the Baron has a predilection for young, innocent girls. Dismas, although a man in his mid-thirties, is more innocent because of his cloistered life than his young companion has been, but even he realizes what peril the girl is in and determines to help her if he can. He uses the Hand of Glory, the hand of a corpse made into a candelabrum, to gain entrance to the castle, where he is confronted by the resident magus, Albrecht, son of the man he is seeking.

Dismas is dismayed to learn that Lucius Germanicus has died at the age of 119; his son, himself now ninety-nine, claims to have found the secret of life: it lies, he says, in the last three drops of a virgin's blood. Fortunately, the old man continues, the Baron has a virgin locked up at that very moment in a cell overlooking a sheer drop to the river; all that Albrecht has to do is to find Radegonde/Gabriel before the Baron ravages her, kidnap the wench, and then drain away the girl's blood until only three drops are left. With Dismas as his assistant, the magus continues, they are certain to succeed. Dismas, who is beginning to have tender thoughts for the girl, is horrified at this threat, but pretends to go along with the old man to effect her rescue.

Radegonde/Gabriel is no fool, however, and no coward; in the middle of the night, she determines either to escape or die trying, and eases herself out of her cell through its waste hole. She then makes a horrifying descent down the rock wall, using cracks, crevices, and the light of the moon to inch her way to the castle base. She loses her grip and falls backward, dropping twenty feet to the river; she is discovered there the next morning by Gita, a peasant girl. The peasants have no love for their Baron, who has used them unmercifully, and Gita and her betrothed, Hubert, decide to help the fugitive.

Dismas, in the meantime, is persuaded by Albrecht to enter the realm of the dead, where he can determine for himself whether any of those who have claimed to have made the elixir work actually escaped the Grim Reaper. The magus's potion succeeds, but Dismas is disappointed to learn that all of those he wishes to consult are in the netherworld—all have failed. Albrecht has been informed during Dismas's sojourn that the local coven of witches under Albrecht's control has captured the two girls; Albrecht orders a black mass during which the virgin will be sacrificed. Mad Hans, the magus's assistant, offers to help Dismas stop the ceremony. When Dismas appears, the monk shows the hags the talisman he had been given by a gypsy in England, a token of power over all witches; they must not interfere. Albrecht is stopped and dies in rage as his hand is slapped away from the girl's throat.

Thomas has found Radegonde's father living as a hermit in a nearby cave and arranges a reunion. Radegonde persuades Dismas that he loves her, and they all return to London, where Thomas learns that the indisposed Earl has recovered from his illness and now credits Thomas with the cure. His friends' fortunes restored and his own heart secured, Dismas returns to his abbey, both to report his failure to his abbot and to resign his position as lay brother. The abbot has sunk into senility, however, and Brother Nicholas, temporarily in charge, threatens to lock Dismas away unless the alchemist reveals his secret. Dismas disavows the elixir, for he has come to realize the futility of living eternally; however, he suggests that the brother take the gypsy amulet, which is known by the ancients to have great power, and call up the Devil, who can grant immortality for the price of a soul.

Xenograffiti, by ROBERT REGINALD

In a curious epilogue, Brother Nicholas calls the Prince of Darkness out of his pit and offers him his soul, but the Black Prince will have none of it, saying that he is not what men make him to be. Nevertheless, although Nicholas has nothing to give in return, he will grant the monk's request—eternal youth and life—until he grows tired of it. As for Dismas, he has ordered his life as befits a man.

Here is a novel of adventure, magic, fantasy, sorcery, love, and life. Dismas is a complex character, a shy, scholarly recluse who grows emotionally into a fully-rounded human being. Not a man of action, he nevertheless does what needs to be done to save his friends from death or torture. Radegonde, his paramour, has a bolder, more sparkling personality; intelligent, humorous, and directly courageous, she decides her own fate by taking it into her own hands. Comeau's style anticipates that of L. Sprague de Camp and Fletcher Pratt ten years later; his work deserves wider attention than it has received.

Xenograffiti, by ROBERT REGINALD

X.

CURIOUS THINGS

THE HORROR FICTION OF ELEANOR M. INGRAM

with Mary A. Burgess

(1983)

Eleanor M. Ingram was just beginning a promising career as a novelist when she died at the age of thirty-five, leaving three or four undistinguished fictions of modern-day life and a last book, her only venture into fantasy, which stands as a monument to her unrealized abilities, and which is perhaps the single most neglected novel of supernatural fiction written by an American author between the late Victorian period and the advent of H. P. Lovecraft in the mid-1920s.

In every way, *The Thing from the Lake* (1921) remains a thoroughly modern work, as readable today as it was when it was first published more than seventy years ago. Roger Locke, a well-known writer of popular songs, buys the old Michell property in rural Connecticut, determined to find a secluded refuge from the pressures of New York City. During his first night in the house, he wakes to find a braid of hair trailing through his open hand. A woman's soft voice warns him to leave the house while he still can, but when he manages to find a light, the girl has vanished, leaving a cut length of hair dangling by his bed. Later that same night, Locke hears a horrifying sucking noise emanating from the swampy lake behind the house and smells a hideous stench

Xenograffiti, by ROBERT REGINALD

pouring in through the window. In the midst of the spell, he realizes that something is watching him, physically or psychically, that some presence in the lake is casting a hypnotic net over his soul, seeking to destroy his willpower and draw him into its grasp. With great difficulty, he manages to pull away, and leaves the house the next morning.

Meanwhile, back in the city, Locke's cousin Phillida has eloped with Ethan Vere. At first suspicious of the man, Locke gradually comes to see his true worth and to accept Phillida's judgment of her lover. With some consideration of their plight (they have no money, and Phillida's mother disapproves of the match), he offers them the use of his rural estate in return for their assistance in refurbishing the house and lands, both of which are in a state of decay. They accept, and Locke is pleased to find on his next visit that the couple has worked miracles with the three-hundred-year-old house, making it into a warm, pleasant retreat.

Locke continues to be disturbed through his second sojourn by the returning wraith of the girl, whose spirit he has grown to love in spite of himself, and more frighteningly, by the Thing lurking in the ooze beyond the house. The creature's malevolent intelligence is directed entirely at subduing Locke's will and drawing him through the barrier between man's world and the other plane to become its slave. The Thing is implacable and unwavering; however much Locke might resist, he cannot resist forever, and the being in the lake will wait as long as necessary to capture his soul. The continuing presence of the girl as part of the puzzle mystifies Locke until he discovers an old diary in the house. The seventeenth-century journal details the sordid events surrounding the life of Desire Michell, a daughter of the old Michell family who had built the house centuries before.

Desire had first dabbled with the love-struck men around her and then with the black arts, with calamitous results. After murdering a lover by witchcraft, she had embraced necromancy completely, determined to call up a creature from the beyond to act as her all-powerful avenging servant. There was a barrier between men and the other orders of beings which neither could breach by himself; but with the proper incantations and with the assistance of one from

63

this realm, the breach had been made, and the colossal, formless intelligence issued forth into the world. Unable to control what she had called forth, Desire Michell was destroyed by the Thing, which then occupied the ruined foundations of the house, later covered by a lake. A new house was built by the survivors of the family nearby. In the ensuing centuries, there were several other descendants with the name Desire Michell, each one becoming a tool that the creature used to enslave men, each one meeting a final horrible end. Only one member of the family now remains, the current Desire Michell, a girl whom Locke has seen fleetingly on several different nights, and with whom he has fallen in love.

After a near brush with death, Locke determines to resolve the situation, and with the help of Phillida and Vere, he captures the current Desire, discovering that she is a living being fully aware of the creature's menace and anxious to warn Locke away. Locke, however, must have his Desire, so the two couples prepare themselves for a last struggle against the creature. A vicious storm destroys the lake, freeing the creature to advance on the house; waves of icy psychic foulness break over the frail human beings as the Thing demands obeisance as its price for their continued life. Locke offers his life in exchange for the girl's, thereby freeing her from the spell it holds over her; Vere calls upon God to thrust the creature back into its realm. In a mighty, cataclysmic flash, the breach is healed, the Thing returned to its world, and the human beings left to reassemble their disrupted lives. Courage and sacrifice, Ingram seems to be saying, are not enough to fight off the despoiler; one must also have faith in God the Almighty.

In its tone, style of writing, and theme, *The Thing from the Lake* presages the writings of H. P. Lovecraft, particularly his Cthulhu Mythos stories. The presence of horribly malevolent and indescribable creatures from a dimension beyond man's ken has become almost a stereotype in American supernatural writing of the twentieth century; its presence here, however, may be the first developed writing on that theme, and as such, the novel is a landmark of horror literature. It is indeed unfortunate that Ingram never had the chance to develop the kind of following gathered by Lovecraft; her early death not only deprived supernatural fiction of a major talent, but also caused her one major contribution to the genre to be eclipsed by the *Weird Tales* school.

Xenograffiti, by ROBERT REGINALD

XI.

THE DEVIL TOOK HER!

CHARLOTTE HALDANE'S *MELUSINE*

(1983)

Charlotte Haldane came from a distinguished English family which included such luminaries as J. B. S. Haldane, the noted scientist (her brother), and she added to their luster with a distinguished career of her own as a journalist and writer. A pioneering feminist, she wrote a dystopian novel of the future, *Man's World*, which was published in 1926 to great acclaim; serious mainstream novels; and nonfiction of all kinds, including articles, commentary, and reviews. *Melusine; or, Devil Take Her!* (1936), however, was her only fantasy novel. It is a rich, full-bodied work, loosely adapted from the medieval legend fashioned by Jean d'Arras for his master, Prince Jean, son of King Jean II of France.

One must not confuse the legend with the real history of the region: there was a Lusignan family in Poitiers from an early date, and Geoffroy de Lusignan did burn the Abbey of Maillezais in 1232; the family later gained prominence b0079 participating in the Crusades, its members becoming Kings of Jerusalem and Cyprus. The tale constructed by Jean d'Arras wove elements of this real-life history together with the legend of Melusine, which was inextricably linked with the rounding of the castle of Lusignan. Charlotte Haldane took this raw material and used it to construct a different kind of story, one which emphasized characterization, particularly that of Melusine, and the motivations of the

Xenograffiti, by ROBERT REGINALD

"devil cult" working to destroy the "evil" influences of Christianity. The result reads as well today as it did when it was first published in 1936.

Emery, Earl of Poitiers, invites his brother-in-law, Henry, Earl de Forests (a small and impoverished realm), to his castle for a celebration. Henry brings his three young sons, the youngest of whom, Raymond, captivates everyone with his charm, intelligence, and good looks. Emery had been urged to invite his relatives by Owain Wanderer, the castle wise man and philosopher. Owain, of Welsh origin, is the head of a secret cult which outwardly worships the Devil but actually seeks to restore a more humanistic philosophy of government and religion to a land oppressed by monks, corrupt functionaries, and religious taxation to support the privileged few. The long-term political aims of this religion/cult involve manipulating the Earldom of Poitiers to ensure the succession of someone sympathetic to its aims.

Within days, Raymond has been adopted by his uncle, and he soon becomes good friends with Bertrand, Emery's only son and heir. Owain, meanwhile, gradually convinces Earl Emery, who is tiring of his position after decades in power, that Raymond is his true successor and that the transfer of power must be symbolic, according to the old forms. Emery and Raymond go on a boar hunt, where Raymond accidentally kills his "father"; unbeknown to Raymond, Emery has arranged the killing, acquiescing to his own murder. Bertrand succeeds to the earldom, and Raymond requests of his cousin the small piece of land surrounding the cave where the cult holds its most secret ceremonies. There he meets Melusine, Princess of Albany, who has been brought there to seduce Raymond and run his life, but who eventually falls in love with him. The castle of Lusignan is built next to the cave. Within a few years, Owain has poisoned Bertrand, and Raymond, the next heir, becomes Earl. Melusine, high priestess of the cult, conducts a service each Saturday evening in which she appears in a suit woven from adders' skins. Owain, having brought his plans to fruition, leaves the country to scout other areas of the world for possible control. Melusine and Raymond, utterly devoted to each other, rear eight sons.

Xenograffiti, by ROBERT REGINALD

Owain arranges for the three older sons to seek their fortunes in distant lands, where they repulse the Saracens and marry female heirs to three different thrones. As the years pass, trouble threatens when Melusine gradually becomes enamored of the Christian faith and discontinues the weekly Sabbaths. When informed of her lapsed ways, Owain returns to Poitiers and forces her to hold another ceremony. There he rapes her on the high altar; nine months later, a son, Geffray, called "The Devil," is born. Geffray is wholly unlike his brothers: unruly, disrespectful, independent, courageous, and rash, it is clear that he will be the heir of both Raymond and Owain. Upon coming of age, he immediately establishes himself as a mighty warrior, putting down rebellious lords and conquering enemies in several different lands. His hatred for religions of all kinds is evident. Learning that his younger brother, Froimond, has become a monk, he bolts off across the countryside, burning the abbey and all its members, including his kin. He then leaves immediately for Albany, in Britain, where a giant is threatening the people.

Geffray's actions have far-reaching consequences. In Albany, Owain greets him as his son and tells him of his destiny. In Poitiers, Raymond renounces both son and wife, whereupon Melusine must take her leave. Appearing in the great hall of the castle dressed in her snake suit, she bids farewell to her lover and plunges from the open window into the moat far below. Raymond is left utterly destroyed. Geffray returns from overseas to claim his lands, which Raymond no longer has the will to rule; Raymond retires voluntarily to a hermit's life in Spain. Geffray restores the land's peace. Melusine, who has not been killed, returns to Albany, where she lives with Owain until the latter dies; she then is united with her triplet sisters, who had also been impressed into duty in far-off lands. When Raymond finally dies, years later, a great thunderstorm breaks over Lusignan.

Haldane has invested the legend with new life, making full-blooded characters out of the players. Melusine, in particular, is one of fantasy's most attractive female characters: intelligent, attractive, politically knowledgeable, and strong-willed. Owain is also a "fine figure of a man": wise, virile, sensitive, and humane, far better in many ways than his Christian opponents. Owain and his ilk desire the return of the earthbound values of hearth, home, loyalty, and respect; he possesses no skills other than his own very human abilities to move men and women. In many respects, the book anticipates the Deryni novels of Katherine Kurtz, although Kurtz is more sympathetic with the Christian side of the conflict than is Haldane. For both writers, the powers of the mind are the only magical forces at work, aided at times by objects of power (Melusine, for example, possesses the ability of precognition, reinforced by use of a crystal); for both, political conflict is at the heart of their work in the interactions of mighty men and women. *Melusine* is a superior novel of fantasy, richly wrought and imbued with the aura of the Middle Ages; it deserves a wider readership and wider critical acclaim.

XII.

GORY INTERLUDES

JOHN NORMAN AND THE
ENNUI OF SEXUAL FANTASY

(1983)

It is difficult to be fair when writing of John Norman's Gor novels. On the one hand, they have sold in the aggregate perhaps five million copies, making this series one of the most popular contemporary novel sequences in imaginative literature. On the other hand, they have been almost universally castigated by the critics, who claim that they are poorly written and highly derivative and that they espouse a philosophy of cruelty and sexual bondage that is at best morally reprehensible.

John Lange (pronounced "lenj") is a curious candidate for such controversy, being in real life a mild-mannered professor of philosophical logic at a New York university. So shy is he of publicity that for years after publication of his first novel, he refused to reveal his identity or address to fans, having all his mail forwarded through his publisher; it has only been in recent years that he has consented to appear at a few fan conventions and to be interviewed by the press. Even now, he makes no effort to publicize his work or to cater to the desires of his readers. He keeps his professional work completely separate from what he considers to be a private avocation.

Yet the controversy continues. The first Gor novel, *Tarnsman of Gor*, appeared in 1966 from Ballantine Books.

Xenograffiti, by ROBERT REGINALD

Thereafter, the books were published at the rate of one volume a year in the following order: *Outlaw of Gor* (1967), *Priest-Kings of Gor* (1968), *Nomads of Gor* (1969), *Assassin of Gor* (1970), *Raiders of Gor* (1971), and *Captive of Gor* (1972). The eighth book, *Hunters of Gor*, although announced by Ballantine, was ultimately rejected by Betty Ballantine and sold to Donald A. Wollheim at DAW Books; it appeared early in 1974. Thereafter, DAW released seventeen more novels in the series before killing it: *Marauders of Gor* (1975), *Tribesmen of Gor* (1976), *Slave Girl of Gor* (1977), *Beasts of Gor* (1978), *Explorers of Gor* (1979), *Fighting Slave of Gor* (1980), *Rogue of Gor* (1981), *Guardsman of Gor* (1981), *Savages of Gor* (1982), *Blood Brothers of Gor* (1982), *Kajira of Gor* (1983), *Players of Gor* (1984), *Mercenaries of Gor* (1985), *Dancer of Gor* (1985), *Renegades of Gor* (1986), *Vagabonds of Gor* (1987), and *Magicians of Gor* (1988), the twenty-fifth and final volume in the series.

Tarl Cabot, a college professor at a New England school, is kidnapped by an alien spaceship while on a camping trip and awakes on Gor, a planet that has been artificially moved into an orbit on the opposite side of the sun from Earth. Gor is a barbarous world peopled by cruel warriors bound into a rigid caste system that segregates men and women partly by innate ability, partly by heredity. Tarl's father, Matthew Cabot, is the administrator of a Gorean city; he orders that his son be trained for the highest caste, the warriors. The younger Cabot soon learns the use of the sword, spear, and knife, and he is trained to fight aboard the fierce tarns, giant birds that carry their warrior-masters into battle. Weaponry on Gor is strictly limited by the unseen Priest-Kings, who use their superior technology to destroy attempts by inventors to introduce gunpowder or other modern improvements in their armaments. Tarl is determined to discover the secret of the Priest-Kings, and he penetrates their stronghold. There he participates in a civil war between two factions of the antlike creatures, a conflict that destroys much of their headquarters. The surviving Priest-Kings enlist Tarl on a crusade against the Kurii, the Beasts, bearlike enemies of the Priest-Kings who threaten to take both

Xenograffiti, by ROBERT REGINALD

Earth and Counter-Earth as their new home. The Kurii's original world has been destroyed; they now survive only in space bases and ships, from which they conduct periodic raiding parties on the two planets. The Kurii remain unaware of the Priest-Kings' helplessness; consequently, they fear to invade either world directly, but conduct clandestine operations against both.

Tarl is waylaid on his first mission as the Priest-Kings' agent and enslaved by the marsh-dwellers; his innate shame at his abasement destroys his illusions and makes him independent of both parties; still, he will fight for Gor when he can. He travels to Port Kar, a free city occupied by pirates and thieves, calling himself Bosk; there he helps set up a government of free captains, ridding the town of undesirables and establishing himself as an equal of these hard-bitten men. Samos, first captain of Port Kar, is an agent of the Priest-Kings. Eventually, Tarl befriends one of the Kurii, resumes his former name of Cabot, and gradually finds himself performing errands for the Priest-Kings in spite of himself.

Inherent in Norman's world is the Darwinian philosophy of survival of the fittest; the caste society of Gor operates strictly in this fashion. The strongest, the brightest, and the cruelest rule this world without pity. Those who are weaker are crushed by those who are stronger. Since women are physically weaker than men, they deserve only slavery; this, says Norman, is their natural position in life, imposed upon them by heredity and physiological and psychological necessity.

Men on Earth have failed to recognize this reality, and therefore men and women on Earth are generally unhappy with their lives; women's equality is a myth standing in the way of sexual liberation. If women submitted to men as they should, then both sexes would reach true satisfaction, the kind of satisfaction sorely missing from twentieth-century civilization.

That Norman believes this philosophy inherently is clear from interviews with him published over the years. For Norman, sexual satisfaction implies bondage, sadomasochistic interaction between men and women, and an ac-

Xenograffiti, by ROBERT REGINALD

knowledgment of the respective roles of the inferior and the superior; no other relationship will produce true emotional release for either party. Norman regards his ideas as revolutionary, his books as earth-shaking masterpieces.

They are hardly that. The first six books do possess a power, an inventiveness, an energy that carry the reader past their obvious flaws. Even here, however, Norman tends at times to be ponderous, self-reflective, and didactic; yet somehow one tolerates these glitches as part of the fictional framework the author is erecting. Norman is at his best when fleshing out the details of Gorean civilization—for example, the meaning of a word, the structure of the Gorean calendar, the training of a tarn. All of these things are endlessly fascinating to an imaginative reader and add greatly to the verisimilitude of Gor. Norman's extensive knowledge of ancient civilizations on Earth is used to color Gor life, dissuading those who might spot correlations between the two planets by noting the "voyages of acquisition," through which the Priest-Kings and Kurii have added to Gor's population over the centuries. Since all men on Gor presumably derive originally from Earth (the only native intelligent life on Gor being Priest-Kings), it is only natural that one would encounter earthly customs, names, and bits of language fragments interspersed randomly throughout the native cultures. For example, the Gorean word for sea, *thassa*, clearly derives from the Greek word for sea, *thalassa* [$\theta\alpha\lambda\alpha\sigma\sigma\alpha$] (confirmed by personal correspondence with Lange).

Furthermore, Tarl Cabot as depicted in the early books is a strong, attractive male figure with ideals, a sense of honor, immense self-confidence, qualities of leadership, and intelligence. He readily adapts to Gorean society and quickly becomes an independent figure, his independence guaranteed by his prowess at arms and by his strength of character. As he changes, however, so do the books change, and unfortunately, the change ultimately improves neither.

The key books are volumes seven and eight in the saga, *Hunters of Gor* (the book that was rejected by Ballantine) and its predecessor, *Captive of Gor*. In these books, finally, the philosophy of slavery, bondage, and the inferiority of women, which had played a low-key role in the first six novels, becomes the central theme of the Gor series, displacing plot, action, story line, and character development, and thus losing the reader's interest. Hereafter, women become mere ciphers for groveling animals that can enjoy only degradation. In these books Tarl Cabot becomes a moody, introspective antihero who seems remarkably joyless in his domination of his women/slaves. The novels become filled with long expository passages devoted to nothing more than a constant harping on the joys of subjugation (for women) or mastery (for men), with interchangeable characters of both sexes who seem to be exact substitutes for one another. The societies into which Tarl Cabot finds himself manipulated by his creator seem to be lifted almost unchanged from their earthly paradigms, showing little of the creative energy which filled the earlier novels. In one book, an Eskimo society is featured; in another, an Arab milieu; in *Savages of Gor*, the Indians of North America are transplanted (with different names) onto a Gorean plain.

One wonders what has happened to the verve displayed in *Tarnsman of Gor*, to the *élan* of *Priest-Kings of Gor*, or to the humor inherent in the plot of *Nomads of Gor*. There is no humor in these later creations, but only the seemingly endless sermons of a man standing on a very low soapbox. One can still occasionally glimpse flashes of the old talent and energy, but they are too few to raise the later books from the mud bath in which they are immersed. The thinness of Norman's plots after the sixth volume is insufficient to carry the reader over the exposition, particularly since the later books average four hundred pages of small type each; indeed, it is clear from the way in which they were published that several of these monsters were actually one novel broken into two very large chunks for publication.

In the end, too, one must question the morality of novels that directly advocate violence (whether mental or physical) as a means of sexual satisfaction and which promote masochism as a substitute for love. Norman's later work completely lacks the finer emotions: kindness, pity, understanding, forgiveness, compassion, sacrifice, and love. His is a harsh world, which many readers will ultimately find lacking in substance. The promise and the spirit demon-

Xenograffiti, by ROBERT REGINALD

strated by the first six Gor novels have been replaced by *ennui* and lassitude, and by a certain sadness on the part of the reader that such a talent could have been debased to the level of its subject.

Xenograffiti, by ROBERT REGINALD

XIII.

JEWELS OF FANTASY

THE DUNSANIAN PASTICHES OF VERNON KNOWLES

(1983)

Vernon Knowles died in 1968, certain that his work had been completely forgotten within his own lifetime, that his reputation as a writer had achieved that curious status neither praised nor criticized, but simply abandoned altogether. Yet for a few years during the late 1920s and early 1930s, it appeared that Knowles might step into the shoes of Lord Dunsany or assume the appellation of a British Robert Nathan; that he failed to do so, that he failed to write further or to find a publisher for his work, is a great tragedy for imaginative literature.

In an eleven-year period, from 1924-1935, Knowles published six slim books of fantasy: one novel, *Eternity in an Hour*; one novella, *The Ladder* (also included in his third collection); and four collections of stories, *The Street of Queer Houses and Other Stories*, *Here and Otherwise*, *Silver Nutmegs*, and *Two and Two Make Five*; the two middle books were also collected in 1978 as *Sapphires* (Arno Press). His stories may be grouped together roughly into three categories: Dunsanian pastiches, allegories, and everyday fantasies. These categories should only be used as a general guide, however, for all of his stories, of whatever type, employ the same basic themes and language, relying heavily on irony and satire to make their points.

Xenograffiti, by ROBERT REGINALD

The first group of tales clearly derives inspiration from the early stories of Lord Dunsany, featuring places, persons, and beings just beyond the edge of the known world. Knowles, however, is not Dunsany: whereas Dunsany's passion tends toward exotic names and characters, Knowles's are plain; whereas Dunsany revels in the language, Knowles revels in ironic effect; whereas Dunsany often works toward a climactic turn of phrase at story's end, Knowles often twists the entire tale one degree from the ordinary. In "The Gong of Transportation," for example, young King Merea, bored with his duties, turns to reading and dreaming in order to escape from life; then, when he has read everything he can find in the kingdom, he uses a magical artifact to create the perfect environment in one corner of his kingdom, spending his entire natural life searching for perfect natural wonders. Having completed his task, he dies, leaving the wonderland to his son and heir, who, contemplating the scene for the first time, also demands the Gong. Perfection, it seems, varies in the eye of the beholder.

In "The Birds," Medena, Chairman of the Council of Twenty, is ousted from power and imprisoned by his enemies; in his jail he draws his only solace from the birds he can spy through his window. Vowing to grant his avian friends protection if he is ever restored to power, Medena quickly forgets his pledge following the ensuing revolution; as his memory of their beauty fades, so does his regard for the men he serves; in the end, he strikes a bird that gets in his way, and is found later the same day lying in the park, stone dead, with two vultures tearing out his heart.

"The Mask" restores the Court Poet's wife to life, but with a price: for each year of additional life she lives two are subtracted from the Poet's. In the end, as he lies dying, he must view her real face again—and what he sees is the visage of a corpse.

The allegories are the least successful of Knowles's stories, perhaps because their removal from reality also removes the necessary glue to bind them emotionally to the reader. Of these vignettes, perhaps the best is "The River and the Road," in which the watercourse and its companion muse about the travelers who use them, finally deciding to abandon their positions altogether.

At least half of the tales fall into the third category, that of "everyday fantasies," in which an ordinary person experiences an extraordinary event. In "The Shop in the Off-Street," Mr. Bennett buys a pair of magical wings, thereby fulfilling his secret desire to fly, and visits fairyland (the shopkeeper cannot allow his customers to fly about London, after all); he finds it so enchanting that he abandons his everyday life altogether, finally choosing fantasy over reality. "The Chimpanzee" is trained by an English criminal exiled to Africa to act as his servant, and finally to speak; but the Englishman treats the beast so vilely that it escapes back into the jungle. There it organizes its fellows and returns to the small settlement of thieves and murderers, subjecting them to Chimpanzee society and language.

In "The Broken Statue," Anne breaks a sculpture of herself that her lover has spent months in carving, and on which he had based his fortune. With the help of an imp, she takes its place on the pedestal; but her lover, bereaved by the loss of his love, loses all interest in life, and never shows the sculpture. When he eventually dies of sorrow, the statue topples over, and therein the dead body of Anne is found.

The most successful of Knowles's work, however, is to be found in his novella-length books, *The Street of Queer Houses* (1924), *A Set of Chinese Boxes* (1926), and *The Ladder* (1927, published in book form in 1929). In the latter story, Alan Porter opens a box sent to the family by his brother, who is adventuring in the Far East; immediately a ladder springs up into the sky, vanishing into the heavens. Alan decides to climb the ladder, and disappears up the rungs. One by one, the other villagers investigate and follow him up, until none is left. When the authorities elsewhere discover the ladder, they wall it off and appoint a Royal Commission to investigate; two years later an 1800-page report comes to the conclusion that the government ought to send someone to investigate. A servant of the Crown is chosen and prepares to embark on his journey before a crowd of reporters. As he grasps the first rung, the entire structure collapses, having rotted away under the combined siege of sun and rain, burying him under a pile of rope.

A Set of Chinese Boxes features a series of semi-connected stories told to entertain an ailing friend. *The Street of Queer Houses* is an architectural anomaly: "John Street," as it is called, has been created by a very odd architect to depict the dozen sides of his character; like its structures, the inhabitants of this avenue are a strange lot indeed, including a gardener who turns into a giant purple flower, and lovers who open a peculiar book and walk into an enchanted land filled with yellow light and singing.

Knowles was a master of style and mood; he aimed to create an effect of otherworldly grace and gentleness solely through his languid language. His characters are often unable to cope with the real world, and are saved—or save themselves—only through the intervention of fantasy, if they can be saved at all. There is a sadness in his work that reminds one of the later short novels of Robert Nathan. Many of his fantasies—like the real world—are irresolute, coming to no final conclusion. The ironic position of man in what he believes to be *his* universe is continually emphasized. For Knowles, redemption, if it exists, is accidental; there are no saviors and often no salvation; but there is beauty, love, and devotion to an ideal, and these make life worth living. These jewels of fantasy, lambent sapphires glittering with touches of literary brilliance and flashes of insight, will be treasured by all lovers of fantastic literature.

XIV.

THE LIFE OF DEATH

ROBERT NATHAN AND THE NECESSITY OF LOVE

(1983)

Robert Nathan is one of the truly forgotten writers of the twentieth century. He outlived all of his contemporaries and most of his critics, favorable or unfavorable, and eventually reached that curious status of many artists who attain an advanced age, of having been entombed in the minds of his public before his actual physical death. This was unfortunate, both for himself and for discerning readers of fantasy, for he penned, in a career of sixty years—from publication of his first story in about 1915 to the release of his last novel, *Heaven and Hell and the Megas Factor*, in 1975—some six to ten novels (out of more than sixty books published) that may survive the test of time, and at least two, *Portrait of Jennie* (1940) and *So Love Returns* (1958), that may justifiably be considered classics of modern literature.

Nathan's work is unique in several respects. Virtually all of his fantasy stories are novellas or short novels, averaging about forty thousand words in length, perhaps twenty thousand words shorter than the "average" novel; and although he wrote some short stories at the beginning of his career and several longer "serious" works, almost all of his later prose fiction fits neatly into this intermediate length, one not especially popular with trade houses (his usual publisher, Alfred A. Knopf, used large type and wide leading to push his wordage into longer lengths). Second, Nathan's stories are in many cases blatantly autobiographical, including names of real-life friends and incidents gleaned from the lives of himself and his acquaintances. This is generally true of all writers, of course, but one feels with Nathan that he writes very directly from his inner life. His stories, although charged with emotion, are not sentimental, but mix elements of tragedy, love, and fantasy in almost equal proportions, everything tinged with a dark streak of sadness.

One can see these elements at work in *So Love Returns*. Lenny, a writer of children's books, is trying to work through the sorrow he experienced at the recent death of his beloved wife, Trina. With his two young children, Trisha and Chris, he rents a small house on the California coast, and there begins writing a new book about a witch from the sea. One day he hears Trisha scream and rushes down to the beach to find Chris's body sprawled near the surf line—he had been out swimming and nearly drowned. Both children tell their father that Chris was saved by a "lady" who suddenly appeared in the water from nowhere and carried the boy back to land. He spies the girl, talks with her briefly, and she walks off down the beach.

A week or two later he again meets Kathleen standing alone on the beach, and they talk briefly; she then calls him on the phone and arranges to meet him a third time at a cove. She is young and slender, with ivory skin and green eyes; her bathing suit is made of some scaly green material, and her hair is wound with a piece of kelp. The children immediately accept and trust her. Kathleen is enigmatic about her origins, parrying some of Lenny's questions, declining gently to answer others. When Lenny and the children leave for the day, they last spy her swimming effortlessly far from shore, as if she had fins.

As Lenny's feeling for Kathleen progresses from fondness to love, other strange events occur so naturally that their peculiarity is obscured. Lenny gets drunk in Los Angeles after talking with a producer who takes out an option on one of his stories; while driving home in a semi-stupor, he suddenly feels that his dead wife Trina is driving the car, and begins talking to her. Then Trina becomes Kathleen, telling him in Trina's voice to get home immediately. When he arrives home, Chris reports that Trisha is sick, but Kathleen is there to tend her. She does not leave again, but moves into a small cottage nearby, decorating it with items from the sea. They never speak of her background, although the girl drops hints now and then of otherworldly origins. The two lovers declare their feelings for each other, but always there is the threat, just under the surface, of their imminent separation.

There follows, as Lenny puts it, a period of enchantment. Some months later they hold a picnic at their seaside home for a number of friends, including Dick and Alice, who inform Lenny and Kathleen that they are engaged. Kathleen offers to have the wedding there, and their friends gratefully accept. Unfortunately, Lenny is virtually penniless, so Kathleen gives him an ancient necklace to pawn to raise enough money for the refreshments. The jeweler tells Lenny that the necklace resembles the published description of one known to have been lost at sea in the year 1687.

At the last moment, the scheduled minister falls ill, and a replacement, a heavy-bearded man known to none of them, appears in his place. Kathleen seems uneasy around him, and, when the ceremony begins, gasps at his unusual substitutions. For, the minister states, men are assisted by unseen ethereal beings, God's messengers, whose names are love; they are sent by the Almighty to tell man that he is not forgotten. As they are sent out, so must they return to the elements of which they are composed. "So love returns, to love." Kathleen kisses Lenny, tears streaming down her cheeks, telling him she must go, that she has things to do. He never sees her again. As the party winds down, he realizes that she has disappeared and goes down to her cottage by the sea; it has been stripped clean of its artifacts, and he hears the sound of weeping, coming from somewhere out of the fog, from the sea. A month or two later, he hears someone, Trina or Kathleen, calling him, and awakens to find the house threatened by a brush fire. He and the children escape, but the house, with all their belongings (including the story of the sea witch), is burned to the ground. Later he finds a written account of the strange marriage ceremony penned by Bernard of Trèves, who had continued: "These beings are indeed sendings, sent to the beloved to take the place of one gone from his side; not being mortal, however, for them to love a mortal is forbidden; if and when they do, they must find themselves recalled into the element from which they came."

    This sad and beautiful tale of love, death, and the necessity of hope is the best novel of Nathan's later period, and perhaps the best he ever wrote. It is deceptively simple, for it manages to confront in a brief space questions basic to man's existence: the death of a loved one, coping with the inevitable sorrow, the constant struggle against despair and self-pity, the loneliness of the individual and particularly of the writer, pride in one's work, and the basic need of all men to come to some sort of understanding with themselves, their friends and lovers, and the universe, however one interprets it. In the end, Nathan seems to be saying, everyone needs someone special, if not to survive, then just to live well.

Xenograffiti, by ROBERT REGINALD

XV.

MEROVINGIAN DREAMS

THE NEUSTRIAN FANTASIES OF LESLIE BARRINGER

(1983)

Born in 1895 in Yorkshire, England, Barringer was the son of a schoolmaster. He served in World War I in France, was wounded in action, and returned home in 1917, joining the staff of Thomas Nelson & Sons, the British publishers, as an editor and salesman. In 1942, he became an editor at the *Radio Times*, a popular weekly magazine published by the British Broadcasting Corporation (BBC); four years later, he entered the British government as Senior Information Officer for the Central Office of Information. Finally, he moved to the Amalgamated Press in 1954, working as an editor for their Encyclopedia Department. He died at his home in Ilkley, Yorkshire, England, in 1968.

Of the six novels published by Leslie Barringer during his lifetime, none were bestsellers. They include three historical fictions set in medieval England—*Kay the Left-Handed* (1935), *Know Ye Not Agincourt* (1936), and *The Rose in Splendour* (1953)—and the three novels for which he is likely to be remembered—*Gerfalcon* (1927), *Joris of the Rock* (1928), and *Shy Leopardess* (1948), a loose trilogy of novels which Newcastle Publishing Company called the Neustrian Cycle when reprinting them in 1976 and 1977.

Barringer was an accomplished historian—he contributed an outline of world history to the *Amalgamated*

Xenograffiti, by ROBERT REGINALD

Children's Encyclopedia—so it is no surprise to find him utilizing the events of medieval history as a background for his novels. Curiously, however, he chose to place the Neustrian books in an alternate world where the Merovingian Empire apparently never dissolved. In real history, the Franks conquered much of what is now France and Germany, beginning in 486 A.D. under their first great leader, King Clovis I. With his successors of the Merovingian Dynasty, the kingdom split at various times into two or more parts, Neustria occupying what is now central and northwestern France, Austrasia covering what is now northeastern France and southwestern Germany, and Burgundy lying to the south and east of these two. The borders of these states were not fixed in the modern sense, but varied with the fortunes of war; the constant struggles between the dynastic branches resulted in the unification of the states on four different occasions, but ultimately led to chaos and a decline in royal power. The Mayors of the Palaces gradually assumed real political power and finally deposed the Merovingians in 751. Thereafter, the western Franks merged with the old Romanized population to form the political entity that is now called France; the eastern Franks established the Holy Roman Empire, although the Franks themselves basically occupied the Duchy of Franconia in southwestern Germany, an area which had previously been a part of Austrasia.

Barringer's version of history is not at all clear from his books. The geography of "Neustria" as displayed on maps accompanying the first two books is clearly that of present-day Normandy and Brittany; other lands to the south and east are mentioned as part of Neustria, but their extent is never indicated. England exists as an independent kingdom, but Germany has become Franconia. There is one fleeting reference to Austrasia. Italy is divided into duchies and small states, much as it was in real history. There are a few clues, however: King Thorismund of Neustria is a Merovingian name taken from one of the real kings of that dynasty; King René may be patterned after a real King René who ruled Burgundy. The royal house of Franconia, according to Barringer, is closely related in the male line to that of Neustria, thereby following a pattern common in the old Merov-

85

ingian Empire. From these hints, it may be inferred that Barringer did more than merely switch a few place names, actually implying a continuation of the Merovingians into medieval times, with Neustria more or less occupying the same space as present-day France, and Austrasia becoming Franconia, a development that could actually have happened. The loose confederation of states that is now called the Holy Roman Empire does not exist in Barringer's world; Franconia, which appears to occupy the area which later contained Württemberg and Bavaria, is a single, unified state under a strong king. Barringer's given names for his characters would seem to support this theory, as they indicate a strong Germanic element in the population. Old King René's bastard son, for example, is Conrad of Burias.

Whatever the guiding principle, Barringer's world is a compelling mix of politics, intrigue, fierce battles, treachery, religion, and strong characters, all set in the early 1400s (no specific dates are mentioned). If France and Germany have changed, the major sweep of world history continues as before: the Ottomans threaten Constantinople, the same religious conflicts exist between Muslim and Christian, and the Franconians hate the Neustrians as the Neustrians do the Franconians.

The first book in the series, *Gerfalcon,* follows young Raoul of Ger, nephew of the reigning Count. Orphaned at an early age (his father was killed in the Crusades), Raoul must live on the stingy generosity of Count Armand, playing second fiddle to Armand's son and heir, Charles. When Raoul disobeys one of his uncle's rules, he is publicly whipped; he therefore decides to find his own way in the world until he comes of age, when he will become eligible to succeed to a small, desolate barony left to him by his grandmother. Under the assumed name Herluin, Raoul wends his way to the castle of Lorin de Campscapel, called the "Butcher Count" by his soldiers, a fierce warrior whose erratic behavior has endeared him to few. During one of Lorin's rages, Raoul kills him and escapes from the castle. In the woods to the east, he encounters Nino Chiostra and John Doust, an Italian and an Englishman who become Raoul's friends (and later his associates); they settle in the merchant town of Belsaunt for the winter, until Raoul comes of age; and there one day, Raoul sees his cousin Charles murdered by a jealous lover, making him heir to his uncle's seat. When he returns to his uncle's castle on the coast and confronts him with the demand to render him his small barony, Count Armand collapses in his rage with a stroke, making Raoul regent of Ger. Raoul then gathers a small party of soldiers and returns to Campscapel, where he defeats and kills mad Count Jehan, Lorin's brother and successor, restoring peace to his part of Neustria. At the end of the book, he marries his cousin, Reine, after saving her from an ambush by the outlaw, Joris of the Rock.

The second novel, *Joris of the Rock*, begins earlier than *Gerfalcon* and ends later, revolving around the same incident in which Raoul and Reine fight the notorious bandit. In the first novel, the attack is told from Raoul's point of view, in the second, from Joris's. Joris is the illegitimate son of a Neustrian noble, a brilliant lad who is embittered when his mother is killed. He sets himself up in a forest retreat high on the "Rock," not far from Belsaunt, where he ambushes unwary travelers on the nearby highways. Certain from a prophetic verse of his own ultimate destiny, he gradually gathers an army of one hundred desperate men, vagabonds who will follow him anywhere. Old King René is ill and his own son has died in a hunting accident; his heir is his nephew, Prince Thorismund, who duly succeeds to the throne when the old man dies. René's illegitimate son, Duke Conrad of Burias, has gathered a following who believe him more suited for the throne than the young, inexperienced, flighty Thorismund, and a vast conspiracy is set in motion. Joris exploits the situation by selling his men to Conrad, while Raoul works for the legitimate heir, believing that only he can keep the kingdom secure. In the climactic battle of the civil war, Raoul saves the day with a flanking attack; Joris and his surviving men escape the battlefield but are pursued by Raoul, who has convinced the King to grant him the authority to eliminate this menace to the kingdom's safety once and forever. Hounded by Raoul's troops, Joris goes underground for several months, finally emerging from hiding when the troops have largely disbanded, thinking him dead.

Xenograffiti, by ROBERT REGINALD

Ironically, he encounters one of his own bastards, Juhel, sired by Joris when he raped the lad's mother, and meets his death at the hands of his son.

Shy Leopardess is set ten years after the culminating events of the previous volume and concerns fourteen-year-old Yolande, heir to the Duchy of Baraine. When her father is ambushed in his own castle by bandits, Yolande becomes the ward of her uncle, Count Azo, hero of a recent war with Franconia. Azo persuades the King through flattery to betroth his ward to Azo's son and heir, Balthasar, thereby making Balthasar Duke of Baraine when the marriage is finally consummated. Azo gradually begins concentrating power into his own hands, with the ultimate goal of killing King Thorismund and placing his underage son, Prince René, on the throne; Azo, as constable of the kingdom, will then become regent. Balthasar, called "Belphegor" behind his back (after the devil of the same name), is as cruel and depraved as he is handsome, a sadistic young monster who enjoys torture, both physical and psychological. Gradually, Yolande realizes that Azo murdered her father by hiring a surviving remnant of Joris's displaced band; with the assistance of her pages, Diomede and Lioncel, both of whom have become her lovers as well, she gradually gains control of her own life and plots the downfall of Balthasar. Count Raoul of Ger, heir to her Duchy, helps to expose Azo's conspiracy. Yolande lures her husband to her father's castle to consummate their marriage, presumably ending whatever shreds of independence she still possesses; instead, she and her pages murder Balthasar in cold blood, recounting to him the long list of innocents he has killed or injured; Yolande then sends her husband's pickled head to Count Azo on the eve of the final battle for possession of the kingdom. Azo is defeated and hanged for his crimes, but in the course of the struggle, both Diomede and Lioncel are killed. At the end of the book, Count Raoul suggests to Yolande, still under the age of twenty, that she seriously consider marrying the widowed King Thorismund and using her strong will to bring peace to Neustria.

Barringer's books are all *bildungsromans*. In each volume, he focuses on an innocent, immature youth and fol-

Xenograffiti, by ROBERT REGINALD

lows the development of that character's personality as he or she finds himself or herself. Raoul of Ger is his paradigm of the medieval nobleman; a shy and untried lad at the beginning of *Gerfalcon,* he quickly uses his spirit and intelligence to make his way in the world. He learns to kill when necessary for his own survival, but he never glories in the violence forced upon him. Short and plain in looks, Raoul's gentle, unassuming nature, his lack of pretense, and his quick wit and sense of humor make him an attractive figure to men and women alike. His experiences with the "Jacquerie," the common folk, provide him with a perspective that few of his fellow nobles possess; he never abuses his power when he finally inherits the crags of Ger.

In *Joris of the Rock*, Barringer balances out the sly, intelligent amorality of Joris with the sensitivity of his retiring bastard son, Juhel, who has been reared after a peasant revolt as the supposed Count of Ath. Whereas Joris is bold, forceful, arrogant, cruel, and wholly selfish, Juhel is shy, religious, unassertive, kind, and almost completely unselfish. Because of his (false) position, Juhel is forced into the role of nobleman, a role he ultimately rejects. After fighting at Raoul's side in the great civil war, Juhel is left numbed by the carnage; some months later, when he revisits the site, he wanders away down the river bank, where he spies a lone hunter fording the river. Recognizing Joris but unaware that he is his real father, Juhel challenges the outlaw and rides him down. Joris, in one last moment of spite, tries to ruin the lad's life by blurting out his secret, but he dies choking on his own blood. Juhel, mortified nevertheless at one more death laid to his hands, asks Raoul for permission to leave the nobility and enter the ranks of the Church. In Barringer's eyes, clearly, Joris's sins will be expiated and balanced by Juhel's life of sanctity. If Joris is the devil, a human version of Satan, Juhel is the saint, a human version of Christ. Thus is the natural order restored.

Finally, Barringer's paradigm of woman is Yolande of Baraine, the *Shy Leopardess*. Orphaned at the age of fourteen, Yolande is forced to grow up ahead of her time in a world where men make the rules and expect women to follow. Once again, Yolande, as with all of Barringer's leading characters, is exceptionally intelligent and seems to have a natural sense of self-possession. Manipulated by her cruel and ambitious uncle, Count Azo, Yolande is forced to find a subtle road to revenge, a road fraught with peril. Having been married to Azo's monster of a son, Duke Balthasar, Yolande literally has no rights under the law; although legally Duchess of Baraine, her uncle is Regent and Grand Seneschal of the Duchy until she comes of age—and when she does come of age and Balthasar claims his marriage right, he legally becomes Duke of Baraine, possessing all temporal authority in her domain. Through luck, fortitude, courage, and an utter determination to rule her own mind and body, and with the help of her cousin, Count Raoul of Ger, Yolande begins directing events to her own ends. Ultimately, she gains possession of the treasonous document constructed by Count Azo to disgrace Raoul and his supporters; Azo had then hoped to murder the unwise King (whom Balthasar has already cuckolded) and make himself and his son the final authority in the kingdom, as regents for Prince René. By the end of the novel, Yolande has lost her innocence but gained a sense of wisdom; never a fool, she has grasped the reins of her own life, in both love and war, and has decided that she will never again relinquish them to anyone. It is Raoul, however, who sees the kind of person she has become—and sees her potential as Queen of Neustria. The leopardess is shy no longer.

XVI.

ONE IS ONE AND ALL ALONE

FRITZ LEIBER'S SOLIPSISTIC FANTASY

(1983)

Fritz Leiber, Jr., is best known in the fantasy genre for his series of stories about Fafhrd and the Grey Mouser, although he also wrote a wide variety of fantastic tales in a career which spanned more than fifty years. One of his most obscure works, *You're All Alone*, is also one of his most interesting, having been intended for the magazine *Unknown* (*Worlds*) in 1943. When the magazine ceased publication later that year, Leiber put aside the unfinished novel, his third, and turned to war work; a few years later he completed the book, but was unable to sell it until the early 1950s. The "soft porn" house which bought it changed its title to *The Sinful Ones*, added several extraneous sex scenes, and published it with a short novel by David Williams, *Blood, Bulls, and Passion*. Ace did a shorter version of the book, closer to the original pulp story, in 1972, under the earlier title. Pocket Books then republished the longer novel in 1980, deleting extraneous material, but maintaining the title used in 1953. For all its checkered history, and under whatever title, Leiber's book remains a fascinating philosophical fantasy, wholly different from any other work published in the modern history of the genre.

    The question here is essentially one of life itself: what is it?, how do men perceive it?, and how do men perceive other men? "Is anyone alive other than myself?"

Xenograffiti, by ROBERT REGINALD

Leiber asks. His answer may be interpreted in several different ways. Carr Mackay is an interviewer at General Employment. One day, a comely young girl appears at his desk; he begins to ask her the usual questions, but is totally mystified by her response, by her obvious terror before a complete stranger. When the girl asks, "Don't you know what you are?" the puzzle compounds itself. The girl has been followed into the office by a big blonde, a woman whose behavior is just as peculiar as the girl's. The blonde's manifest arrogance, her lack of regard for the other people in the office, and her air of superiority, all make her seem somehow otherwordly. After responding to Carr's questions with *non sequiturs* about the danger he is in, the girl scribbles a note on a piece of paper, drops it on his desk, and walks out. The blonde is waiting for her at the doorway and strikes her across the face. No one notices, not even the girl herself. She continues calmly on her way. The note tells Carr to beware of the wall-eyed blonde, the young man without a hand, and the affable-seeming older man; the small dark man with glasses is his friend, she says. While Carr is watching the charade, another applicant sets himself down in front of Carr and immediately begins answering the questions that Carr would have asked if the interruption had not occurred. Suddenly Carr realizes that the dumpy man is smoking a nonexistent cigarette that Carr should have offered to him and that he is responding like a robot to comments that Carr has never made. Carr tells him to stop, but he pays no attention. When Carr grabs him by the shoulder, the dumpy man begins throbbing and mouthing meaningless drivel. When Carr seeks help from his fellow employees, no one responds. It is as if the entire world is running by itself and Carr has somehow dropped out of it, becoming aware for the first time that the world and almost all the people in it are mere cogs in some vast machinery that just keeps ticking away. Any attempt to interrupt the cycle results in vibration; the machine's huge inertia struggles mightily to fit people back into their molds.

Carr meets the girl in the park and gradually learns something about her and about reality. A few men and women have somehow become aware of their situation, have

Xenograffiti, by ROBERT REGINALD

suddenly sprung alive into a dead world. Such persons have great power, since the world as a whole ignores them: many use this power in obscene ways. Often these abusers of power band together into small gangs, fighting one another to establish their supremacy, seeking to eliminate the few independents who try to live their awakened lives responsibly. Miss Hackman, the blonde girl, is one member of a gang, together with Wilson, the leader, and a young man, Driscoll Aimes. They hunt their prey with a trained panther (some animals may also become "alive"). Their quarry is Fred, the small, dark man with glasses, the one who, in his loneliness, had awakened Jane from her "sleep." He is eventually killed by the trio, who have now become aware of Jane's existence and suspect Carr's. All the rest of humanity is irrelevant, a mere plaything for these less-than-noble godlings. Jane and Carr play hide-and-seek with the gang throughout Chicago: to escape the cat, Carr must dive into the lake. He is rescued by another independent, Old Jules, who has "connections" who will neutralize the gang. Carr returns to the city and retrieves Jane, but is trapped with her in an old house. As the gang and their beast close in, the house is rushed by a rival gang who mercilessly murder the three humans and their cat; Jane and Carr, hiding on the upper floor, are overlooked during the fight. They decide, conscientiously, to resume their places in the real world, carefully managing their lives toward marriage and trying to awaken others of their friends and relatives in a fashion that will minimize the danger of exposure.

The interwoven questions of delusion, solipsism, behaviorism, insanity/sanity, responsibility toward others, and the machinelike nature of modern society make this a particularly enjoyable book for the inquiring mind. Leiber does not dismiss these questions out-of-hand; one could interpret this novel as the epitome of paranoia or as a fictional treatise on mass self-delusion, as a parable on the temptations of power or as a thinly disguised tract on elitism, pro or con. At the heart of the book, however, is a tale of love, courage, and the necessity of standing up for oneself, of fighting for what one believes in, of having principles for which to fight. The gang uses its situation to gratify the basest instincts; Carr and

Xenograffiti, by ROBERT REGINALD

Jane decide, at the end, to dedicate their lives to awakening what they realize will be a very small portion of mankind. With their commitment to each other and their commitment to humanity, they can bear the pain of seeing reality before them, in its bright, searing ugliness.

XVII.

PALADOREAN IDYLLS

SIR HENRY NEWBOLT'S *ALADORE*

with Mary A. Burgess

(1983)

Aladore (1914) is, on its most elemental level, a fairy tale, a story so limpid and gentle in the telling that one is tempted to read it simply for pure enjoyment. Sir Henry John Newbolt's pastiche of the style made popular by William Morris employs a rich though archaic language which contributes greatly to the beautiful flow of this tale of a medieval quest for love and the meaning of life.

Ywain is the jaded administrator of an unnamed medieval state who is so overcome with ennui that he renounces his rights and turns over his lands and appurtenances of office to a younger brother, takes up the cloak and staff of a pilgrim, and sets off to follow his "desire," a will-o'-the-wisp in the guise of a child. He first encounters a hermit in the wilderness who teaches him the joys of the aesthetic life: solitude and peace. They break bread together and bathe in a mountain stream (the first of many such allusions to Christian fellowship). Ywain is soothed, but torn between the fellowship and peace of the hermitage and the lure of the child, his desire. This tension is reminiscent of the pull between the saintly life and the knightly quest depicted so well in

Xenograffiti, by ROBERT REGINALD

Geoffrey Chaucer's *The Canterbury Tales* (1387-1400), and it is never resolved here completely.

Ywain leaves the hermit's solitary paradise and is directed toward Paladore, a walled city. There he encounters a beautiful lady, Aithne, who entreats him not to desert her as other knights have done in the past. He is distracted by the nearby sounds of battle and, overcome with a strange compulsion, joins the Eagles who are attacking the besieged Tower and helps to win the day. The warring parties converge at the end of the battle, and both sides honor Ywain as a hero. They explain that the battle is part of an age-old custom whereby the Eagles (who represent the liberal forces for change) challenge the Tower (the bastion of conservative power). Ywain is given a house and welcomed to the community. He has an inexplicable interlude with the lady Aithne, whose supernatural powers enable her to travel at will to the magical city of Aladore. He cannot "see" the city when she asks him to look for it, and she turns away in resignation. Meanwhile, the Tower, although outwardly friendly, secretly conspires to rid itself of Ywain's influence. He is challenged with three adventures which he accepts. Each time, when he is confounded by seemingly overwhelming odds, the lady Aithne appears in the guise of another and saves him.

Finally, Ywain is lured to join a band of knights who seek the City of Saints. Although the company's motives are varied and suspect, Ywain still longs for fulfillment and so elects to join the group. After much travail, Ywain and his companion Bartholomy happen upon the city and think they have completed their quest. The city is both lovely and unusual, but it is governed by ringing bells. A caretaker, Vincent, asks what they hope to find. "Peace," responds Bartholomy, but Ywain says, "I look only to love and to seek." Subtly, both men succumb to the lure of the bells which lull them into a state of forgetfulness. They think they have found peace, but the bells are really their captors. After a period of time, Ywain stumbles upon a garden where he meets again the lady Aithne. Suddenly, he remembers all that has gone before and realizes that she is the image of all that he desires. She asks him to forswear the bells and fol-

Xenograffiti, by ROBERT REGINALD

low her on a new pilgrimage. At this point, they are startled by a spy for the city slithering away in the grass, like a serpent invading the lovers' Edenic paradise. Ywain agrees to break the bonds of the city and follows his lady to the Lost Lands of the South. Here they encounter oreads, naiads, and fauns in a magical kingdom of milk and honey. Ywain falls in with the fauns and is enchanted by their rough pursuit of earthly pleasures. Together with Aithne (in the guise of a shepherdess), he spends blissful days in pastoral harmony. Gradually, Ywain becomes fearful of the fauns and their madcap antics. One evening, he has a vision of the city of Aladore, and the longing for his desire overcomes him once again. He begs Aithne to leave with him and aid him in casting off the animal trappings which make him kin to the fauns.

The fauns, growing bolder, follow the lovers in their flight. Suddenly, Aithne and Ywain are taken up by a strange creature with wings and flown to the city of Doedala, where a race of men carries on the tradition of Daedalus. Ywain is then taught the art and flies off to seek Aladore, leaving Aithne behind. He falls to the ground and is rescued by his old friend, the hermit. Here he bides, again renewing his strength and purpose. The hermit counsels him to return to Paladore and seek his desire among men. Ywain returns and discovers the Tower and the Eagles still at odds. He speaks to them and pacifies them temporarily, although the Tower has grown to hate him and resolves to destroy him.

One afternoon, Ywain follows the sound of many children frolicking and singing. There, on the Sherperdine Sands, he discovers again the city of Aladore. This time, he is permitted to cross through the mist and over the sea to its gates. He is taken to the chamber of the Rhymer's Hail, where he finds a book containing a picture of Aithne; he turns and finds that the image has become reality and follows her to their bridal chamber. They are wedded, and she tells him he has become the master of his dream, which is her dream as well. They begin an idyllic existence, as Aithne shows Ywain the Rhymer's magic, wherein all the seekers and lovers of times past, of myth and of history, are brought to life before their eyes. Ywain visits the scene of Aithne's childhood, Castle Kerioc, where he sees her as a child and there experiences with her all the warmth and love of her childhood years.

Ywain has forgotten that his pilgrimage must also take him past the gates of death. Aithne releases the key to a crypt wherein an old man dwells. The man warns Ywain that the time will come when he will be recalled to the world of man, and with the sounding of the midnight bells, Ywain finds himself in Paladore once more. Aithne follows him and together they are drawn into the final climactic battle for mastery of the city. Ywain is offered the principality, but refuses when he realizes that the offer is an illusion; the real prince is a captive of the archbishop and subject to the wishes of the Tower. Instead, he elects to sacrifice himself, like Christ, to purchase the freedom and salvation of his brothers and companions in arms, the Eagles.

Ywain sees the child of his desire one last time and follows him to the sanctuary where Aithne awaits him. There he sees a bier carried in by knights, and, as he pulls back the pall, discovers his own face. Aithne calls him and they depart hand-in-hand through the battle. They are never seen in Paladore again, but the effigies of a knight and his lady are discovered on the tomb of the altar in the sanctuary. Ywain's friend Hubert explains: "They are not here but otherwise, and their sleep is but a semblance. And doubtless the pilgrim hath achieved his pilgrimage for he learned of this lady: and she came and went of her own magic, and had from her birth the Rhymer's heritage."

This allegory of Christian love is notable for the fact that it is (except for the somewhat juvenile Greenwood tales of G. P. Baker) the only medieval fantasy published between the death of William Morris in 1896 and the twenty-year interlude between World War I and World War II. Newbolt is clearly familiar with Morris's work, and uses the same style of language, indefinable time period, and medieval trappings. That such a novel, with its emphasis on love and companionship at all levels, should appear on the eve of World War I is indeed ironic; Newbolt, who later wrote the official history of the British Navy in that conflict, never wrote another novel.

XVIII.

PROSPERO UPDATED

THE FANTASY OF JOHN BELLAIRS

with Mary A. Burgess

(1983)

Sepharial, the professional name of Walter Gorn Old, has said in his book *The Kabala of Numbers* (1913) that "what we call an event is but a displacement and rearrangement of the parts of our own sphere of reality." This is an appropriate comment on John Bellairs's novel, *The Face in the Frost* (1969), both because the author mentions the *Kabala* as the solution to his character's dilemma and because he has, in fact, utilized this concept of rearranging known historical facts as the basis for constructing an idealized medieval world of surpassing charm and beauty. Indeed, Bellairs's novel deals very directly with the question of the nature of reality—and who or what makes things real.

Prospero and Bacon, wizards and old friends, embark upon a journey to save mankind from the evil spell of their former colleague and fellow magician, Melichus. Melichus has found an old book written in curious ciphers that seem untranslatable; when he tries to decipher the strange writing, he can make out only tantalizing glimpses of some basic formulas of power. The more he pursues the question, the more entranced he becomes; what has begun as intellectual curiosity quickly becomes an obsession, first with the translation itself, and then with the power the spells might bring the translator. The formulas somehow contain the secret to another reality or series of realities; the master of these arcane symbols can literally destroy the world of the North and South Kingdoms. This Prospero and Bacon must prevent at any cost.

This is not the Roger Bacon who was the Franciscan monk in the "real world," a man known not only for his contributions to science ("It is the intention of philosophy to work out the nature and properties of things"), but also as an alchemist and dabbler in magic. Yet he is clearly intended to be an analogue of the real Bacon in a world where magic works. Like his model, this alternate version is devoted to the truth, whatever it may be, wherever it may lie; like the real Bacon, Bellairs's wizard is a man of honor and courage. Prospero, on the other hand, is modeled after William Shakespeare's fictional sorcerer, the practitioner of "this rough magic." In *The Tempest* (1611), Prospero sets out to right the wrongs of his world, and in so doing, employs his magic one last time to bring about a proper balance of persons and events. Bellairs's character is also concerned with balance, with setting right his world; a bumbling and forgetful man, clearly no match for the brilliant and logical Melichus, he nevertheless sets forth with a desperate kind of courage to fight the good fight. His very lack of pretension, his refusal to fool himself by championing his own considerable abilities, are major assets in this struggle to the death.

The mark of Melichus's growing power over the land is the ever-recurring image of "the face in the frost," a yawning, vacant visage which, when glimpsed, evokes a nameless terror, a horror that cannot be dispelled by reason: "He felt very nervous, drowsily nervous, with prickling dark borders on his sight. A glass bell was ringing somewhere deep, deep in the forest. An icy green glass bell ridged with frost, trembling on a green willow branch." Time is growing short; the two friends begin their adventure by shrinking themselves and sailing a model ship down an underground stream that leads from Prospero's root cellar. In the ensuing chapters, the magicians defeat a troll, make use of a prophetic mirror (a looking-glass), ride in a pumpkin (squash) coach, fight off

Xenograffiti, by ROBERT REGINALD

the spells cast by an enchanted forest, and climb a magical vine (beanstalk) to reach the fairy tale-like cottage once shared by Prospero and Melichus in happier days. These images from common folk myths and childhood fairy tales weave a rich but dark tapestry of allusion and double entendre throughout Bellairs's tale.

At the cottage, Prospero retrieves the green glass paperweight that contains the magical powers of Prospero and Melichus combined. Like Zed in John Boorman's acclaimed motion picture *Zardoz,* Prospero enters the world of the prism, a strange place in which technology has prevailed, filled with electric lights, lawnmowers, and the accoutrements of modern civilization. Zed's crystal had contained all of man's knowledge; with it, and with the knowledge he gained of himself, Zed was able to destroy the prism itself, thus freeing man from the bonds of self-imposed technological shackles. In Bellairs's prism, Prospero encounters M. Millhorn, a true believer in the occult, a man who has been waiting all of his life for this moment. In exchange for the paperweight, Millhorn uses his knowledge of the *Kabala* to save Prospero from the pursuing Melichus; Prospero is returned to his own world, where he finally remembers the spell he must use to destroy Melichus and his evil book, thereby restoring reality. In the end, Prospero's world returns to normal, and he and Bacon celebrate their triumph with a party for their friends.

The Face in the Frost was published originally as a children's book, although it has been reprinted in paperback as an adult novel; it can be read on many different levels. What appears on the surface to be the rather lighthearted adventures of two bumbling wizards on a quest becomes, on rereading, a darkly streaked tale of moral courage, tragedy, and the ultimate doom of the world. Everything in the book is seen through the two-sided mirror, a glass which, when held up to "reality," reflects fantasy and real life, the past and the present, humor and sorrow, the pursuit of power and a devotion to duty, in equal measures. The reader sees "through a glass darkly" to reach the truth on the other side. Prospero must pass out of his world through the glass before he can defeat Melichus; he must see his world—and see evil—for what it is before he can remember the spell. He must recognize that good and evil are the only true constants.

Bellairs's powers of description bring this book alive; every leaf on every branch of every tree is limned in exquisite detail. His ability to make his readers see, smell, hear, taste, even touch the outlines of his fantasy creation makes it real for them. In the context of his story, this must surely be the ultimate paradox.

Xenograffiti, by ROBERT REGINALD

XIX.

STRANGE LESSONS

EDWARD HERON-ALLEN'S COSMOPOLI TALES

(1983)

Edward Heron-Allen wrote many novels and stories during his long career, but he is remembered today primarily for his pseudonymously published University of Cosmopoli tales, published in four volumes between 1921 and 1934. Their publishing history is almost as strange as the stories themselves: the first collection, *The Purple Sapphire and Other Posthumous Papers*, was issued by Philip Allan of London in 1921 under the pen name Christopher Blayre, and included most of the stories in the sequence; however, one short novel, *The Cheetah Girl*, was listed on the contents page but not actually included in the text, apparently being dropped by the publisher at the last moment for fear of prosecution under Britain's rather severe anti-smut laws of the time. The story was issued in 1923 by Heron-Allen himself in a private edition of ten or twenty copies and remains virtually inaccessible today. The Blayre tales proved popular enough to warrant a second edition from Allan in 1932 under the title *The Strange Papers of Dr Blayre*; this book included all the stories previously published in the 1921 version, plus several new adventures, but again omitting *The Cheetah Girl*. A final collection, *Some Women of the University: Being a Last Selection from the Strange Papers of Christopher Blayre*, was again privately printed by Heron-Allen in 1934 under the R. Stockwell imprint, and distributed in an edition

103

of perhaps a hundred copies; this 171-page volume is also exceedingly rare.

The technique of connecting otherwise unrelated tales with a loose framing structure is an old one, and one which is still used in modern times by such masters of fantasy as Ray Bradbury. Indeed, one is reminded of Bradbury in reading these stories, for they share with his work a disdain for the results of technology, a love of the *outré*, and a certain sentimentality mixed with a sobering dash of the tragic. The stories can be grouped roughly into three categories: tales of the supernatural, tales of scientific exploration or warning, and tales of fantastic whimsy.

Heron-Allen is most successful with the first category of stories. "The Purple Sapphire," for example, the title story of the first Blayre collection, tells of a cursed Indian jewel which wreaks disastrous ill luck on the Arkwright family of England. Attempts to give the stone away are futile: thieves who steal it are promptly jailed and the sapphire is returned; a society belle who agrees to take it from Sir Clement Arkwright eventually commits suicide, and the stone is returned to Sir Clement by the police investigating team; an attempt to throw it into the Thames is thwarted when a pauper discovers the jewel, tries to pawn it, and is sent to Arkwright. Eventually, Arkwright dies a ruined man, leaving the jewel to his heirs with specific instructions that it be donated to the University.

In "Mano Pantea," Heron-Allen turns to another kind of curse, one attached to a charm in the form of a silver hand. The Italians, who have three different forms of the hand to ward off the evil eye, are deeply superstitious about the hands' supposed powers. Ippolito makes the mistake of breaking his hand, which then turns on him, taking its revenge by strangling the poor man.

"The Thing That Smelt" demonstrates the evil that results when a spiritualist carries his experiments too far and must pay the price for his inquisitiveness.

"The Demon" is a chilling tale of possession and the price a dying woman pays for the continuation of her life.

Heron-Allen's scientific romances tend to be cautionary tales that warn against dabbling in matters beyond

Xenograffiti, by ROBERT REGINALD

the ken of man. "Aalila," the most interesting of these stories, features Professor Alured Markwand, whose experiments in phototelephony and sound transmission anticipate current developments in the laser transmission of sound through small filaments of glass. Markwand aims his device at Venus and is startled to receive a response from an inhabitant of that planet, a captivating woman named Aalila. Eventually he succeeds in sending not only sound but also visual images, so that he can both see and talk to the beautiful alien. The Venusians, it seems, have long been studying the radio broadcasts of Earth and now understand English perfectly. Markwand falls in love with the girl, but fails to anticipate the jealousy of her husband; during the course of an intimate conversation, the two are interrupted by her Venusian mate, who cuts off the circuit, thereby killing Markwand. Markwand's device is destroyed and the evidence covered up before the police arrive.

In "The Mirror That Remembered," Professor Erichsen discovers a method for playing back the light images that have been "seen" by a mirror, similar to the "slow glass" concept invented by Bob Shaw in his story, "The Light of Other Days"; while playing back the events recorded by the mirror, both Erichsen and his lady friend, also present, realize that certain events of the preceding three weeks should not be viewed by the assembled audience, and she immediately destroys the mirror.

The tales of whimsy include the delightful fantasy, "The House on the Way to Hell," in which a former University librarian, having died and gone to his "reward" in Hell, finds himself appointed librarian of the Library and Museum of Projected and Unfinished Books and Projected and Unfinished Works of Art, Science, and Manufacture. The librarian is astonished to find completed copies of Charles Dickens's *The Mystery of Edwin Drood* (1870), Franz Schubert's *Unfinished Symphony*, Samuel Taylor Coleridge's "Kubla Khan," and many others. Before leaving him to his eternal chores, the Devil hands the librarian one final volume—the librarian's unfinished *History of the University of Cosmopoli*. Another such tale is "The Man Who Killed the Jew," in which a bumbling doctor's cure is sufficient to end the eternal travels of the Wandering Jew, who was cursed by Christ to live until the Second Resurrection.

Heron-Allen will never be considered a major fantasy writer, but his work bears further examination by historians in the field. At their best, his stories have an ironic poignancy reminiscent of the short novels of Robert Nathan, who was also active in the 1920s and '30s; however, Heron-Allen is more dispassionate than Nathan and more interested in exploring the edges of spiritualism and pseudoscience than his contemporaries, Vernon Knowles or Lord Dunsany. This curious combination makes his a unique voice for his time and his collections unique works of fantastic literature.

Xenograffiti, by ROBERT REGINALD

XX.

STYX TRYX

THE HUMOROUS FANTASIES OF JOHN KENDRICK BANGS

with Mary A. Burgess

(1983)

The humorous ghost story is a peculiarly American subgenre, spawned in the tall tales told around a roaring campfire and first developed into a literary form by Washington Irving. Irving's stories, epitomized by "The Legend of Sleepy Hollow," became immensely popular—more popular with the *hoi polloi,* it is true, than with the critics, who have always regarded Irving as somewhat less than a serious writer. After Irving, occasional writers attempted to produce humorous fantasy, often with rather haphazard results. By the late Victorian period, however, the "serious" ghost story, both in England and in America, had reached one of its periodic peaks of popularity, with both countries' best writers producing classic examples. Robert Louis Stevenson, Charles Dickens, Henry James—these are but a few of the major serious authors who popularized this literary form. As a counterpoint to this movement, other writers began turning to the humorous ghost story, both to profit by these fast-selling stories and to satirize them. The most successful lampoonist of the ghostly tale in both America and Britain

Xenograffiti, by ROBERT REGINALD

was John Kendrick Bangs, who made the humorous sprite the basis of his literary reputation.

Bangs had a remarkably productive career, writing more than forty books, editing such well-known journals as *Harper's Weekly*, *Harper's Monthly*, *Puck*, and many others, and producing essays, articles, short stories, and reviews, many of which were collected in volume form. Born in 1862 in New York, he spent most of his life close to the metropolis, except for making brief, well-paid lecture tours throughout the United States and Europe.

Although Bangs was successful almost from the very start of his career and supported himself very well from his free-lance writing and his editing, he did not reach public notice until the appearance in 1893 of *Toppleton's Client; or, A Spirit in Exile*, a humorous fantasy novel, and the stories published at about the same time in various popular magazines which were later collected in *The Water-Ghost and Others* (1894). (An earlier collection of fantasy had appeared anonymously in 1888 under the title, *New Waggings of Old Tales*, by Two Wags—*i.e.*, John Kendrick Bangs and Frank D. Sherman.) Both *Toppleton's Client* and *The Water-Ghost and Others* were well received; Bangs, a thoroughly professional businessman and never one to miss an opportunity, saw his opportunity and began producing a steady stream of tall tales and satires. His humorous fantasy *Mr. Bonaparte of Corsica* was published in 1896, as was *The Rebellious Heroine*, a fantasy novel. The following year saw the publication of *A House-Boat on the Styx*. *The Pursuit of the House-Boat: Being Some Further Account of the Divers Doings of the Associated Shades, Under the Leadership of Sherlock Holmes*, was issued in 1897. A year later, *Ghosts I Have Met and Some Others* appeared, which was followed in 1899 by *The Enchanted Type-Writer*. Two books were published in 1901: *Over the Plum-Pudding*, a collection, and *Mr. Münchausen*, a fantasy novel. *Bikey the Skycycle and Other Tales of Jimmie* followed in 1902, as did the novel *Olympian Nights*. Finally, some years later, the following titles appeared: *Alice in Blunderland* (1907), a novel; *The Autobiography of Methuselah* (1909), a novel; *Jack and the Check-Book* (1911), a collection; and *Shylock Homes: His*

Xenograffiti, by ROBERT REGINALD

Posthumous Memoirs (1973), a posthumous collection of the Sherlock Holmes pastiches.

Of all Bangs's books, by far his most popular were the "House-Boat" stories, which have remained almost continually in print from the date of their first publication. Bangs had an inspiration which was later shared by the modern writer/actor/producer Steve Allen: what would happen if the world's most famous historical personages, including politicians, artists, literary figures, even fictional characters, somehow got together to discuss the foibles of mankind? The only logical place for such a meeting was Hell itself, or the gentler Hades of Greek mythology, that gloomy, shadowy, hateful nursing home for men's immortal souls, surrounded by the River Styx, which could only be penetrated or crossed by the dour ferryman, Charon. It was Charon's eternal task to transport the souls of the deceased to their final abode in Hades.

So here, under Bangs's watchful eye, gather the spirits of Hades, who have now formed a social organization known as the Associated Shades. The Associated Shades have taken over management of a houseboat, which they intend to turn into an exclusive, luxurious club; their one remaining problem is Charon, who is likely to object to any interference with his monopoly. Therefore, the usual committee is formed, consisting of Sir Walter Raleigh, Cassius, Demosthenes, Blackstone, Doctor Johnson, and Confucius; they will approach Charon and seek to gain his active participation in the venture. Charon agrees, at double the proposed wages, with Saturdays off; after much discussion, the committee acquiesces and awards him the honorific title of Janitor, which is, they explain, a very noble office indeed. Charon responds by noting the time, twelve midnight on Saturday morning, and proceeds to take the day off.

Each chapter in both of these books is a separate vignette, a tale-within-a-tale, with different characters in many cases, a different mini-question or mini-problem, proposed solutions (usually humorous), and a closing punchline(s). The denouement may be subtle or gross, the humor, sly or brazen. The Association's control over Hades is not absolute; when William Shakespeare tosses a coin and shows his

Xenograffiti, by ROBERT REGINALD

independence by taking the course opposite from that indicated, the reader is told that the Fates have already contrived to have the coin fall on the reverse side so that their intentions for him might be fulfilled; each action here is a part of their plan, whatever that plan might be. Shakespeare argues with Nero over the authorship of *Othello,* and Sir Francis Bacon is called as a witness. Bacon hints that although he had nothing to do with "that Othello fellow," he did write *Hamlet.* By this time, Shakespeare is red-faced and angry, and he calls upon Sir Walter Raleigh to settle the dispute once and for all. Raleigh confesses his lack of shame and acknowledges that he wrote it himself. The company continues to harass the Bard throughout the tale, constantly casting aspersions on his supposed authorship of his own plays. Then Christopher Columbus appears, grumpily participating in George Washington's birthday party, while James Boswell takes copious notes for his gossip column. Baron Münchausen insists that he has dined on stewed icicles and fried pyramids, much to the delight and amusement of the guests. Ptolemy notes that he has had experience with pyramids himself.

And so it continues. Bangs uses his shades to direct satirical jabs at their own historical personages, at the mores and customs of his own time, and at the form of the ghost story itself. For example, Shakespeare maintains that he had drugged the actor who was to play Hamlet in a Bostonian production of his play and had assumed the part himself. The reviews published the next day were devastating, asserting that the actor's conception of the role was not sufficiently "Shakespearean." "That's criticism," notes the Bard. Ralph Waldo Emerson replies, that "that isn't criticism, it's just Boston." Shakespeare's ghost also manages to arrange with a Bostonian syndicate to provide "posthumous autographs" at one thousand dollars each. Washington remarks that the scheme will probably work, because "the Yankee *is* an inventive genius."

Bangs's own inventive genius is clearly at work here; he is not content to have his characters merely sit and discuss the times. Among his other flights of imagination, he constructs the "smoking room" on the houseboat, whose inven-

Xenograffiti, by ROBERT REGINALD

tor is an unknown shade who "had sold all rights to the club through a third party." Tobacco smoke is stored in reservoirs and carried by flue to the smoking room, where it proceeds to prospective smokers through rubber tubes with mouthpieces attached to meters. Smokers pay so much per foot for the smoke and eliminate the waste and mess of cigar and cigarette butts.

Another of Bangs's innovations is his explanation of Hamlet's melancholy: he resents Shakespeare's meddling with his life and reputation. He never met Yorick, he insists, and has an alibi to prove it: "I was never near the graveyard." He does not mind the play so much but dislikes the way he is presented. He describes a Western version that stages the play with "three Hamlets, two ghosts, and a pair of blood-hounds. It's called the Uncle Tom-Hamlet combination, and instead of falling in love with one crazy Ophelia," he is "made to woo three dusky maniacs named Topsy on a canvas ice-floe while blood-hounds bark behind the scenes."

The downfall of the Associated Shades in the first book is brought about by its own sins of omission. Curious about the houseboat and barred from membership by their sex (Bangs manages to insert a few words here about women's suffrage, its perils and pleasures), Queen Elizabeth I, Xanthippe, and Ophelia (later joined by Cleopatra and others) board the craft one afternoon when all the males are away enjoying a prize fight. Completely enchanted by their surroundings, the "ladies of Hades" fail to notice the approach of Captain Kidd and his crew of pirates, who are also seeking revenge for their blackballing by the Association. The houseboat is cut loose from her moorings and spirited away. The male shades return to discover not only that their marvelous club has vanished, but also that "the most precious gems in the social diadem of Hades" have disappeared. Socrates tells them not to worry; Caesar's wife is in the party, and she is a good chaperone.

The Pursuit of the House-Boat takes up where the first book ended. Sherlock Holmes assumes command of the party, and they commandeer a boat to track down the purloined houseboat. Meanwhile, aboard the houseboat, the women hatch a plot to overthrow the nefarious pirate and his crew. Mrs. Noah, who has had much experience at sea, assumes command of the female contingent. Her son Shem is horrified at the news: "It was she who ran us ashore on Ararat," he notes. A treachery committee headed by Lucrezia Borgia and Delilah contribute clever ideas for betraying their captors, who ultimately never have a chance against the women's wiles. As anticipated, all ends happily: the houseboat is recovered, the ladies become full members of the Association, and Captain Kidd and his fellows shrink to mere "shadows of their former shades."

The books are loosely plotted and contain only the skeletons of any sustained story. Their humor remains remarkably fresh considering their age, although some comments relating to topical controversies and personages are lost on modern readers. Satire as a vehicle does not often wear well historically, and it is a tribute to Bangs's talent that the books can still be enjoyed today. Bangs's importance lies in his historical relationship to his predecessors, particularly Irving, and his role as the grandfather of modern fantasy humorists. One can see his work reflected specifically in Kummer's *Gentlemen of Hades* and *Ladies of Hades,* two 1920s' pastiches of his work; in the novels of Thorne Smith, who revived the humorous fantasy story in the 1930s; and in such recent writers as Reginald Bretnor, L. Sprague de Camp and Fletcher Pratt, John Collier, and the cartoonists Charles Addams and Gahan Wilson, among many others. As long as men continue to search for solace from their everyday ills, writers such as Bangs will continue to be read and enjoyed.

XXI.

A THOUSAND NIGHTS IN SERENDIP

PIERS ANTHONY'S *HASAN*

(1983)

Hasan was the third or fourth novel written by Piers Anthony, but it remained unpublished in book form for more than ten years after its completion. Anthony had originally become enthralled with *The Thousand and One Nights* (c. 1450) during his teenage years, later deciding to adapt the tale of Hasan from its original sources into a full-length fantasy. The book was written without a publisher in mind in 1965 and 1966, and then sold to a paperback firm which cancelled the project after the editor who had purchased it moved elsewhere. It finally saw print in *Fantastic Stories* (1969), but remained unpublished in book form until 1977. Of the many publishers who turned the book down, Anthony has said, most expressed interest in the novel but failed to see how they could market it. During this time, the only fantasy being published successfully was Tolkienesque in nature; the utter failure of two nineteenth-century Arabian Nights fantasies reprinted in the Ballantine Adult Fantasy Series prejudiced this particular subgenre for ten years. Yet for all its difficulties in finding a publisher, *Hasan* remains an important book, both for the history of fantasy and for the consideration of Anthony's work.

The story is fairly simple. Hasan, a naive and feckless youth of Bassorah, a small town on the Persian Gulf, is seduced from his metal-working job by a kindly old man who promises him gold and wealth if the lad will only help him. Actually, Bahram the Persian needs Hasan as a sacrifice to obtain the final ingredient for his elixir of gold; he kidnaps the boy and takes him to Serendip (Ceylon), leaving him to be torn to pieces by a roc. Hasan escapes, kills his master, and wanders through the jungle looking for help. Instead, he stumbles across an exquisite palace peopled by the seven lovely daughters of a king of Sind (India), who has secluded his girls to protect their innocence. On the roof of the palace is a garden, and there Hasan discovers a flock of giant birds landing by the pool; these suddenly transform themselves into the beautiful Sana, a princess of the Isles of Wak, and her handmaidens, who have used magical feathers to make the long trip from their homeland (Indonesia). Hasan falls in love with the Princess and manages to capture her with the help of his friends; he then marries her and returns home to Bassorah, where he assumes the life of a wealthy merchant.

Hasan's mother makes the unfortunate mistake of showing the girl her feather-dress; the homesick girl puts on the magical suit and flies back to her homeland. Hasan is grief-stricken; returning to Serendip, he once again seeks the help of the seven maidens; Rose, one of the girls, refers him to her uncle, Abd al-Kaddus, a magician of Sind. Abd al-Kaddus sends Hasan to Abu al-Ruwaysh, his mentor, who enthralls a flying ifrit, one of the many ranks of jinn (spirits); this particular ifrit, Dahnash bin Faktash, is noted for his peculiar sense of humor. With the help of Dahnash, Hasan is able to find his way to the distant land of Wak, where he persuades the Amazon general, Shawahi, to support his cause. The Queen of Wak, Sana's sister, refuses to let her go, thereby starting a war between the Queen's Amazon army and Hasan's army of jinni. When it appears that Hasan is losing, he orders Dahnash to awaken a sleeping marid (an extinct volcano); the resulting explosion devastates the surrounding area, including the Queen's soldiers, and Hasan is reunited with his love. In gratitude, he frees the spirits from his control, and they return to the netherworld.

Hasan, innocent and naive at the start of the book, has grown by its end to the point where the kings of the ifrits

Xenograffiti, by ROBERT REGINALD

do him homage; while taking his leave, Dahnash tells Hasan: "One man *is* worth a thousand jinn, provided it is the right man." Coming from an immortal spirit, this is high praise indeed. Hasan has never shown any real intelligence, but his heart has always been in the right place; he has never shirked his duties or avoided the unpleasant. He has learned from his many teachers—his wife, his magician, his friend Rose, Shawahi, Dahnash—and has in turn earned their respect. Anthony seems to be saying, however, that learning in itself, although admirable, is not enough; after all, Bahram the sorcerer is very learned but also corrupt. Hasan is never corrupted by what he learns; he may have lost his physical innocence, but psychologically he will always be innocent enough to take people as they are, to enjoy life without hurting others. His attitude is demonstrated very early in the book when Anthony notes: "He had refused to believe that a man could be inherently evil, even a Persian." It is his noble simplicity that makes him so attractive to his fellows, men and women alike: they see in him a basic goodness that few human beings have.

What distinguishes this book from Anthony's other early novels is its lack of seriousness—or perhaps stuffiness. While he does deal with the essential questions of life—good and evil, the nature of love, the necessity for responsible action—he never beats them into the ground with heavy-handed moralizing. The spice of humor savors the brew and makes it a much more palatable concoction. Anthony had a tendency in his early work, particularly in his science-fiction novels, to become ponderous, weighty, reflective, and intricate for the sake of intricacy. In some of his books, he seems almost to be playing rather futile games with his readers. This is the first of his books to demonstrate a lighter, more caring side, one that seems closer to Anthony the man than is seen elsewhere. In his later and more successful work, particularly in the Xanth series, this same energetic, highly imaginative, light-hearted, down-to-earth, caring force of the writer pushes its way to the surface, making *Hasan* and his other novels in the same vein utter delights to read, on whatever level.

Xenograffiti, by ROBERT REGINALD

Anthony's book was the first successful attempt in modern times to break away from the Celtic/Germanic/Norse/Welsh mythos as the only approved source for re-mythologized fantasies. Anthony demonstrates here that other mythologies are equally valid sources for stories; since the first publication of his novel in 1969, others have turned to *The Thousand and One Nights,* to Japanese, Sumerian, and African mythology, and to any of the archetypal tales handed down by men from their earliest oral recollections. The source is irrelevant; the only thing that matters is the story itself and how it is told.

XXII.

VIVO, ERGO SUM

THE PROBLEM OF IMMORTALITY IN EDWIN LESTER ARNOLD'S *PHRA THE PHOENICIAN*

(1983)

Of all the different kinds and subgenres of the fantastic story, among the most compelling is the tale of immortality, in which some poor mortal is transformed by fate or circumstance or curse into living history. Typical of these tales is the legend of the Wandering Jew, first put into definitive form in 1844-1845 by the French writer Eugène Sue. Sue's long novel *Le Juif errant* (*The Wandering Jew*, 1844/45) tells the story of a Roman soldier who taunts Christ on his way to the Crucifixion and is cursed by God to wander the ages until Christ returns to save mankind. Another variation on the same theme is the story of the Flying Dutchman, put into novel form in 1888 by William Clark Russell as *The Death Ship*. Here, a Dutch mariner curses God for the foul winds he has been sent, and God in turn curses him to spend the rest of eternity trying to sail around the Cape of Good Hope, doomed only to meet those unfortunate sailors who are sailing doomed ships themselves.

Edwin Lester Arnold, son of the well-known English man of letters, Sir Edwin Arnold, was taken to India by his father in his youth and studied agriculture and ornithology while traveling extensively throughout the world. He became a journalist for the *London Daily Telegraph* in 1883, wrote a book on ornithology, and then turned his hand to fiction. *The Wonderful Adventures of Phra the Phoenician*, his first novel (of four published), was serialized in the *Illustrated London News* in 1890 before appearing in book form later the same year; it was immensely popular at the time and went through numerous "cheap" editions before fading into obscurity after the turn of the century.

Phra is an adventurer, a merchant seaman who travels to the far corners of the globe looking for bargains. When he comes to the British Isles, not long before the first Roman invasion, he quickly becomes involved in the struggle of the native peoples to resist the conquest. A British princess, Blodwen, becomes enamored of the Phoenician, and the two are married. A jealous Druid blames Phra for a defeat by the Romans, and the angry mob carries Phra away to a ritual execution. After his "death," Blodwen, a priestess in her own right, conducts an arcane ceremony which heals his wound and puts him into a coma-like sleep that lasts for centuries. When Phra finally awakens, four hundred years have passed, and the Romans are preparing to evacuate the British Isles. Phra becomes involved in a love triangle between Electra, a British matron preparing to desert her villa, and Electra's beautiful servant girl, Numidea. During the course of the chaotic flight, Electra slays Numidea rather than lose Phra to her, and Phra "dies" again trying to save his love from the waters of the swiftly-flowing river.

He awakens a second time in a Saxon monk's cell, where he had been placed by King Alfred; the time now is 1066, and Harold II is King of England. William of Normandy invades the eastern coast of England, and Harold is defeated and killed; Phra, who once again has been in the midst of the fight, escapes with other Saxon nobles. He retires to Voewood, a Saxon estate and noble house, and there falls in love with Editha, now heir to this land. Their idyllic existence lasts only twelve years, the longest stretch of time he has spent "alive" since his transformation. Inevitably, the Norman overlords discover the small manse during the great census of households; a fight breaks out when Phra loses his temper, and he and Editha are forced to flee with their family. They are given shelter by a local monastery, but there

Xenograffiti, by ROBERT REGINALD

once again Phra falls into his dreamless sleep of the centuries.

When he awakens, having been preserved by the monastery as a "living" display, three centuries have passed, and it is now the year 1346. King Edward III is preparing to fight the French at the Battle of Crécy. Phra is introduced to Lady Isobel, daughter of a nobleman, and presses his attention upon her; she disdains him, but secretly follows him into battle, dressed as a knight. During the worst part of the fighting, she takes a spear thrust meant for him; he discovers her love for him just as she is dying. Overwhelmed by grief, Phra begs the King to send him to England; during his passage, the ship is wrecked and he alone is swept ashore. There he stumbles into an ancient tomb, and once more falls asleep.

Phra is roused a last time in the reign of Queen Elizabeth I. Taken in by an old scientist, Adam Faulkener, who is perfecting a steam engine, Phra finds himself in a love triangle between Faulkener's comely daughter, Elizabeth, and the scientist's Spanish assistant, Emanuel. In the end, Emanuel treacherously poisons the couple as they say their marriage vows. Throughout the centuries, Phra has been "awake" for no more than fifteen years, having slept away the rest of some fifteen hundred years.

Arnold's book was popular enough to spawn several imitations, including George Griffith's *Valdar the Oft-Born* (1895), and it is chiefly through his influence on other writers that Arnold is remembered today. His later novel, *Lieut. Gullivar Jones: His Vacation* (1905) is cited as the progenitor of all of the later romantic Mars novels, including those of Edgar Rice Burroughs. Both Arnold and Sue influenced George Sylvester Viereck and Paul Eldridge in their well-known Wandering Jew trilogy.

Still, *The Wonderful Adventures of Phra the Phoenician* stands on its own as a minor masterpiece of fantasy adventure. Arnold is commenting on the force of love in human affairs: how love, if sufficiently strong and passionate, can conquer even the ages. At every stop in his journey through the centuries, Phra meets a new avatar of Blodwen, his first love; and on several occasions, Blodwen appears to

Xenograffiti, by ROBERT REGINALD

him, reassuring him that all will be well in time, that they will be reunited again when he is finally given the gift of death. The reasons for his odyssey are unclear, even to Arnold; somehow, apparently, Phra must live through the life denied him by murder, step by step, woman by woman, a few months here, twelve years there, a few days somewhere else. His nature changes little from century to century, but his desire for death gradually grows stronger as each brief stop results in another tragedy. All life is tragedy, says Arnold; all love affairs are brief, even those which last a lifetime; and life is always too short, even when it spans the centuries. At the end, Phra is ready to accept the death finally forced upon him; and death, in the person of Blodwen, finally accepts him. His last conscious vision sees the fair British maid coming for him out of the mists, claiming her husband at last.

XXIII.

BETWEEN ORDER AND CHAOS

THE FICTION OF BRUCE MCALLISTER

(1986)

Bruce McAllister is a writer's writer, a critic's writer, a man whose work has always been highly regarded by his fellow professionals, but who remains relatively unknown and unappreciated among science-fiction fans. The reasons for this are legion: he is a slow and meticulous craftsman, often doing twenty drafts for every story completed and published; he has pursued a dual career as a university English professor, thereby severely limiting his writing time; throughout most of his career he has preferred shorter lengths, in a field where regular production of novels is essential to achieving and maintaining broad public recognition; he eschews sequels, serials, and sword-and-sorcery fantasy; his fictions focus on character development, not mindless action-adventure; and he has never been prolific, even in his early years. Since 1965 he has published some fifty short stories, two novels, and forty-five poems, in addition to editing several noteworthy anthologies. It is only in the 1990s that he has stopped writing short fiction, "probably forever," he says, "(or for a decade)."

"The Faces Outside," written when the author was sixteen, sets the tone for the rest of his work. The nameless hero finds himself floating in a tank with his mate and an assortment of aquatic creatures; their only contact with the outside world is a disembodied Voice. The Voice tells them that the faces watching through the ports are the Enemy, aliens who have annihilated the rest of humanity and have altered these two survivors into underwater humanoids. The two eventually transcend captivity by developing mental powers which will vanquish their alien captors, thereby assuring the survival of a new human race.

Here in microcosm we see the basic themes of McAllister's work. His protagonists are tortured individuals caught between a Heaven and Hell not of their own choosing. Their suffering and tribulations take them from the Limbos of their own minds to an ultimate realization, epiphany, or metamorphosis—or a combination of all three. In the author's early fictions, the theme of self-transcendence often translates into rather obvious power fantasies, in which one lonely or alienated character somehow manages to conquer his nemesis (*i.e.*, himself), represented by alien or human monsters, or by some other life- or mind-threatening situation.

In the later stories, and particularly in the two long novels, *Humanity Prime* (1971) and *Dream Baby* (1989), the author's treatment of these themes becomes more sophisticated, his view of mankind more cynical, his treatment of man's self-sacrificing inclinations more realistic, his feeling for the ultimate tragedy of the human condition more poignant (but never needlessly sentimental). These fictions also demonstrate an understanding of the female psyche unsurpassed in the work of any other male SF writer except D. G. Compton.

Humanity Prime, greatly expanded from "The Faces Outside," mixes mermen, cyborgs, intelligent sea turtles, and telepathic powers to produce one of the most compelling and convincing portraits of an underwater human species ever published. The author's intimate knowledge of human and animal biology, and his childhood experiences as the son of a behavioral psychologist, are reflected in this realistic and plausible extrapolation of man functioning in an alien environment. To McAllister, animals are as human in their own ways as men are sometimes animal-like in theirs; much of his fiction specifically concerns itself with the question of what it means to be human, and the answers are never simple, never easy to assimilate by either the characters or the reader. The mutual themes of man's alienation from man and the transcendence of human nature reach a crescendo in McAllister's brilliant and highly-acclaimed second novel, *Dream Baby*, which took a decade to write, partially under the aegis of a National Endowment for the Arts fellowship. Set in Indochina during the Vietnam War, this "nonfiction" novel is told largely in the first person by an Army nurse, Lt. Mary Damico, with interstices of real and fictional statements from Vietnam veterans (the author interviewed some 200 survivors of the War over a ten-year period).

McAllister cleverly interweaves the surrealism of the wartime experience with actual contingency plans developed by the U.S. Army to end the War by interjecting special forces units into North Vietnam. In *Dream Baby* the military cynically gathers together a group of veterans who have been experiencing a variety of paranormal experiences under combat. Mary's "talent" is her ability to dream the future, to forecast events which are rarely pleasant and often depict horrifying glimpses of brutal deaths to come. The group is dropped into the North, where it is ordered to destroy the dikes in central Vietnam during the monsoon season, thereby flooding Hanoi into the sea (attempts were actually made by U.S. forces during the War to bomb these embankments).

The combination of severe psychological stress, discovery of the infiltrators by the North Vietnamese, and the threat of imminent death, suddenly melds the team into one psychical whole, and provides it with the means to escape and survive. To complete the circle, the would-be destroyers of tens of thousands of human lives return to South Vietnam to destroy just one life, the soulless instigator of the project, Bucannon, whose brutal psychological manipulations have matched anything the Vietcong had ever devised. Mary Damico, the healer who had been so overwhelmed with horror that she could not heal, must restore order to the universe in the only way she can, by executing the agent of chaos. Only in this way can her life and the lives of the other survivors return to some semblance of normalcy, with their talents gradually fading away. In McAllister's universe, although a

Xenograffiti, by ROBERT REGINALD

precarious balance between the forces of order and chaos can sometimes be achieved, ecstasy always walks hand-in-hand with agony, transcendence is always temporary, and nothing worthwhile is ever achieved without pain.

Xenograffiti, by ROBERT REGINALD

XXIV.

MORAL/IMMORAL

THE FICTIONAL UNIVERSE OF MICHAEL REAVES

(1986)

Michael Reaves, whose early work appeared under the name J. Michael Reaves, had been writing science fiction since his teen years, but it was not until he attended the Clarion Workshop, in 1972, that he was able to sell his first story, "The Breath of Dragons," written while he was a student at California State University, San Bernardino, it was published in the third of the Clarion anthologies.

"Breath" uncannily presages Reaves's later fictions, both in theme and in setting. Perrin is a hunter on a planet where dragons are killed for their fire-producing bladders. The dragons look and fly like the creatures from children's fairy tales, but they're no match for man's superior technology. Perrin also believes they're sentient beings, a theory no one else sanctions. His attempt to prove the dragons' intelligence causes the accidental death of a crewmate; as he struggles to find a way out of his predicament, he is consumed (in an apparent act of kindness) by the very creatures he is striving to protect. Perrin has paid the ultimate price for his carelessness, and a moral balance has been restored to his world.

Although the author's most successful prose works—*Dragonworld* (with Byron Preiss, 1979), *The Shattered World* (1984), its sequel, *The Burning Realm* (1988), and *Darkworld Detective* (1982)—have been packaged by their

Xenograffiti, by ROBERT REGINALD

publishers as fantasy, Reaves enjoys combining elements from the SF, fantasy, and detective fiction genres into seemingly irreconcilable plot lines, making the believability of one dependent upon the other. Images of dragons and similar creatures, of flying in general, of man and beast soaring above the grittiness of the everyday world, permeate his fiction. Even in the ostensibly hard SF novel, *Hellstar* (written with Steve Perry, 1984), set in the artificial environment of a multi-generation spaceship traveling slowly between the stars, the characters literally "fly" (in a recreation room designed for that purpose), and take weightless walks on the outside of the ship's hull, where they experience almost a religious ecstasy while observing the grand vistas of open space.

Each of Reaves's protagonists sees an imbalance in the universe, a flaw, an emptiness in himself or others, and seeks to restore some semblance of order or sanity to nature, to himself, to humanity as a whole. Thus, Perrin regards the dragons as his private crusade, while Amsel in *Dragonworld* must go on his own dragonquest, and Kamus of Kadizar, the otherworldly shamus of *Darkworld Detective*, seeks to right the wrongs of his fantasy world by solving the mysteries of his clients.

We can see these themes—of action and reaction, of responsibility and irresponsibility, of wrongs which must be righted and sins which must be redressed—most clearly developed in the author's most popular work, *The Shattered World* and its sequel, *The Burning Realm*. Here the surviving magicians must face the consequences of an ancient war of sorcery that literally broke their world into fragments. Pandrogas and Amber cannot escape the harm caused by their illicit romance, and Beorn, as attractive a thief as one will find in modern fantasy literature, must pay a high price indeed for the pursuit of his profession. Yet each persists in his or her chosen (even stubborn) course, doing what each thinks is right and necessary and proper, for himself and for others—and sometimes being damned for it.

Similar themes are evident in Reaves's 200 teleplays, often on a more simplistic level (much of the author's work has been produced for half-hour, animated children's cartoon programs). In "Street of Shadows" (*The Twilight Zone*), for example, Steve Butler, a homeless, down-on-his-luck carpenter with a family to support, breaks into the home of Frederick Perry, a wealthy industrialist, and briefly changes places mentally with him. As "Perry" (the name is clearly a homage to Reaves's sometime collaborator, Steve Perry), Steve is able to balance his micro universe by buying the mortgage of the near-bankrupt shelter where he and his family have been staying. In the script version of the "Where No One Have Gone Before" episode of *Star Trek: The Next Generation* (written with Diane Duane, and originally called "Where None Have Gone Before"), Peter Kosinski, a brilliant engineer, saves the *Enterprise* from the consequences of his own warp drive experiments, and in the process rescues himself from a life of loneliness by somehow regenerating a son who had died at birth seven years earlier; the episode was substantially rewritten by the series producers before filming.

In the author's most recent novel, *Night Hunter* (1995), Los Angeles police detective Jake Hull is called to a crime scene in a seedy Hollywood hotel, where a dead man lies with a stake driven through his heart and a bulb of garlic in his mouth. Hull assumes, with everyone else, that LA's latest serial killer is a nutcase who thinks he's a latter-day Van Helsing hunting vampires. But as he probes deeper into the case, Hull begins to realize that there may be more to the crime than is apparent. The trail leads the detective into an occult society and the night life of the Hollywood fringe element. It also forces him to confront the darker side of his own nature, the part of himself that identifies with the madness in the streets.

There are many things in Heaven and Earth, the author seems to be saying, not all of them rational or explicable or knowable; but ultimately man must take responsibility for his own actions, and *some* things will eventually balance out. For Reaves, the universe has ever been a moral place where immorals fear to tread.

XXV.

TEACHER-PREACHER

R. LIONEL FANTHORPE AND THE LITERATURE OF ABUNDANCE

(1986)

What can one say about R. Lionel Fanthorpe? On the one hand, he is generally acknowledged to be the most prolific SF author of all time, having generated some 122 full-length novels and forty-eight story collections, all but one of which fall into the science-fiction, fantasy, or horror genres. His enormous output is all the more remarkable when one considers that it was produced, with a few exceptions, in just one decade of work (1957-1966), during which he was also fully employed as a training officer and high-school teacher. Almost all of his books were published by John Spencer & Co. Ltd., a small British paperback house that began issuing digest-sized books in the early 1950s. Fanthorpe's first story, "Worlds Without End," appeared in *Futuristic Science Stories*, a Spencer magazine, when the author was just seventeen (1952).

Spencer moved into mass-market paperback publishing with its Badger Books line in 1958; all of the magazine titles were dropped except for *Supernatural Stories*, which became a paperback-sized series in which novels alternated with purported magazine issues. In reality, the latter were single-author collections of short stories commissioned from either Fanthorpe or John Glasby (the other Spencer regular), each of whom contributed entire "issues" (usually

128

five or six stories) under a variety of recurring pennames. They also wrote virtually all of the subsequent SF and fantasy novels published by Badger, with Fanthorpe accounting for about 80% of the entire SF and Supernatural lines.

At its height, Spencer demanded delivery of completed books in as little as three days (typically over a weekend); to maintain this extraordinary output, Fanthorpe dictated many of the manuscripts into a tape recorder, had them transcribed by a typist, corrected them in one quick reading for spelling and punctuation, and sent them off in the Monday post. No revisions or editing were possible. Also, a handful of the tales included in *Supernatural Stories* were contributed by friends, and "ghosted" under Fanthorpe's pen names.

Consequently, many of the books from this period, particularly the science-fiction novels, suffer from contrived plots and titles, hackneyed situations, continuity errors, obvious padding (extended scientific discourses by the characters, or extensive quotations from classic poetry and prose, particularly Shakespeare), and very abrupt endings. Fanthorpe never seemed comfortable with the SF form, even when he had the time (in the earlier books) to consider his plots more carefully.

Fanthorpe's *forte* was always fantasy. In particular, the series of stories which began with "The Séance," featuring the recurring characters, Val Stearman and the beautiful and mysterious La Noire, probably represents the author at the height of his powers. The series continued haphazardly through several dozen short stories and eight novels, most written under the penname Bron Fane. The climax of the Stearman/La Noire tales was "The Resurrected Enemy" (*Supernatural Stories* #105, 1966), in which Val and La Noire face the same enemies they had vanquished together in their very first adventure. Although the evil is again defeated, this time a terrible price must be paid. The couple meets its fate together, with courage and with love, and enters a suspended animation until their special talents are needed once more by humanity.

Throughout these stories, and in his other fantasy and horror tales, Fanthorpe was able to draw upon his almost encyclopedic knowledge of British and Celtic folklore to produce rousing adventures and morality plays in which good always triumphs over obvious evil, and in which the major characters are represented by strong, physically attractive, very intelligent heroes and heroines. One also sees in these shorter pieces a humorous side to Fanthorpe not evident elsewhere; in "The Curse of the Khan" (*Supernatural Stories* #105), for example, a magician challenges seven heroes (seven of Fanthorpe's own pseudonyms) to a duel to the death with seven monsters, who are systematically vanquished with great *panache*.

In later years Fanthorpe became a high-school principal and Episcopal priest, professions which severely limited his writing time. He continued his interest in the occult with the nonfiction books, *The Holy Grail Revealed* (1982), an examination and history of the mysterious events surrounded Rennes-le-Château; its companion volume, *Rennes-le-Château: Its Mysterious Secrets* (1991), which elaborates on his remarkable discoveries in France; and a history of the 200-year quest to uncover the lost treasure of Oak Island on the east coast of Canada.

All of these works were co-authored with his wife Patricia, whose byline also appears on his most recent short pieces. These include: "Et in Arcadia Ego," one of his better fantasy stories, published in the Ian Watson anthology, *Pictures at an Exhibition* (1981); two humorous SF plays, "The Monster of Gruesome Grange" and its sequel, "Eli Still Goes On"; and *The Black Lion* (1979), the first novel of as yet unfinished fantasy trilogy. In the latter work, military veteran Mark Sable is transported to the world of Derl to fight the evil wizard Andros, the personification of the dark forces of greed. As always in Fanthorpe's fiction, the hero triumphs after great travail and colorful adventures, but unfortunately, and despite a very promising beginning, the novel sags badly in the middle. For Fanthorpe, the author-as-teacher/ preacher, the moral message of his stories remains the paramount concern, of greater importance, perhaps, than the fiction itself.

Xenograffiti, by ROBERT REGINALD

XXVI.

THE STAFFORD CONNECTION

AN INTRODUCTION TO *STAFFORD COUNTY, VIRGINIA, TITHABLES, 1723-1790*, BY JOHN VOGT AND T. WILLIAM KETHLEY, JR.

(1990)

The loss of roughly two-thirds of the Stafford County deed and will books prior to the year 1860, combined with that county's central location in northeastern Virginia, has proved particularly vexing to historians and genealogists of early Virginiana. So many families have disappeared into the "black hole" of Stafford County records that the mere mention of a Stafford family is enough to send shudders down the spine of the most accomplished genealogist. Until recently, even searching those records which do survive was a time-consuming and often unrewarding task. What a revelation, then, is Vogt and Kethley's new compilation of Stafford County tax lists—and what a Godsend!

The history of the Northern Neck of Virginia, the land between the Potomac and Rappahannock Rivers, begins similarly to the other coastal regions in Virginia, with predominantly English settlers pushing the Indians back from the river plains. By the late 1640s the first two counties had been erected at the seaward end of the Neck, following a pattern already established in Virginia of dividing coastal peninsular county jurisdictions along watershed lines. This made sense during a period when most travel followed the broad coastal rivers, and when most of the major tobacco plantations (and their wharfs) were located along their banks, as were most county courthouses. As settlers pushed further up these waterways, additional counties were systematically cut off from their parent jurisdictions. Thus, Westmoreland and Old Rappahannock (later Richmond) Counties were split from Northumberland and Lancaster Counties, respectively, and Stafford and King George were formed in turn from Westmoreland and Richmond.

Stafford County was created in 1664, and theoretically included at that time the Potomac River watershed from the western boundary of Westmoreland County (at Machotick [*i.e.*, Machodoc] Creek) to the Blue Ridge Mountains and possibly beyond (since the area was unsettled except for Indians, the western boundary remained vague for many years). Richmond County encompassed similar boundaries for the Rappahannock River watershed, until King George County was cut off from it on 23 April 1721. When Prince William County was formed from the upper reaches of Stafford and King George Counties in 1731, its creation effectively prevented any further spread of the combined jurisdictions beyond their present-day limits.

THE FAIRFAX PROPRIETARY

After the execution of British King Charles I in 1649, his son and heir, the future King Charles II, attempted to rally his forces from exile and raise funds by granting all of the land between the Rappahannock and Potomac Rivers jointly to Lord Jermyn, Lord Culpeper, Thomas Culpeper, John Berkeley, William Morton, and Dudley Wyatt. This charter had no practical effect, however, until the restoration of the monarchy in 1660, when the proprietors hired an agent to represent their interests in Virginia. However, settlement of the Northern Neck had already begun during the Commonwealth period, and those who had obtained their farms from the Commonwealth-dominated colonial government resented and feared the intrusion of outside interests; also, one of the original proprietors had died, muddying the legal waters, so a second, clarifying charter (a 21-year lease) was issued by the King in 1669, to Jermyn, Berkeley, Morton, and John Trethway, with the Culpepers being added in 1671. Thomas, 2nd Baron Culpeper, eventually purchased the rights of his fellows, and alone secured a third lease, in perpetuity, in 1688, dying shortly thereafter, in February of 1789. His rights were inherited by his daughter, Catherine, soon-to-be wife of Thomas, 5th Baron Fairfax, whose rights were confirmed in 1794; and then by Catherine's son, Thomas, 6th Baron Fairfax. After the latter's death in 1781, Virginia quickly moved to bring control of the Proprietary under the state, the Fairfax claims and payments finally being settled in 1806.

The Fairfax family employed a series of agents to grant un-claimed lands to individuals who filed the appropriate papers plus an application fee. The agent then issued a warrant to have the property marked off, with the farmer being responsible for paying to have the land actually surveyed. The warrant and completed survey were then returned to the agent, who issued a title in fee simple. The annual quit rents that elsewhere in Virginia would have gone to the Crown were paid instead to the Proprietor or his agent. The Northern Neck warrants and surveys have been abstracted and thoroughly indexed by Peggy Shomo Joyner (*Abstracts of Virginia's Northern Neck Warrants & Surveys.* Portsmouth, VA: Peggy S. Joyner, 1985-87, 4 vols.), while the original patents and grants have been abstracted and indexed by Nell Marion Nugent and Susan Bracey Sheppard (*Cavaliers and Pioneers: Abstracts of Virginia Land Patents and Grants: Supplement, Northern Neck Grants No. 1, 1690-1692.* Richmond, VA: Virginia State Library, 1980, iii, 18 p.), and Gertrude E. Gray (*Virginia Northern Neck Land Grants, 1694-1742* [and] *Volume II, 1742-1775.* Baltimore: Genealogical Publishing Co., 1987-88, 2 vols.). All are readily accessible to the researcher. The quit rent rolls which undoubtedly existed for every county and every year have largely been lost; the few which survive for Stafford County are reproduced in this volume.

Grants were normally inherited according to primogeniture, usually by the landholder's eldest surviving son, or, failing any sons, by his other heirs, as provided by the Virginia law of the time; plantations could also be willed to a combination of heirs, subject to certain restrictions (provision had to be made for the widow, for example). Lands which escheated (*i.e.*, reverted to the lord of the fee where there were no heirs capable of inheriting under the original grant) could be (and were) regranted by the Proprietor to new landholders; these new grants appear in the Northern Neck grant books. However, subsequent dispositions of Northern Neck land—plus wills—are recorded in the record books of the counties in which the land was located. In Stafford County, the early records volumes often included a mixture of deeds and wills and inventories and even election returns in one volume, although the usual practice by the eighteenth century was to alternate predominantly deed and will books in the numbering sequence. The earliest Stafford records books are labeled *Liber* [Latin for "book"] A, B, C, etc., through Z, and then AA, BB, CC, etc. Because of the irregular way in which the Stafford records were kept, two or more books would often overlap in date spans.

THE PROBLEM OF BOUNDARIES

One of the major problems facing the Stafford researcher is determining the boundary line between Stafford and King George Counties at any particular time. At least three realignments in county jurisdictions are known to have occurred in this part of the Northern Neck during the eighteenth century (not counting the formation of new counties). Prior to 1777, both counties were long, narrow strips flanking the Potomac and Rappahannock Rivers. Up to the point where the Potomac River turns north, at Potomac Creek in Stafford County, the Northern Neck varies in width from roughly six to twenty miles, the narrowest sections occurring in present-day King George and Westmoreland Counties. There are swamps and creeks lining both sides of the Neck. A small ridge or rise of rolling hills runs down the middle of the peninsula. The original line between the two counties was defined by these small runs: *i.e.*, if one's land was located in the Stafford/King George area and included a creek (or was between two such creeks) that drained to the Rappahannock River, that land *per se* was considered located in King George Co. Unfortunately, the farms straddling the boundary line often existed in a kind of legal limbo, since there are points on the ridge where the gap between observable water courses exceeds one-half mile. The practical problems caused by such an ill-defined boundary between the two counties became so acute that about 1751 a commission was appointed to survey the line and to settle the disputes permanently. The result was predictable: a dozen or two families formerly recorded in one county suddenly found themselves transferred to the other without ever actually having moved.

For example, this writer's ancestor, Edward Burges(s), purchased 100 acres of land in King George County in 1731, the deed specifically describing the farm as being both in Stafford *and* King George Counties. Prior to the year 1750, Edward Burgess appears only in King George records; after that date, he appears only in Stafford County records, his will being recorded there in 1759. Yet it is clear from later deed and tax records that Edward and his heirs never moved, that his 100-acre farm, located behind the present-day village of Comorn, Virginia (about where county highway 608 terminates), was continually occupied by the Burgess family between 1731-1788, being finally sold by Edward's absent grandchildren in 1797, in still another King George Co. deed. During these fifty-seven years "Pudding Hill" (the Burgess farm) changed jurisdictions twice, first from King George Co. to Stafford Co. about 1751, and then from Stafford back to King George in 1777.

Eventually, the awkwardness caused by the elongated county jurisdictions became sufficiently annoying to the major plantation owners that several petitions were circulated beginning in 1769 in both Stafford and King George Cos. to reorient the boundaries along more rational (squared-off) lines. Two of these are reproduced in this book; the numbers of attached signatures indicate wide popular support for the change. The onset of the Revolutionary War caused several delays in consideration and approval of the bill, but it was finally passed in 1776, with effect from 1 January 1777. At that date, the boundary line between Stafford and King

Xenograffiti, by ROBERT REGINALD

George Counties was altered to its present-day location, along Muddy Creek and the Black Swamp Branch of Potomac Creek—that is, the northern half of King George County (including the town of Falmouth) was transferred to Stafford County, and the southern half of Stafford (encompassing the inhabitants of St. Paul's Parish) was put under the jurisdiction of King George. A second change in 1779 similarly reoriented the boundaries (by trading off several smaller, overlapping areas) of Westmoreland and King George Counties. New county courthouses were erected at their present inland, more central locations by the 1780s (previously, the courthouses of both counties had been located at several different sites along the banks of their respective boundary rivers).

    These changes transferred a third to a half of the residents of the northern end of the Northern Neck into new counties; thus, the determination of an individual's actual place of residence is an essential first step in conducting genealogical research in Stafford and King George Counties during the colonial period.

THE LOSS OF RECORDS

    The second major problem plaguing students of Staffordiana is the destruction of many of its earliest deed and will records. It is a misnomer to call Stafford a "burned records county," since the courthouse was not actually destroyed by the invading Union army during the Civil War. Unfortunately, however, the little town of Stafford Courthouse *was* situated on a major invasion route between Washington, D.C., and Fredericksburg, and suffered multiple occupations by the military forces of both sides throughout the war; and while the courthouse itself was not burned or apparently even looted, it was abandoned on several occasions by county officials, to the point where several federal officers removed old record books ostensibly for the purpose of preserving them. Contemporary descriptions of the courthouse further indicate that it had reached a state of disrepair even before the Civil War, and that some of the missing books may have crumbled simply from lack of maintenance.

Xenograffiti, by ROBERT REGINALD

Whatever the reason, it is an unfortunate fact that better than two-thirds of the records books known to have existed in the 1792 inventory do not survive today, although missing volumes have continued to surface every other decade or so at various locations around the country.

The surviving pre-1800 books include: Liber D (1686-92), Liber F (1699-1709), Liber I (also called J; 1722-28), Liber M (1730-48), Liber O (1747-54), Liber P (1754-64), Liber S (1780-89), and several unnumbered order books dating from 1664-68 and 1689-92. All the extant books were abstracted and thoroughly indexed in nine published volumes between 1987-1989 by Ruth and Sam Sparacio of McLean, VA, and are available from the compilers, as well as in many genealogical libraries. In addition, a contemporaneous index book exists at the Stafford County Courthouse, with a copy at the Virginia State Archives collection at Richmond; this volume includes a brief running list of the deeds and wills included in each book through the early nineteenth century, with the indexes for some of the libers missing (there are also pages missing from some of the extant indexes); about half the listings record data from volumes that no longer survive. Although included in the Embrey Index, it has not otherwise been abstracted.

ABOUT THIS BOOK

Vogt and Kethley's book brings together into two volumes both previously published and hitherto untranscribed Colonial and Revolutionary War tax, quit rent, and related lists; it undoubtedly represents the last major uncollected cache of early Stafford County documents that will ever be assembled for the researcher, barring the discovery of additional Stafford County records volumes. Its importance for the student of early Virginiana should not be underestimated.

Stafford County enjoyed a prominence in eighteenth-century Virginia which has long since faded. Its plantation owners included some of the major political and cultural figures of the Revolutionary War period and before, and its central location, including a major tobacco port at New Marle-

Xenograffiti, by ROBERT REGINALD

boro (or New Marlborough), on the large inlet of Potomac Creek, made it a common arrival and transit point for immigrants prior to the building of Washington, DC, during the 1790s. During the 1680s, Huguenots were actively encouraged to settle in Stafford County through grants of land, and hundreds came. Many of these émigrés moved on to other parts of northern Virginia, having lived for a few years or decades or generations in Stafford; by the end of the Revolutionary War, as the western territories of Kentucky and Tennessee began to attract new settlers, the exodus became marked, numerous families leaving the eastern seaboard permanently between the years 1780-1800.

With the loss of the 1790 and 1800 Virginia censuses, all that officially remains of many of these persons is their mention on the personal property tax rolls levied statewide beginning in 1782. Every free white male of the age of twenty-one years or over was required to pay a minimum poll tax, plus additional sums for specific categories of personal belongings (including, at various times, horses, cattle, wagons, watches, hogs, and, of course, Negroes). The real estate registers were maintained completely separately. Beginning in 1787, the rolls also included white males of the ages of 16-21, often enumerated by name with their parents or guardians. Even those exempt—paupers, widows, certain professionals—had to be listed, making the tax registers virtually year-by-year censuses of each Virginia county. Through a systematic perusal of these rolls, one can guess at family relation-ships, estimate the ages of sons who appear with their fathers between their twenty-first and twenty-second birthdays, and determine when families have left the area (and possibly match their reappearances elsewhere in the surviving tax lists of other Virginia and Kentucky counties). When joined with surviving deed, will, and other records, the tax lists can often verify or support genealogical hypotheses established elsewhere.

Vogt and Kethley have been extraordinarily careful and meticulous in their transcriptions. All of the lists, including the few previously published elsewhere, have been copied or recopied from the original documents, or from microform reproductions of same. Column notations, which often vary from page to page in the originals, have been maintained exactly as written. Spellings have been rendered precisely as penned, included the raised abbreviations for given names so common during this period. Page breaks on the original lists are carefully noted. Names which could not be read are so noted; textual breaks and cut-outs are precisely marked. Sources or locations of the originals are always stated. Relatively few lists survive prior to the inauguration of the personal property tax registers, but Vogt and Kethley have managed to assemble an astonishing number of hitherto unknown and unpublished records, including an extraordinary 1779 petition that includes several hundred residents, surely a large percentage of the free white males then resident in the county. The index is comprehensive and easy to follow.

One can lament the many gaps in Stafford County tax, deed, and will records prior to 1800, and wish that fate had been kinder to documents which might have revealed many permanently-buried secrets of the families in this region. In the end, however, one can only be thankful for what does survive. Let us applaud the wide sweep and careful accuracy of Vogt and Kethley's scholarship, encourage them to produce additional volumes in this series, and thank them both for a job exceptionally well done.

Xenograffiti, by ROBERT REGINALD

XXVII.

THE BRUSH OF ÆONS

GEORGE ZEBROWSKI'S FICTIONAL UNIVERSE

(1991)

Like Olaf Stapledon before him, George Zebrowski paints his fictive vistas with the brush of æons, adding and subtracting galaxies and centuries with great slashing strokes. Not for him are the crabbed miniatures of most science-fiction novelists, whose collective vision barely extends over the next hill. Zebrowski is concerned with the "big picture," the long-term fate of mankind, the end (and the beginning) of things, the how and where and particularly the *why* of life, the universe, and everything. Where so many of his compatriots are now producing western, mystery, and mainstream novels with SF trappings, sequel upon sequel upon inanity, *this* author has written and continues to pen brilliant *science* fictions which could be presented in no other conceivable form.

Beginning life as the child of Polish parents displaced by World War II, Zebrowski grew up in England, Manhattan, Miami, and the Bronx, even then a wasteland of broken dreams and deadened hopes. He began reading science fiction at an early age, and was writing his first stories in the 1960s. In 1970 he published "The Water Sculptor," the first of a hundred stories which quickly earned him numerous award nominations. The author's first novel, *The Omega Point* (1972), later expanded into *The Omega Point Trilogy* (1983), provided an initial showcase for Zebrowski's cosmic visions of man and the universe. These early fictions pale, however, before the sweep and impact of the writer's first major novel, *Macrolife* (1979), which would ensure him a place in the SF Hall of Fame even if he never wrote another word.

Zebrowski had penned the first drafts of *Macrolife* as early as 1964, although the book was not completed until fifteen years later. In a near-future Earth, the discovery of bulerite (named for the Bulero family) has revolutionized architecture and economics. Lightweight, versatile, stronger than steel, bulerite has enabled the construction of huge cityplexes, and facilitated the exploration of near-Earth space, with the subsequent colonization of Mars, the asteroids, and several of the larger moons in the Solar System. Unknown to the Buleros, however, bulerite is inherently unstable, and as structures made of the element begin to disintegrate or explode, they pull civilization down with it. Three of the Buleros—Richard, Sam, and Janet—escape to Asterome, a hollowed-out, ten-mile-long asteroid in Earth orbit, along with other scattered refugees from the devastated planet below. Earth is enveloped in an impenetrable cloud, with no hope of any life surviving the incessant lightning storms raging over its surface.

Asterome represents the first stage of macrolife, a self-sufficient, self-contained structure that will eventually spread intelligent life to every part of the universe. Eventually, Asterome leaves the Solar System, traveling to nearby stars, and utilizing the raw materials from their planets to construct new macrolife globes as its own compartments become crowded, or as social divisions develop among the populace. The flexibility of this arrangement, and the gradual lengthening of life-spans, enable humanity to grow literally without limits, to avoid frictions that might lead to war, to develop intellectually and emotionally in ways never before contemplated. Eventually, an alien macrolife unit is located, one of many such structures traversing the galaxy, and contact is made, to the mutual benefit of both races. The mental links between these groups seem to promise another stage in the development of mankind.

Xenograffiti, by ROBERT REGINALD

Eventually, a hundred billion years later, all intelligence has merged into one group mind. But the universe is winding down toward ultimate nullity, when all matter will collapse into the final explosion. John Bulero, a clone of Samuel Bolero, suddenly finds his consciousness reconstituted for some ultimate decision. Is there something more? the intelligences ask. Can anything survive the final debacle? The answers to these questions lead Bulero to the third level of macrolife, a consciousness so powerful that it can create its own universes, can transcend time and space itself.

Zebrowski's next major novel, *Stranger Suns* (1991), represents a further fifteen years of effort, an early draft having been published in much abridged form in 1975. Juan Obrion and his three companions discover an abandoned alien spaceship buried deep in the Antarctic ice. The ship admits them, then abruptly takes off for an unknown destination. The explorers discover matter replicators within the ship that solve their immediate problems of food and water supply, but no sign of the race which had constructed the vessel. They determine that the aliens have built a network of way stations within the suns of both our galaxy and its neighbors; these sophisticated facilities have similarly been abandoned, as have the surface structures found on a barren planet at the end of the chain. Eventually Juan and his friends determine that a set of black panels in the ship's bowels connect directly through hyperspace to similar panels on two other vessels left within the Solar System, one buried in the Amazon jungle, the other on the Moon, and to other alien vessels and facilities, enabling instantaneous movement through tremendous distances.

However, nothing in Zebrowski's works is ever quite what it seems, because the very act of moving back and forth through the portals alters either the viewer or the viewed in ways which are sometimes subtly, sometimes grossly skewed from the original. Eye color may be changed, or the outcome of a football game—or the fundamental history of the world as Obrion has known it. Why did the alien race develop this alternate mode of transportation? Why have all their facilities been abandoned? Where have they gone?

Xenograffiti, by ROBERT REGINALD

Can mankind use these structures to ensure its survival? The answers to these questions lead Obrion and company on a strange odyssey beyond the universe to an existence outside time and space as we know it.

The author's third major work, *The Killing Star* (with Charles Pellegrino, 1995), poses another curious question: if the universe is filled with intelligent life, as Carl Sagan and many other scientists have proposed, must they necessarily be as friendly as has been postulated? And if they're not friendly, or even if they're just a little bit afraid of what we might do to them in the future, won't they do it to us first? Within the first few pages of this gripping adventure set a hundred years hence, most of humanity is wiped out by an unseen alien race which has decided to dispose of a potential problem with humanity before it arises. By accelerating rocks and other debris to near-light speeds, the unseen enemies create devastating bombs that home in on all radio emissions in the solar system, eliminating 99% of the human species within a few minutes. All that survive are isolated outposts and ships, and these are quickly targeted for "mop-up" operations by the alien intruders. The bulk of this gripping saga deals with the efforts of the remnants of humanity to survive and fight back, countering the overwhelming alien presence with new and innovative scientific discoveries.

Zebrowski has penned more than just these three novels, of course. His young adult series, *The Sunspacers Trilogy* (comprising *Sunspacer* [1984], *The Stars Will Speak* [1985], and *Behind the Stars* [1996]), has been well-received in the juvenile market. His numerous short stories include significant works of science fiction, horror, fantasy, and mainstream fiction. His editorial credits include numerous original and reprint anthologies, and long service as co-editor of the *Bulletin of the Science Fiction Writers of America*. He also has gathered together several collections of his essays, including the groundbreaking pieces on Eastern European SF featured in *Beneath the Red Star: Studies on International Science Fiction* (edited by Pamela Sargent, published in 1996), and the forthcoming selection of autobiographical essays, *Perfecting Visions*.

Xenograffiti, by ROBERT REGINALD

Most of Zebrowski's fiction focuses on man's attempts to rise from the mud of his mundane existence and lift his face to the stars. If our race is to survive the wars and chances of planet-bound existence, he seems to be saying, we must leave this place for the limitless reaches of outer space, we must find new challenges for the species as a whole. Life on Earth is inherently flawed, for by creating a world on the edge of collapse we have imperiled our own future existence. In Zebrowski's cosmos, limited or unlimited, Earth (the soil) is Hell, the stars (the universe) are Heaven, and humanity can become either god or devil, savior or destroyer, as he or she so chooses.

Xenograffiti, by ROBERT REGINALD

XXVIII.

DERYNIAN DREAMS

THE FANTASY WORLDS OF KATHERINE KURTZ

(1991)

The beginning of the tale, as related by the author in *The Deryni Archives*, derived from an especially vivid dream which came to her on the night of October 11, 1964. Kurtz summarized what she remembered of this vision on a 3 x 5" card, and shortly thereafter expanded the scenario into the novelette, "Lords of Sorandor." "Sorandor" was in turn reworked into the climactic section of Kurtz's first novel, *Deryni Rising*.

These journeyman efforts contain all of the seeds of the author's later work. Katherine Kurtz has spent much of her creative life developing an alternate fantasy world centered around the medieval state of Gwynedd, the central kingdom of an area patterned roughly after tenth-to-twelfth-century England, Scotland, and Wales (in our own world, Gwynedd was an ancient name for Northern Wales). Although we can see rough similarities to medieval Britain—in language, culture, religion, and politics—there are equally striking differences.

Gwynedd and its neighbors are peopled by both humans and Deryni; the latter are outwardly similar to man, but have the innate ability to perform acts which their fellow humans regard as magical. These psychic talents vary considerably from individual to individual, and may be developed further with appropriate training. The history of

Xenograffiti, by ROBERT REGINALD

Gwynedd has been marred by a series of conflicts between the two races, the Deryni having controlled Gwynedd for less than a century of its history. (They still control Torenth, a large neighboring kingdom, which they have ruled from its inception.) Such clashes have been exacerbated by lack of empathy between the two groups, by arrogance on the part of the Deryni, and by outright racial hatred and envy on the human side, with concomitant persecutions and pogroms of the Deryni minority.

Kurtz's geography also varies significantly from the Europe we know, and these differences have themselves altered the political dynamic of the region. Unlike Britain, for example, Gwynedd is joined directly to the mainland; without the benefit of a channel buffer, it is immediately subject to invasion from hostile neighbors. The Mediterranean Sea does not seem to exist in this world, although references are made at several points to a "Holy Land" where Christ was born, preached, and martyred, much as in our own world. We can also see rough equivalents to the Moors, Gauls, and other ethnic groups from Earth, but no other obvious political, historical, or geographical correspondences with real-life medieval Europe.

The religious hierarchy of Kurtz's world is also subtly different from that of medieval Europe, generally following the tenets of the Roman Catholic Church, but being organized administratively along the lines of our own world's Eastern Orthodoxy or the Anglican Church. Thus, each major state contains its own autocephalous religious body, governed by an archbishop or patriarch chosen and supported by an independent ruling Synod. There is no "Pope" or central Church authority (indeed, no "Rome") in Kurtz's "Europe," although Latin remains the official Church language, and the celebration of the mass its key ritual.

Kurtz has developed her world in four sets of trilogies and nine short stories, eight of the latter being collected in *The Deryni Archives*. "The Chronicles of the Deryni," comprising *Deryni Rising* (1970), *Deryni Checkmate* (1972), and *High Deryni* (1973), relate the rise to power of King Kelson Haldane, who succeeds to the throne of Gwynedd at the age of thirteen when his father is assassinated. The

Xenograffiti, by ROBERT REGINALD

Haldanes, although not traditionally Deryni, have the ability to exercise similar powers when these have been activated through a magical ritual. Kelson represents the new man, merging the best of both blood lines into one person, unfettered by the past and able to forge the nation into a unified whole. In these three novels Kelson defeats the two representatives of the Festil dynasty, consolidates his position as King, and begins exploring his arcane heritage.

"The Legends of Camber of Culdi," comprising *Camber of Culdi* (1976), *Saint Camber* (1978), and *Camber the Heretic* (1981), take place two hundred years earlier, at a time when Deryni monarchs ruled Gwynedd. Camber, the Deryni Earl of Culdi, proves instrumental in locating the last Haldane heir, Prince Cinhil, whom he restores to the throne after the latter kills the Deryni King Imre. By the end of Cinhil's reign the restoration has created a backlash against the Deryni minority, resulting in increasingly harsh measures and massacres, as the newly-appointed human bishops and peers assume the reins of power.

"The Histories of King Kelson," including *The Bishop's Heir* (1984), *The King's Justice* (1985), and *The Quest for Saint Camber* (1986), return to the time of Kelson, picking up where *High Deryni* left off. Now eighteen, Kelson must face a revolt in the provinces, endure a marriage of convenience and the murder of his wife, and counter further unrest at home, as the surviving conservative bishops attempt to oust him and his government. He also faces treachery from within his own family, and ultimately learns that the art of statesmanship must be tempered with the king's justice.

"The Heirs of Saint Camber," comprising *The Harrowing of Gwynedd* (1989), *King Javan's Year* (1992), and *The Bastard Prince* (1994), are set in the years following the death of King Cinhil Haldane. The king's passing brings the forces of repression to the fore, and the few remaining Deryni must go underground to protect the remnants of their persecuted race. One by one the King's three young sons succeed to the throne and are killed by the human monsters actually governing the realm. But King Rhys Michael's death is not without meaning, for he leaves a will that provides his supporters with a way of overthrowing the conservative rulers. The succession of his infant son, King Owain, promises new hope for the future.

Two additional novels return to the later era in Kurtz's fictional universe. *King Kelson's Bride* (2000) is by far the worst contribution to the entire series, reflecting an unfortunate amalgamation of incompatible stories of political intrigue in Torenth and an attempted romance in Gwynedd between the young king and his younger cousin. Alas, this book illuminates quite clearly the author's total inability to present either believable women characters or believable romantic situations, and the attempt to shoehorn this "love story" into the usual political machinations fails miserably.

In the Service of the King (2003) returns to the era of two generations earlier, at the end of the reign of Kelson's grandfather and the succession of his father, King Brion, but the tale seems in the end almost as tired and shopworn as *Bride*, reflecting a turning-in of the author's fictional world upon itself, and a cannibalization of old scenarios and *milieux*. We have seen this all before—and better done at that!

Politics and religion are inextricably intertwined in Kurtz's creation, as they were in our own history, with state and church constantly vying with each other and the Deryni minority for power and authority. The key players of these historical fantasies recognize that the price of failure is either disgrace or death. What sustains them is faith, an abiding and sincere belief in God, his Church, his anointed King, and their close friends and family as *the* key structures of society.

Even those depicted on Kurtz's *tableaux* as cruel or manipulative largely perceive themselves as acting in the best interests of Church or state or family, often justifying their despicable acts through religious dictates that condemn the Deryni as evil personified. We may not applaud such individuals, but we can readily understand their motivations. The author's villains are carefully drawn in shades of gray, not splotches of black and white; some even seem marginally sympathetic, being true in their own fashion to the world as they see it. In her fiction Kurtz consistently champions intelligence, duty, sensitivity, love, faith, truth, and all of the other finer virtues. Such attributes do not always save her

Xenograffiti, by ROBERT REGINALD

characters from the acts of evil-minded men, but they save their souls for eternity, and that is a far, far better thing to do.

In recent years Kurtz has begun a new series of fantasies co-authored with Deborah Turner Harris. The Adept sequence, beginning with *The Adept* (1991), and continuing with *The Lodge of the Lynx* (1992), *The Templar Treasure* (1993), *Dagger Magic* (1995), and *Death of an Adept* (1996), feature a group of Scottish and British occult detectives seeking to right wrongs and counter the influence of evil in the modern world. Kurtz's solo novel, *Lammas Night* (1983), which is set during World War II, can be considered a prequel to these books. These novels, while entertaining in their own right, seem less effective than the Deryni books, perhaps because the contemporary setting decreases the verisimilitude of vast conspiracies and evil magicians working their wills over time on generations of insipid followers.

The characters in the Adept books are less ambiguous, more rigid in their beliefs, and ultimately less real. Ironically, the authors' message shines through in these books even clearer than before. Man makes of this world what he will, Kurtz seems to be saying, either a heaven or a hell, and this condition clearly presages what he (or she) will ultimately become in the afterlife.

Xenograffiti, by ROBERT REGINALD

XXIX.

THE FAT MAN, THE CONSULTING DETECTIVE, AND THE SELLER OF SPECULATIONS

THE CURIOUS WORLD OF ARTHUR BYRON COVER

(1991)

The world of Arthur Byron Cover reads like a *Classic Comics* version of Hieronymus Bosch: grotesqueries there are aplenty, unexplained and inexplicable, wandering the bizarre landscape of a caricature Earth, interacting with each other in curious and unique ways, seeking neither resolution nor evolution nor solution, but just existing as they are. Forget about plots, forget about the conventionalities of science fiction or fantasy, or of fiction in general: you won't find them here. What you *will* find are orts from Cover's intellectual table, pieces and snatches of characters, conversations, situations, perambulations, rearranged in new and interesting ways.
 Take, for example, the author's first novel, *Autumn Angels* (1975). We see a strange, far-future or other-dimensional Earth dominated by godlike beings scrapping over philosophical nullities while trying to establish his or her own position. Each has assumed the guise of a well-known fictional character of the past—from comic books, pulp fiction, motion pictures, or television—and is known to the reader only by the label of his or her choice ("the demon," "the lawyer," "the fat man," "the other fat man," etc.). The only named characters are two "bems" ("bug-eyed monsters"

Xenograffiti, by ROBERT REGINALD

in SF parlance), Dwit and Xit, the aliens who had originally metamorphosed the race of man into "godlike man" as a joke. The plot, if such exists, meanders back and forth across a landscape of broken conversations and philosophical musings. Each of these beings is searching for a unique identity in a world where individualities have failed; each seeks something to give him or her purpose: a name, a self, a reason for living. But the best that the demon, the lawyer, and the fat man can do at story's end, with all of their immense powers, is to cause the two alien bems to instill a sense of depression into their world, a form of negative identity that may help alter the stasis into which the godlike men have fallen.

The results of the trio's action can be seen in two later works by Cover, "The Clam of Catastrophe" (in the collection *The Platypus of Doom and Other Nihilists* [1976]) and the long novel, *An East Wind Coming* (1979). "Clam" introduces the character of the Consulting Detective, a pastiche of Sherlock Holmes, who is hired by the three beings to discover why sexism, which they have introduced into the world of the future to offset the effects of depression, has divided the godlike beings into two warring camps. To achieve the greatness of mere man, the detective ultimately concludes, godlike man must explore the ramifications of love, not sex.

An East Wind Coming, the author's major work of fiction, further explores the theme of identity, as the consulting detective and the good doctor must face the threat of a new Jack the Ripper, who is using an anti-matter knife to disembowel female godlike beings. After murdering his final victim, the Seller of Speculations (*i.e.*, a bookseller: Cover himself is co-owner of a science-fiction shop, Dangerous Visions), the ripper is forced by the detective to destroy himself, thus ending the threat to the godlike beings. The right of the individual to be individual has thus been reaffirmed.

Three other Cover novels deserve some mention. The author's second book, *The Sound of Winter* (1976), relates the story of Michael St. Claire, a would-be revolutionary, and his mute sister, Elizabeth, who travel from the City to the Wasteland, seeking a new way of life. Ultimately, Elizabeth regains her tongue, but is killed by her husband, and Michael comes to the realization that he never really understood anything about his sister's character—or about life in general. The book reads like a nineteenth-century Russian travelogue, and remains one of the most accessible of his works.

Two later books, *Planetfall* (1988) and *Stationfall* (1989), plus *Futurefall*, an uncompleted third book in the projected trilogy, reflect a change in direction for Cover, utilizing synthesized pulp and animation influences to produce more directly a deliberately farcical and very broadly-based SF satire. Although billed as game tie-ins, these two fictions have very little to do with the actual games from which they were theoretically derived, but take various elements from hackneyed science-fiction plots, reworking them *à la* Monty Python into a crazy patchwork of slapstick humor. Both are hilarious satires well-worth a second read.

The author's other works include a readable novelization of the screenplay for *Flash Gordon* (1980), three time-travel gamebooks for young adults, two tie-ins to multi-author series (*Isaac Asimov's Robot City: Prodigy* [1988]) and *Robert Silverberg's Time Tours: The Dinosaur Trackers*, written with Tim Sullivan and John Gregory Betancourt under the joint pseudonym, Thomas Shadwell [1991]), and a handful of short stories, the latest of which appeared in *Down & Dirty* (1988), the fifth of George R. R. Martin's Wild Cards mosaic novels. His most recent contributions have been to graphic stories in the comic book, *Disney Adventures*.

Cover's novels share a certain common framework, jumbling together elements from science fiction, the pulps, magic realism, detective fiction, music, comic books, movies, comedy, and the theatre into semi-coherent polemics about the manner in which people live their lives. The author's chief characters are quintessential outsiders trying to make sense of an essentially meaningless existence. Cover was particularly influenced by the Fireside Theatre, having noted how the actors utilized odd remarks, lines, and themes from extremely diverse sources to create something unique

Xenograffiti, by ROBERT REGINALD

and darkly satirical. He has tried to regenerate this feeling in his fiction, which is filled with non-sequiturs, scrambled plots, and snatches of philosophy.

At its best, Cover's work is exciting and stimulating, filled with fresh ideas presented in new and unique ways. At its worst, his style can seem incomprehensible, tangled, even ponderous, and certainly different from the expectations of the average reader. But then, you can't always tell a book by its Cover.

Xenograffiti, by ROBERT REGINALD

XXX.

SLICING AWAY AT SUBURBIA

THE FANTASTIC FICTION OF WILLIAM F. NOLAN

(1991)

William F. Nolan started his creative life as an artist, but quickly turned to the more lucrative science-fiction and men's magazines in the mid-1950s. Nolan was one of a group of Southern California SF writers that included (at times) the late Charles Beaumont, Ray Russell, George Clayton Johnson, Richard Matheson, the late Chad Oliver, and others. These authors not only socialized together frequently or occasionally, but also used their common interests in fantastic literature, film, television, and professional racing to develop a myriad of creative projects, often in collaboration. Although each writer eventually went his own way, artistically and personally, for the ten-year period from 1955-1965 most followed a similar path, moving from pulp fiction to slick nonfiction to the lucrative television market.

Nolan has been a full-time freelancer from the beginning, producing some fifteen hundred short fiction and nonfiction works in the course of his career, plus sixty-odd books, forty teleplays, and a dozen screenplays. Although his career has been a financial success, his work has been spread across so many subjects and genres that he remains relatively unheralded as a writer. Still, the frequency with which Nolan's 130 stories continue to be regularly anthologized ("Small World" has been reprinted at least twenty

Xenograffiti, by ROBERT REGINALD

times) is a sign of his continuing popularity and deepening influence as a writer.

Nolan's reputation as an SF writer seems secure, resting primarily on wide popular acceptance of two fictional creations, Logan the Sandman and Sam Space. *Logan's Run* (written with George Clayton Johnson [1967]), together with its two sequels, both written by Nolan alone, *Logan's World* (1977) and *Logan's Search* (1980), represent the high water mark of the author's science-fiction career, having been turned into both a successful motion picture and a television series, as well as being adapted into a popular comic book series.

In the not-so-distant future, young people have revolted and killed all the adults. The new regime decrees that henceforward anyone reaching the age of twenty-one (age thirty in the screen version) shall voluntary undergo euthanasia; those who refuse to die shall be hunted down by the police (the Sandmen) and summarily executed. A massive computer ("The Thinker") is built to control the world and enforce the new rules. The new world state provides each citizen with everything he/she might want: travel, drugs, pleasures of all kinds, even work for those who want it—but everything ends at twenty-one. Logan 3 is a Sandman who begins questioning the system after being forced to terminate a young girl. As his own time begins running out, Logan searches for Sanctuary, the semi-mythical place to which some runners have apparently escaped, and meets Jessica 6, with whom he forms a lasting and loving relationship. After a series of harrowing adventures, including a confrontation with the Thinker which succeeds in shutting down the machine, Logan and Jessica find Sanctuary, and live to fight another day.

In *Logan's World*, Logan and Jessica return to find the Sandman system largely destroyed, except for a group of renegade Sandmen who are trying to repair the damaged Thinker. In the ensuing chaos, Logan's son is killed, the Thinker is destroyed, and mankind is left to find its own way to the future. *Logan's Search* concludes the Trilogy with Logan's attempt to defeat the Sandman system on a parallel Earth where the Thinker still exists.

Xenograffiti, by ROBERT REGINALD

Logan is Everyman, the man forced by conscience and circumstance to blaze a new path for himself—and for mankind. The signs of systemic failure are everywhere, literally and figuratively: this brave new world of the future, itself once representing a great turning point in the history of the human race, has come full circle, to a cultural and historical dead end. The machines are breaking down—and so is human society. Logan must destroy the old, rekindle the new, and show man the way to a new civilization. In another sense, Logan is also Nolan (one name being nearly the anagram of the other): the author as iconoclast, the artist as creator/destroyer, the rebel *with* a cause, the self-made man remaking himself in fiction. Complacency is sterility, the author seems to be saying, a life without challenge a life not worth living. Mankind cannot stand still: it must either move forward—or die.

The three Sam Space books—*Space for Hire* (1971), *Look Out for Space* (1985), and the collection, *3 for Space* (1992)—represent the second and third main strands in Nolan's fiction: farce and hard-boiled detective fiction. Sam Space (*i.e.*, "Sam Spade" in SF terms) is a Mars-based private eye who always seems to be getting himself into impossibly wacky situations. Nolan manages to satirize the conventions of both the mystery and science-fiction genres, as well as modern mores, his fellow authors, and the world in general. Other stories in this vein include: "The Day the Gorf Took Over," "The Fasterfaster Affair," "Papa's Planet" (a robot-Hemingway send-up), and "Jenny Among the Zeebs" (a rock n' roll spoof).

In the 1980s Nolan moved away from SF into dark fantasy, producing a horror novel, *Helltracks* (1991), and some fifty short stories, the best of which have been collected into *Things Beyond Midnight* (1984) and *Night Shapes* (1995). Like his frequent early collaborator, Charles Beaumont, Nolan has proven particularly effective at depicting the unpleasant side of human nature, and his stories are filled with clever twists, a legacy of his work in the mystery genre. These tales reflect a more cynical view of man's nature, one in which there are not always happy endings or Pollyannish characters, in which evil is both acknowledged and sometimes prevails.

In the 1990s Nolan's work has again zagged into new directions, with the author producing a series of mystery thrillers which feature "The Black Mask Boys"—Dashiell Hammett, Raymond Chandler, Erle Stanley Gardner— functioning as amateur detectives in the Hollywood of the 1930s. The first of these, *The Black Mask Murders* (narrated by Hammett) was published in 1994, with *The Marble Orchard* (narrated by Chandler) following in 1996.

In these and in all of Nolan's fictions we find the writer sitting to one side, deliberately sharpening his authorial knife and covertly slicing away at man, his machines, and his conventions. Some of his stories may have more-or-less happy endings, but even these drip with skepticism and often twist into strange angles by tale's end. In Nolan's fictional world nothing is as it seems, no one is safe, and happiness always comes with a price tag attached.

Xenograffiti, by ROBERT REGINALD

XXXI.

A MODEST PROPOSAL

(1991)

NOTE: *In response to a proposal to revise membership rules to allow only the top-producing SF writers to retain "active" membership in the professional organization, Science Fiction and Fantasy Writers of America, Inc., Reginald wrote the following letter to the* SFWA Forum. *It was never published.*

Dear Folks:

I agree, let's throw the riffraff out; the presence of hundreds of itinerant, would-be, or played-out writers only tends to corrupt the very few of us (at least seven) who constitute the *real* professionals, if in no other way than by filling SFWA's coffers. We need to return to being a small, impoverished, largely irrelevant writers' union. In fact, Dafydd ap Hugh *et al.* don't go nearly far enough with their proposals; we must use this opportunity to purge the membership of those who are culturally, intellectually, and authorily inferior to those of us qualified to judge such matters. I therefore suggest these small emendations to the proposed membership qualification changes:

Xenograffiti, by ROBERT REGINALD

Alternative One

Writers shall qualify for active membership in SFWA when they have published ten SF novels, and shall thereafter be permanently qualified. Each member's vote shall be weighted according to the cumulative record of SF books published, each monograph counting for one vote. Members shall qualify for office when they have published fifty novels. Writers who don't qualify shall be called amateurs.

Comment

Under this proposal, short fiction, anthologies, nonfiction works, etc., wouldn't count for qualification purposes, since they reflect a less than serious effort on the part of the writer to attain true professional status. Personally, I think this category should be limited even further, to ten cloth novels, since otherwise Lionel Fanthorpe would have the largest vote (160+), and he is, after all, a foreigner, and probably not worthy anyway. One could also set a minimum length of 200 pages (or 80,000 words) to qualify; this would help keep out those goddam "paperback writers." They're all hacks, every one of them.

Alternative Two

Writers shall be eligible for membership in SFWA when personally recommended by already-qualified members of the organization, and when they have submitted to the Membership Committee a notarized statement prepared by a certified public accountant, showing that their annual income has exceeded for at least the five previous consecutive years a level of $100,000, at least one dollar of which must have been derived from professional sales of SF-related fiction or nonfiction. A member shall be accorded the number of votes appropriate to his or her income level (*i.e.*, status), with one vote being awarded for every $50,000 of income. Dues shall be assessed inversely proportionate to income. Nebulas will annually be auctioned off to the highest bidders.

Comment

This proposal really cuts to the heart of the matter, doesn't it? We want a wealthy, elite, intellectual organization, not a bunch of poor, self-trained hacks. I want to know that the idiot sitting next to me at the Nebula Banquets has some real knowledge, for Christ's sake, of the watery vintage he or she is gurgling down by the gallon. We've got to draw the line somewhere, and cash is the easiest way to do it. Another variation of this plan would simply have the Membership Committee assess the net wealth of prospective members, and rank them from 1-100, limiting the organization to no more than that number (we can always have less!). There is one minor problem with the proposal: who shall qualify the first member?

Alternative Three

Prospective members of SFWA shall be rated for literary quality by the members of SFRA, and ranked in order. The top 10% shall qualify for Active membership, and the rest shall be deemed Amateur Apprentices. Dues would be levied only on those in the bottom ranks, the absence of dues being one of the perquisites owed the true professionals in the field. Only those in the top 5% would be eligible for office.

Comment

The virtue of this plan is that it combines elitism with pseudo-literary values; indeed, under this proposal the organization should probably be renamed The Academy of Science-Fiction Self-Realization (ASS), to reflect its sublimely high (and enormously smug) literary standards. Only those sanctified by a presumably objective outside panel could join, and there would be no appeal, no messy qualification process: either you pass the litmus test—or you don't!

Xenograffiti, by ROBERT REGINALD

<u>Alternative Four</u>

I hope the membership will give all of these proposals the consideration they truly deserve. In the meantime, it is sad to watch this noble organization die the death of a thousand knives. Whatever SFWA is, whatever it has been, whatever it will become after this interminable logorrhea finally subsides, we are all diminished by these seemingly endless internal squabbles. If we really *are* professionals, in any sense of the word, then why are we wasting our collective time on issues which were discussed at great length on several previous occasions? Have we truly nothing better to do? If the answer to the latter question is yes, then I submit to you that SFWA has already degenerated to the status of a fan group or social club, and is unworthy of any further support, at any level. My "final solution," fellow SFWAns, is to dissolve the organization entirely, and retire to the bar, where most of us can usually be found anyway.

Dyspeptically Yours:

Robert Reginald

Xenograffiti, by ROBERT REGINALD

XXXII.

PILGRIM AWARD ACCEPTANCE SPEECH

(1993)

This award is the culmination of all I've worked for during the past quarter century. I started my first book in 1968 as a senior Honor's project at Gonzaga University. While attending Baycon in Berkeley that fall, and meeting for the first time a number of writers who had just been names on the title pages of their books, I realized that no one had ever compiled a "who's who" of the science fiction field. I decided to produce one myself. It was my first experience as both author and publisher.

I was too dumb and too inexperienced to realize the utter impossibility of the task, so I rented a post office box, ordered some stationery and questionnaires, and began mailing them out. Much to my surprise, writers began responding in great numbers, many of them providing illuminating comments and quotations that I could use to highlight their entries. I compiled their bibliographies from the sources available to me, and typed up the individual entries on offset masters. Gonzaga found a little money somewhere to help complete publication, and I had my first reference book.

Stella Nova, as it was called, had serious flaws, including design problems with the index and an overuse of obscure abbreviations. But I learned more from working on that first nascent publication than from all of my academic classes. There's a vast gulf between theory and practice that separates the amateurs from the professionals in almost every field of knowledge.

Xenograffiti, by ROBERT REGINALD

Even this early publication wasn't produced in a vacuum, however, since I partially patterned the book's design on the style used in *Contemporary Authors*, adapting it to suit my own needs. Within a year of its publication in 1970, I had proposed and sold to Gale Research Company two new books: a bibliography of the first twenty years of the mass market paperback, and a reworking of *Stella Nova* into a bio-bibliography of science fiction, replacing and updating Everett F. Bleiler's pioneering guide, *The Checklist of Fantastic Literature*.

Bleiler's influence on all subsequent reference works in our genre should not be underestimated. Produced at a time when bibliographical resources were minimal, *The Checklist* set a standard rarely to be exceeded or even equaled in the following decades, save by Bleiler himself. The book is an extraordinary piece of scholarship: authoritative and comprehensive, with an attractive, easy-to-use format. That such a work could have even been published in early 1948—coincidentally, within a month of my birth—is a remarkable testament to the man and his abilities, and to the acumen of my late friend, Ted Dikty, who published it.

Bradford M. Day and others had produced supplements to Bleiler's guide, but I envisaged a complete re-verification of the original database, using the *National Union Catalog*, *British Museum Catalogue*, and other works not available in the mid-1940s, plus the collection of the late Dr. J. Lloyd Eaton, which had recently been purchased by the University of California, Riverside. I also intended to extend coverage through 1974, the year I actually started work on *Science Fiction and Fantasy Literature*. The two-volume set was published by Gale in late 1979; the supplement, covering the years 1975-1991, was issued by them in 1992, and covered more works in seventeen years than the original volumes had recorded in more than two and one-half centuries of SF publications. Together, the books cover some 38,000 original monographs of fantastic literature published in English.

In the forty-five years since the publication of Bleiler's *Checklist*, some 530 additional bibliographies, indexes, dictionaries, encyclopedias, and other reference tools

163

relating to SF and fantasy have been issued in monograph form. We critics have been extraordinarily blessed with this cornucopia; our brothers and sisters working in mystery and detective literature, a field with twice the number of primary works, have many fewer resources upon which to draw for background information, and those active in the field of Western literature have virtually none. Only a few of these publications, of course, are professionally written, but a surprising number possess at least some utility or merit, and a few are of surpassing excellence, as good as anything produced on "mainstream" literature.

Among the modern compilers of outstanding SF reference tools are: Mike Ashley, Neil Barron, John Clute, Bill Contento, Lloyd Currey, Hal W. Hall, Peter Nicholls, Leslie Kay Swigart, Donald H. Tuck, and, of course, Everett F. Bleiler himself. In particular, special mention needs to be made of Hal Hall, whose work so directly supports that of *all* SF critics. Without his *Science Fiction Book Review Index* and *Science Fiction and Fantasy Research Index*, the standard guides, respectively, to book reviews and secondary sources relating to fantastic literature, none of us would be able to do systematic searches of the secondary literature. His name is one that has been consistently overlooked by the awards committees.

The work that remains to be done is significant. We badly need a current, annotated guide to critical monographs in the field, something that will provide both detailed descriptions and full comparative evaluations of books and dissertations on SF writers and themes. The genre has yet to produce any literary biography of an SF writer equivalent in size and scope and authoritativeness to John J. McAleer's *Rex Stout: A Biography* (1977), although critical guides have been published on most of the major science fiction and fantasy authors, plus scattered autobiographies and remembrances. The latter provide interesting details on the early publishing history of the field, but lack the kind of objective evaluations of each writer's life and career that is so badly needed.

We have too many mediocre critical guides available on writers like Stephen King, and far too few on other, less

Xenograffiti, by ROBERT REGINALD

prominent individuals who nonetheless deserve some further consideration for their work; and too many of the critiques and bibliographies that have been published fail, ultimately, even in their understanding of how and why this genre originated and developed. Where other genres and literatures have produced dozens of *festschriften* to honor their esteemed senior colleagues, we have thus far issued none.

All of us have an obligation to act as mentors to the newer members of our group, to provide guidance and assistance in developing projects of all kinds, to make certain that their works are well-organized and -conceived, with appropriate academic apparatus and indexing, and that finally they are brought to some king of successful conclusion through professional publication as essays or books. The Science Fiction Research Association bears the additional responsibility of providing some general guidance and publishing opportunities to its membership. We need to do more to encourage the younger talents among us, to nurture those who receive no support or even castigation from academic colleagues on their own campuses.

We should also issue a list of recommended reference and critical works and standards, for use by our members as pattern works, and by the library world as potential acquisitions. We have the perfect jury in place for determining such a list: the surviving Pilgrim Award recipients. We could further produce an *Annual Review of Science Fiction*, not a yearbook, but an anthology of essays by members on major topics of current interest, similar to those produced by Annual Reviews Inc. and JAI Press. The proceeds from such publications would benefit the organization, while simultaneously providing refereed publication outlets for SFRA members. The possibilities are limited only by the limits of our vision.

We should never forget that *we* are the pioneers, *we* are the pilgrims of fantastic literature. There is scarcely a person in this room who has not or will not at some point in his or her career pen the first critical or biographical or bibliographical essay or book on some SF or fantasy writer. As my Latin teacher would have said, *mirabile dictu!*—what a marvel to say! Instead of treading the broad boulevards of

Xenograffiti, by ROBERT REGINALD

mainstream literature, we have chosen the byways little trodden, the back alleys, the suburbs of criticism, where it is still possible to unearth genuine literary treasures and to make the first significant observations about them. One hundred, two hundred, three hundred years hence, the critics of the future will be examining *our* works to find the first extended contemporaneous examinations of the SF writers of our time. In great measure, we have it within our power to shape the literary consciousness of the future. We must not fail this challenge—or the equal challenge of convincing our academic colleagues of today of the inherent value of fantastic literature. If the history of literature is any judge, many of the "darlings" so highly touted today will not survive the passing of the century in which they lived; while others not as highly regarded by their contemporaries, including many of our genre writers, will continue to be read and enjoyed and discussed into the indefinite future.

For my own part, I expect no phone calls from Ted Koppel or Oprah Winfrey. I won't be stopped by the man on the street, or even by my fellow professors at Cal State. And I certainly won't find my advances increasing. But I am very pleased—and deeply honored—that you have found my work worthy of notice, and I hope to spend the next quarter century trying to live up to this honor.

Thank you all very kindly.

Xenograffiti, by ROBERT REGINALD

XXXIII.

A REQUIEM FOR STARMONT HOUSE AND FAX COLLECTOR'S EDITIONS, 1972-1993

A HISTORY AND BIBLIOGRAPHY

(1993)

When Starmont House, Inc., ceased operations on March 1, 1993, the event marked the end of a publishing era. For almost seventeen years, Starmont published some of the best work of both established and new SF critics, in addition to reprinting a number of previously uncollected pulp classics. Its passing meant the loss of a major outlet for innovative nonfiction books about fantastic literature.

Starmont House was founded by Thaddeus Maxim Eugene "Ted" Dikty (1920-1991). Dikty had received his editorial baptism by becoming managing editor of the then-new specialty house, Shasta Publishers, in 1948, and by working on that company's first book, E. F. Bleiler's pioneering bibliography, *The Checklist of Fantastic Literature*. For the next five years Shasta issued dozens of significant books in the field, but eventually collapsed after trying to expand too quickly into mainstream trade publishing. Dikty also edited (with Bleiler) the first "best SF of the year" story anthologies, and later worked for a Chicago-area publishing house.

In 1972 Dikty and Darrell C. Richardson formed FAX Collector's Editions to reproduce selected pulp-era (and

Xenograffiti, by ROBERT REGINALD

earlier) SF stories and novels; their reprints of lesser-known works by Robert E. Howard were commercially successful, but as the Howard boom began to die, Dikty began searching for new publishing ventures.

By then Dikty and his family (including his wife, SF writer Julian May) had relocated to West Linn, Oregon (and later to Mercer Island, Washington). He envisioned a new publishing company, one wholly owned by the Dikty family, that could capitalize on the growing interest in SF criticism. In 1976 Starmont House, Inc. issued its first book, a guide to the work of Robert E. Howard by Robert Weinberg, with a second guide by Lee N. Falconer (*i.e.*, Julian May) being published the following year.

Neither of these works was packaged as part of a series. However, Dikty had seen the first few books in The Milford Series: Popular Writers of Today, and envisioned a similar series of paperbound books devoted exclusively to science fiction and fantasy writers. To edit the Starmont Reader's Guides, as they were called, he hired a well-known academic critic, Roger C. Schlobin, who was directed to prepare a series format and to begin soliciting manuscripts.

Schlobin proposed a package similar to that of the Twayne U.S. Authors series, but limited the size of the books to about half that of the Twayne standard. The first twenty titles averaged eighty pages in length, although the small typeface used in the guides enabled Starmont to pack 40,000 words or more into some of its books. The guides were attractively packaged into an innovative series format that first featured Stephen Fabian drawings on the front covers, and later substituted author photographs. Cloth bindings were added as an option in 1980, vastly increasing potential sales in the lucrative library market.

The Starmont Reader's Guides became the flagship series for the company, eventually reaching Number 61 in 1992 (although some numbers were skipped). As the series progressed, the average length of the guides grew, with one of the later books (*Frederik Pohl*, by Thomas D. Clareson) reaching 178 pages, longer than the average page count of a Twayne critique. Editor Schlobin kept tight control over the guides: the series format required a chronology of the au-

Xenograffiti, by ROBERT REGINALD

thor's life and works, an introduction summarizing the subject's biography, coverage of the major books or collections of short stories, detailed primary and secondary bibliographies, and index.

In the early 1980s Starmont added two other series to its list, Starmont Studies in Literary Criticism, intended to feature somewhat longer author- or subject-oriented anthologies and monographs on fantastic literature; and Starmont Reference Guides, which included magazine and publisher indexes and SF bibliographies. More series followed. These later entries to the Starmont list suffered somewhat from a lack of strict editorial guidelines.

In the mid-1980s Starmont acquired its own printing and binding facilities at Eugene, Oregon, using high-speed copiers to produce Starmont's own titles, while soliciting outside work to keep the plant fully operational. In retrospect, this proved to be an unfortunate choice, for the immediate result was a serious diminution in the production quality of the books, with very little actual savings in cash. When the recession of the early 1990s began hitting specialty and academic publishing, Starmont was affected with the rest, while outside printing jobs also diminished. Ted Dikty's death on 11 October 1991 removed the founder's guiding hand from Starmont at a crucial point in its history; and although his daughter, Barbara Dikty, had already been made President of Starmont House, Inc., she could not stem the tide. When Barbara was herself severely injured in a car accident on 26 December 1992, there was no one left to continue. Starmont had published its last few titles the preceding summer.

In total FAX Collector's Editions issued seventeen books and Starmont House, Inc. another 131 volumes (one book appearing under both imprints), many of them the first extended examinations of their particular subjects, plus two art folios and a fantasy map. Starmont's authors included such leading critics as: Thomas D. Clareson, Donald M. Hassler, Gary K. Wolfe, Michael R. Collings, S. T. Joshi, Gorman Beauchamp, Kenneth J. Zahorski, Randall D. Larson, Joan Gordon, Hoda M. Zaki, Marshall B. Tymn, Tony Magistrale, Robert M. Price, Darrell Schweitzer, and Shel-

Xenograffiti, by ROBERT REGINALD

don Jaffery, among many others. One Starmont book (*Isaac Asimov*, by Donald M. Hassler) was honored with the Eaton Award as best critical monograph of 1991, and Dikty himself received the 1984 Milford Award for his contributions as editor and publisher. The demise of Starmont House, Inc. represented the loss of both a major market for nonfiction works in the field, and the permanent absence of a strong editorial voice. Starmont House—and the great man who founded it—are both sorely missed.

A FAX COLLECTOR'S EDITIONS BIBLIOGRAPHY

1972

The Checklist of Fantastic Literature, by E. F. Bleiler. xix+455 p. Dust jacket illustration by Hannes Bok. ISBN 0-913960-01-2 cloth $10. The ISBN number was assigned retroactively. A facsimile reprint of the 1948 Shasta edition.

The Moon Metal, by Garrett P. Serviss, with a new introduction and bibliography by Darrell C. Richardson. 163 p. Cover illustration by Eric Bess. ISBN 0-913960-02-0 boards $3.95. The ISBN number was assigned retroactively. A facsimile reprint of the 1900 Harper & Bros. edition of this science fiction novel.

Through the Earth, by Clement Fezandié. [32] p. LC 80-130879. ISBN 0-913960-00-4 paper $2.50. The ISBN number was assigned retroactively. A facsimile reprint on slick paper of the pulp novella published in *St. Nicholas* magazine in 1898, including the original illustrations.

Valdar the Oft-Born: A Saga of Seven Ages, by George Griffith, introduction by Darrell C. Richardson. 128 p. Cover illustration by Dean Richardson. ISBN 0-913960-03-9 cloth $3.95. The ISBN number was assigned retroactively. A facsimile of the 1895 C. Arthur Pearson edition of this novel of immortality.

Xenograffiti, by ROBERT REGINALD

1974

Famous Fantastic Classics #1, anonymously edited by Robert Weinberg. 128 p., illus. LC 74-20652. Four-color cover art by Stephen E. Fabian. ISBN 0-913960-10-1 paper $3. A facsimile reprint of several pulp stories. Contents: "Tomorrow," by Arthur Leo Zagat; "The Man in the Moon," by Homer Eon Flint; "The Snow Girl," by Ray Cummings; "Creatures of the Ray," by James L. Aton.

Far Below and Other Horrors, edited by Robert Weinberg. 151 p. LC 74-82615. Jacket illustration by Lee Brown Coye. ISBN 0-913960-05-5 cloth $6.95. Contents: "Introduction," by Robert Weinberg; "Far Below," by Robert Barbour Johnson; "The Execution of Lucarno," by Julius Long; "Thing of Darkness," by G. G. Pendarves; "The Accursed Isle," by Mary Elizabeth Counselman; "Masquerade," by Mearle Prout; "Naked Lady," by Mindret Lord; "Out of the Deep," by Robert E. Howard; "Doom of the House of Duryea," by Earl Pierce, Jr.; "The Chapel of Mystic Horror," by Seabury Quinn; "Return to Death," by J. Wesley Rosenquest; "Under the Tomb," by Robert Nelson.

The Incredible Adventures of Dennis Dorgan, by Robert E. Howard. vii+165 p. LC 74-83075. Four-color jacket art by Tom Foster. ISBN 0-913960-06-3 cloth $11.95. Contents: "Introduction," by Darrell C. Richardson; "The Alleys of Singapore"; "The Jade Monkey"; "The Mandarin Ruby"; "The Yellow Cobra"; "In High Society"; "Playing Journalist"; "The Destiny Gorilla"; "A Knight of the Round Table"; "Playing Santa Claus"; "The Turkish Menace."

The Lost Valley of Iskander, by Robert E. Howard. xiv+194 p. LC 74-83076. Four-color jacket art by Michael William Kaluta. ISBN 0-913960-07-1 cloth $12.95. Contents: "Introduction," by Darrell C. Richardson; "The Daughter of Erlik Khan"; "The Lost Valley of Iskander"; "Hawk of the Hills."

Xenograffiti, by ROBERT REGINALD

1975

Famous Fantastic Classics #2, anonymously edited by Robert Weinberg. 128 p., illus. LC 74-20652. Four-color cover art by Michael William Kaluta. ISBN 0-913960-11-X paper $5. A facsimile reprint of two pulp stories. Contents: "The Stagnant Death," by H. Bedford-Jones; *The Radio Flyers*, by Ralph Milne Farley.

Famous Pulp Classics #1, anonymously edited by Robert Weinberg. 128 p., illus. LC 74-20653. Four-color cover art by Michael William Kaluta. ISBN 0-913960-12-8 paper $5. A facsimile reprint of several pulp stories. Contents: "Lances of Tartary," by Malcolm Wheeler-Nicholson; "Black Flag," by Talbot Mundy; "Cave of the Blue Scorpion," by Loring Brent; "Uneasy Lies the Head," by Theodore Roscoe; "Four Lashes an Hour," by Johnston McCulley; "Berber Loot," by H. Bedford-Jones.

The Shudder Pulps: A History of the Weird Menace Pulps of the 1930s, by Robert Kenneth Jones. xv+238 p. LC 74-82614. Four-color jacket art by Michael William Kaluta. ISBN 0-913960-04-7 cloth $11.95. Illustrated with reproductions of cover art and interior drawings from the pulps.

1976

Swords of Shahrazar, by Robert E. Howard. xv+133 p. LC 76-16707. Four-color jacket art by Michael William Kaluta. ISBN 0-913960-08-X cloth $12.95. Contents: "Introduction," by Frederick Cook; "The Curse of the Crimson God"; "The Treasures of Tartary"; "The Treasure of Shaibar Khan."

1977

I Found Cleopatra, by Thomas P. Kelley. 111 p., illus. LC 77-87563. Four-color cover art by Stephen E. Fabian. ISBN 0-913960-18-7 paper $4. A facsimile reprint of the pulp fantasy novel, apparently intended to be a second volume in the "Famous Pulp Classics" series.

Xenograffiti, by ROBERT REGINALD

The Return of Skull-Face, by Robert E. Howard and Richard A. Lupoff. 96 p. LC 77-89158. Four-color jacket art by Stephen E. Leialoha. ISBN 0-913960-17-9 cloth $17. An original novel by Lupoff continuing the adventures of Howard's well-known character, Skull-Face.
Son of the White Wolf, by Robert E. Howard. xiv+170 p. LC 77-73604. Four-color jacket art by Marcus Boas. ISBN 0-913960-09-8 cloth $12.95. Contents: "Introduction," by Frederick Cook; "Blood of the Gods"; "Country of the Knife"; "Son of the White Wolf."
The Weird Tales Story, by Robert E. Weinberg. ix+134 p. LC 77-73602. Four-color jacket art by Alex Nino, Frank Magsino, and Orvy Jundis. ISBN 0-913960-16-0 cloth $17.50. An illustrated history of the best-known professional magazine of horror.

1979

American Fantasy and Science Fiction: Toward a Bibliography of Works Published in the United States, 1948-1973, by Marshall B. Tymn. ix+228 p. LC 76-55151. ISBN 0-913960-15-2 paper $12.95.

A STARMONT HOUSE BIBLIOGRAPHY

A comprehensive, descriptive bibliography of the printing and binding states of Starmont House books is probably impossible, given the diversity of styles and formats used throughout its existence, particularly in its last five years. The following list arranges Starmont's titles in chronological order by year of publication, and gives complete bibliographical information, plus occasional notes:

Xenograffiti, by ROBERT REGINALD

1976

The Annotated Guide to Robert E. Howard's Sword & Sorcery, by Robert Weinberg. viii+152 p. LC 76-16708. ISBN 0-916732-20-7 cloth $13.95 (not available until 1980); ISBN 0-916732-00-2 paper $7.95.

1977

A Gazeteer of the Hyborian World of Conan, Including Also the World of Kull and an Ethnogeographical Dictionary of the Principal Peoples of the Era, with Reference to The Starmont Map of the Hyborian World, by Lee N. Falconer [*i.e.*, Julian May]. xiv+119 p. LC 77-79065. ISBN 0-916732-19-3 cloth $10.95 (not available until 1980); ISBN 0-916732-01-0 paper $4.95.

The Hyborian World of Conan: Being Here Newly Researched and Embellished for the Information and Edification of the Faithful, and Including All Locales Set Forth in the Immortal Saga, As Well As in Divers Works of a Comical Nature, and in Certain Incunabula Attributed to the Master, Robert E. Howard, Juliana ux. Thaddei Maximi fecit [*i.e.*, by Julian May]. ISBN 0-916732-11-8 colored map (77 x 103 cm.) $4.95. Printed on glossy paper, and mailed rolled in a tube.

1978

No titles published.

1979

Arthur C. Clarke, by Eric S. Rabkin. STARMONT READER'S GUIDE, 1. 80 p. LC 79-84709. ISBN 0-916732-12-6 cloth $9.95 (not available until 1980); ISBN 0-916732-03-7 paper $3.95.

Portfolio, by Stephen E. Fabian. [8] leaves of colored art, housed loosely in a portfolio case. $17.50?

Xenograffiti, by ROBERT REGINALD

Roger Zelazny, by Carl B. Yoke. STARMONT READER'S GUIDE, 2. 111 p. LC 79-17107. ISBN 0-916732-13-4 cloth $9.95 (not available until 1980); ISBN 0-916732-04-5 paper $3.95.

1980

Arthur C. Clarke, Second Edition, by Eric S. Rabkin. STARMONT READER'S GUIDE, 1. 80 p. LC 79-84709. ISBN 0-916732-22-3 cloth $9.95; ISBN 0-916732-21-5 paper $3.95.

Fabian in Color, by Stephen E. Fabian. [8] leaves of colored art housed loose in a portfolio case. ISBN 0-916732-23-1 paper folio $17.50. A few copies were also released in a deluxe cloth rebinding at $35.

Frank Herbert, by David M. Miller. STARMONT READER'S GUIDE, 5. 70 p. LC 80-20880. ISBN 0-916732-07-X cloth $9.95; ISBN 0-916732-16-9 paper $3.95.

Fritz Leiber, by Jeff Frane. STARMONT READER'S GUIDE, 8. 64 p. LC 80-22107. ISBN 0-916732-02-9 cloth $9.95; ISBN 0-916732-10-X paper $3.95.

Joe Haldeman, by Joan Gordon. STARMONT READER'S GUIDE, 4. 64 p. LC 80-21388. ISBN 0-916732-15-0 cloth $9.95; ISBN 0-916732-06-1 paper $3.95.

Philip José Farmer, by Mary T. Brizzi. STARMONT READER'S GUIDE, 3. [ii]+80 p. LC 79-17691. ISBN 0-916732-14-2 cloth $9.95; ISBN 0-916732-05-3 paper $3.95.

1981

The Science Fiction Reference Book: A Comprehensive Handbook and Guide to the History, Literature, Scholarship, and Related Activities of the Science Fiction and Fantasy Fields, edited by Marshall B. Tymn. viii+536 p. LC 80-28888. ISBN 0-916732-49-5 cloth $22.95; ISBN 0-916732-24-X paper $14.95. Probably the best-selling book of the entire Starmont list. Contents: "Introduction," by Frederik Pohl; "Toward a History of Science

175

Xenograffiti, by ROBERT REGINALD Fiction," by Thomas D. Clareson; "Children's Fantasy and Science Fiction," by Francis Molson; "Science Fiction Art: Some Contemporary Illustrators," by Vincent Di Fate; "The Fantastic Cinema," by Vincent Miranda; "Critical Studies and Reference Works," by Tymn; "Science Fiction Fandom/A History of an Unusual Hobby," by Joe Siclari; "The Writing Awards," by Harlan McGhan; "Literary Awards in Science Fiction," by Howard DeVore; "Science Fiction and Fantasy Periodicals," by Tymn; "From the Pulps to the Classroom: The Strange Journey of Science Fiction," by James Gunn; "Masterpieces of Modern Fantasy: An Annotated Core List," by Roger C. Schlobin; "Outstanding Science Fiction Books: 1927-1979," by Joe De Bolt; "Science Fiction and Fantasy Collections in U.S. and Canadian Libraries," by Elizabeth Cummins Cogell; "Resources for Teaching Science Fiction," by Tymn; "Doctoral Dissertations in Science Fiction and Fantasy, 1970-1979," by Douglas R. Justus; "Science Fiction Organizations and Societies," by Tymn; "Directory of Specialty Publishers," by Tymn; "Definitions of Science Fiction and Fantasy," by Roger C. Schlobin; Contributors; Index.

Theodore Sturgeon, by Lahna Diskin. STARMONT READER'S GUIDE, 7. 72 p. LC 80-21423. ISBN 0-916732-09-6 cloth $9.95; ISBN 0-916732-18-5 paper $3.95.

1982

Alfred Bester, by Carolyn Wendell. STARMONT READER'S GUIDE, 6. 72 p. LC 80-19655. ISBN 0-916732-17-7 cloth $10.95; ISBN 0-916732-08-8 paper $4.95.

Brede's Tale, by Julian May. 1982. [23] p., 2 x 3". LC 82-5516. ISBN 0-916732-31-2 deluxe leather-bound edition $85; ISBN 0-916732-32-0 special edition $45. This short tale, which was excerpted from May's novel, *The Many-Colored Land*, was produced as a miniature book housed in a box, limited to 300 copies signed and numbered by the author and illustrators, of which 100 copies were bound in leather. Without a doubt the most collectible of the Starmont books.

Xenograffiti, by ROBERT REGINALD

David Lindsay, by Gary K. Wolfe. STARMONT READER'S GUIDE, 9. [ii]+64 p. LC 82-5563. ISBN 0-916732-29-0 cloth $10.95; ISBN 0-916732-26-6 paper $4.95.
Hal Clement, by Donald M. Hassler. STARMONT READER'S GUIDE, 11. [ii]+64 p. LC 82-5577. ISBN 0-916732-30-4 cloth $10.95; ISBN 0-916732-27-4 paper $4.95.
H.P. Lovecraft, by S. T. Joshi. STARMONT READER'S GUIDE, 13. 83 p. LC 82-10236. ISBN 0-916732-36-3 cloth $12.95; ISBN 0-916732-35-5 paper $5.95.
Philip K. Dick, by Hazel Pierce. STARMONT READER'S GUIDE, 12. 64 p. LC 82-6005. ISBN 0-916732-34-7 cloth $10.95; ISBN 0-916732-33-9 paper $4.95.
Samuel R. Delany, by Jane Branham Weedman. STARMONT READER'S GUIDE, 10. [ii]+79 p. LC 82-5545. ISBN 0-916732-28-2 cloth $10.95; ISBN 0-916732-25-8 paper $4.95.
Stephen King, by Douglas E. Winter. STARMONT READER'S GUIDE, 16. 128 p. LC 82-10699. ISBN 0-916732-44-4 cloth $11.95; ISBN 0-916732-43-6 paper $5.95.

1983

C.S. Lewis, by Brian Murphy. STARMONT READER'S GUIDE, 14. 95 p. LC 82-7346. ISBN 0-916732-38-X cloth $13.95; ISBN 0-916732-37-1 paper $5.95.
Patterns of the Fantastic: Academic Programming at Chicon IV, edited by Donald M. Hassler. STARMONT STUDIES IN LITERARY CRITICISM, No. 2. [vi]+105 p. LC 83-587. ISBN 0-916732-63-0 cloth $13.95; ISBN 0-916732-62-2 paper $5.95. Contents: "Preface," by Hassler; "Introduction: Science Fiction and Fantasy and the Academic Enterprise," by Hassler; "Stephen King in Context," by Joseph F. Patrouch, Jr.; "Science Fiction Women: Victims, Rebels, Heroes," by Richard Law; "The Woman Science Fiction Writer and the Non-Heroic Male Protagonist," by Jim Villani; "The Days of Future Past, or Utopians Lessing and Le Guin Fight Future Nostalgia," by Kathe Davis Finney; "Narcissism and Romance in McCaffrey's *Restoree*," by Mary T. Brizzi; "Woman on the Edge of Narrative: Language in Marge Piercy's Utopia," by David L.

177

Xenograffiti, by ROBERT REGINALD

Foster; "The Metalinguistic Racial Grammar of Bellona: Ethnicity, Language and Meaning in Samuel R. Delany's *Dhalgren*," by Marleen Barr; "Harlan Ellison's Use of the Narrator's Voice," by Joseph F. Patrouch, Jr.; "The Social Science Fiction of Robin Cook," by Thom Dunn; "Moon-Watcher, Man, and Star-Child: *2001* as Paradigm," by Richard D. Erlich; "Science Fiction Theater the Moebius Way," by Jane Bloomquist and William McMillan; "Freaking the Mundane: A Sociological Look at Science Fiction Conventions, and Vice Versa," by Phyllis J. Day and Nora G. Day; Appendix: Academic Program at Chicon IV. The series title does not actually appear on the book.

Piers Anthony, by Michael R. Collings. STARMONT READER'S GUIDE, 20. 96 p. LC 83-2466. ISBN 0-916732-53-3 cloth $13.95; ISBN 0-916732-52-5 $5.95.

Robert Silverberg, by Thomas D. Clareson. STARMONT READER'S GUIDE, 18. 96 p. LC 83-542. ISBN 0-916732-48-7 cloth $13.95; ISBN 0-916732-47-9 $5.95.

Shadowings: The Reader's Guide to Horror Fiction, 1981-1982, edited by Douglas E. Winter. STARMONT STUDIES IN LITERARY CRITICISM, No. 1. x+148 p. LC 83-21326. ISBN 0-916732-86-X cloth $14.95; ISBN 0-916732-85-1 paper $6.95. Contents: "Foreword," by Winter; "The Art of Darkness," by Winter; "The Cannibal and the Cop," by Stephen King; "Many Years Ago, When We All Lived in the Forest," by Charles L. Grant; "The Man Dog and Maine," by Burton Hatlen; "Different Writers on *Different Seasons*," by Charles L. Grant, David Morrell, Alan Ryan, and Douglas E. Winter; "The Sandman Will Still Be There," by Alan Ryan; "Forgotten Words, Spoken by Forgotten Ancestors," by Winter; "The North and South of Horror," by Alan Ryan; "Whispersoft and Shadowfast," by Roger C. Schlobin; "The Cold Beyond Bearing," by Ronald L. Weston; "The Presence of Things Unseen," by Jack Sullivan; "Rustlings and Slitherings in the Shadows," by Alan Ryan; "Casting a Long Shadow," by Melissa Mia Hall and Douglas E. Winter; "Billy Bob Burnette Buys Books," by Billy Bob Burnette; "Ramsey Campbell: No Light Ahead," by Jack Sullivan; "Dennis Etchison: The

Xenograffiti, by ROBERT REGINALD

Unknown Writer," by Karl Edward Wagner; "David Morrell: Tasting First Blood," by Winter; "David Morrell's *The Totem*: The Link Is Control," by Brooks Landon; "Things That Go Bump in the Movies," by Craig Shaw Gardner; "Held Over by Popular Demand: David Cronenberg," by Richard Meyers; "Horror and the Limits of Violence: A Forum of Interviews," edited by Douglas E. Winter; "I Want My Cake! Thoughts on *Creepshow* and E.C. Comics," by Winter; "The Year in Review"; Notes on the Contributors.
Urania's Daughters: A Checklist of Women Science-Fiction Writers, 1692-1982, by Roger C. Schlobin. STARMONT REFERENCE GUIDES, No. 1. xiv+79 p. LC 83-2467. ISBN 0-916732-57-6 cloth $14.95; ISBN 0-916732-56-8 paper $6.95.

1984

Jack London, by Gorman Beauchamp. STARMONT READER'S GUIDE, No. 15. 96 p. LC 82-7345. ISBN 0-916732-40-1 cloth $13.95; ISBN 0-916732-39-8 paper $5.95.

1985

America's Secret Service Ace: The Operator 5 Story, by Nick Carr. STARMONT PULP AND DIME NOVEL STUDIES, No. 2. 63 p. LC 85-26269. ISBN 0-930261-70-4 cloth $19.95; ISBN 0-930261-73-9 paper $9.95. A facsimile reprint of the 1974 Robert Weinberg edition.
The Annotated Guide to Fantastic Adventures, by Edward J. Gallagher. STARMONT REFERENCE GUIDES, No. 2. xxii+170 p. LC 84-16228. ISBN 0-916732-71-1 cloth $17.95; ISBN 0-916732-70-3 paper $9.95.
Discovering Modern Horror Fiction, edited by Darrell Schweitzer. STARMONT STUDIES IN LITERARY CRITICISM, No. 4. [iv]+156 p. LC 84-2763. ISBN 0-916732-94-0 cloth $19.95; ISBN 0-916732-93-2 paper $9.95. Contents: "Introduction," by Schweitzer; "The Other Side of Magic: A Few Remarks About Shirley Jackson," by Mary

Xenograffiti, by ROBERT REGINALD

Kittredge; "Urban Gothic: The Fiction of Ramsey Campbell," by Gary William Crawford; "Russell Kirk: Ghost Master of Mecosta," by Don Herron; "The Dark Side of the American Dream: Dennis Etchison," by Michael E. Stamm; "Stephen King As an Epic Writer," by Ben P. Indick; "T. E. D. Klein," by Robert M. Price; "Karl Edward Wagner and the Haunted Hills (and Kudzu)," by Schweitzer; "Saberhagen's New Dracula: The Vampire As Hero," by Neal Wilgus; "The Recent Fantasies of Manly Wade Wellman," by Robert Coulson; "John Coyne: The Craftsman and the Monsters," by A. J. Montesi; "Roald Dahl: Nasty, Nasty," by Alan Warren; "Jonathan Carroll: Galen to Vienna to the World," by Edna Stumpf; "Appendix: Critical Studies in Horror Literature: A Selected, Annotated Bibliography," by Marshall B. Tymn; Contributors; Index.

Discovering Stephen King, edited by Darrell Schweitzer. STARMONT STUDIES IN LITERARY CRITICISM, No. 8. 219 p. LC 85-2821. ISBN 0-930261-07-0 cloth $19.95; ISBN 0-930261-06-2 paper $9.95. Contents: "Introduction," by Schweitzer; "What Makes Him So *Scary*?" by Ben P. Indick; "Has Success Spoiled Stephen King?" by Alan Warren; "The Biggest Horror Fan of Them All," by Don Herron; "Stephen King's American Gothic," by Gary William Crawford; "The Early Tales: Stephen King and *Startling Mystery Stories*," by Chet Williamson; "Stephen King and Peter Straub: Fear and Friendship," by Bernadette Bosky; "*The Stand*: Science Fiction into Fantasy," by Michael R. Collings; "Stephen King with a Twist: The E.C. Influence," by Debra Stump; "*Cycle of the Werewolf* and the Moral Tradition of Horror," by Randall D. Larson; "Stephen King and the Lovecraft Mythos," by Robert M. Price; "Three by Bachman," by Don D'Ammassa; "A Matter of Choice: King's *Cujo* and Malamud's *The Natural*," by Debra Stump; "The Ultimate Horror: The Dead Child in Stephen King's Stories and Novels," by Leonard G. Heldreth; "Collecting Stephen King," by Schweitzer; "Synopses of Stephen King's Fiction," by Sanford Z. Meschkow; "Stephen King: A Bibliography," by Marshall B. Tymn; Contributors; Index. An expanded and re-

Xenograffiti, by ROBERT REGINALD

worked version of *Essays Lovecraftian*, originally published by T-K Graphics in 1976
Gangland's Doom: The Shadow of the Pulps, by Frank Eisgruber, Jr. STARMONT PULP AND DIME NOVEL STUDIES, No. 1. 64 p. LC 85-26069. ISBN 0-930261-71-2 cloth $19.95; ISBN 0-930261-74-7 paper $9.95. A facsimile reprint of the 1974 Robert Weinberg edition.
James Tiptree, Jr., by Mark Siegel. STARMONT READER'S GUIDE, 22. 89 p. LC 85-17159. ISBN 0-916732-68-1 cloth $15.95; ISBN 0-916732-67-3 paper $7.95. Dated January 1986 on the copyright page.
J.G. Ballard, by Peter Brigg. STARMONT READER'S GUIDE, 26. 138 p. LC 85-2724. ISBN 0-916732-84-3 cloth $14.95; ISBN 0-916732-83-5 paper $6.95.
The Many Facets of Stephen King, by Michael R. Collings. STARMONT STUDIES IN LITERARY CRITICISM, No. 11. [vi]+190 p. LC 85-12598. ISBN 0-930261-15-1 cloth $19.95; ISBN 0-930261-14-3 paper $9.95.
Marion Zimmer Bradley, by Rosemarie Arbur. STARMONT READER'S GUIDE, 27. [ii]+138 p. LC 85-2721. ISBN 0-916732-96-7 cloth $14.95; ISBN 0-916732-95-9 paper $6.95.
Naked to the Sun: Dark Visions of Apocalypse, by Michael R. Collings. [x]+75 p. LC 85-30248. ISBN 0-930261-77-1 cloth $16.95; ISBN 0-930261-76-3 paper $8.95. Poetry.
Patterns of the Fantastic II: [Academic Programming at ConStellation], edited by Donald M. Hassler. STARMONT STUDIES IN LITERARY CRITICISM, No. 3. [vi]+90 p. LC 84-2683. ISBN 0-916732-88-6 cloth $19.95; ISBN 0-916732-87-8 paper $9.95. Contents: "Introduction: Dangerous Tastes: Science and Fiction," by Hassler; "The Hubris of Science: Wells' Time Traveller," by Merritt Abrash; "Ars Scientia = Ars Poetica," by Rosemarie Arbur; "Thornton Wilder as Fantasist and the Science-Fiction Antiparadigm: The Evidence of *The Skin of Our Teeth*," by Jared Lobdell; "The Mathematics in Science Fiction: Of Measure Zero," by Edward A. Boyno; "Two Views of the Sentient Computer: Gerrold's *When HARLIE Was One* and Ryan's *The Adolescence of P-1*," by Con-

stance M. Mellott; "Binary First Contact," by Lawrence I. Charters; "Creation Unfinished: Astronomical Realities in the Hainish Fiction of Ursula K. Le Guin," by Thomas P. Dunn; "Private Eye: A Semiotic Comparison of the Film *Blade Runner* and the Book *Do Androids Dream of Electric Sheep*," by Judith B. Kerman; "From Pessimism to Sentimentality: *Do Androids Dream of Electric Sheep* Becomes *Blade Runner*," by Philip E. Kaveny; "Fantastic Fictions at the Edge and in the Abyss: Genre Definitions and the Contemporary Cross-Genre Novel," by Janice M. Bogstad; Contributors.

The Shorter Works of Stephen King, by Michael R. Collings and David Engebretson. STARMONT STUDIES IN LITERARY CRITICISM, No. 9. [vi]+202 p. LC 85-2822. ISBN 0-930261-03-8 cloth $17.95; ISBN 0-930261-02-X paper $9.95.

Stephen King as Richard Bachman, by Michael R. Collings. STARMONT STUDIES IN LITERARY CRITICISM, No. 10. [vi]+168 p. LC 85-2832. ISBN 0-930261-01-1 cloth $17.95; ISBN 0-930261-00-3 paper $9.95.

1986

Anne McCaffrey, by Mary T. Brizzi. STARMONT READER'S GUIDE, 30. [viii]+95 p. LC 85-17160. ISBN 0-930261-30-5 cloth $14.95; ISBN 0-930261-29-1 paper $6.95.

The Annotated Guide to Startling Stories, by Leon Gammell. STARMONT REFERENCE GUIDES, No. 3. [iv]+90 p. LC 86-6012. ISBN 0-930261-51-8 cloth $20; ISBN 0-930261-50-X paper $10.

The Annotated Guide to Stephen King: A Primary and Secondary Bibliography of the Works of America's Premier Horror Writer, by Michael R. Collings. STARMONT REFERENCE GUIDES, No. 8. [vi]+176 p. LC 86-1854. ISBN 0-930261-81-X cloth $19.95; ISBN 0-930261-80-1 paper $9.95.

Brian Aldiss, by Michael R. Collings. STARMONT READER'S GUIDE, 28. [iv]+115 p. LC 85-17224. ISBN 0-916732-99-1 cloth $14.95; ISBN 0-916732-74-6 paper $6.95. Cover title reads: *Brian W. Aldiss*.

Xenograffiti, by ROBERT REGINALD

Charles Williams, by Kathleen Spencer. STARMONT READER'S GUIDE, 25. 104 p. LC 86-5750. ISBN 0-916732-80-0 cloth $15.95; ISBN 0-916732-79-7 paper $7.95.

E.E. "Doc" Smith, by Joe Sanders. STARMONT READER'S GUIDE, 24. [viii]+96 p. LC 85-30434. ISBN 0-916732-73-8 cloth $14.95; ISBN 0-916732-72-X paper $6.95.

Far Below and Other Horrors, edited by Robert E. Weinberg. 151 p. LC 85-25072. ISBN 0-930261-57-7 cloth $19.95; ISBN 0-930261-56-9 paper $9.95. Contents: "Far Below," by Robert Barbour Johnson; "The Execution of Lucarno," by Julius Long; "Thing of Darkness," by G. G. Pendarves; "The Accursed Isle," by Mary Elizabeth Counselman; "Masquerade," by Mearle Prout; "Naked Lady," by Mindret Lord; "Out of the Deep," by Robert E. Howard; "Doom of the House of Duryea," by Earl Pierce Jr.; "The Chapel of Mystic Horror," by Seabury Quinn; "Return to Death," by J. Wesley Rosenquest; "Under the Tomb," by Robert Nelson. A facsimile reprint of the 1974 FAX Collector's Editions hardcover; a later printing of the Starmont version relabelled the book STARMONT POPULAR FICTION "#0" [sic].

The Films of Stephen King, by Michael R. Collings. STARMONT STUDIES IN LITERARY CRITICISM, No. 12. [vi]+201 p. LC 85-17192. ISBN 0-930261-11-9 cloth $19.95; ISBN 0-930261-10-0 paper $9.95.

Gene Wolfe, by Joan Gordon. STARMONT READER'S GUIDE, 29. iv+116 p. LC 85-17163. ISBN 0-930261-19-4 cloth $14.95; ISBN 0-930261-18-6 paper $6.95.

H.G. Wells, by Robert Crossley. STARMONT READER'S GUIDE, 19. 79 p. LC 84-2691. ISBN 0-916732-51-7 cloth $15.95; ISBN 0-916732-50-9 paper $7.95.

Olaf Stapledon, by John Kinnaird. STARMONT READER'S GUIDE, 21. 107 p. LC 84-2656. ISBN 0-916732-55-X cloth $14.95; ISBN 0-916732-54-1 paper $6.95.

Robert Bloch, by Randall D. Larson. STARMONT READER'S GUIDE, 37. [iv]+148 p. LC 86-5751. ISBN 0-930261-59-3 cloth $16.95; ISBN 0-930261-58-5 paper $8.95.

Suzy McKee Charnas, Octavia Butler, Joan D. Vinge, by Marleen S. Barr, Ruth Salvaggio, Richard Law.

Xenograffiti, by ROBERT REGINALD
STARMONT READER'S GUIDE, 23. 52+44+72 p. LC 85-2715. ISBN 0-916732-92-4 $17.95; ISBN 0-916732-91-6 paper $9.95.

1987

Discovering H. P. Lovecraft, edited by Darrell Schweitzer. STARMONT STUDIES IN LITERARY CRITICISM, No. 6. xiv+153 p. LC 87-9923. ISBN 0-916732-82-7 cloth $19.95; ISBN 0-916732-81-9 paper $9.95. Contents: "Introduction," by Schweitzer; "Notes on an Entity," by Robert Bloch; "A Literary Copernicus," by Fritz Leiber, Jr.; "The Four Faces of the Outsider," by Dirk W. Mosig; "The First Lewis Theobald," by R. Boerem; "Story-Writing," by H. P. Lovecraft; "Character Gullibility in Weird Fiction, or, Isn't Yuggoth Somewhere in Upstate New York?" by Schweitzer; "Some Thoughts on Lovecraft," by Arthur Jean Cox; "The Derleth Mythos," by Richard L. Tierney; "Genesis of the Cthulhu Mythos," by George Wetzel; "Lovecraft's Ladies," by Ben P. Indick; "When the Stars Are Right," by Richard L. Tierney; "Lovecraft and Lord Dunsany," by Schweitzer; "H. P. Lovecraft and Pseudomathematics," by Robert Weinberg; "Textual Problems in Lovecraft," by S. T. Joshi; "H. P. Lovecraft: A Basic Reading List," by Schweitzer; Contributors; Index.

Don't Bite the Sun, by Tanith Lee. STARMONT HARDCOVER COLLECTION, 1. 158 p. LC 87-16037. ISBN 1-55742-044-0 cloth $19.95. A facsimile reprint of the 1976 DAW Books edition. The book was printed in paperback, but rebound and sold only in cloth editions with the paperback covers laminated into the hardcover binding; some paperbound copies exist.

Force Fields, by Andrew Joron. viii+55 p. LC 87-1959. ISBN 0-930261-87-9 cloth $16.95; ISBN 0-930261-86-0 paper $8.95. Poetry.

Frederik Pohl, by Thomas D. Clareson. STARMONT READER'S GUIDE, 39. x+173 p. LC 86-14587. ISBN 0-930261-34-8 cloth $17.95; ISBN 0-930261-33-X paper $9.95.

Xenograffiti, by ROBERT REGINALD

Future and Fantastic Worlds: A Bibliographical Retrospective of DAW Books (1972-1987), by Sheldon Jaffery. STARMONT REFERENCE GUIDES, No. 4. xiv+297 p. LC 87-9901. ISBN 1-55742-003-3 cloth $29.95; ISBN 1-55742-002-5 paper $19.95.

Grand Army War Songs. [ii]+157 p., 7 x 10". LC 87-750989. ISBN 1-55742-000-9 cloth $19.95; ISBN 1-55742-001-7 paper $9.95. One of two non-category books published by Starmont; a facsimile reprint of the 1886 edition; part of the last section of the book was accidentally omitted in the Starmont version.

The Return of the Time Machine, by Egon Friedell. STARMONT HARDCOVER COLLECTION, 2. 127 p. LC 87-16039. ISBN 1-55742-045-9 cloth $19.95. A facsimile reprint of the 1972 DAW Books edition. The book was printed in paperback, but rebound and sold only in cloth editions with the paperback covers laminated into the hardcover binding; some paperbound copies exist.

Robert E. Howard, by Marc A. Cerasini and Charles E. Hoffman. STARMONT READER'S GUIDE, 35. [vi]+156 p. LC 85-17161. ISBN 0-930261-28-3 cloth $17.95; ISBN 0-930261-27-5 paper $9.95.

Shanghai Year: A Westerner's Life in the New China, by Peter Brigg. [x]+115 p. LC 87-1949. ISBN 0-930261-88-7 cloth $17.95; ISBN 0-930261-89-5 paper $9.95. One of two non-category books published by Starmont.

The Stephen King Phenomenon, by Michael R. Collings. STARMONT STUDIES IN LITERARY CRITICISM, No. 14. 144 p. LC 85-17164. ISBN 0-930261-13-5 cloth $17.95; ISBN 0-930261-12-7 paper $9.95.

The Weirds: A Facsimile Selection of Fiction from the Era of the Shudder Pulps, edited by Sheldon Jaffery. STARMONT POPULAR CULTURE SERIES [sic], Vol. 1. [ii]+173 p. LC 87-1952. ISBN 0-930261-93-3 cloth $17.95; ISBN 0-930261-92-5 paper $9.95. Contents: "Introduction," by Jaffery; "The Mole Men Want Your Eyes," by Frederick C. Davis; "Mistress of the Blood-Drinkers," by Ralston Shields; "White Mother of Shadows," by George Vandegrift; "Dance of the Bloodless Ones," by Francis James; "A Beast Is Born," by W. Wayne Robbins; "Beauty for

185

Xenograffiti, by ROBERT REGINALD Sale," by J. O. Quinliven; "The Horror at His Heals," by Wyatt Blassingame; "Guest-Room in Hell," by Leon Byrne; "Chamber of Horrors."

1988

The Corpse Maker, by Hugh B. Cave, compiled and edited by Sheldon Jaffery. STARMONT POPULAR CULTURE STUDY #2. xii+156 p. LC 87-13199. ISBN 1-55742-017-3 cloth $19.95; ISBN 1-55742-016-5 paper $9.95. Contents: "Preface," by Jaffery; "Introduction," by Audrey Parente; "Comments," by Hugh B. Cave; "The Corpse-Maker"; "The House of Evil"; "The Barricade"; "Disturb Not the Dead"; "The Thing from the Swamp"; "My Pupil—The Idiot!"; "The Black Gargoyle."

Discovering Modern Horror Fiction II, edited by Darrell Schweitzer. STARMONT STUDIES IN LITERARY CRITICISM, No. 16. [iv]+169 p. LC 84-2763. ISBN 0-930621-48-8 cloth $19.95; ISBN 0-930261-47-X paper $9.95 [ISBNs for the first volume appear on the back cover]. Contents: "Introduction," by Schweitzer; "Peter Straub: From Academe to Shadowland," by Bernadette Bosky; "Poetry of Darkness: The Horror Fiction of Fritz Leiber," by Michael E. Stamm; "Tales of Childhood and the Grave: Ray Bradbury's Horror Fiction," by Schweitzer; "The Poetics of the Unconscious: The 'Strange Stories' of Robert Aickman," by Gary William Crawford; "Michael McDowell and the Haunted South," by Michael E. Stamm; "Yours Truly, Robert Bloch," by Randall D. Larson; "Concerning David Case," by Jeffrey K. Goddin; "The Subtle Terrors of Charles L. Grant," by Don D'Ammassa; "Ramsey Campbell: An Appreciation," by T. E. D. Klein; "James Herbert: Notes Toward a Reappraisal," by Ramsey Campbell; "American Gothic: Joseph Payne Brennan," by Alan Warren; "The Grim Imperative of Michael Shea," by Arthur Jean Cox; "Sardonic Fantasistes: John Collier," by Ben P. Indick; "History as Horror: Chelsea Quinn Yarbro," by Gil Fitzgerald; "Quietly Soaring: Peter Tremayne," by Christina Kiplinger; "Three Poets of

Xenograffiti, by ROBERT REGINALD

Horror: Tierney, Breiding, and Brennan," by Steve Eng; Contributors; Index.
Ira Levin, by Douglas Fowler. STARMONT READER'S GUIDE, 34. viii+87 p. LC 87-16033. ISBN 0-930261-26-7 cloth $19.95; ISBN 0-930261-25-9 paper $9.95.
Mary Shelley, by Allene Stuart Phy. STARMONT READER'S GUIDE, 36. 124 p. LC 86-6502. ISBN 0-930261-61-5 cloth $17.95; ISBN 0-930261-60-7 paper $9.95.
Peter Beagle, by Kenneth J. Zahorski. STARMONT READER'S GUIDE, 44. [iv]+124 p. LC 87-9924. ISBN 1-55742-009-2 cloth $17.95; ISBN 1-55742-008-4 paper $9.95.
Phoenix Renewed: The Survival and Mutation of Utopian Thought in North American Science Fiction, 1965-1982, by Hoda M. Zaki. STARMONT STUDIES IN LITERARY CRITICISM, No. 22. 1988. [viii]+151 p. LC 87-9920. ISBN 1-55742-007-6 cloth $17.95; ISBN 1-55742-006-8 paper $9.95. Reset and reprinted by Borgo Press in 1993 as I.O. Evans Studies in the Philosophy and Criticism of Literature, No. 18.
The Pulp Magazine Index, First Series, by Leonard A. Robbins. 2,152 p. in 3 v., 8.5 x 11". LC 88-20056. LC 91-658651 (series). ISBN 1-55742-111-0 cloth (3-vol. set) $175.
Pulp Man's Odyssey: The Hugh B. Cave Story, by Audrey Parente. STARMONT POPULAR CULTURE STUDY, No. 6. xiv+146 p. LC 87-26706. ISBN 1-55742-039-4 cloth $19.95; ISBN 1-55742-038-6 paper $9.95.
Ramsey Campbell, by Gary William Crawford. STARMONT READER'S GUIDE, 48. [vi]+74 p. LC 87-16030. ISBN 1-55742-037-8 cloth $17.95; ISBN 1-55742-036-X paper $8.95.
Roald Dahl, by Alan Warren. STARMONT CONTEMPORARY WRITERS, No. 1. vi+105 p. LC 88-33743. ISBN 1-55742-013-0 cloth $16.95; ISBN 1-55742-012-2 paper $8.95.
Science Fiction: A Teacher's Guide and Resource Book, edited by Marshall B. Tymn. STARMONT REFERENCE GUIDES, No. 5. x+140 p. LC 87-10143. ISBN 1-55742-021-1 cloth $25.95; ISBN 1-55742-020-3 paper $15.95. Contents: "Introduction," by Marshall B. Tymn; 1. "A

Xenograffiti, by ROBERT REGINALD

Short History of Science Fiction," by Tymn; 2. "Children's Science Fiction," by Francis J. Molson and Susan G. Miles; 3. "The Fan Movement," by Joe Sanders; 4. "Science Fiction in the Movies," by Brooks Landon; 5. "A Teacher's Reference Shelf," by Tymn; 6. "Science Fiction Periodicals," by Joe Sanders and Marshall B. Tymn; 7. "Conferences and Conventions," by Tymn; 8. "Reading Lists in Science Fiction," by Tymn; 9. "In the Classroom: Teaching Tools," by Tymn; 10. "Approaches to Course Structure: The SF Class," by Tymn; 11. "Teaching Science Fiction As Current Events," by Lloyd Biggle, Jr.; Contributors.

"Seven Men," by Theodore Roscoe. STARMONT POPULAR FICTION #1. viii+136 p. LC 88-20067. ISBN 1-55742-101-3 cloth $18.95; ISBN 1-55742-100-5 paper $8.95. A novel reprinted from the pulp magazines.

The Shattered Goddess, by Darrell Schweitzer. STARMONT POPULAR FICTION #5. [iv]+183 p. LC 88-31950. ISBN 1-55742-113-7 cloth $19.95; ISBN 1-55742-112-9 paper $9.95. A facsimile reprint of the 1982 Starblaze Edition.

Sudden Fear: The Horror and Dark Suspense Fiction of Dean R. Koontz, edited by Bill Munster. STARMONT STUDIES IN LITERARY CRITICISM, No. 24. x+182 p. LC 88-1077. ISBN 1-55742-025-4 cloth $19.95; ISBN 1-55742-024-6 $10.95. Contents: "Introduction," by Tim Powers; "Foreword," by Bill Munster; 1. "Dean R. Koontz: A Chronology," by Bill Munster; 2. "Interview with Dean R. Koontz," by Bill Munster; 3. "Keeping Pace with the Master," by David B. Silva; 4. "Dean R. Koontz and Stephen King: Style, Invasion, and an Aesthetics of Horror," by Michael R. Collings; 5. "In the Midst of Life," by Richard Laymon; 6. "A Mutation of a Science Fiction Writer," by Stan Brooks; 7. "Mainstream Horror in *Whispers* and *Phantoms*," by D. W. Taylor; 8. "Dark Genesis: *Watchers & Shadowfires*," by Stan Brooks; 9. "The Three Faces of Evil: The Monsters of *Whispers*, *Phantoms*, and *Darkfall*," by Michael A. Morrison; 10. "Dean R. Koontz's *Twilight Eyes*: Art and Artifact," by Michael R. Collings; 11. "Femmes Fatales? The Women Protagonists in Four Koontz Novels," by Elizabeth

Xenograffiti, by ROBERT REGINALD

Massie; "Afterword: A Brief and Informal Appreciation," by Joe R. Lansdale; Contributors; Bibliography; Index.
The Super Feds: A Facsimile Selection of Dynamic G-Man Stories from the 1930s, edited by Don Hutchison. STARMONT POPULAR CULTURE STUDY, No. 8. [viii+158] p. LC 88-1078. ISBN 1-55742-091-2 cloth $19.95; ISBN 1-55742-090-4 paper $9.95. Contents: "Introduction: The G-Man Years," by Don Hutchison; "The Suicide Squad and the Murder Bund," by Emile C. Tepperman; "Captain of the Corpse Crew," by Harry Lee Fellinge; "Bomb-Proof Town Tamer," by William R. Cox; "It's Up to You," by J. Edgar Hoover; "The Voice Says Die!" by Edward S. Williams; "The Ghost and the Skeleton," by Wyatt Blassingame; "Herr Yama from Yokohama," by Day Keene; "*Ace G-Man Stories* Bibliography," by Phillip H. Nelson.
Toughest in the Legion, by Theodore Roscoe, edited by Sheldon Jaffery. STARMONT FACSIMILE FICTION #3. 144 p. LC 87-18361. ISBN 1-55742-099-8 cloth $17.95; ISBN 1-55742-098-X paper $8.95. The first printing lacks pages 5-6 (the second and third pages of Roscoe's original introduction); the later printing (blue and red cover) restores the full text. Contents: "Introduction"; "The Kid and the Cutthroats"; "Toughest in the Legion"; "Monkey See, Monkey Do"; "The Devil Who Played God"; "The Ears of Donkey Daudette".
We Are All Legends, by Darrell Schweitzer. STARMONT POPULAR FICTION #4. [iv]+189 p. LC 88-31949. ISBN 1-55742-115-3 cloth $19.95; ISBN 1-55742-114-5 paper $9.95. A facsimile reprint of the 1981 Starblaze Edition.

1989

A. Merritt, by Ronald Foust. STARMONT READER'S GUIDE, 43. vi+104 p. LC 87-9927. ISBN 0-930261-36-4 cloth $19.95; ISBN 0-930261-35-6 paper $9.95.
The Arkham House Companion: Fifty Years of Arkham House: A Bibliographical History and Collector's Price Guide to Arkham House/Mycroft & Moran, Including the Revised and Expanded Horrors and Unpleasantries, by

Xenograffiti, by ROBERT REGINALD Sheldon Jaffery. STARMONT REFERENCE GUIDES, No. 9. xvi+184 p., 8.5. x 11". LC 89-31701. ISBN 1-55742-005-X cloth $34.95; ISBN 1-55742-004-1 paper $22.95. An expanded and reworked version of *Horrors and Unpleasantries*, published in 1982 by Bowling Green State University Popular Press.

Children's Fantasy, by Francis J. Molson. STARMONT READER'S GUIDE, 33. [vi]+97 p. LC 87-10145. ISBN 1-55742-015-7 cloth $19.95; ISBN 1-55742-014-9 paper $9.95.

Christopher Priest, by Nicholas Ruddick. STARMONT READER'S GUIDE, 50. x+104 p. LC 88-16046. ISBN 1-55742-110-2 cloth $19.95; ISBN 1-55742-109-9 paper $9.95.

The Eighth Green Man (and Other Strange Folk), edited by Robert E. Weinberg. STARMONT POPULAR FICTION #2. vi+171 p. LC 89-34754. ISBN 1-55742-067-X cloth $19.95; ISBN 1-55742-066-1 paper $9.95. Contents: "Introduction," by Weinberg; "The Eighth Green Man," by G. G. Pendarves; "The Night Wire," by H. F. Arnold; "The House of the Worm," by Mearle Prout; "The Gray Death," by Loual B. Sugarman; "Norn," by Lireve Monet; "His Brother's Keeper," by Major George Fielding Eliot; "The Dead Wagon," by Greye La Spina; "The Floor Above," by M. L. Humphreys; "The Cavern," by Manly Wade Wellman; "The Wolf-Woman," by Bassett Morgan; "Jorgas," by Robert Nelson.

The Flying Spy: A History of G-8, by Nick Carr. STARMONT PULP AND DIME NOVEL STUDIES #3. 160 p. LC 85-26231. ISBN 0-930261-72-0 cloth $19.95; ISBN 0-930261-75-5 paper $9.95. A facsimile reprint of the 1978 Robert Weinberg edition.

A Grave Must Be Deep, by Theodore Roscoe. STARMONT FACSIMILE FICTION #1. 120 p. LC 87-16029. ISBN 1-55742-041-6 cloth $19.95; ISBN 1-55742-040-8 paper $9.95. A novel reprinted from the pulp magazines.

The Lure of Adventure, by Robert Kenneth Jones. STARMONT PULP AND DIME NOVEL STUDIES, No. 4. [iv]+80+[iv] p. LC 89-34753. ISBN 1-55742-143-9 cloth $19.95; ISBN 1-55742-142-0 paper $9.95.

Xenograffiti, by ROBERT REGINALD

Margaret Drabble, Symbolic Moralist, by Nora Foster Stovel. STARMONT CONTEMPORARY WRITERS, No. 2. vii+224 p. LC 88-33732. ISBN 1-55742-035-1 cloth $19.95; ISBN 1-55742-034-3 paper $10.95.

The Moral Voyages of Stephen King, by Anthony Magistrale. STARMONT STUDIES IN LITERARY CRITICISM, No. 25. [iv]+vi+157 p. LC 88-1076. ISBN 1-55742-071-8 cloth $21.95; ISBN 1-55742-070-X paper $11.95.

The Pulp Magazine Index, Second Series, by Leonard A. Robbins. 583 p., 8.5 x 11". LC 89-34752. ISBN 1-55742-162-5 cloth $80.

Ray Bradbury, by William F. Touponce. STARMONT READER'S GUIDE, 31. iv+110 p. LC 87-16031. ISBN 0-930261-23-2 cloth $19.95; ISBN 0-930261-22-4 paper $9.95.

The Robert Bloch Companion: Collected Interviews, 1969-1989, edited by Randall D. Larson. STARMONT STUDIES IN LITERARY CRITICISM, No. 32. [iv]+157 p. LC 89-26126. ISBN 1-55742-147-1 cloth $21.95; ISBN 1-55742-146-3 paper $11.95.

The Unseen King, by Tyson Blue. STARMONT STUDIES IN LITERARY CRITICISM, No. 26. viii+200 p. LC 88-1074. ISBN 1-55742-073-4 cloth $21.95; ISBN 1-55742-072-6 paper $11.95.

The Waltzing Wizard: Cartoons, by Alexis A. Gilliland. [ii]+116 p. LC 89-34751. ISBN 1-55742-164-1 cloth $19.95; ISBN 1-55742-163-3 paper $9.95.

The Western Pulp Hero: An Investigation into the Psyche of an American Legend, by Nick Carr. STARMONT POPULAR CULTURE STUDIES, No. 3. 138 p., 8.5 x 11". LC 87-18370. ISBN 1-55742-033-5 cloth $21.95; ISBN 1-55742-032-7 paper $11.95.

Z Is for Zombie, by Theodore Roscoe. STARMONT FACSIMILE FICTION #2. 140 p. LC 87-16028. ISBN 1-55742-043-2 cloth $19.95; ISBN 1-55742-042-4 paper $9.95. A novel reprinted from the pulp magazines.

Xenograffiti, by ROBERT REGINALD

1990

The Adventure Magazine Index, by Richard J. Bleiler. 1,085 p. in 2 v., 8.5 x 11". LC 90-10407. ISBN 1-55742-189-7 cloth $150.
Clark Ashton Smith, by Steve Behrends. STARMONT READER'S GUIDE, 49. vi+112 p. LC 87-16034. ISBN 0-930261-99-2 cloth $19.95; ISBN 0-930261-98-4 paper $9.95.
Dark Transformations: Deadly Visions of Change, by Michael R. Collings. 95 p. LC 89-26101. ISBN 1-55742-197-8 cloth $16.95; ISBN 1-55742-196-X paper $8.95. Short stories and poetry.
The Devil's Notebook: Collected Epigrams and Pensées of Clark Ashton Smith, compiled by Donald Sidney-Fryer, edited with an introduction by Don Herron. STARMONT POPULAR CULTURE STUDIES, No. 16. xvi+82 p. LC 89-29636. ISBN 1-55742-161-7 cloth $19.95; ISBN 1-55742-160-9 paper $9.95.
Faces of the Beast, by Bruce Boston. 56 p. LC 89-26102. ISBN 1-55742-195-1 cloth $16.95; ISBN 1-55742-194-3 paper $8.95. Poetry.
H.P. Lovecraft and the Cthulhu Mythos, by Robert M. Price. STARMONT STUDIES IN LITERARY CRITICISM, No. 33. [iv]+170 p. LC 89-34791. ISBN 1-55742-153-6 cloth $21.95; ISBN 1-55742-152-8 paper $11.95.
H.P. Lovecraft: The Decline of the West, by S. T. Joshi. STARMONT STUDIES IN LITERARY CRITICISM, No. 37. viii+155 p., 8.5 x 11". ISBN 1-55742-208-7 cloth $27.95; ISBN 1-55742-207-9 paper $17.95.
The Horror of It All: Encrusted Gems from the "Crypt of Cthulhu", edited by Robert M. Price. STARMONT STUDIES IN LITERARY CRITICISM, No. 31. [iv]+199 p. LC 89-26171. ISBN 1-55742-123-4 cloth $21.95; ISBN 1-55742-122-6 paper $11.95. Contents: "Introduction," by Price; "Lovecraft's Revisions: How Much of Them Did He Write?" by S. T. Joshi; "The Real World and the Dream World in Lovecraft," by S. T. Joshi; "The Origin of Lovecraft's 'Black Magic' Quote," by David E. Schultz;

Xenograffiti, by ROBERT REGINALD

"Lovecraft's Ghouls," by Will Murray; "Baring-Gould and the Ghouls: The Influence of *Curious Myths of the Middle Ages* on 'The Rats in the Wall'," by Steven J. Mariconda; "'The Hound'—A Dead Dog!" by Steven J. Mariconda; "On 'The Loved Dead'," by David E. Schultz; "Digging Up Irem," by Lin Carter; "CAS & Diverse Hands," by Steve Behrends; "The Clark Ashton Smythos," by Will Murray; "The Cthulhu Mythos Fiction of Robert Bloch," by Randall D. Larson; "Reconstructing *De Vermis Mysteriis*," by Price; "Solar Pons Meets Cthulhu," by S. T. Joshi; "The True History of the Tcho-Tcho People," by Robert M. Price and Tani Jantsang; "Obed and Obadiah Marsh," by Robert M. Price and Tani Jantsang; "The Strange Case of Robert Ervin Howard," by Charles Hoffman and Marc A. Cerasini; "Gol-Goroth, a Forgotten Old One," by Price; "The Statement of Lin Carter," by Price; "The Carter-Smith 'Collaborations'," by Steve Behrends; "Henry Kuttner's Cthulhu Mythos Fiction: An Overview," by Shawn Ramsey; "The Transition of Colin Wilson," by Charles Hoffman and Marc A. Cerasini; "Brian Lumley—Reanimator," by Price; "The Fantasy and Mystery Bookshop," by Peter H. Cannon; "The Pool," by Donald R. Burleson; "The Volume Out of Print," by Jim Cort; "Strange Manuscript Found in the Vermont Woods," by Lin Carter; "The Cthulhuers," by John Strysik; "Lovecraft As I Seem to Remember Him," by Robert M. Price as F. Gumby Kalem; "Lovecraft's Letters to Santa Claus: An Introduction," by Price.

Kioga of the Wilderness, by William L. Chester. STARMONT HARDCOVER COLLECTION, 3. 303 p. LC 87-16036. ISBN 1-55742-046-7 cloth $19.95. A facsimile reprint of the 1976 DAW Books edition. The book was printed in paperback, but rebound and sold only in cloth editions with the paperback covers laminated into the hardcover binding; some paperbound copies exist.

Lewis Carroll, by Beverly Lyon Clark. STARMONT READER'S GUIDE, 47. viii+96 p. LC 87-16032. ISBN 1-55742-031-9 cloth $19.95; ISBN 1-55742-030-0 paper $9.95.

Xenograffiti, by ROBERT REGINALD

The Pulp Magazine Index, Third Series, by Leonard A. Robbins. 639 p., 8.5 x 11". ISBN 1-55742-204-4 cloth $80.

The Shining Reader, edited by Anthony Magistrale. STARMONT STUDIES IN LITERARY CRITICISM, No. 30. xii+220 p. LC 89-29631. ISBN 1-55742-107-2 cloth $21.95; ISBN 1-55742-106-4 paper $11.95. Contents: "Introduction," by Magistrale; "Once, Out of Nature: The Topiary," by Michael N. Stanton; "Wendy Torrance, One of King's Women: A Typology of King's Female Characters," by Jackie Eller; "Jack's Nightmare at the Overlook: The American Dream Inverted," by Patricia Ferreira; "The 'Masked Author Strikes Again': Writing and Dying in Stephen King's *The Shining*," by Mary Jane Dickerson; "The Collapse of Family and Language in Stephen King's *The Shining*," by Alan Cohen; "The Redrum of Time: A Meditation on Francisco Goya's 'Saturn Devouring His Children' and Stephen King's *The Shining*," by Greg Weller; "Good and Evil in Stephen King's *The Shining*," by Burton Hatlen; "The Red Death's Sway: Setting and Character in Poe's 'The Masque of the Red Death' and King's *The Shining*," by Leonard Mustazza; "Stephen King and the Tradition of American Naturalism in *The Shining*," by Jeanne Campbell Reesman; "Canaries in a Gilded Cage: Mental and Marital Decline in *McTeague* and *The Shining*," by Brian Kent; "Shakespeare in 58 Chapters: *The Shining* As Classical Tragedy," by Magistrale; "The Dark Side of Childhood: *The 500 Hats of Bartholomew Cubbins* and *The Shining*," by Vernon Hyles; "Kubrick's or King's—Whose *Shining* Is It?" by James Smith; "'Orders from the House': Kubrick's *The Shining* and Kafka's 'The Metamorphosis'," by Mark Madigan; "Kubrick's *The Shining*: The Specters and the Critics," by James Hala; Index.

Stanislaw Lem, by J. Madison Davis. STARMONT READER'S GUIDE, 32. x+116 p. LC 87-17646. ISBN 1-55742-027-0 cloth $19.95; ISBN 1-55742-026-2 paper $9.95.

Under the Green Star, by Lin Carter. STARMONT HARDCOVER COLLECTION, 4. 144 p. LC 87-16036. ISBN 1-55742-047-5 cloth $19.95. A facsimile reprint of the 1972 DAW Books edition. The book was printed in paperback, but rebound and sold only in cloth editions with the paperback covers laminated into the hardcover binding; some paperbound copies exist.

1991

The Annotated Guide to Unknown & Unknown Worlds, by Stefan R. Dziemianowicz. STARMONT STUDIES IN LITERARY CRITICISM, No. 13. 212 p. ISBN 1-55742-141-2 cloth $24.95; ISBN 1-55742-140-4 paper $14.95. The book was intended to be No. 13 in the Starmont Reference Guide series, but was mislabeled.

The Annotated Index to The Thrill Book: Complete Indexes to and Descriptions of Everything Published in Street & Smith's The Thrill Book, by Richard J. Bleiler. STARMONT REFERENCE GUIDES, No. 18. viii+256 p. ISBN 1-55742-206-0 cloth $24.95; ISBN 1-55742-205-2 paper $14.95.

Isaac Asimov, by Donald M. Hassler. STARMONT READER'S GUIDE, 40. iv+129 p. LC 86-14585. ISBN 0-930261-32-1 cloth $19.95; ISBN 0-930261-31-3 paper $9.95. Winner of the 1993 J. Lloyd Eaton Award for Best Critical Work of 1991.

It's Raining Corpses in Chinatown, edited by Don Hutchison. STARMONT POPULAR CULTURE STUDIES, No. 9. xxxviii+169 p. ISBN 1-55742-125-0 cloth $20.95; ISBN 1-55742-124-2 paper $10.95. Contents: Cover Reproductions; "Introduction: Yellow Shadows," by Hutchison; "The Octopus of Hongkong," by Loring Brent; "Tongman's Bargain," by William R. Randall; "King Cobra," by Sidney Herschel Small; "The Wrong Move," by Ralph R. Perry; "It's Raining Corpses in Chinatown," by Russell Gray; "The Jade Joss," by T. T. Flynn; "In the Dragon's Lair," by Justin Case (pseud. of Hugh B. Cave); Bibliography.

Lin Carter: A Look Behind His Imaginary Worlds, by Robert M. Price. STARMONT STUDIES IN LITERARY CRITICISM, No. 36. vi+172 p. ISBN 1-55742-230-3 cloth $21.95; ISBN 1-55742-229-X paper $11.95. Pages 135-172 include an extensive bibliography of Carter's works by Mike Ashley.

The Monster of the Lagoon, by George F. Worts. STARMONT FACSIMILE FICTION #14. viii+145 p. ISBN 1-55742-243-5 cloth $20.95; ISBN 1-55742-242-7 paper $10.95. A reprint of the 1947 Popular Publications edition of this novel.

The Pulp Magazine Index, Fourth Series, by Leonard A. Robbins. 567 p., 8.5 x 11". ISBN 1-55742-241-9 cloth $80.

Red Twilight; World's End: Two Classic Novels from Argosy, by Harl Vincent and Victor Rousseau. STARMONT FACSIMILE FICTION #13. vi+123 p. ISBN 1-55742-216-8 cloth $20.95; ISBN 1-55742-215-X paper $10.95.

Secret of the Earth Star and Others, by Henry Kuttner, edited & introduced by Sheldon Jaffery. STARMONT FACSIMILE FICTION #6. x+157 p. ISBN 1-55742-135-8 cloth $20.95; ISBN 1-55742-134-X paper $10.95. Contents: "Introduction," by Jaffery; "Secret of the Earth Star"; "World Without Air"; "What Hath Me?"; "Dragon Moon"; "I, the Vampire"; "The Elixir of Invisibility"; "The Uncanny Power of Edwin Cobalt"; "Under Your Spell."

Worlds Within Worlds: Four Classic Argosy *Tales of Science Fiction*. STARMONT FACSIMILE FICTION #12. viii+122 p. ISBN 1-55742-214-1 cloth $20.95; ISBN 1-55742-213-3 paper $10.95. No editor is credited. Contents: "Worlds Within Worlds," by Philip M. Fisher Jr.; "Out of the Silence," by Garret Smith; "Children of Tomorrow," by Arthur Leo Zagat; "Colossus of the Radio," by Leslie Ramón.

1992

Black Forbidden Things: Cryptical Secrets from the "Crypt of Cthulhu", edited by Robert M. Price. STARMONT STUDIES IN LITERARY CRITICISM, No. 44. iv+200 p. ISBN 1-55742-249-4 cloth $21.95; ISBN 1-55742-248-6 paper $11.95. Contents: "Introduction," by Price; "Who Wrote 'The Mound'?" by S. T. Joshi; "H.P. Lovecraft and

Xenograffiti, by ROBERT REGINALD

The Dream-Quest of Unknown Kadath," by S. T. Joshi; "The Sources for 'From Beyond'," by S. T. Joshi; "Tentacles in Dreamland: Cthulhu Mythos Elements in the Dunsanian Stories," by Will Murray; "Self-Parody in Lovecraft's Revisions," by Will Murray; "Prehuman Language in Lovecraft," by Will Murray; "H.P. Lovecraft's *Fungi from Yuggoth*," by David E. Schultz; "Lovecraft's New York Exile," by David E. Schultz; "E.R.B. and H.P.L.," by William Fulwiler; "Randolph Carter, Warlord of Mars," by Price; "The Pseudo-Intellectual in Weird Fiction," by Price; "August Derleth: Myth-Maker," by Price; "'Lovecraftianity' and the Pagan Revival," by Price; "Cosmic Fear and the Fear of the Lord: Lovecraft's Religious Vision," by Price; "Chariots of the Old Ones?" by Robert M. Price and Charles Garofalo; "The *Necronomicon*: The Origin of a Spoof," by Colin Wilson; "The Diary of Alonzo Typer," by William Lumley; "A Sacrifice to Science," by Adolphe de Castro; "The Automatic Executioner," by Adolphe de Castro; "The Tower from Yuggoth," by Ramsey Campbell; "The Ringer of the Doorbell," by Jim Cort; "The Slitherer from the Tomb," by Lin Carter; "Limericks from Yuggoth," by Lin Carter; "Mildew from Shaggai," by Price; "Shards from Shaggai," by Price; "Famous Last Words," by Price; "Screwtape's Letter to Cthulhu," by Price; Mail-Call of Cthulhu.

A *Casebook on The Stand*, edited by Tony Magistrale. STARMONT STUDIES IN LITERARY CRITICISM, No. 38. xii+210 p. ISBN 1-55742-251-6 cloth $26; ISBN 1-55742-250-8 paper $16. Contents: "Introduction," by Magistrale; "'Almost Better': Surviving the Plague in Stephen King's *The Stand*," by Mary Pharr; "'I Think the Government Stinks!': Stephen King's *Stand* on Politics," by Douglas Keesey; "Stephen King and His Readers: A Dirty, Compelling Romance," by Brian Kent; "The 'Power of Blackness' in *The Stand*," by Leonard Cassuto; "Repaying Service with Pain: the Role of God in *The Stand*," by Leonard Mustazza; "Free Will and Sexual Choice in *The Stand*," by Magistrale; "Choice, Sacrifice, Destiny, and Nature in *The Stand*," by Bernadette Lynn Bosky; "Dark Streets and Bright Dreams: Rationalism,

Xenograffiti, by ROBERT REGINALD

Technology, and 'Impossible Knowledge' in Stephen King's *The Stand*," by Michael A. Morrison; "Dialogue within the Archetypal Community of *The Stand*," by Ed Casebeer; "Beyond Armageddon: Stephen King's *The Stand* and the Post Catastrophic World in Speculative Fiction," by Steven Kagle; Works Cited; Index.

Discovering Classic Horror Fiction I, edited by Darrell Schweitzer. STARMONT STUDIES IN LITERARY CRITICISM, No. 27. vi+191 p. LC 89-11431. ISBN 1-55742-085-8 cloth $21.95; ISBN 1-55472-084-X paper $11.95. Contents: "Introduction," by Schweitzer; "Arthur Machen: Philosophy and Fiction," by S. T. Joshi; "Richard Middleton: Beauty, Sadness, and Terror," by Schweitzer; "Full Fathom Five: The Supernatural Fiction of William Hope Hodgson," by Alan Warren; "On the Edge: The Ghost Stories of Walter de la Mare," by Gary William Crawford; "Chambers and *The King in Yellow*," by Lee Weinstein; "H. Russell Wakefield: The Man Who Believed in Ghosts," by Ben P. Indick; "The Landscape of Sin: The Ghost Stories of J. Sheridan Le Fanu," by Gary William Crawford; "Blood Brothers: The Supernatural Fiction of A. C., R. H., and E. F. Benson," by Mike Ashley; "The Shadow over Derleth," by Paul Spencer; "Oliver Onions: The Man at the Edge," by Mike Ashley; "W. C. Morrow: Forgotten Master of Horror—First Phase," by Sam Moskowitz; Contributors; Index.

Double Trouble: A Bibliographic Chronicle of Ace Mystery Doubles, by Sheldon Jaffery. STARMONT POPULAR CULTURE STUDIES, No. 11. xvi+150 p. LC 89-11447. ISBN 1-55742-119-6 cloth $22; ISBN 1-55742-118-8 paper $12. Title page reads: Starmont Reference Guide #12.

Fear to the World: Eleven Voices in a Chorus of Horror, by Kevin E. Proulx. STARMONT STUDIES IN LITERARY CRITICISM, No. 35. x+243 p. ISBN 1-55742-174-9 cloth $30; ISBN 1-55742-173-0 paper $20. Interviews with eleven horror writers. Contents: Acknowledgements; Foreword; 1. Clive Barker; 2. Ramsey Campbell; 3. John Farris; 4. Joe R. Lansdale; 5. George R. R. Martin; 6. Richard Christian Matheson; 7. Steve Rasnic Tem; 8. J. N. Williamson; 9. F. Paul Wilson; 10. T. M. Wright; 11. Chelsea

Xenograffiti, by ROBERT REGINALD Quinn Yarbro; Recommended Reading; Afterword; Index.

J. R. R. Tolkien, by David & Carol D. Stevens. STARMONT READER'S GUIDE, 54. vi+178 p. ISBN 1-55742-238-9 cloth $19.95; ISBN 1-55742-237-0 paper $9.95. Most copies of this book were defective, reproducing page 8 on pages 9-10, and omitting the text that should have appeared on the latter. A handful of copies were corrected, but the bulk of the print run remained uncirculated. The book was reprinted facsimile in 1993 by The Borgo Press as Volume 56 of The Milford Series: Popular Writers of Today. This is the scarcest of all the Starmont books.

Kurt Vonnegut, by Donald E. Morse. STARMONT READER'S GUIDE, No. 61. iv+128 p. ISBN 1-55742-219-2 cloth $19.95; ISBN 1-55742-220-6 paper $9.95.

Lovecraft: A Look Behind the Cthulhu Mythos: The Background of a Myth That Has Captured a Generation, by Lin Carter. STARMONT POPULAR CULTURE STUDIES, No. 10. xxii+198 p. ISBN 1-55742-253-2 cloth $22; ISBN 1-55742-252-4 paper $12. A facsimile reprint of the 1972 Ballantine Books edition.

Pulpmaster: The Theodore Roscoe Story, by Audrey Parente. STARMONT POPULAR CULTURE STUDIES, No. 13. xvi+173 p. ISBN 1-55742-170-6 cloth $21.95; ISBN 1-55742-169-2 paper $11.95.

William Gibson, by Lance Olsen. STARMONT READER'S GUIDE, 58. vii+131 p. ISBN 1-55742-199-4 cloth $20; ISBN 1-55742-198-6 paper $11.

MISCELLANEOUS TITLES

In addition to the books listed above, Starmont also distributed and sold as part of its own list the titles published under the FAX Collector's Editions imprint (the last book of which appeared in 1979), plus two other volumes previously published by Dikty:

The American Boys' Book Series Bibliography, 1895-1935, by Alan S. Dikty. Naperville, IL; West Linn, OR: BBC

Xenograffiti, by ROBERT REGINALD Publications, 1977. 167 p., 8.5 x 11". LC 77-75300. ISBN 0-916732-65-7 cloth $22.95; ISBN 0-916732-64-9 paper $14.95 (the price charged in 1983). The ISBN numbers were assigned retrospectively; Starmont began listing the remainder of the print run in its catalogs in 1983.

Boys' Book Collector, #1-13, Alan S. Dikty, Editor, Ted Dikty, Publisher. 1983. ISBN 0-916732-66-5 cloth $19.95. A binding together of the thirteen issues of this periodical, which had been originally published between 1969-1973. Roughly 75 sets were bound in lots of 5-10 copies each.

BORGO PRESS EDITIONS

The Starmont cloth editions were almost all rebound by The Borgo Press from the paper editions, employing the hardcover binders that Borgo used in Southern California. A few Starmont cloth editions were independently produced and bound in Eugene, Oregon, during the last years of its existence. Borgo Press also distributed the entire Starmont House and FAX Collector's Editions list beginning in 1980, and rebound the books into its own cloth imprints, the title pages being labeled with the BP label. The Borgo editions usually carry the Borgo logo and imprint impressed on the top and bottom of each book's spine. The paperbound versions of the Starmont editions of these books are always the true first editions.

SERIES NUMBERS

Starmont House assigned many series numbers to books that were never actually published. Some of these manuscripts will be issued by other publishers; others were never completed, or will fail to find a home elsewhere. The actual numbers used in the various Starmont series are as follows:

CONTEMPORARY WRITERS—1-2 (2 vols.)

Xenograffiti, by ROBERT REGINALD

FACSIMILE FICTION—1-3, 6, 12-14 (7 vols.)

HARDCOVER COLLECTION—1-4 (4 vols.)

POPULAR CULTURE STUDIES—1-3, 6, 8-11, 13, 16 (10 vols.)

POPULAR FICTION—0-2, 4-5 (5 vols.)

PULP AND DIME NOVEL STUDIES—1-4 (4 vols.)

READER'S GUIDES—1-16, 18-37, 39-40, 43-44, 47-50, 54, 58, 61 (47 vols.)

REFERENCE GUIDES—1-5, 8-9, 18 [12-13 misassigned] (8 vols.)

STUDIES IN LITERARY CRITICISM—1-4, 6, 8-14, 16, 22, 24-27, 30-33, 35-38, 44 (27 vols.)

Xenograffiti, by ROBERT REGINALD

XXXIV.

LAUGHING LIKE HELL

BRIAN STABLEFORD'S WORLD IN AGONY

with Brian Craig

(1995)

Brian Stableford sold his first SF story while still at school, and three of his early novels—*The Blind Worm, To Challenge Chaos*, and *Firefly: A Novel of the Far Future*—are partly or wholly cannibalized from material written at about the same time. For some years he divided his time between the desultory pursuit of an academic career and his writing, swaying first one way and then the other as his fortunes shifted. Between 1969 and 1982 he wrote approximately thirty novels, most of them for Donald A. Wollheim, the SF editor at Ace and (from 1972) the publisher of DAW Books, his own imprint. His few attempts to break out of the mold which Wollheim preferred—series space opera—failed to make any significant headway; the intense psychological melodrama *Man in a Cage*, the light-hearted children's fantasy *The Last Days of the Edge of the World*, and the time-hopping evolutionary fantasy *The Walking Shadow* disappeared almost immediately following initial publication.

In 1981, having obtained tenure in a teaching position at the University of Reading, the author decided to concentrate on nonfiction, but when his painstaking study of *Scientific Romance in Britain, 1890-1910* sold poorly, and his volume on *Eroticism in Supernatural Literature* had to be aborted after the U.S. distributor pulled out, he concluded that such work was ultimately self-defeating. In 1986 he began to write short stories in profusion, redeploying and refining speculations about the future of biotechnology which he had first extrapolated for use in the futurology text, *The Third Millennium*. The implanting of "hard science fiction" ideas into sarcastic and somewhat mannered narratives gave him for the first time a distinctive narrative voice. He also attempted to take up his earlier career where he had left off by extending one of his last DAW novels, *Journey to the Center*, into a trilogy, but DAW was no longer interested, and the trilogy (including a revised version of the first volume) only appeared in England. This was an unfortunate fate for what is by far the most stylish, extravagant, and action-packed of Stableford's space operas, in which countless alien worlds are conveniently packed into a giant, multi-layered artifact endangered by the breakdown of the systems controlling its power source.

In 1987 Britain was at the height of an economic boom and British publishing was rapidly expanding. Stableford obtained a commission from Simon and Schuster's fledgling U.K. offshoot to produce *The Empire of Fear*, an alternative history novel in which seventeenth-century Europe is ruled by an aristocracy of "vampires." The creatures' hegemony is threatened and eventually overturned by the emergence of new investigative instruments and the scientific method, which reveal that their origins and powers are natural rather than supernatural. The quest for an explanation of vampirism takes the characters deep into the heart of Africa. There they discover a biological agent which confers longevity and immunity to pain on those who nourish it with the blood of their fellow men, and find that it has been integrated into tribal societies in a fashion which contrasts strongly with its amalgamation into western culture.

The Empire of Fear is perhaps the most memorable of Stableford's works, but his attempts to answer Simon and Schuster's demands for more of the same were less successful. A project similar in spirit— in that it adopted a similar revisionist approach to various other staples of horror fiction—was recast at the publisher's request into a trilogy begun with *The Werewolves of London*, but was then interrupted in the hopes of cashing in on the sudden popularity of vampire fiction. *Young Blood* is as different from *The Empire of Fear* as the author could contrive: a contemporary thriller in which a neurotic young woman's love affair with a vampire might or might not be the hallucinatory result of a psychotropic virus which has escaped from the laboratory where her boyfriend works. The novel's conclusion, which reinterprets everything that has gone before in a surprising and intellectually ambitious fashion, is startlingly original. The trilogy whose production was interrupted by this intrusion ended far less happily, its belated third volume, *The Carnival of Destruction*, appearing in Britain in paperback form some three years after *The Angel of Pain*. The loss of creative impetus is evident in the climax of *Carnival*, which is both awkward and unclear when it should have provided some better resolution to the series.

Stableford has tried for some years to extend his adventures in speculative biotechnology into novel form, but without much commercial success. The novel version of the flirtatiously decadent futuristic murder mystery, *Les Fleurs du Mal*, was rejected by his agent on the grounds that it was too eccentric and tedious; in the end the author salvaged the material by cutting it to novella length. When it sold in that version, he quickly recast several other projects in a similar mold, producing a number of works written in a much terser style than before, but still retaining an imaginative sweep unusual in novellas of that length. For example, "The Hunger and Ecstasy of Vampires" is a parallel text to H. G. Wells's *The Time Machine*, in which a select party of Victorians—including Oscar Wilde, one of whose avatars is the paradoxical hero of "Les Fleurs du Mal"—passes judgment on a time traveler's far-ranging account of the species which inherits the earth after the self-destruction of mankind. "Mortimer Gray's History of Death" describes the career of a man born into a world where no one dies of disease or old age. His compilation of a definitive history of death only uses up a tiny fraction of his prospective lifespan, but nevertheless achieves a glorious triumph over the creeping menace of *ennui*.

The novella version of "Les Fleurs du Mal" brought Stableford his first Hugo nomination, but it remains to be seen whether he can discover any market space in which to continue his ironic celebrations of the potential of biotechnology to transform the quality of human life and the nature of human society. Although his most pedestrian action-adventure novels exhibit a certain flair for exotic imagery, Stableford's sense of humor is sufficiently unorthodox to ensure that he never will appeal to a wide audience; and even those who have acquired a taste for his fictions sometimes find his odysseys in *bizarrerie* difficult to follow to their conscientiously perverse conclusions. Laughing like hell, the author seems to be saying, is the only recourse left to a species whose perversity has created a laughable hell on Earth.

XXXV.

MARGARET ATWOOD

The Young Woman in Agony

with Mary A. Burgess

(1996)

Atwood's work frames a portrait of the young woman in agony. Her first novel, *The Edible Woman* (written 1965, published 1969), has been described as *proto*-feminist, while *Bodily Harm* (1981), which concerns itself heavily with the juxtaposition between the inner and the outer woman, her health and her work, has justifiably been called *post*-feminist.

The Edible Woman is narrated by Marian, who struggles to define her existence in terms of what is expected of her as a woman. As with most of Atwood's fiction, this is a novel about relationships, about the ways in which men and women give up to each other the power of control, both physically and psychologically. Atwood addresses these issues in a typically ambivalent manner, allowing Marian to slide into the salvation and trap of anorexia. As Marian ceases to consume food, she begins consuming her own psyche, although she eventually finds the courage to resolve both her eating disorder and her problems with Peter, her fiancé.

Surfacing (1972) is undeniably more strident, more invasive, more violent in its depiction of the confrontations that underlie the relations between men and women, with

Xenograffiti, by ROBERT REGINALD

clear foreshadowing of the futuristic horrors depicted in *The Handmaid's Tale*. Anna must tread a careful line to avoid running afoul of David's "rules," or face immediate corporal punishment for her meaningless "transgressions."

Atwood's later works, such as *Lady Oracle* (1976) and *Cat's Eye* (1988), take a more jaundiced look at women and their friendships, both with the opposite sex and with each other, focusing particularly on the very basic relationship between mothers and their daughters. In *Lady Oracle*, for example, the author confronts the "rules" of femininity head-on. Her character's love-hate relationship with her "good"/"bad" mother has forced the adolescent Joan into a fit of self-loathing and obesity. The act of overeating (or that of starving oneself, in *The Edible Woman*) represents the attempt of the disenfranchised to strike out against those in power, and is a metaphor for how some women perceive themselves in society—"consume, or be consumed." Joan's eventual loss of weight, and later on, her success at writing women's gothic romance novels, allows her to regain "control" of her existence, in essence to become her own oracle, to remake her own future. In this sense, *Lady Oracle* can be seen as a direct progression along Atwood's fictional road from female self-sacrifice to female self-vindication.

Although all of the author's works are cut from the same fictional cloth, her novel *The Handmaid's Tale* (1985) is the only one of her long tales which can be considered fantastic. In the not-too-distant future the religious right has taken over the United States, and Canada has become the last bastion of democracy in the new world. Freedom of speech and freedom of worship have been abolished, having been outlawed by a totalitarian regime that emphasizes the harsher dictates of the Old Testament. Women have become chattel, relegated either to mindless existences as uneducated *hausfraus* or as outright slaves and surrogates of their masculine masters, the elite of this highly stratified brave new world.

Within this sick society the "handmaids" have been stripped of all identity, even their personal names. Now they are called by variations of their masters' given names—*e.g.*, "Offred" (Of Fred), "Ofglen" (Of Glen), "Ofwarren" (Of Warren). They have become mere appendages of the males

207

they are bound to serve, and can undertake no task independently, even bathing or the simple pleasure of shopping. No women, not even the wives of the masters, are allowed to read *anything*, including the Bible. Even something as innocuous as hand lotion is forbidden, its use being considered pleasurable and self-enhancing. The handmaids' only requirement is to bear children for the sterile wives of their masters.

Offred lost her husband and daughter while trying to escape to Canada; she is utterly without friends or family. But although she may be physically restrained, she still has the ability to think and scheme— about her past, her present, and the possibilities of her future. As long as she can keep her sanity, she tells herself, she will find some way to escape. Her forbidden relationship with Nick is secretly encouraged by Commander Fred's wife, Serena Joy, who suspects that her husband is also infertile, and who, in any case, is anxious to drive a wedge between Offred and the Commander.

Atwood highlights the drabness of this world by letting us feel the sensuality of her heroine's personality. Through her vivid first-person narration we feel Offred's reaction to the fabrics drawn against her skin, and experience the touch and shape of objects as disparate as Scrabble tiles or soft-boiled eggs; we smell the intoxicating perfume of the flowers in Serena Joy's garden, juxtaposed against the almost-sickening scent of the Commander's "moth-ball" aftershave; we share Offred's vivid craving for the mere taste of tobacco or a whiff of its smoke (mirrored by her equally vivid longing for sex with Nick). All of these images pierce us through Offred's eyes like a Technicolor searchlight stabbing through the gray personalities and decaying images of this bleak dystopian future.

It is not surprising, then, that the colors of Off*red*'s world are all primary hues, like the reds, blues, and greens in a child's paint-box. The handmaids, all dressed in lush reds, resemble nothing so much as Serena Joy's blood-hued tulips—at first flourishing, then drooping and dropping their petals in her immaculate flowerbeds. Serena Joy (like the other wives) wears only virginal blue. She is cold and pristine, "serene" but icy, "sterile" and utterly devoid of sympathy. The lack of "joy" in her existence is clearly contrasted with her handmaid's lust for life. In this society, as in Harlan Ellison's "Down Under" from "A Boy and His Dog," the evil of *The Handmaid's Tale* lies just beneath an idyllic *façade*, a landscape of lies overlaying a corrupt and dissolute society.

There is a compelling charm and subtlety about Atwood's heroine, but also a measure of calculation and practicality in her character that is immediately offsetting. This is no innocent waif to be gobbled up by the lions. Offred recognizes instinctively that her true enemy is not the Commander, but his wife, who in many respects is as much a prisoner as she. She will make no mistake if she can help it, and considers her options well before she enters into clandestine relationships with Commander Fred and with Nick, her Guardian lover. She carefully bides her time, observing both her captors and her fellow prisoners, weighing their motivations and reactions with a cool, clinical eye. We come to realize that Offred has more control over her situation than it might at first seem. In each of Atwood's books her characters gradually learn to control first themselves, then their surroundings, and finally their opponents through subtle manipulations. These almost cynical maneuverings become part and parcel of her protagonists' protective coloring. Moving delicately through the light and shadow of the societal jungles of her existence, Offred watches, waits, and moves her pawns carefully. Outwardly she may be a prisoner, but inwardly she is captain of her soul. As she plays the forbidden Scrabble with the Commander, the words she forms in her mind become objects, like the smooth tiles in her fingers. She wins the first game handily, then "allows" the Commander to win the second. Although she is virtually his slave, she consciously manipulates his desire in order to control the situation.

Here and elsewhere in her fictions Atwood seems much more concerned with the relationships her characters establish, and with the use and abuse of power within those relationships, than with the characters themselves. So while we are clearly meant to empathize with Offred's "tragedy," some of that empathy is lost through the latter's cold appraisements of her own situation. For example, Offred would like to have a knife, or perhaps Serena Joy's gardening shears, or some other sharp object—not, we suspect, to commit suicide (as her captors fear), but to do other damage. She is almost sly in her little deceptions and transgressions. She watches and waits and plots. The smoldering violence which has often been foreshadowed in Atwood's contemporary novels here bursts forth into the flame of revolution. Offred and her companions must literally fight and hack and slash their way to freedom. At the end of the book we hail the new revolution that will inevitably topple the rotted-out hulk of the Guardians' society—and wonder, just a bit, where all of this destruction will lead.

Atwood has oft been hailed as a feminist spokesperson, and her works have been described by other critics as being driven by many of the issues ascribed to this movement. Certainly the author is concerned with the use of control in relationships, and, perhaps more importantly, with women's image of self, and how that image can be changed, bolstered, or destroyed by inward or outward manipulation. At the same time, one finds a certain ambivalence in Atwood's fiction, and detects in her soliloquies almost a loathing of her female self. Her characters are constantly remaking themselves, and seem never satisfied with who they are or what they were or have become. Janus-faced, she has peered simultaneously at both the past and future of women in society, and found them both wanting. For example, the author seems to empathize almost viscerally with the physical and emotional needs of women to bear and rear children. And yet one senses, particularly in such episodes as the birthing scene in *A Handmaid's Tale*, an almost overpoweringly negative response to the multitude of sensual stimuli associated with birth—the contortions, the pain, the sweating, and the smells—particularly the smells. Atwood's loathing of her own sex, however, seems directed most uncompromisingly toward the kind of women represented by Joan's mother or the Commander's wife, who are willing to use others of their gender unfeelingly for their own self-fulfillment or -aggrandizement.

Xenograffiti, by ROBERT REGINALD

Atwood has presented, in this harsh depiction of a future America, an allegory of the abuse of political and personal power by both men and women, of the manipulation of others by those who perceive themselves to be in control of society. The salvation of the individual can only be found in such simple things as improved self-image and the courage to remove oneself from inappropriate abuse, and through the willingness to seek further empowerment, vindication, and escape from a system that represses the possibilities of any individual who fails to fit the mold. Her female protagonists are tortured creatures trying to maintain a scrap of dignity in an unjust world. They may be down, she seems to be saying, but they can never be counted out—at least as long as there are any sharp knives around.

Xenograffiti, by ROBERT REGINALD

XXXVI.

A TURBOT AT A TIME

THE MYSTERY NOVELS OF LINDSEY DAVIS

(1996)

It is the year 70 A.D., during the height of the Roman Empire. Eighteen months earlier the Emperor Nero had committed suicide, plunging Rome into a year of civil war. Out of the chaos of four candidates vying for the throne emerged the Emperor Vespasian, and into the turmoil of Roman politics and society plunges the hero of this new detective series, Marcus Didius Falco.

Falco is a member of the lower classes, a former soldier who had served a term in the frontier province of Britain, but has now returned home to Rome. His father, who had abandoned the family many years before, now works as a successful auctioneer in Rome; his older brother, a war hero, had been killed a year earlier while serving under the Emperor's son and heir, Titus, during the wars in Judea. His five sisters have all married and most have broods of their own. Falco lives on the upper floor of a rundown apartment building, the higher levels being the most undesirable lodgings. He calls himself a "private informer": his services are available at reasonable rates to uncover information or to do whatever needs to be done to satisfy his clients.

Sometimes he works directly for the Emperor himself, traveling from Rome to distant provinces in Italy, Britain, and Gaul, accomplishing tasks for the government that must be handled discreetly or at least not through official channels. On other occasions he follows the more traditional pursuits of the P.I., uncovering murder, mayhem, and larceny for private customers within the walls of Rome herself or in her nearby environs. He also serves as occasional bodyguard, blackguard, body disposer, and guardian of public morality, depending on the commission and the circumstances, although he maintains a strict code of ethics, and will not kill gratuitously or enrich himself needlessly as his so-called betters (and employers) frequently do. He supports the restoration of the Republic, and is not afraid to say so publicly, but is realistic enough to work for the Imperium, and eventually becomes friends with Vespasian and Titus. He can be crude, boorish, inconsiderate, fast-talking, quick-thinking, and without manners, yet utterly charming for all that.

In the first novel of the series, *The Silver Pigs*, Falco meets Helena Justina, the recently-divorced daughter of a rich senator, and a member of the privileged class. Their on-again, off-again romance and the inherent differences in their social positions, a gulf that makes a marriage impossible in Roman society, fuel the underlying tension of this series. Part of what drives Falco in the subsequent novels is the necessity of accumulating enough wealth (400,000 pieces of gold) to buy a social position which will enable him to marry Helena. They make a delightful if constantly bickering couple, although the ultimate conclusion, despite the fact that Helena is living with Falco by the fifth book in the series, remains uncertain.

The connection with Helena proves useful to Falco in other ways, opening doors to the wealthier classes that he otherwise might have difficulty in reaching. Falco's unique position allows him to pry the lid off higher Roman society, and to watch the roaches feeding at the public trough scurry for cover. Most of the novels deal with high-level chicanery in one form or another, even when the initial problem seems to be something else. In *The Silver Pigs*, for example, Falco must return to Britain and work as a slave in the silver mines there to uncover a smuggling scheme involving Helena's uncle. In *Shadows in Bronze* (each of the first five books in the series includes a metal in its title) the detective travels to the

Xenograffiti, by ROBERT REGINALD

isle of Capri and southern Italy to unravel a plot to overthrow the Emperor. *Venus in Copper* has Falco investigating a vixen whose wealthy husbands, all much older than she, keep dying providentially very shortly after their marriages. In *The Iron Hand of Mars* Vespasian sends the investigator on a secret mission to discover who is behind the rebellion of the Germanic auxiliaries at the Rhine, and in the process Falco discovers the solution to a generations-old mystery of what happened to the Emperor Augustus's three lost legions, and uncovers a pattern of high-level graft. *Poseidon's Gold* focuses on the mystery behind the career of Falco's older brother, Festus, who took an arrow during the siege of an obscure village in Galilee, and on the background of their father, Favonius the sleazy auctioneer.

Davis opens our eyes to the realities of life for the average Roman citizen. There are no hoards of Christian refugees roaming the streets, and none of the modern amenities. What does fill these books is a certain *joie de vivre* and a humor sorely lacking in most historical and crime fiction. Most of Falco's friends are poor, but they live their brief lives to the fullest. *Venus in Copper* features an utterly classic dinner scene, in which a giant turbot given to Falco by the Emperor's son is cooked and served to the comings and goings of Falco's multitudinous family, with Titus Caesar himself showing up in the middle of the feast with his military escort. The episode is funny and sad and chaotic all at the same time. One has the sense that Davis has lifted her characters straight out of history, that this is how things actually were in ancient Rome.

Each book has advanced the timeline by four to six months, and as with most historical detective series, they should be read in order for greatest appreciation, since the characters and their situations change and develop sequentially. Meanwhile, we wait, as Falco himself does, to see what new perfidies and corruptions will come his and Helena Justina's way. As Cicero himself once said, *"O tempora! O mores!"*

Xenograffiti, by ROBERT REGINALD

XXXVII.

THIRTY YEARS, 1965/66-1995/96

AN INTRODUCTION TO *T TAURI*

(1996)

In May of 1966, at the close of the first academic year at California State University, San Bernardino, the Associated Student Body issued a commemorative publication, *T Tauri*. Apparently intended as the first of a series of such volumes, it proved to be one of a kind in many different respects. It was the first campus publication to list the founding faculty at Cal State, and to provide biographies of each. It included a complete register of CSUSB's first class, about two hundred students. It included a plethora of early photographs and historical details concerning the building of the campus. More importantly, it summarized the *esprit de corps* so evident in these first administrators, faculty, and students. The excitement of establishing an entirely new educational structure from scratch permeates this publication.

Thirty years later to the month, we celebrate three decades of service by this institution to the Inland Empire, and we honor the six faculty members from that first academic year who are still teaching at Cal State, San Bernardino: Ronald Barnes, Bruce Golden, Dennis Ikenberry, Jorun Johns, Ward McAfee, and Edward White.

There was only one *T Tauri* ever published. The uniqueness of that publication reflects a special time in the history of this university, an era which will never come

Xenograffiti, by ROBERT REGINALD

again. In 1996 the campus includes 400 tenure-track faculty and twelve thousand students. Our challenges have moved from building a dream to just keeping it going. But let us not forget our origins: this is who we were and where we started. We reprint this publication in homage to the founding faculty and students of California State University, San Bernardino.

Xenograffiti, by ROBERT REGINALD

XXXVIII.

MEASURING THE MARIGOLDS

THE FALL AND RISE OF BORGO PRESS

(2003)

The curious business of publishing books has always for me been a bit of a roller coaster ride, filled with exciting climbs to the very heights of prosperity and productivity, followed by just-as-rapid descents into the hollows of legal challenges and declining sales, complicated by the endless (and sometimes unreasonable) demands of authors, jobbers, and would-be writers. Sometimes the lows would follow the highs in quick succession, or even occur simultaneously. So it goes.

But by the end of 1998, it was clear to Mary Burgess and me that the "monster" was threatening to consume all of our energies, fortune, and sanity, while giving us very little in return. My position at Cal State kept eating more and more of my time, and the recession of the early 1990s had changed academic publishing permanently—and not for the better. Jobbers were becoming increasingly demanding, as they saw their own library sales decline and their profits erode, and each of the changes they imposed took away another of our safety margins.

We had once envisioned riding into the retirement sunset on Borgo's back, continuing our efforts to provide a home for the publication of serious genre criticism and bibliography; clearly, however, this vision could not now be realized without a continuous drain on our finances. We were now operating at a loss. The question soon became, "how could we rid ourselves of this unsightly beast?" without being devoured by the disembowelment and decay of the soon-to-be decapitated corpus. How, indeed?

Ironically enough, we published in the latter years of Borgo Press more books than we ever had previously, finally reaching Opus 300 in December of 1998 (our last work was *The Mystery Scene Movie Guide*, by well-known detectionist Max Allan Collins); among those titles were some of the finest works that we ever issued. When, in the early months of '99, we reached a decision to shut down the company, we wanted to ensure that our authors and suppliers were completely recompensed—and they were, all of them—and so we decided to begin a fire sale of our existing book stock, essentially cannibalizing the volumes in hand to repay everyone to whom we owed money. Some authors took copies of their books in lieu of royalties, which was fine with us, while others bought out all of the stock of their titles at vastly reduced rates. The process worked. All accounts finally zeroed out. We also returned the rights to all unpublished works to their authors. When we finally shut our doors for the last time in August of 1999, we felt free for the first time in many years.

Why? Why found Borgo in the first place? Why end the experiment in the last place?

I have come to believe in the cycle of life, in the surge and release of energies, as simply a natural thing, a part of the working out of our respective existences. Each life contains within itself, I think, both sorrows and joys, troubles and elations. Some individuals seem to get more of one than the other at various times in his or her lifespan, but all of us experience our due share of ups and downs.

We started Borgo Press for a variety of reasons, some having to do with the reinvestment of the large royalty checks that I was then earning for my reference books, others being the perceived need to fill a niche, and to provide for the world a place where genre critics, then just coming into their own, could have their words circulated and preserved in library collections. We made our share of mistakes, no doubt, but we also contributed a great many books to the

Xenograffiti, by ROBERT REGINALD

world that would never have otherwise been issued—and some of these were well worth the effort.

And we closed the press twenty-four years later for another assortment of reasons and self-rationales, justifications that were equally as valid as those of initiation. Among them were the necessity of preparing seriously for retirement from my university position, the gradual loss of satisfaction with what we were accomplishing, uncertain health, and the sense (true or not) that we were little appreciated for our work. In other words, the time had finally come, as it always does, for everything.

During the next four years Mary and I worked on other lucrative writing projects, I took up the study of ancient coins and published my first essay on the subject, and we lived through a series of personal crises that had nothing to do with the business, as we gradually began clearing away the impediments (as we saw them) to our eventual retirement. An uncomfortable, suffocating entanglement with another writer was swept away into the trash heap of bad experience. Good riddance. Our only granddaughter, Whitney Louise Rogers, was killed on November 9, 2001. Terrible, unfathomable tragedy. A long-time family problem was finally resolved through separation, although it will re-emerge, we know, at some later date. And so forth.

They've been hard years, but somehow we've slithered through the worst of them, albeit not wholly unscathed. Throughout this period we've somehow kept each other sane, and we've tried to maintain a positive face as one difficulty after another battered at the fortress of ourselves.

And then, quite unexpectedly, we were given the opportunity in the spring of 2003 to slip through the back door of publishing again, and revive in a small way the Borgo Press imprint, under the aegis of another house, Wildside Press. How long and to what extent this revival will sustain itself, well, who can say? There are never any guarantees.

But to be pulling on the strings again, to be back in the game again, if only marginally, is energizing and invigorating and, well, just plain fun! It's one of the few things that I've missed from my previous life during these past few years.

Xenograffiti, by Robert Reginald

Not the business, but the editing. Not the demands, but the creativity. Not the yin, but the yang. At least for now.

So I'll do what I can one more time to bring people together, to facilitate the publication of worthy works that otherwise wouldn't be preserved or read, to measure the marigolds anew.

And perhaps, just maybe, the ghosts will leave me alone at last.

XXXIX.

ON BE(COM)ING A LIBRARIAN

(2003)

Of the twin contrails of my career (*viz.*, my life), I have considered perhaps overmuch the leavings of my first and seemingly more exciting path, that of editing and writing and publishing; and have scarcely bothered even to mention the secondary and somewhat humdrum road that I have wandered during the past three decades, namely, the profession of librarianship.

After all, as one pundit would have it, who but an old dog could love a librarian? We are become (and have long been) the butt of idle jokes and the distress of the academic community. Those who profess commonality with all subjects are privy to none—or so the self-proclaimed gurus of academe would have us believe. Nonetheless, we are the last remnants of the Renaissance Man and Woman still to inhabit the modern world, and that world has ever failed to appreciate our role and even our sheer necessity.

For if Dante had to have his guide through the entangled underworld of the Inferno, displaying and interpreting to him the wonders and terrors of that unique underground universe, so too must the modern wanderer through the fields of knowledge possess his or her librarian as a constant companion, both to sift away the detritus of uncouth opinion and unsound fact, and also to point out the highpoints of the journey, sights that might otherwise be missed by those who have little more time on their hands than their own limited existences.

Xenograffiti, by ROBERT REGINALD

Librarians serve as the active intermediaries between the student and the g(l)ob(u)s of information that permeate(s) the æther surrounding modern civilization. Some of that data can be found on the Internet, some exists in printed form within the millions of volumes housed in the great university libraries of this land, and some, well some derive from the irreplaceable judgment that an experienced librarian can bring to the interchange. It is not enough to find one disconnected fact buried in some obscure tome or entangled idly on the web. That ort of knowledge must be related to other bits of information to form a theory, a supposition, perhaps even a thesis.

Librarians excel at such interventions. In a world which seems to be sliding ever deeper into triviality, fragmentation, specialization, and into noise, the ever-present noise substituted for careful thought, they represent one of the few elements that cries out for unification, common sense, yea, for some basic understanding of how things fit together and impact each upon the other. They represent an element of sanity and stability amid chaos and corruption.

I had none of these thoughts when I first entered the world of librarianship. I had majored in English literature at Gonzaga University during my undergraduate years, and minored in classical Greek. The only possible profession to be reaped from such rampant nonsense was profession itself. In a rare moment of brilliant insight into my own character, I realized that I was not, perhaps, exactly suited to the role of instructor, even at the college level, and so I sought some other possibility for myself. I also disliked manual labor and general business, so the digging of ditches and pinching of pennies were ruled out at a very early stage, oh yes.

What then? What career could possibly suit a young *naïf* devoted to the collecting and reading of books?

I found myself most comfortable lurking in the stacks of the Crosby Library, where I could follow whatever bits of curiosities I was then pursuing to their logical ends—or at least to the limits of the resources held at Gonzaga, which (I understood even then) is not quite the same thing. *This* is where I belonged, I suddenly realized during my sophomore year. This is what I should be doing with my life.

Xenograffiti, by ROBERT REGINALD

I had, of course, no idea whatever of what librarians actually did. The lust of books and the quest for knowledge drove me into the profession. I burned for them, and had done so, really, from about the age of four, when words suddenly and magically made sense to me. The magic enthralled me from the beginning, and it has never released its grip on my soul through the ensuing decades. Thus, I decided, I would surround myself with an academic library, a *large* library, and figure out the rest at some later date.

School was never a problem for me: I could ace any tests and absorb any knowledge with astonishing ease. I had an almost eidetic memory for details, and I understood the relationships between complicated pieces of information almost instinctively. The University of Southern California offered me a graduate fellowship to attend their master's program in library science, and I headed to Los Angeles in the summer of 1969.

I was terrified. I had never actually been away from home for longer than a week or two in my entire life to that point, and I had no idea what to do. I borrowed a little money from my parents, stopped at a motel nearby, and looked immediately for housing somewhere off campus. I finally rented a room in the house of an African-American engineer in the Adams District, a couple of miles distant from USC.

This was not a happy time in America. I had no transportation, and walked to the university, or took buses to the outlying fantasy land of Hollywood. I lived through a number of unpleasant incidents and confrontations with the Black Panthers and others, but received more of an education than I had ever anticipated.

The classes themselves, however, seemed somewhat funky, for the lack of a better word. Rather than hearkening forward to the onset of computers and their soon-to-be impact upon the library universe, they retrogressed me and my fellow students into a world that was part and parcel of the Depression era. The instructors were in their dotage, and their instruction at best failed to inspire. Was this the true reality of librarianship: the bland leading the blind?

Xenograffiti, by ROBERT REGINALD

Well, of course it wasn't. I completed my studies in 1970, and was interviewed for three positions, at USC itself, Occidental College, and California State College, San Bernardino. I deliberately restricted my choices to Southern California, which offered a warm winter climate, loads of great bookstores, and good career possibilities; and further narrowed my options only to positions in academic libraries. San Bernardino offered the best pay and the promise of much future growth, and so I started my stint there on September 1, 1970, at the well advanced age of twenty-two (a time of life in which one knows everything about everything).

I have never left.

In those days I was "green behind the gills," as they say, bright and opinionated and intolerant of others' views. I was hired as Periodicals Librarian, but the new building we were supposed to occupy in the summer of '70 had been delayed due to heavy rains, winds, and labor strikes, and we didn't actually move into the six-storey structure until June of the following year. In the meantime, I worked the reference desk along with my compatriots, and learned how to catalog books. (I thought I already *knew* how to perform the latter task, but I soon discovered, as with so much else in life, that the application was vastly different from the theory.)

Cal State was five years old and had about 2,300 students at the time that I joined the faculty; it now has 17,000. Automation was unknown in 1970; now everything that we do is affected by the pervasiveness of computers and data systems. One thing that hasn't changed appreciably is the size of our staff: we had ten librarians (four of them half-time) when I started; we now have eleven full-time faculty, and three or four part-timers.

But the world as a whole and the world of academe have altered in quite significant ways, and we librarians have had to move with them. When I started within the profession, we had the leisure to contemplate the long-term implications of administrative decisions and the changes that they might work; now everything must be handled on an *ad hoc* basis, because the time to *think* about the philosophical as-

Xenograffiti, by ROBERT REGINALD

pects of what we do no longer exists. This leads at times to unfortunate choices with unforeseen consequences.

At the same time, the requirements for librarian promotion and tenure have been severely ratcheted upwards since 1970. Present-day hires must perform to the same standards in professional growth (*i.e.*, publications) and campus service as the teaching faculty; and evaluations themselves are conducted at the higher levels of review by a committee composed of senior professors on campus. I was promoted initially based only on my performance as a working librarian; the standards changed for the Cal State System during the early 1980s.

Of course, raising such performance standards is not necessarily a bad thing. The quality of the library faculty that we have hired in the past decade at CSUSB is superior on the whole to what came before. And the librarians themselves have benefited both from higher pay and access to the perquisites previously available only to the instructional faculty.

But the flip side to this reality for most of my junior colleagues is a severe squeezing of the time available for them to do anything job-related, beyond the bare necessities. Once one subtracts reference desk hours and the time required to prepare, teach, and evaluate bibliographical instruction sessions, how many hours remain within the average work week to do service and growth? The answer usually is: not enough.

Yet somehow the institution—and I—have survived and prospered, despite several hiccups along the way. At some point during those decades, I learned cataloging well enough to instruct others in the process. At another point, I developed sufficient administrative skills to run a major department successfully, although the stress ultimately had severe consequences on my health. Maybe I was even able to acquire a little wisdom along the way.

Now I spend most of my days acting as collection development officer and mentoring the junior faculty, trying on the one hand to enrich and build our collection with very few financial resources, and simultaneously attempting to make the evaluation process less of a mystery to those entering it for the first time.

After my near-fatal heart attack in the summer of '03, my tasks were reconfigured just to include acquisitions, while removing the overall supervision of Technical Services. For me this one action has revitalized and reinvigorated my library career. But I don't have many years left to devote to the profession. In '05 I intend either to retire completely or to drop to half-time status. Thirty-five years is perhaps long enough to have served at one institution. Time to do other things, if I live so long.

So why do we exist? What was so important about my three decades at CSUSB, or any librarian's contributions to the profession? This is what I've come to understand:

Librarians exist as a bridge between students, the teaching faculty, and the general public, and the almost innumerable resources currently available through any academic library. Those resources are now so extensive, both in print and in on-line form, that the average person cannot possibly find his or her way through the myriad of materials available, and make any sense of them.

A Google search is not a substitute for effective research. Random facts do not create by themselves a reasonable and reasoned exegesis. There is a vast difference, a difference little perceived by most students or even by some teaching faculty, between "data" taken as a whole, and the use of that material to produce a structured thesis. And it is precisely in this arena that librarians can be our guides.

Like Dante wending his way through the world of the *Inferno*, we need such guides to explain, explicate, and extend our vision of the information available to us, and what it actually means. During the past five years, I have increased the Cal State community's access to full-text, on-line journals from nothing to over 24,000 titles. Even keeping track of these offerings presents a major challenge to my staff; actually delineating how each periodical is presented in their respective databases is a far more difficult task. And this particular problem represents just the very beginning of the problem of information overload.

Xenograffiti, by ROBERT REGINALD

This is not to say that the knowledgeable individual cannot find his or her way through the myriad of data resources that the average university library now offers. As an undergraduate, I delighted in ferreting out obscure tomes situated in remote parts of the USC collections. But students today have on the average as little free time to explore the vast vistas of knowledge as do their instructors.

Librarians can provide significant help, when they themselves know the resources under their tutelage, and when students or teaching faculty bother to inquire. All too many times, of course, we never see them. Reaching our core audience has long been one of the great challenges of modern librarianship.

Still, it's been a fun ride. Being the spider at the heart of the web of knowledge throughout all of these years has given me an access to the world of learning that most writers or researchers can scarcely even imagine. I have learned so much—and have so much to learn—that my life as a librarian and author has been enriched beyond any reckoning that I can now make. This is what I was born to do. This is what I live to do.

And when I have finally retired from Cal State San Bernardino, I will continue to use the collection to bolster my writing skills and my personal knowledge. One does not just walk away from a lifetime of learning.

XL.

KO'D AT THE OK CORRAL

OR,

THE PERILS OF PULLULATING PSEUDONYMITY

(2003)

In a previous life I was once (true confession time now, my kiddie-cats!) just a whit more ambitious than I am in these latter days of post-near death experiences; and I was then much more eager to do that which was necessary, whatever *that* might be, to achieve my (self-perceived) overdue share of literary fame and fortune.

O tempora, o mores! What a foolish creature is made of a little literary f(l)op.

And so I allowed myself to be seduced by the dark side of the farce.

When a well-known writer asked me to create a detailed background for his fictional world, I was flattered enough—and oh so willing, for I saw therein the many possibilities-to-be—to perform like the trained monkey that I had now become; and I produced in quick-quack time a set of somewhat marvelous (or so it seemed to me) vignettes and stories and creative schtuff in general, all for the use of this individual who was much better known in Literary-Lollipop-Land than lowly *moi* (but not for long, I knew, oh, not for long!).

And then I was asked by this same individual to put to paper a full-length fiction set in this same *milieu*, which *le*

Xenograffiti, by ROBERT REGINALD

grand auteur would peddle under our joint bylines (his having primacy, of course), and for which he would inhale half of the mucho moolah that would soon miraculously appear (since it would be his name and his agent selling the novel)—but, but, my career would suddenly blossom beyond my wildest imaginings (and they were pretty wild, let me tell you), and well, well, further possibilities were certainly possible, weren't they?

Alas, dear readers, that it didn't happen that way. Mr. X. failed to finish one of his own projects on time. The house of cards abruptly collapsed, and my reams of work suddenly became worth no more than the cheap paper it was printed out on.

For years thereafter, the fiction was maintained between us, that something, maybe something *great*, would work out—eventually! Perhaps *this* project would finally go, or *that* one would finally be issued by a major publisher, or maybe the writer's career would be resurrected—maybe this, maybe that, maybe not!

So I continued to pen materials in this *milieu*, to the tune of some 600,000+ words, I continued to allow my ambition sway my better judgment, and I wasted seven years of my authorial career trying to become a clone of Mr. X.

There's a lesson here for all would-be writers. Develop your own style in your own good time, *ma ou mon littérateur prétendu*, and avoid all authorial collaboration at the potential cost of your literary soul, unless, of course, unless you control the terms. I didn't.

At this late date I surely do not wish Monsieur X. any ill. He's gone his way, I've gone mine. He's managed to revitalize his career to a certain degree, for which he deserves full credit. I don't think his more recent books are as well-conceived or -executed as some of his earlier fictions, but that's just my two cents' worth. Others would disagree, I'm sure.

For myself, I did learn from this experience something of the craft of fiction, and I did finally come to understand the serendipitous nature of New York publishing. Talent is rarely enough; indeed, talent is sometimes contraindicative or even antithetical to achieving widespread distribution in the real world. Dumb, dumber, dumbest seem to be the operative words.

No matter.

My books will continue to be published professionally, as they always have. I've never yet penned a volume that ultimately failed to sell. I'll continue to write for as long as I'm physically and mentally able, and I'll continue to do the best I can to make my books interesting, readable, perceptive, and halfway intelligent. That's who I am. That's what I'm about.

As long as I remain vitally interested, I think my writing will itself stay interesting—to someone. And if I ultimately have no readers, well, there'll be no one left to say boo, will there?

XLI.

A FEW WORDS, A VERY FEW WORDS, ON WRITING

(2003)

I'm no Stephen King or Terry Brooks, to name two well-known authors who have published in recent years little memoirs about their writing lives (*On Writing* and *Sometimes the Magic Works*). I'm not even Jack Dann or George Zebrowski. I don't have their reputations either as a fiction writer or as a nonfiction hacker. In fact, I'm not all that well known outside of a very small group of devoted fans and curious academics.

Still, I've been writing professionally since 1970, and during that three-and-one-half decades have sold millions and millions of words for hundreds and hundreds of thousands of dollars. It was never enough, I thought, to provide a consistently good living, and I'm rather glad at this point that I have a state pension to fall back on in my rapidly approaching (g)olden age; or perhaps I merely lacked the courage to plunge into the occupation of literature on a full-time basis.

Whatever.

I've paid my dues, have nothing left to prove, and have lost most of my ambition to the after-effects of a near-fatal heart attack (it's amazing how a near brush with death can reconfigure one's priorities). So why spout off now? Why talk about this particular topic at this particular time?

Precisely because....

The prospect of one's potentially imminent passing concentrates one's mind wonderfully, to paraphrase an old saying. I have a few things to say, and no one has ever been able to shut me up before. They're not likely to start now. So bear with me, if you please.

I've been writing since about the age of four or five, when I started copying the names and words off my mother's kitchen appliances in our old, two-storey, rented gothic in Fairfield, Massachusetts. I've been making up stories for about the same time.

I remember getting up well before my parents at the initial hint of sunlight, sneaking down the stairs, and carefully opening each blind, first looking about very carefully (of course) for all of the monsters that I knew were lurking in the shadows. It wasn't really safe until all the windows were open.

Then I'd create continuing serials featuring myself and Superman or one of my favorite western heroes, and play them out over days or weeks. This was oodles of fun for a little kid of five or six. It was how I entertained myself, even at that young age. Not much has changed.

I write these essays—and pen my stories and novels—for much the same reason now. I haven't grown a bit in that sense: there's still a rambunctious rapscallion lurking somewhere down in my subconscious, always clamoring to be let out. Writing for me is occasionally a catharsis of sorts, and sometimes hard work, but mostly (at least these days) it's just plain fun. I write because I want to, because I need to, because NOT writing would somehow represent a little death to me.

I don't care any longer about sales or markets or money or fame or any of that crap. Read my stuff or not, as ye choose. Laugh or cry with me or not, as ye choose. Agree with me or argue with me, as ye choose. Criticize my ramblings and call them crap or praise the hell out of them, as ye choose. It signifieth not, as the prophet sayeth.

I write to please myself first, and no one else, with one caveat. If I don't also please Mary, my one true critic, then I know for certain that there's something's wrong with my story, my precious prose, my plot, my whatever. I do pay close attention to what she says; or, rather, I ignore what she says at my authorial peril. She's too intelligent to miss very much, and she always has my best interests at heart.

Otherwise, though, I write exactly what I want to write these days, without much of an eye as to where it might sell or how it might appear. I've never had any problem finding outlets for my schtuff. Everything I've ever written of any worth whatever has been published professionally.

This doesn't mean to say, o thou would-be writers, that I completely ignore the realities of commercial publishing, or that I fail to seek contracts first before beginning long projects on which I would like to work—or at least have some good idea of where such lengthy books might be placed. I dislike wasting time, particularly *my* time, which has become especially precious to me in these my latter years. And yet....

I penned three books on behalf of another writer between 1996-2002 (see "KO'd at the OK Corral; or, the Perils of Pullulating Pseudonymity"), and only one of these was actually published, despite numerous promises to the contrary. Fair enough. There are very few certainties in the publishing world, and one takes one's lumps and failures along with one's successes, swallowing the pills of bitterness and learning from the experience. One of these books has now been completely rewritten, and will finally appear in '04; the other still needs recasting into a different *milieu*. All will eventually be published, but only after considerable extra work on my part. I will not lend my creativity to another author ever again.

Nor should I have done so initially. I should have known better than to agree to do what I was asked to do, without a contract clearly defining and delineating exactly how and in what way and with whose permission my work could be employed by this other entity in developing his fictional universe. I was ambitious. I was wrong. I wasted a great deal of effort and energy for almost no return.

I like what I'm doing now very much better. I piddle around with my own creativity, and there's no one to say yea or nay or even maybe save myself—and Mary! I've written a half-dozen essays this past week as capstones for this second edition of *Xenograffiti*, just because I wanted to, and because

Xenograffiti, by Robert Reginald

I felt that I had something to say—about myself, about my life, about what I've done and where I've been. If someone else obtains even a modicum of enjoyment from these musings, well, so much the better. And if not, whom I have harmed, dear friends?

I write what I see. When I'm gone, in the not-so-distant future, these words will remain behind, small signposts that I once lived, that I once thought, that I once felt, and that I made all of these hoary things, in and of myself—and no one else did them or could have done them in quite the same way. This is who I am.

In a few words, in a very few words, we wordsmiths draw pictures in the minds of other men and women just like ourselves—those currently living, those yet to be born, those inhabitants of some distantly unfathomable future civilization. This is time travel in its truest form: I communicate directly with you, I talk to you, not just now, but for as long as these words continue to exist in some form. I give to you my wisdom, my ideas, my self.

And you talk back, although I rarely hear your responses.

You see and hear Robert Reginald and Michael Burgess and Boden Clarke, and all of those other personas that I have worn as a writer. You see whatever face I choose to put on.

In a few words, in a very few words, you understand.

XLII.

DOUBLE YOUR PLEASURE, DOUBLE YOUR FUN, SCHIZOID LIVING FOR EVERYONE!

ON BEING A PSEUDONYM

(2003)

Once upon a time there was just one of me, a scrawny high school kid of sixteen who was living in Spokane, Washington in the fall of 1964. His name was Michael Burgess. And one day, while perusing the paperback racks, I encountered my name splashed all over the lurid cover of a "nonfiction" sex guide published by the soon-to-be-defunct Monarch Books.

This "Michael Burgess," as I later discovered, was the pen name of an historical novelist named Noel B. Gerson (ironically, I encountered many years afterwards a portrait of Gerson on one of his hardcover romances; he looked remarkably like the author, complete with curly hair). Gerson had been writing a series of what passed in those days for soft porn books for such "B" pb imprints as Monarch, Lancer Books, Midwood, and others, sometimes under the MB name, sometimes under the joint pseudonym of "Ann-Marie and Michael Burgess."

I was stunned, utterly stunned.

Already I had harbored certain aspirations of possibly becoming a writer one day, and here was my byline, being used and abused over and over again on stuff that (at best) was utter trash. It was then that I started signing my name with my initials, "M. R. Burgess," or even "Emar Burgess," and it was then that I started looking for some unique moniker of my own. I couldn't possibly employ my real name on my own writings ever again.

I had been reading the complete works of "Saki," the byline of H. H. Munro, who, together with a great many other British writers of his generation, had been killed in the trenches in France during World War I. Saki's work appealed to me for its wry humor, ironic situations, and clever plot devices. One of his major story cycles featured a very sophisticated Brit, "Reginald," and so I thought highly appropriate the appropriation of a pen name's fictional character as my own pseudonym. I added the initial "R." in front of Reginald, thereby making it a complete byline.

Of course, I immediately started getting inquiries as to what the "R." stood for. Folks just naturally assumed that it was taken from my middle name. But I had actually been named for my grandfather, whose forename I regarded as rather old-fashioned and wholly unsuitable for the image that I wished to project, and so I employed "Robert" instead.

Eventually, of course, Gerson died; he had long ceased using the name "Michael Burgess" by then, and as the books in questionable objection faded from public view, so did my objections to employing my real name as a byline. Unfortunately, by then I had already established a reputation under my pen name; indeed, far more people in the publishing business knew me as "Robert Reginald" than they did as "Michael Burgess," and while I never made a secret of the connection, neither did I much advertise it. Also, for many years my writing career was regarded as an impediment to my advancement in academe, and so I kept the two spheres of my life completely separate, being careful to work on my writing and editorial projects only on my own time.

I established a joint bank account in both names, both to pay and receive, had stationary printed under both names, and eventually added "Boden Clarke" and a few other one-shot-ers to my long list of *noms de plume*.

Now, I suppose psychiatrists would find some deep significance in the fact that I shadowed most of my creative life under the aegis of a pen name—and still do, for that mat-

Xenograffiti, by ROBERT REGINALD

ter—but the truth is, I was a very shy lad as a teenager. My parents consistently pooh-poohed my interest in science fiction and fantasy literature, and rarely expressed approval of any kind of my writing, a pattern which continued into my adulthood. There was always an aura of disdain surrounding my literary efforts, as great as they were, and I lacked the confidence to plunge boldly forward where no man had gone before, at least until I left home in 1969.

So the adoption of a pseudonym was perhaps my teenage way of saying, "foo on you" back at them, while trying to establish my own unique personality and to find some imagined country where I felt comfortable within my own skin.

At any rate, once I had established a career as "Robert Reginald," it was too late to turn back the hour hands again. "Rob Reginald" I had become, and "Rob Reginald" I shall remain, until the end of my days.

And, truth be told, when I'm writing as Reginald, I'm a different person in many respects than "Professor Michael Burgess," the respectable and respected and rather stuffy academic librarian. One of my colleagues, after reading the introduction to *Katydid & Other Critters,* my short story collection, proclaimed rather perplexedly, "Why, that doesn't sound like you at all!"

Of course not! When I write, I think differently and act differently and communicate differently than when I talk, and I'm still a far better writer than I am a speaker (that shyness again). It's as if I put on a cloak of creativity, and associations and stories and anecdotes miraculously appear through my fingers and are dispersed upon the written page. I don't know how the process works, but it does work.

Within myself, there is no conflict. One part of my life enriches the other—or so I hope. My experiences as a librarian, and the knowledge that I have gained thereby, have added appreciably to my worth as an author, and I trust the opposite is true as well.

But there are times and there are days when I feel like the schizoid man, divided into two incompatible halves, one creative, one practical, one impulsive, one calculating, one plus one plus one....

237

Xenograffiti, by ROBERT REGINALD

Most of the time, though, being a pseudonym just doubles my pleasure and doubles my fun, with enough occasional confusion for anyone!

Xenograffiti, by ROBERT REGINALD

XLIII.

SELECTED REVIEWS

(1971-1993)

(1971)

Anderson, Poul. *The Broken Sword.* New York: Ballantine Books, 1971.

Sometimes, when I'm particularly weary at the end of a day's efforts, when my head is aching and my bod fatigued, I enjoy just listening to a good story. Don't particularly want to work at it, you understand, and really don't want to be eased into that profoundest of critical judgments, sleep. *The Broken Sword* is a good book for such a time, for Poul Anderson, whatever else he may or may not be as a writer, has been from the very start of his career a damn good storyteller.

I remember how, years ago, my father would take my brothers and me out into the woods; and how at night, by the only light available—the moon and a small campfire—we'd gather round the warmth, hands and faces burning in the heat, backs a shiver with the forest chill—and he'd tell stories, grand, wondrous tales of adventure (mostly his own), of war and hunting and logging, of human foibles and human grandeur, of little things that made us want to laugh or feel sad. He was very good at what he did, and I'm sorry I could never convince him to write them down.

And somehow, in a very small but analogous way, I think that this was much as it must have been centuries ago, when violent men would gather together at the end of a (per-

Xenograffiti, by ROBERT REGINALD

haps literally) bone-shattering day and call for the bards and the singers. They'd be entertained, by the gods, and pity the tunesmith who failed to do so: ridicule was the best he could hope for, laughter all he deserved.

The feeling of listening to an heroic saga produced by the skillful interposition of a personal narrator between story and reader is achieved remarkable well in *The Broken Sword*. Form, language, and story all work as one to simulate a Nordic air; particularly effective is the use by the major characters of short, unrhymed verses, or staves, in a regular trochaic meter: these are generally reserved for songs and charms, or times of particular stress and importance, such as the beginning of major battles or love scenes. In combination with occasionally semi-archaic language and phrasing, this sprinkling of poetry does much to imply the world Anderson attempts to create. It's remarkable to find verse handled with any sort of finesse within the text of a larger fictional work; that both mesh as well as they do is a tribute to the author's skill.

The tale itself fits the setting well. In a medieval world of elves and trolls and mortal men, Anderson mixes together a grand war, a curse, an ill-destined but truly wondrous love, a possessed sword, a few defrocked gods (and some others, including the Christian one, who are very potent indeed), and a berserker-doppelgänger, to produce an assortment of bloody battles, behind-the-scenes machinations, and cutthroat politics. The Nordic philosophy of subtle predestination permeates the story, and indeed, one wonders at times if the characters ever truly act with freedom, or if the story is all part of some vast chess game played by one group of the gods against another. And yet this, too, adds to the calculated effect, and heightens the tragedies that fill this book. The plot itself is so tightly spun that although the inevitable ending can be spied long ahead, one's only desire is to reach the last page. And once finished, the book is put away with sadness.

In a new introduction to this revised edition (*The Broken Sword* was originally published in hardcover in 1954), Anderson half apologizes for a work written early in his career, in a style quite unlike that of his later work.

Xenograffiti, by ROBERT REGINALD

You're too modest, old man: you've written one hell of a good story, perhaps a minor classic in its field, and this reader, at any rate, is willing to trade a flagon of ale for the pleasure. Name your way house.

Anderson makes one final comment: "As for what became of those who were still alive at the end of the book, and the sword, and Faerie itself—which obviously no longer exists on Earth—that is another tale, which may someday be told." Aye, let us hope so.

Carter, Lin, editor. *Golden Cities, Far.* New York: Ballantine Books, 1970.

I guess I'm just spoiled, or maybe a wee bit cynical, but whatever it is, I haven't the patience these days to put up with a dull book. Even dull heroic fantasy. And whatever merits this book has (there are a few), I find myself quite unable to participate in the delights so joyously heralded on its cover. I feel almost guilty about this, as if I've deserted an old friend: Lin Carter's gilded cane comes tap-tap-tapping on my shoulder, and turning, I find his pointed beard nodding up and down as he asks where my "sense of wonder" has flown. Quite truthfully, Lin, I don't know; wherever it is, though, it's not in your book.

Golden Cities, Far is the third fantasy anthology to appear in the Ballantine Adult Fantasy series, in what seems to be an annual Fall event. Mr. Carter originally set the theme for these anthologies when he confined the first of his books, *Dragons, Elves, and Heroes*, to stories published before the advent of William Morris, leaving his second volume, *The Young Magicians*, to writers flourishing primarily in the twentieth century. *Cities* is akin to the first volume, and includes material gathered from several cultures, East and West, covering a span of some 3000 or more years (c1500 B.C. to the nineteenth century). Carter draws from what is obviously a vast storehouse of knowledge on the field to provide extensive notes, biographies, publishing histories, and running commentaries on each piece.

But the anthology fails to work, and it falls apart on the very point on which it is most touted: entertainment value. Any story, old or new, must be sufficiently interesting

Xenograffiti, by ROBERT REGINALD

to hold the reader's attention, or he or she will turn on the tube, pick up his newspaper, or whatever. The enthusiasm I felt for *Cities* may be summarized by a wide yawn and an ardent desire to go to bed.

It's not that the stories are poor—they are all competent representatives of their respective periods—but what was great writing centuries ago is often only laughable today, a footnote somewhere in a dusty literature text. Perhaps the most indicting statement I can make about *Cities* is that it would serve admirably in that function, as a fine text for some future survey course in the antecedents of fantastic literature. There's no sophistication in these tales: they are simplistic, naive, contrived; fairyland is just over the next hill with an odd name attached, viewed through the infamous rose-tinted spectacles. Simplicity is not a fault *per se*—William Morris is a fine example of a writer whose simply-drawn characters and settings mesh to produce some of the most memorable fantasy novels ever written—but when it results in lack of understanding and failure in story conception and realization, then the reader's time is better spent elsewhere.

However, all is not rotten in Fairyland, and there is fiction of value to be found among the aureate towns. Three stories are worth note: the two selections from *Amadis of Gaul*, "Arcalaus the Enchanter" and "The Isle of Wonders," are fascinating prose extravaganzas, and leave one hoping that the entire work will someday be reprinted under the unicorn's head. "The Palace of Illusions," a new prose translation from the classic epic, *Orlando Furioso*, is a curiously puzzling work that jumps from character to character and event to event in a foreshadowing of the Edgar Rice Burroughs writing technique, some 400 years removed. Although frustrating in its incompleteness, the story leaves one interested in reading the tale intact. Ballantine intends to publish the work in 1971.

In an introduction to *Golden Cities, Far*, the publisher tells us that "there is, perhaps, no reading matter so flagrantly devoted to pure pleasure than adult fantasy." I agree. I only wish that Betty Ballantine had paid more at-

Xenograffiti, by ROBERT REGINALD

tention to her own words. What I hold in my minds is potentiality unfilled. Lin Carter can do much better.

Morris, William. *The Well at the World's End.* New York: Ballantine Books, 1970, 2 vols.

Some books survive just for their usefulness, and others because they are representative of their times, and there a few, a very few, that outlast the years from sheer beauty of composition. William Morris's *The Well at the World's End* is such a book: its calm brilliance, its quiet, gentle people, the almost-medieval world, one step the other side of reality, are enough to take one's breath away. In some respects it is neither an easy book to read nor to judge: originally published in 1896, it is long, one of the longest heroic fantasies ever penned; it is written in a purposely archaic tongue, created and patterned (but not quite the same as) late medieval English; its pace and rhythm are considerably slower than most modern readers are accustomed to; and its plot and resolution, which seem on the surface perhaps overly simplified or romanticized, are in reality exceedingly complex and interwoven. Yet for all these "defects," if they are defects, *Well* remains one of the finest examples of its genre, a true classic of imaginative literature.

Superficially, this is a quest story, telling of one Ralph, son to the Kinglet of Upmeads, and how he came to the Well at the World's End, and what became thereof; but it would not be stretching matters to say that the book celebrates the journey of a boy into the world, and his discovery of himself and what it means to be a man—a journey that every man must take. As such, the work has universal application and meaning, particularly in a time as seething and unsettled as our own. It may be difficult for us to visualize the Victorian period as one of upheaval, but to Morris it certainly was. He deeply resented the materialism of his age, the mass-merchandizing which he believed dehumanized the ordinary worker into just another cog in the industrial machine. In the face of continual change, Morris found only one thing constant: the beauty of a simple and uncomplicated way of life, a beauty he believed was incarnated in the

243

medieval period, a beauty he embraced with his entire soul. In a way he never grew up. This is not a book to swallow down in gulps. Sip at it slowly, gradually—let it softly overcome your mind. You will find both sex and violence here—Morris was far from being a prude—but you will also uncover something rarely seen in today's literature: a deep sense of peace and surety in man and his world. And wonder, wonder that something so filled with beauty could exist in words. There are those who say it is impossible to love a book. However that may be, if it *is* possible, here is one well worth the devotion.

(1975)

Wisconsin. The State Historical Society, Madison Library. Author-Title Catalog. New York: Greenwood Press, 1974, microfiche.

This is another in an apparently unending series of library catalogs issued during the last decade by various reprint houses. And, in the sense that it provides access to the rather specialized holdings of this lesser-known library, it is to be welcomed, particularly by interlibrary loan departments. This kind of publication must by its very nature have a limited audience; the more specialized the library, the less need will be evidenced for its catalog. In this particular instance, the Library of the State Historical Society of Wisconsin has large holdings in regional history, local genealogy and family history, American history (especially of the Wisconsin region and the Old Northwest), the American Trade Union movement (the John R. Commons Collection), plus extensive newspaper resources from colonial times to date. Still, the appeal of the catalog will probably be primarily local, with some additional interest from very large university or public libraries specializing in labor or American history, and possibly from highly-developed genealogy collections. There will be much less interest from the medium-size college library, or from most public libraries.

The material itself is divided into two parts: an author-title listing on fiche, and a bound subject catalog. Not having seen the latter, I will confine my remarks to the fiche publications. From the eight samples I was provided, it appears that the catalog is divided into three sections. The first is a simple author-title listing. Part Two is an index to city directories arranged by state, city, and date of publication. The third section, a newspaper listing, appears to be arranged by country, city, and title, but the sample provided is too brief for me to be certain. Each fiche contains thirty images. A typical image includes three columns of cards produced from the library's main catalog. Legible headers provide access to the content of each fiche.

On the whole, the catalog is hard to read and even harder to follow. While the fiche themselves have an acceptable reduction ratio, and appear to be of good physical quality, the original typed material is in many instances quite faint, and no micro-reproduction handled on this kind of scale can really improve on the original. One must work very hard indeed to follow the progression of entries from one column of cards to another. The newspaper listing is perhaps the easiest and clearest section to use; however, it comprises only a small part of the whole, and is not typical of the rest in quality. Even a dedicated scholar would be hard-pressed to spend more than a few moments working through the main part of the catalog.

The advertisement included with the set states that the bound subject catalog includes a special introduction by Charles Shetler describing the collection in detail and explaining the use of the catalog. But, unless he provides details I have not already seen, I cannot recommend this set to any but the most specialized libraries, or those located in or near Wisconsin itself.

(1979)

Allard, Yvon. *Paralittératures.* Montréal: La Centrale des Bibliothèques, 1979.

Allard's monumental bibliography provides thorough coverage in French of what he calls "paralittératures," or genre literatures, including fairy tales, fantasy (encompassing horror and supernatural fiction), adventure and suspense stories, romances, historical novels, detective and spy novels,

Xenograffiti, by ROBERT REGINALD

westerns, science fiction, and humor. Each section includes an introductory essay outlining the history of each genre, plus general background information. Then Allard provides an annotated bibliography of reference works on that particular genre, including specialty periodicals, historical studies and critiques, a selected list of important book reviews and critical articles from a wide variety of sources, a brief author dictionary, with a critical evaluation of each author's career and a bibliography of further sources of study, a list of publishers' series, mention of important anthologies in each field (listed by title), and, as a major part of each chapter, a selective, annotated bibliography of major fictional works in each "paralittérature." The latter are arranged in alphabetical order by author, then by title of the work in French: French or Canadian publishers are cited for the main entries, and complete bibliographical and price information is provided for each book. The titles of English or foreign-language original editions are mentioned after the French versions. A few important books that have not been translated into French are listed under their English-language titles and publishers, as are most of the nonfiction sources included. Allard's annotations are brief, descriptive, and often witty, with summary evaluations; on the whole his judgments seem fair and balanced. This book is particularly important for the large number of French and European authors included who have not had their works translated into English, and whose careers as SF writers are therefore unknown to most historians of the genre. Many of these writers deserve wider dissemination of their fictions. *Paralittératures* is attractively bound in green cloth. The text is readable and nicely balanced in a double-column format, with the use of boldfaced type easily to distinguish the authors' names from the works being annotated. A comprehensive index of authors and titles occupies the last hundred pages of the book. This is a major contribution to the study of popular literature, a mandatory purchase for all academic libraries worthy of the name. American scholars have long neglected European genre literature; Allard's bibliography demonstrates that there is much here worthy of further consideration. A thoroughly fine piece of work.

Xenograffiti, by ROBERT REGINALD

Ashley, Mike. *The John Spencer Fantasy Publications.* Wallsend, Tyne & Wear, England: Cosmos Literary Agency, 1979.

This is the first in a very useful series of bibliographies published by Philip Harbottle, the man who unraveled the bibliographical tangle that was John Russell Fearn. The Spencer publications have proven particularly difficult problems for SF researchers: they are difficult to locate for examination purposes, and difficult to elucidate, since most were penned under house pseudonyms. Ashley has done an admirable job in identifying the vast majority of the real authors behind these books, and in providing a complete checklist of Spencer's SF and fantasy publications, both magazine and book. He also includes a short history of the firm, and two sample stories from among the hundreds that they published. An auspicious beginning.

Bulmer, Kenneth, writing as Alan Burt Akers. *Golden Scorpio.* New York: DAW Books, 1978.

While no one will confuse the Dray Prescot series with great literature, Akers's world is more sophisticated than most in this genre, and significantly better constructed. This pseudonymous author obviously is well-versed in military history, particularly naval history, and uses this knowledge to good advantage. The series as a whole has clearly been plotted well in advance, leaving just enough loose ends from book to book, and cycle to cycle, to keep the faithful reader intrigued. A cut above most heroic fantasy, and pleasant, if light, reading.

Caprio, Betsy. *Star Trek: Good News in Modern Images.* Mission, KS: Sheed, Andrews & McMeel, 1978.
Blair, Karin. *Meaning in Star Trek.* New York: Warner Books, 1979.

Caprio's book is an interesting, if somewhat perplexing, approach to the phenomenon of *Star Trek*. The material seems aimed at the young or pre-teen level, with chapters on various topics followed by "Energizer" or workbook sections intended to be completed by the reader. The emphasis on religious themes makes it unsuitable for classroom use, except in church schools, where it is unlikely to find a home. The only other logical market is the "Trekker" or completist collector, who may be intrigued with Caprio's obsession with trivia. The one truly valuable section is a complete listing of the seventy-nine original *Star Trek* episodes, cross-referenced to the James Blish paperback adaptions; the book is also indexed. Overall, though, Caprio's study has little value for the average reader. While it is legitimate to point out common themes between secular and religious literature, the problem with linking them so specifically is that other, equally significant themes may be lost or discarded in the process.

Blair's study, on the other hand, is more interesting. This reprint of the 1977 Anima Books edition is an intelligent and believable tapestry of mythological meaning against the space/time continuum through which the starship *Enterprise* moves from the known to the unknown. Proceeding from the premise that *Star Trek* enjoyed a popularity which far transcended its position as a "pop" culture fad, the author provides insights into the probable causes for the show's continued success. Drawing upon a wide range of mythological lore and philosophical thought, especially Jungian psychology, Blair makes her connections with ease and credibility.

Blair sees the starship and its crew as archetypes of human sensibility; in particular, she finds significance in the shape of the ship itself, a circular body (representing the feminine side of consciousness) propelled by cigar-shaped (masculine) power modules. The circle, as symbol of a total and complete unity, also represents the Bridge, where most of the decisions are made. Kirk, at the center of the Bridge, represents the synthesis of both masculine and feminine (conscious and unconscious) qualities. The polarities on either side of the captain are embodied in the characters of Spock and McCoy, whose personalities also represent the emotional (McCoy) and the logical (Spock) aspects of human nature.

Blair draws upon specific incidents to illustrate the tensions inherent in these polarities: young/old, female/male, good/evil. Although it is problematical whether the show's creator, Gene Roddenberry, or subsequent writers had such things in mind, it seems logical that the subsequent popularity of the program could reflect deep, subconscious urges in all of us which strike chords of sympathy. Blair falls prey to her own description of the feminine being possessed by the animus when, in her conclusion, she idealizes Spock. She finds in him the archetype, Number, which combines the qualitative and the quantitative, feeling and intellect; he becomes the perfect mediator for woman, whose role has historically been subjugated to that of man. Although Blair feels that *Star Trek* itself is guilty of such subjugation (and she makes a good case for it), she believes that Spock can point a way to a "new" relationship between men and women, a balanced union of androgynies who have successfully defeated the "fear of flying."

—with Mary A. Burgess

Coffman, C. C. *Spacedust One.* New York: Vantage Press, 1979.
Cirilius, Marcus. *Prehistoric Epic!* New York: Vantage Press, 1978.
Jenkins, Harry. *An Affair of Survival: A Novel.* New York: Vantage Press, 1979.
Campbell, Clive S. *The Day the Sun Came Through.* New York: Vantage Press, 1979.
Annan, Ralph. *The Spider-Men: A Science-Fantasy Adventure.* New York: Vantage Press, 1979.

Vantage Press is the largest of the subsidy or "vanity" publishers, houses which require their authors to pay the cost of printing their own books. Others of the same ilk include Exposition Press, Carlton Press, Dorrance & Co., and Ashley Books. Subsidy publishers differ from trade publishers in many respects: they generally lack trade distribution to bookstores, and advertise fitfully, if at all, making it very difficult for the outsider to determine exactly what they have published; this situation is compounded by the large number of books each imprint produces (Vantage Press's annual output numbers in the hundreds of volumes). They are also unusual in that they advertise widely to *get* new books and authors, soliciting manuscripts in newspaper and magazines nationally. Vantage maintains offices in four cities: New York, Washington, Atlanta, and Hollywood. Most publishers are so inundated by unsolicited manuscripts that they place restrictions on who may submit and what may be submitted; many refuse to read unsolicited books altogether. Subsidy publishers will usually stock a particular book for two years or less, and then either pulp the remainder or offer the stock to the author at a reduced price.

Most vanity press authors know very little about publishing; indeed, many have never had any of their work published professionally. They believe that the mere act of printing a book may gain them fame, fortune, or at least notoriety; in truth, however, few of these books and fewer of these authors have ever gathered much notice. There have been a handful of subsidy press bestsellers, to be sure, and another handful of books published by these houses have sold moderately well; most, however, die the death of anonymity, being sold or given away to the authors' friends. Of the hundred or so vanity press science fiction and fantasy novels published, none have ever been sold for reprint to the mass market paperback publishers.

The five books under consideration here are typical of most subsidy publications. Cover art ranges from adequate to atrocious. Binding and typesetting are average to good in quality, with the usual number of typos present, and only one major error noted (the transposition of two pages of text in *Spacedust One*). The books are all bound in cloth, thereby restricting the potential market almost exclusively to libraries, although most libraries will not buy vanity press books as a matter of course. Prices are average for today's market, although perhaps excessive for the smaller books.

The best of the lot is *Spacedust*, a collection of four short stories by a Marine Corps major. Coffman is evidently familiar with weapons, tactics, and hand-to-hand combat, and uses his knowledge to good stead. He is less proficient with dialogue and characterization. Two of the stories, "Gopa" and "Magician," are close to professional pulp level; the remaining pair, "The Welcome" and "Winner Take All," are amateurish gimmick stories with trick endings that the average reader will spy long in advance. The drawings by Kay Niman Fish are no more than adequate.

Prehistoric Epic! by "Marcus Cirilius" is a mixture of the author's personal philosophy, lengthy exposition, and a thin veneer of story. Characterization is nonexistent. I found it utterly unreadable. *An Affair of Survival* is a political novel of the year 2025 by a former Associated Press editor. This reactionary little diatribe has America smashing each of its enemies into the ground in turn, as it defends its national interests with a cold-bloodedness that Napoleon would certainly have admired. By conquering the Arab oil states, the U.S. naturally secures a rapprochement with the Soviet Union, and peace seems secure for the first time in decades. I didn't believe a word of it.

The Day the Sun Came Through is a short expository tale telling how men became gods through the intervention of outside alien entities. There are no characters as such, and the story is amateurish at best. *The Spider-Men* is straight pulp adventure: a cripple is bit on the wrist by an unusual arachnid, and finds himself shrinking down to the level of the insects—and once again whole in body, if diminutive in size. There he finds himself fighting the mutated spider-men, and must try to rescue the beautiful Aronell. This could have appeared in any of the 1930s pulp magazines.

Of the five books reviewed, none really reach professional standards, although three are at least readable. For completists only.

Diamond, Graham. *Dungeons of Kuba: Adventures of the Empire Princess #2.* New York: Playboy Press, 1979.

Stacy, the Empire Princess, and her lover, Fleet Commander Elias, must forego the pleasures of hearth and home when threatened by the expansionist tyrant Sigried, the Rani of Kuba. To complicate the plot further, Stacy embarks on a journey to Kuba disguised as a Satrian noblewoman, Lady Kesa. She is accompanied by her retainers, Melinda and Alryc, and her old-time companion and mentor, the wolf Cicero. After a myriad of predictable difficulties and tiresome confrontations, Siggy is contained in an emotional denouement. This silly sequel to *The Haven* and *Lady of the*

Haven is, if anything, even less interesting than its predecessors. The dialogue is trite and stilted, the characters wooden and unbelievable. The whole wretched mess reads like a soap opera penned by Robert E. Howard for Raquel Welch. One can only hope that Stacy and Elias have finally come to the end of the road, and will venture forth no more.

—*with Mary A. Burgess*

Diamond, Graham. *Lady of the Haven: Adventures of the Empire Princess.* New York: Playboy Press, 1978.

Nigel, father of the Lady Anastasia, has carved out the beginnings of a civilization with the help of the forest dwellers, packs of wolves which were once the enemies of man and have now become his allies. At the beginning of this sequel to *The Haven* (1978), Anastasia is preparing to return home after spending some time as apprentice to the wolves under the guardianship of Nigel's close friend, Hector. She is troubled by the thought of returning to civilization; at the same time, she is intrigued by a story told by an old White Wolf, who faintly remembers crossing the sea to this land from another.

Returning home, she confronts her father, a member of the ruling Council, with a plan for heading a colonizing expedition to this unknown land. Cicero, a renegade wolf, will travel with her to communicate with the White Wolves, should the unknown realm prove hostile.

Diamond's book is an interesting twist on an old theme, men-raised-with-animals. But his novel is marred, not only by jarring anachronisms (Anastasia, for example, becomes "Stacy"), but more seriously by a compromise with the originality of the premise, and through shallow, stereotyped characters. It is difficult to feel much sympathy with Anastasia and her problems: we know that everything will turn out well in the end. Curiously, the wolves are much more interesting types than their human masters. But that's often the case, isn't it?

—*with Mary A. Burgess*

Gilman, Charlotte Perkins. *Herland.* New York: Pantheon Books, 1979.

Xenograffiti, by ROBERT REGINALD

This is an important addition to utopian and feminist literature collections. Gilman is best known for her novella, *The Yellow Wallpaper* (1892), which documents her bitter and frustrating experiences with psychoanalysis following post-partum depression. However, as Ann Lane states in her perceptive introduction: "...*The Yellow Wallpaper* represents a woman in torment; *Herland* a woman at play." *Herland* is the second part of a trilogy comprising *Moving the Mountain* (1911), *Herland* (1915), and *Ourland* (1916), which deals with the possibility of a future utopian society ruled by women. This section is the most successful of the three, and comparable in theme to Edward Bellamy's *Looking Backward, 2000-1887*, although its somewhat simplistic solutions are reminiscent to William Morris's novel, *News from Nowhere* (the classic reply to Bellamy's regimented society of the future).

Three young men stumble into a "lost" kingdom of women. At first they are bemused—the place is civilized, therefore men *must* be in control somewhere! The trio soon learn that the land has remained sealed off from the outside world for about 2000 years. All men having been killed in battle, the race has been perpetuated through parthenogenesis, resulting only in girl offspring. The newcomers are captured, educated in the language and mores of the land, and eventually made grooms for three chosen girls. The results are disastrous: two of the men manage to adapt, but the third resorts to violent rape of his bride, who does not comprehend his "animal" desires. Violence is not condoned by the ladies, and the man is exiled: one couple returns with him to "civilization," and one stays behind.

All of this is unbelievable, but Gilman writes with conviction and charm, managing to get her point across: the world would be a better place if left to the sensitivity of women governors. Her strongest message is the women's perception of themselves as "people"; the brides regard their husbands primarily as "friends." There is a strong sense of peace and lack of stress in this ideal society, which is perhaps unattainable under the best of circumstances. Gilman paints an idealized portrait which makes us wish it were all possible. Upon completion of her autobiography in 1935,

Xenograffiti, by ROBERT REGINALD

and terminally ill with cancer, Gilman ended her life the way she lived it, with courage and strength of purpose.
—with Mary A. Burgess

Hubin, Allen J. *The Bibliography of Crime Fiction, 1749-1975: Listing All Mystery, Detective, Suspense, Police, and Gothic Fiction in Book Form Published in the English Language.* Del Mar, CA: Publisher's Inc., 1979. According to Hubin:

> The intent of this bibliography is to list all adult crime fiction in book form in the English language published anywhere in the world through December 31, 1979. Thus included are: 1) novels, hardcover and paperback originals, both those first appearing in English and those published in English translations; 2) plays; and 3) short story collections (not anthologies) in which at least one story is crime fiction. Magazine and dime novel crime fiction is not included. "Crime fiction" is understood to comprise that fiction in which crime or the threat of crime is a principal plot element. Thus included are mystery, detective, police (procedural), suspense, thriller, and gothic (romantic suspense) fiction.

Hubin's work deserves mention here on several counts. His coverage of gothic and horror fiction includes many books that fall simultaneously into fantastic literature; in addition, he lists many supernatural and SF works with mystery elements. Also, many of the authors he covers later published books in other genres, including SF and fantasy; hence, Hubin's work provides supplemental listings of those authors' books for collectors and readers interested in pursuing their favorites further.

And it is clear, even at this early stage, that Hubin's book will become the standard bibliography of the field. Unlike Ordean Hagen's *Who Done It?* (Bowker, 1969),

Xenograffiti, by ROBERT REGINALD

Hubin's volume is well-organized, well-researched, and clearly based on a thorough knowledge of the genre in all its aspects. The author index provides complete names of authors, where known, years of birth and death, and a list of the mystery works published under that name, in alphabetical order by title. Title, publisher, and year of publication are listed. Books by the same author under other names are listed under those pseudonyms, with appropriate and copious cross references. Alternate titles of retitled publications are also given. The title index includes title and author only. There is also a brief series index, listed by character and keyed to the author's name. The reader must then refer back to the main entry in the author index to find the titles in the series, which are indicated by letter following the publication dates of the books. Supplements are planned for five-year intervals. For all serious collectors and researchers, and for any library worthy of the name, this is an absolutely necessary acquisition. Highly recommended.

Macaulay, David. *Motel of the Mysteries.* Boston: Houghton Mifflin Co., 1979.

This is simultaneously a spoof on modern civilization and the Tut-Ankh-Amen craze. In the year 4022 all of the ancient country of Usa has been buried under many feet of detritus from an ecological catastrophe that occurred way back in 1985. An amateur archeologist, Howard Carson, falls into a shaft near the perimeter of an abandoned excavation site, and is overjoyed to find what is obviously (judging from the DO NOT DISTURB sign hanging on the ancient doorknob) the entrance to a still-sealed and untouched burial chamber. Carson's incredible discoveries, including the actual remains of two bodies, one of them on a ceremonial bed facing an altar that appears to be a means of communicating with the gods, and the other lying in a porcelain sarcophagus in a separate "Inner Chamber," permit him to piece together the entire fabric of this extraordinary lost civilization. Macaulay provides dozens of satiric illustrations to go with his text, and the result is a marvelously entertaining exercise in social commentary. The book compares favorably with Robert Nathan's earlier satire, *The Weans* (1958). Perceptively funny, and highly recommended for all.

Mahr, Kurt. *Between the Galaxies.* Van Nuys, CA: Master Publications, 1978. Perry Rhodan #119.
Voltz, William. *Killers from Hyperspace.* Van Nuys, CA: Master Publications, 1978. Perry Rhodan #120.
Darlton, Clark. *Atom Fire on Mechanica.* Van Nuys, CA: Master Publications, 1978. Perry Rhodan #121.
Brand, Kurt. *Volunteers for Frago.* Van Nuys, CA: Master Publications, 1978. Perry Rhodan #122.
Mahr, Kurt. *Fortress in Time.* Van Nuys, CA: Master Publications, 1978. Perry Rhodan #123.
Brand, Kurt. *The Sinister Power.* Van Nuys, CA: Master Publications, 1978. Perry Rhodan #124.
Voltz, William. *Robots, Bombs, and Mutants.* Van Nuys, CA: Master Publications, 1979. Perry Rhodan #125.
Scheer, K. H. *The Guns of Everblack.* Van Nuys, CA: Master Publications, 1979. Perry Rhodan #126.
Darlton, Clark. *Sentinels of Solitude.* Van Nuys, CA: Master Publications, 1979. Perry Rhodan #127.
Mahr, Kurt. *The Beasts Below.* Van Nuys, CA: Master Publications, 1979. Perry Rhodan #128.
Brand, Kurt. *Blitzkrieg Galactica.* Van Nuys, CA: Master Publications, 1979. Perry Rhodan #129.
Brand, Kurt. *Peril Unlimited.* Van Nuys, CA: Master Publications, 1979. Perry Rhodan #130.

 The longest-running series in the history of science fiction, Perry Rhodan has reached some 900 weekly numbers in the German original. The first of the American translations appeared in May, 1969, with publication of the first two PR adventures together in one volume, *Enterprise Stardust*. From that beginning, the US series has been edited by Forrest J Ackerman, and the translations produced by Ackerman's wife, Wendayne, together with Sig Wahrman and Stuart J. Byrne. The Ace Books series began with five two-in-one volumes, then switched to monthly publication in 1971. The new version resembled a paperback magazine, with one Perry Rhodan novel, several short stories, and other continuing features. The format changed again in March, 1977, when the features were reduced, and the books expanded to again include two Perry Rhodan adventures.

At this point Ace apparently failed to reach an agreement with the German publisher to reprint new books in the series, and decided to use up its remaining inventory. The last book in the regular series was #117/118, published in August, 1977. Four more doubles were released during the last third of the year, comprised of five novels in an offshoot series, Atlan, and several miscellaneous novels in the sequence that had originally been skipped by Ackerman because they failed to advance the overall plot line. One final volume, a special double-length feature called *In the Center of the Galaxy*, was published by Ace in January, 1978.

Ackerman has since claimed that Ace negotiated with Artur Moewig Verlag in bad faith, that they failed to notify the Germans that they were terminating their relationship (see Ackerman's editorial in #127). Other industry sources, however, put the blame on Moewig, saying that they made unreasonable financial demands for continuation of the series, and generally proved obstinate and obdurate. The truth probably lies somewhere in between. In any event, the Ackermans have apparently taken over publication of the series themselves under the name Master Publications, and are releasing six volumes in one batch every three months.

Perry Rhodan is an endless serial, the ultimate space opera of science fiction. The saga is broken into cycles of 50-100 episodes, each being plotted well in advance, individual episodes being assigned to one of twelve house writers. In the first episode, Major Perry Rhodan discovers during a Lunar expedition two members of an alien race, saves them, and with their aid founds the Third Power to stand between the Eastern and Western power blocs. In the third cycle, which includes the twelve books reviewed here, mankind's stellar empire is threatened by invasion from an extragalactic race of invisibles. In Germany the series has reached fourteen cycles ending with episode #1000.

This is pulp science fiction, action-oriented stories with minimal characterization and awful dialogue, but relatively complex plot development. The emphasis is always on man's expanding horizons, the wonder of science and space, and the great destiny of the human race. For relatively unsophisticated readers, and for adolescents in particular, this could be gripping stuff. The books are printed in trade paperback size (5 x 8") on poor quality paper, stapled through the spine, with two-color covers featuring a Perry Rhodan logo. The type, which runs in two columns throughout, is small but readable. The main appeal of the series will be to those already hooked on Perry Rhodan; however, collections should note that the limited distribution of these books will undoubtedly make them scarce in years to come.

Page, Spider. *Legend in Blue Steel.* New York: Python Books, 1979.

"It struck out of nowhere, a wave of mass murder that spelled wholesale slaughter. New York was panic-stricken. Beneath its reign of terror, the police were helpless. But grimly, out of the list of victims, rose a man—Blue Steel—who vowed to track the master killer to a murder showdown!"

The cover blurb says it all: this is a deliberate pastiche of pulp superhero fiction. Elsevier van Rijn is Blue Steel, a relentless crime fighter who is hated both by New York's criminal underground and the befuddled cops he's trying to aid. Van Rijn, a man of a thousand disguises, is assisted by his Indian butler, Tara Khan, his not-too-bright girlfriend, Brenda Morgan, and associate Dustin Ayres, as he tracks down a mastermind of crime. The scientific miracles are kept to a minimum in this potboiler, but the gosh-wow style never lets up. I was reminded of the exploits of Richard Wentworth, the Spider, from the pulp of the same name. For those who like their fiction without any redeeming values.

Resnick, Michael. *The Official Price Guide to Comic & Science Fiction Books, Third Edition.* Orlando, FL: House of Collectibles, 1979.

This is an amalgamation of two books originally published separately as *The Official Guide to Comic Books* and *The Official Guide to Fantastic Literature* (also called on the

Xenograffiti, by ROBERT REGINALD

cover *Official Guide to the Fantastics*), the latter having been published in 1976. Both are reproduced virtually verbatim, with minimal changes in prices, and almost no changes in text. There is no indication in this new edition that the material has been previously published, other than the nebulous tag "Third Edition" on the title page. The science fiction section begins on page 267.

The SF half of the book includes the following sections: introduction, the hero pulps, science fiction and fantasy magazines, general magazines, fanzines, Edgar Rice Burroughs, hardcover books—the specialty publishers and hardcover books—the general publishers, paperback books, *Star Trek* materials, radio and television premiums, and miscellaneous collectibles. Resnick does not attempt to be comprehensive: his avowed intent is to give "a fairly comprehensive cross-section of authors and some of their representative works." The specialty press section seems to have been derived from Owings and Chalker's *Index to the Science-Fantasy Publishers*. No bibliographical information is provided to identify editions; prices are listed for books in "good" and "fine" condition. The selection criteria for the section on general publishers are eccentric at best: many relatively obscure books are included, and other, more popular items are left out, for no apparent reason. Many of the modern writers are covered only by brief, all-inclusive statements of dubious authority: "The works of Andre Norton, in first-edition hardcover with dust jackets, are worth about $10 apiece the moment they go out of print. She has about 18 titles in print at this time." This may well be true, but it provides no help for the reader or librarian or book store owner who is trying to assign a value to a particular item. Generalities, unsupported by any apparent experience in pricing or selling science fiction books, abound. Changes in pricing structure since the 1976 edition are minimal: I compared two pages from the earlier book to the same pages in the new edition, and found only one price revision in each, during a period when inflation drove the prices of OP science fiction books right through the roof. Most of the books listed seem, in comparison to dealers' catalogs issued by L. W. Currey, Barry R. Levin, or Kaleidoscope Books, greatly undervalued, although some few are overpriced. As a guide to the uninformed, this book is utterly useless. The section on Edgar Rice Burroughs, however, is both comprehensive and accurate, and seems to reflect a personal interest in Burroughsiana by Resnick. *Caveat emptor.*

Sabrina. *Witch Bitch,* bound with *Dance of Love,* by Martine. New York: Pleasure Books, 1979.
Trainor, Sandy. *Future Sex.* New York: Pleasure Books, 1979. Cover byline reads Sharon Taylor.
Trainor, Starr. *Pleasure Planet.* New York: Pleasure Books, 1979. Cover byline reads Sharon Taylor.

Four erotic novels from the sinister hand of Manor Books. *Witch Bitch* starts out as a standard sex novel, but then develops into a rather compelling tale of sexual and moral corruption, as the first-person narrator, Harry, is led with his wife into the bowels of a devil-worshipping cult. It is only at the end, when Satan himself finally appears, that Harry takes the ultimate step, willingly sacrificing his wife at the climax of a black mass, and thereby sacrificing his own identity, as he is renamed Agonaces by his master. Bound with this book is *Dance of Love,* an end-of-the-world tale of the final days on Earth, in which a frantic mankind waits for the Sun to explode. Without the explicit sex scenes, this too could have been compelling fiction. Men struggle to find some way out of their dilemma, but there is no reprieve to this grim narrative, and ultimately even the narrator is incinerated in the flaming denouement.

Future Sex is typical erotica: Alan Spindrift (love those names!) is a Lieutenant in the Inter-Planetary Services Command, his particular assignment being security surveillance. Spindrift uses his position in this totalitarian world of the future to gain sexual access (what else?) to the beauties he spies over his monitoring system. Alas, there is little evidence of imagination of any kind, much less sexual, and the writing is clumsy at best. *Pleasure Planet* is an equally awkward hodge-podge, a cross between pulp SF and hardcore porn. Major Ray Jetstream has landed on the planet Zephyr, the so-called "Pleasure Planet," for a period of rest and recreation. The rest of the book is devoted to an explicit account of his playtime. Plot and characterizations are non-existent, of course. Two to avoid.

Vinicoff, Eric, and Marcia Martin. *Spacing Dutchman.* Berkeley, CA: Aesir Press, 1978.
Here's a fusion of pulp SF and the mystery genre that's not half bad. Hans Bergenholm is sent to the *Spacing Dutchman*, a hollowed-out asteroid-cum-space station in permanent Earth orbit, to locate a super spy who keeps popping up every decade or so. Fritz Reismann had first appeared during the Second World War on the German side, and was killed at the end of that conflict; mysteriously, however, he rose from the grave in 1956 and was killed again two years later; and again in 1975, 1982, 1996, 2012, and so forth. Now there is evidence to place him on the *Spacing Dutchman*, the one vital link between Earth and its colonies. Bergenholm fears that Reismann is on to something big, something vital to world interests. Vinicoff and Martin keep the action moving fast enough so the reader doesn't have time to think. Hans is aided by Contessa Valarie de Samario, Police Chief of the asteroid colony, plus a portable computer plug-in unit that generates an image of Sherlock Holmes to help him over the more difficult areas of deduction. Ultimately, of course, Hans and cohorts solve the mystery and save the day. Fun if you don't take it too seriously.

Wurfel, Clifford. *An Introduction to the J. Lloyd Eaton Collection of Science Fiction and Fantasy.* Riverside, CA: Special Collections Dept., University Library, University of California, Riverside, 1979.

Smith, Lynn S. *Space Voyages, 1591-1920: A Bibliography of Works Held in the Library of the University of California, Riverside.* Riverside, CA: Special Collections Dept., University Library, University of California, Riverside, 1979.

Dr. J. Lloyd Eaton (8 July 1902-22 December 1968) was a private collector in the 1940s and '50s who had the time, money, and inclination to establish one of the better private collections of fantastic literature then in existence. After his death, his widow sold the collection to a discerning

Xenograffiti, by ROBERT REGINALD

University Librarian, the late Donald Wilson, at the University of California, Riverside. It took ten years for the University to catalog the 8,000 volumes that formed the core of his collection, but as these books began to find their way into public view, it became increasingly obvious that this is one of the finest assemblies of science fiction and fantasy literature available for general use by scholars and researchers anywhere in the world. It includes some outstanding rarities, among them the original editions of *Varney the Vampyre* and *King of the Dead*, as well as many unique or nearly unique signed copies or variant editions of classics in the field. The collection is strongest in pre-1955 materials, although the Library has made an effort in recent years to supplement its holdings by purchasing several large paperback and magazine collections, as well as several repositories of foreign-language SF books, almost impossible to locate anywhere else in the United States.

Wurfel's introduction to the collection provides a brief overview of the history of science fiction literature, plus a brief history of the Eaton Collection itself. Lynn's work is an annotated bibliography of particularly rare or unusual interplanetary novels included in the collection, with complete bibliographical information, references to other standard bibliographies, and a brief plot summary of each book. The publication of these two volumes, and the extraordinary vision demonstrated by the University of California in acquiring and maintaining this collection, should be welcomed by all persons interested in serious science fiction scholarship and research into popular and utopian literature.

(1980)

Bretnor, Reginald, editor. *Modern Science Fiction: Its Meaning and Its Future.* Chicago: Advent:Publishers, 1979.

This reprint of the 1953 Coward-McCann edition includes a new introduction, corrections, and an index not provided in the original version, but is otherwise a facsimile of the first anthology of science fiction criticism ever published. The contributors include such notables as John W. Campbell,

Xenograffiti, by ROBERT REGINALD Jr., Anthony Boucher, Don Fabun, Fletcher Pratt, Rosalie Moore, L. Sprague de Camp, Isaac Asimov, Arthur C. Clarke, Philip Wylie, Gerald Heard, and Bretnor himself. While some of the pieces remain entertaining and perceptive some thirty years after their initial publication, much of the commentary has been seriously dated by the subsequent history and development of the field. Boucher's article on "The Publishing of Science Fiction," for example, is of historical interest only; other chapters suffer from SF's "chip-on-the-shoulder" syndrome so evident in the 1950s, being filled with self-justifications and rationales offered in a half-apologetic way. Academic libraries which never obtained the original edition should certainly buy this quaintly antique volume, the ancestor of all SF critical anthologies, but the rest of us can safely pass it by.

Grebens, G. V. *Ivan Efremov's Theory of Science Fiction.* New York: Vantage Press, 1978.

In the first book-length study of the best-known writer from the middle period of Soviet science fiction, Dr. Grebens examines Efremov's work (much of which has never been translated into English) from several different angles, showing how he used technology, futurology, and psychohistory to produce a utopian vision of a far-future Communist society. Grebens's judgments seem sound, his knowledge of the material thorough. The book is copiously footnoted, and the bibliography of secondary sources contains much of interest for the student of Soviet literature. Recommended for academic collections.

Scherwinsky, Felix. *Der Neologismen in der modernen französischen Science-Fiction.* Meisenheim am Glan, West Germany: Verlag Anton Hain, 1978.

Dr. Scherwinsky has taken eighteen original French-language novels from the 1960s and '70s, and provided a fascinating study of invented words as they occur in these books. The basic list is by theme: in each section the words are listed alphabetically in French, followed by their German-language equivalents. Scherwinsky then gives a sentence-length quotation from the original showing how each

Xenograffiti, by ROBERT REGINALD

word was used in context, with exact citations to books and page numbers. Each section is defined by subject. End matter includes a complete word list, a bibliography of the novels covered, a bibliography of secondary sources, an author index, and a name index to invented planets, places, things, aliens, and characters. Without comparing this book to the novels covered, it is difficult to judge the study's comprehensiveness; yet there is no doubt that this is a valuable and utterly unique survey of the way in which modern French literature has adapted to the special terms and phrases required by the SF genre. A worthy addition to all academic libraries.

Schlobin, Roger C. *The Literature of Fantasy: A Comprehensive, Annotated Bibliography of Modern Fantasy Literature.* New York: Garland Publishing, 1979.
Tymn, Marshall B., Robert H. Boyer, Kenneth J. Zahorski. *Fantasy Literature: A Core Collection and Reference Guide.* New York: R. R. Bowker Co., 1979.
Waggoner, Diana. *The Hills of Faraway: A Guide to Fantasy.* New York: Atheneum, 1978.

In comparing Schlobin's work with his two competitors, Waggoner and Tymn/Boyer/Zahorski, one is struck by the differences and similarities between these books. All three cover the major works in the fantasy field. Tymn's work is a selective, annotated bibliography restricting to 250 works; the annotations are longer than those in the other two books, and analytical. The judgments seem fair, and the books selected, with few exceptions, really do stand out as classics in the field. The book succeeds admirably in its purpose of providing a core collection and reference guide.

By contrast, Waggoner's guide seems more flighty. A good portion of her book is devoted to theoretical musings on definitions of fantasy, plus lists of recommended reading by category. Her bibliography includes just under a thousand items, many of them juvenile. Her annotations are short to medium in length, and highly opinionated; she will sometimes dismiss a particular author's work for no apparent reason than personal inclination, ignoring and failing to take into account the general critical opinion on that writer. Her judgments appear at times hasty and ill-considered, based

Xenograffiti, by ROBERT REGINALD

more on emotion than reasoned insight. For that reason, I find her annotations untrustworthy in a very basic sense. Also, her knowledge of fantasy literature seems heavily oriented toward mid-twentieth-century publications, ignoring many books and authors who helped establish the foundations of modern fantasy literature.

Schlobin covers 1249 volumes, about 250 more than Waggoner; but since his definition of fantasy excludes juveniles, this figure actually includes many more adult fantasies than Waggoner. Schlobin's literary background and training are evident in his annotations, which are reasoned, based firmly on prevailing literary opinion, and readable. His indexing of the contents of fantasy collections and anthologies is alone worth the price of the volume. His knowledge of the field seems much greater than Waggoner's, although both have lacunae (neither, for example, has heard of G. P. Baker). Still, Schlobin is far stronger on late nineteenth- or early twentieth-century antecedents of the field. For the small- or medium-sized library, Tymn is clearly the choice; but larger libraries and the scholarly community will clearly find *The Literature of Fantasy* the most perceptive, comprehensive, and valuable of the three.

Taylor, R. G. *Futura Man: An Orphan in Time.* New York: Vantage Press, 1979.
LeBlanc, Richard. *The Fangs of the Vampire.* New York: Vantage Press, 1979.
Marinelli, Jean. *From Blight to Height.* New York: Vantage Press, 1979.
Isaac, Rondall. *Stories of the Unforeseen.* New York: Vantage Press, 1979. New York: Vantage Press, 1979.

Four vanity press titles. In *Futura*, "Robert Taleur finds himself having to deal with inner urges that push him toward a vast space voyage and an ultimate encounter with the universe's archenemy Sephus, the eater of white light and creator of black holes." Absolutely unreadable. *Fangs* is set trillions of years in the future, where space explorer Capt. James Barclay discovers that one Richard LeBlanc had written the most significant book ever penned, *The Total Story of Evolution*. Then LeBlanc himself appears, and the story goes downhill from there. Cosmic solipsism. *Blight* is a near-future utopian novel filled with dialogue that would crack the faces of anyone actually trying to speak it. Naturally, everything works out beautifully in the end—except the story. *Stories* is primitive but readable, a collection of supernatural and fantasy tales, many with war or hunting settings. "The Disc," a post-nuclear holocaust quest story, is the best of the lot, pulp-level quality. A very mixed bag.

(1982)

Schreuders, Piet, translated by Josh Pachter. *Paperbacks, U.S.A.: A Graphic History, 1939-1959.* San Diego, CA: Blue Dolphin Enterprises, 1981. As: *The Book of Paperbacks.* London: Virgin Books, 1981.

Schreuders focuses on the history of mass market paperback cover illustrations during the first twenty years (the golden period) of paperback publishing, and in the process provides a lively illustrated history of the publishers, artists, and books that quickly made paperbacks an integral part of American culture. Beginning with such experiments as Bonibooks and Haldeman-Julius publications in the 1920s and '30s, Schreuders follows these tentative steps into mass market distribution with the advent of Pocket Books in 1939, quickly followed by Avon in 1941, Dell in 1943, Popular Library in 1943, and Bantam in 1945. By the early 1950s paperbacks had supplanted the pulp magazines as the primary medium of mass entertainment in literary form for the American public; indeed, the surviving pulp companies often moved into paperback publishing as a means of continued survival.

Schreuders has clearly done his homework; his knowledge of the history of each company (he provides thumbnail sketches of each) is encyclopedic; in many instances, he quotes from surviving artists, editors, and publishers to bolster his arguments, or to provide enlightening tidbits on the editorial, sales, or design policies of each firm. This material alone is worth the price of the book. An appendix, "Who's Who in Cover Art," provides biographical and career details on many of the more obscure artists who worked (and who in some cases still work) as paperback cover illustrators. Also valuable are the other appendices, including a listing of the first hundred stock numbers for each major paperback line, an "Overview of American Paperback Publishers" (which provides historical, bibliographical, and other pertinent details for every paperback publisher active during the period 1939-1959), a history of paperback publishing in general, year by year through 1959, a small section on "Collecting Paperbacks," and an extensive annotated bibliography of historical and bibliographical sources for the study of mass market publishing and collecting.

More than the solidly-based and readable information, however, are the illustrations that make this book a superior piece of work. Included are dozens of photographs of artists and editors, reproductions of paperback advertising and displays, and literally hundreds of carefully photographed covers, many in full color, most at least half the size of the originals. The care taken in reproducing these covers is extraordinary; they've been cleaned and prepared in such a way that they are, in most cases, more vivid and true-to-life than many of the surviving books themselves.

Paperbacks, U.S.A. does have some minor errors and omissions, but these are negligible compared to the wealth of information and visual material presented here. Schreuders's book should become a standard history, of interest to anyone with even the slightest desire to learn more about this fascinating publishing phenomenon. Highly recommended for libraries and students of popular culture.

(1983)

Saxton, Mark. *Havoc in Islandia.* Boston: Houghton Mifflin Co., 1982.

Austin Tappan Wright's posthumous utopia, *Islandia* (1942), was immediately recognized on publication as a classic of imaginative literature. His curious blend of philosophy, sex, utopian politics, and a certain amount of wistful thinking, combined with a meticulously-researched background (based upon thousands of pages of invented history and language), produced an attractive alternative to the real world that has captured a consistently faithful following over the last four decades. Wright delineated his imaginary country through the eyes of a naive American, John Lang, who eventually decided to switch allegiances, and became the first adopted Islandian in several centuries. The book was set in the early twentieth century, at a time of American (and European) colonialism and expansionism.

Mark Saxton was an editor at Farrar & Rinehart when Wright's daughter, Sylvia Wright Mitarachi, brought her father's huge novel into his office; he later assisted her in cutting the book to a publishable length. Saxton later penned a number of books himself, including *Paper Chase*, before attempting to update the story of Islandia in *The Islar* (1969), in which the country once again faced a crisis of its relations with outside imperial powers; John Lang's grandson, Lang III, is the principal character. Unfortunately, by thrusting Islandia into the Vietnam era, Saxton also stripped from it much of the winsome charm that made Wright's creation so attractive.

Saxton then went back to Wright's unpublished notes and manuscripts to pen a "prequel," *The Two Kingdoms* (1979), essentially an historical novel of the days when Islandia's unique political system was evolving during a period of national crisis and dynastic change. Here Saxton seemed to capture much of the magic of the original, together with a healthy influx of rousing medieval adventure, a wholly successful amalgamation that is heartily recommended to the follower of Islandia.

Saxton's new book, *Havoc in Islandia*, retreats even further into Islandia's imaginary history, to a period when the Catholic Church, and through it the European powers, threaten the very soul of Islandia, its philosophy, political system, mores, even its very existence. Bren, a young officer, is drawn into a political conspiracy surrounding the King, Alwin, and the Catholic Bishop of Islandia, Anthony, who has dreams of temporal as well as spiritual authority. As the country, from its lords to its peasants, begins taking sides for or against the Church, the possibility of civil war looms ever greater, until armed conflict between the two unyielding parties finally breaks out. Bren finds himself fighting for King and country at the last climactic battle, when the fate of Islandia is finally sealed.

Once again, Saxton has taken the best elements of Wright's work, and combined them with a tale of adventure and intrigue that elaborates on the Islandian myth without destroying the beauty of its vision. The choices that need to be made here, decisions that become vital to the existence of Islandia and its unique philosophical system, are the pivot around which story and characters revolve. Bren is suitably sure-footed, and Bishop Anthony suitably scheming, a veritable Borgia; and King Alwin is sufficiently weak, at least initially, to provide some dramatic tension about the outcome.

Highly recommended to all fans of Islandia.

(1993)

Chalker, Jack L., and Mark Owings. *The Science-Fantasy Publishers: A Critical and Bibliographic History.* 3rd ed. Westminster, MD: The Mirage Press Ltd., 1991.

Two previous editions of this guide to SF specialty publishers were self-published in 1966. This new version has been expanded some ten times over the original work, reflecting the vast burgeoning of the specialty market.

The basic arrangement of the guide is alphabetically by name of publisher, then chronologically by publication date of each book listed. A typical chapter includes: publisher's name and logo, ISBN prefix(es) (where appropriate), a one-to-two-page history of the company, a chronological checklist of the firm's monographic publications, and a one-page summary. A typical book entry gives: book title (bold-faced caps), author, year of publication, pagination, binding (if other than cloth), price at time of publication, number of copies printed, introducers, illustrators, bibliographical notes, contents listings (for collections and anthologies), and current in-print status, mention of previous editions or noteworthy reprints, bibliographical and binding points, and a one-paragraph descriptive summary (in italics), listing general background information but no plot details (*e.g.*, "Civil war fantasy novella.").

Xenograffiti, by ROBERT REGINALD

148 publishers are covered in the main sequence (494 pages), and an additional 48 houses in Appendix A: Fellow Travelers (135 pages), in a similar but occasionally less detailed format. Other appendices include: B. Almost-Rans; C. Ordering Directly from a Specialty Publisher; D. Where to Find Them (*i.e.*, addresses); E. "But What's It Worth?": Notes on Pricing and Availability; F. The Essential SF Reference Shelf; G. Where They Are: Geographic Breakdown. In addition, the authors provide an informative Preface and User's Guide to the Third Edition, a twelve-page Introduction: A History of the Science-Fantasy Publishers, a six-page Glossary of Terms Used, an Author & Artist Index, an Index by Title, and a short section of addenda. The indexes correlate authors, titles, and publishers (in the author index), mentioning both page numbers and types (*e.g.*, "collection"); the absence of hanging indents for entries longer than one line makes some sections of the indexes difficult to read. The book is attractively typeset and bound to library standards, but rather poorly proofread. A few rather muddy illustrations of publishers, authors, and book jackets are scattered throughout the text.

This guide generated much controversy on publication, with reviewers both praising and damning it with equal vehemence. Published criticism has focused on the factual accuracy of the data presented, and also on the sometimes lurid comments of the authors about other writers, their works, the publishers, and their presses. Let us examine these in detail.

The authors have undeniably accomplished their stated goal: to record the histories and publications of those houses that have specialized in science fiction, fantasy, and horror books. There are no obvious lacunae in coverage; indeed, many of the books and firms mentioned will be obscure even to the most knowledgeable of fans. However, Chalker and Owings have been less consistent in recording bibliographical data; some paginations are simply wrong, or at the least have been recorded in a different manner from those of other publications. Some titles lack subtitles, while others list subtitles which do not appear on the title page.

Xenograffiti, by ROBERT REGINALD

Some printing counts are certainly off, by an unknown factor; and there are at least a dozen ghost titles included.

To measure the depth of this problem, I contacted a half dozen publishers whose lines are covered in the guide; all had seen the index, and all reported substantial errors in the description of their own firm's publications, despite the fact that each had submitted correct information to Chalker, and (in several cases) had asked to help proofread their own sections, but were never contacted further.

More troubling, perhaps, are the liberal scattering of the authors' outspoken opinions throughout the text. Unsupported judgments are presented as facts, hard data and soft opinions are merged together haphazardly, and the worth of publishing lines and their publishers and sometimes their books are too often measured against the yardstick of The Mirage Press (Chalker's own line) or against Chalker himself, a standard of dubious validity. This stirring together of fact and fancy may occasionally make for entertaining reading, but it leaves the researcher with the unsettling feeling of never knowing what is true and what isn't, and completely invalidates the guide's worth as a reference tool.

Finally, this book is touted in its front matter as having been produced in "instant" small printings of no more than 20-100 copies a run. Later (1992) printings are known to have incorporated additions and changes to the main text of a greater or lesser degree, but these subsequent printings can in no way be identified by the average user, nor can the changes be readily noted, *nor can the sequence of the changes*, making future elucidation of the priority of such alterations virtually impossible. For this alone the compilers should be swiftly dispatched to the lower circles of the bibliographer's Hell.

The best that can be said of this hodgepodge is that it does contain a myriad of interesting facts floating about in a stew of unsupported speculation, and that we shall undoubtedly be seeing this particular broth again, rebrewed and restirred, but no more palatable for all that.

Muddle is as muddle does.

271

Xenograffiti, by ROBERT REGINALD

Kies, Cosette N. *Supernatural Fiction for Teens: More than 1300 Good Paperbacks to Read for Wonderment, Fear, and Fun.* 2nd ed. Englewood, CO: Libraries Unlimited, 1992.

The 1987 edition of this annotated bibliography of horror fiction covered 500 works of dark fantasy suitable for the young adult reader; the 1992 version more than doubles the page count (from 127 to 267 p.) and the number of entries (from 500 to 1304).

Books are arranged in two sections, novels/collections and anthologies, alphabetically by author or editor, and then by title. Materials are numbered consecutively throughout the book from the number one. A typical entry gives item number, reading level code letter (*e.g.*, A=written for teens), author's name, title (boldfaced), place of publication, publisher, year of publication, pagination, ISBN, publisher and publication date of previous cloth editions, a mention of any sequels, movie versions, or other titles of interest by the same author, a two-to-three-sentence descriptive annotation, and subject categorization (*e.g.*, "paranormal abilities). The anthology section gives a one-sentence annotation followed by complete contents listings.

A brief and somewhat inadequate series index is arranged alphabetically by series title, with a short annotation for the series as a whole, and a list of the books and their authors in publication order, without, however, noting series numbers or dates (for example, one title is missing from the "Twilight" series, although annotated in the author section, but its absence is not immediately obvious to the casual user). Other end matter includes a four-page glossary of terms, a movie index, a title index, and subject index. The indices are keyed to item number, and are stripped to the bare minimum; the title index, for example, lacks mention of corresponding authors (except where titles are exactly duplicated), while the series index consists of roughly a hundred terms followed by a list of cross-referenced numbers. For a topic such as "Santa Claus," which has only two items associated with it, the subject index provides good access; but broader terms (*e.g.*, "horror" or "ghosts") have hundreds of references appended, requiring the user to examine each item to make an assessment. The volume is attractively designed and typeset, but is available only in paperbound form.

Entries from the first edition are repeated verbatim in the second, although all text has been reset. No attempt has been made to evaluate the works covered, and not all of the novels are supernatural, despite the book's title; Kies uses a loose definition of horror fiction which encompasses such non-fantasy works as Leroux's *Phantom of the Opera*.

Although there is some overlap between Kies's book and Lynn's *Fantasy Literature for Children and Young Adults* (3rd ed., Bowker, 1989), and with Barron's *Horror Literature: A Reader's Guide* (Garland, 1990), all three volumes cover works not noted in the others, with at least half of the titles in Kies not annotated elsewhere. One wonders, in fact, about Kies's rather eclectic selection criteria, and why certain very minor fictions were included, while others more notable were omitted. The author herself states, "the intent has been to give an idea of the various works available," and within this very loose parameter she has succeeded in providing a unique and occasionally valuable resource for a modern genre which has thus far received scant attention from scholars and bibliographers.

Rosenberg, Betty, and Diana Tixier Herald. *Genreflecting: A Guide to Reading Interests in Genre Fiction.* 3rd ed. Englewood, CO: Libraries Unlimited, 1991.

This reader's guide to genre fiction is divided into seven chapters, of which the last three, covering science fiction, fantasy, and horror literature (comprising 90 out of 281 pages of text), are of interest to the SF scholar.

Each chapter is divided into two sections, "Themes and Types" and "Topics." The former includes 10-20 sub-chapters, arranged in no apparent order (except for part of the middle section of the SF list, which is alphabetical by theme name); each theme (*e.g.*, "Hard Science" or "Messianic/Religious") includes a one-paragraph definition (100-200 words) as introduction, followed by a list of 5-30 suggested titles (averaging 15) in alphabetical order by author's name. No bibliographical data other than author and title are noted, except for the theme anthologies list, which also in-

Xenograffiti, by ROBERT REGINALD

cludes (for no apparent reason) publisher and year of publication, in addition to subject appellations following half of the entries (*e.g.*, "alien beings").

The second section, "Topics," is a guide to anthologies, bibliographies, history and criticism, awards, journals, film books, associations and conventions, publishers, and other topics of interest. As with the previous section, each topic includes a general, one-paragraph descriptive annotation, plus lists of materials in alphabetical order by main entry. Bibliographical data for individual titles include: author and title, publisher, year of publication, and (occasionally) a brief, one-sentence annotation or contents listing.

The author/title index interfiles books and their authors in one alphabetical sequence, keyed to item number; however, the author listings lack book titles, and the books lack any indication of authorship, requiring the user to flip back and forth constantly to the main text.

Although *Genreflecting* has added some ninety pages of text since publication of the first (1982) edition, a significant portion of the material appears dated or incomplete. For example, the "Critical Journals" listing in the Topics section of the Science Fiction chapter lists *Starship* and *Science Fiction Review* as open entries, although both journals ceased publication many years ago; and also fails to include *Science-Fiction Studies*, a major academic journal of SF, or the *Journal of the International Association for the Fantastic in the Arts*. On the same page the authors devote an entire paragraph to the *International Science Fiction Yearbook*, which was published once in 1978, and is now totally useless; and in a subsection on "Reviews" they specifically highlight *Fantasy Review*, which they indicate as still being published (but which actually shut down in 1987)—and fail to mention *SFRA Review*, now the major review publication in the field. These lapses suggest a knowledge of the field which is at best superficial.

This is a mediocre guide to genre fiction, of use primarily to high school level libraries. Prefer Neil Barron's guides, *Anatomy of Wonder*, *Fantasy Literature*, and *Horror Literature*.

XLIV.

SELECTED OBITUARIES

(1983-2003)

ROBERT ADLEMAN

Robert H. Adleman, 76, died on Nov. 16, 1995 at Ashland, Oregon. He was primarily known for his war novels, including *The Devil's Brigade*, his first book, which was made into a 1968 film starring William Holden. He later attended Rutgers and Temple Universities, earning a law degree at the latter institution. His only novel in the SF field (out of ten books published) was *Annie Deane* (World Publishing Co., 1971). He was a dedicated environmentalist, and after moving to Oregon in 1975, transformed his ranch into a wildlife preserve.

SPIRO AGNEW

Spiro Theodore Agnew, 77, died of leukemia on Sept. 17, 1996 at Berlin, Maryland. He was born on Nov. 9, 1918 at Baltimore, the son of Greek immigrants. After serving in the U.S. Army during World War II, he received an LL.B. degree from the University of Baltimore in 1947, and an LL.D. from the University of Maryland. After working for ten years as an attorney, he was appointed to the Baltimore County Government in 1957, became County Executive in 1962, was elected Governor of Maryland in 1967, and Vice-President of the United States in 1969. He resigned in 1973 after pleading "no contest" to charges of taking bribes while

Governor. Three years later he published his only fiction, *The Canfield Decision* (Playboy Press), a near-future political novel in which a Vice-President proposes arming Israel with nuclear weapons.

BIBI BESCH

Bibi Besch, 56, died of cancer on Sept. 7, 1996 at Los Angeles. She was born on Feb. 1, 1940 at Vienna, Austria, the daughter of actress Gusti Huber. Her parents brought her to the United States after World War II, settling in Westchester County, New York. She attended Connecticut College for Women, and later studied with Bill Hickey, Herbert Berghof, and Milton Katselas, making her stage debut in *Pygmalion* in 1964. From the theatre she moved into TV soap operas, guest appearances on series, and television movies, and then to motion pictures in 1975. In the SF world she is primarily known for her role as Dr. Carol Marcus, Captain James Kirk's former flame and the mother of his only child, in *Star Trek II: The Wrath of Khan* (1982). Sadly, the actor who played her and Kirk's son in that film, Merritt Butrick, had already perished of AIDS in 1989.

WHIT BISSELL

Character actor Whitner Bissell, 86, died on March 5, 1996 at Woodland Hills, Calif. He was born on Oct. 24, 1909 at New York City, and began his career in acting on Broadway during the 1930s. He debuted on film in the 1943 production, *Holy Matrimony*, and appeared in ninety-eight motion pictures overall, plus numerous television movies and TV series roles. His work in SF films included: *The Creature from the Black Lagoon* (1954), *Target Earth* (1954), *Invasion of the Body Snatchers* (1956), *I Was a Teenage Werewolf* (1957), *I Was a Teenage Frankenstein* (1957), *The Time Machine* (1960), *Seven Days in May* (1964), *City Beneath the Sea* (TV movie, 1970), *Soylent Green* (1973), *Psychic Killer* (1975), and *The Time Machine* (TV movie, 1978). He also appeared in the TV series, *The Time Tunnel* (1966-1967).

Xenograffiti, by ROBERT REGINALD

THOMAS D. CLARESON

A giant has died. The father of science-fiction criticism has passed. Indeed, it is difficult to imagine how the academic study of fantastic literature could have developed in quite the same way without Tom Clareson. His stature and influence were in many ways comparable to that of John W. Campbell, Jr.'s contributions to the Golden Age of SF literature. Like Campbell, he served as editor of the major periodical of the field for over thirty years; however, Clareson actually founded and for many years published *Extrapolation*, nurturing it from its beginnings in 1959 as a typed 8.5" x 11" newsletter into a sophisticated quarterly journal published by Kent State University Press. Its first issue featured a lengthy bibliography by Clareson himself, material which would later form the basis for his definitive guide, *Science Fiction in America, 1870s-1930s: An Annotated Bibliography of Primary Sources* (Green-wood Press, 1984).

Thomas Dean Clareson was born on Aug. 26, 1926 at Austin, Minnesota. He displayed his interest in SF criticism early, publishing his first essay on the subject in 1954 in the pulp magazine, *Science Fiction Quarterly*. A year later he joined the faculty of The College of Wooster, Wooster, Ohio, and in 1956 received his doctorate in English from Penn. By 1958 he had persuaded the Modern Language Association to sponsor a seminar on science fiction, an event which may well be used by future historians to mark the coming of age of SF criticism. A year later he assembled and published (through the English Department of The College of Wooster) the first issue of *Extrapolation* as *The Newsletter of the Conference on Science-Fiction of the Modern Language Association*. Kent State University Press acquired the journal in 1979, and has published it ever since.

As editor, Clareson avoided controversy, emphasizing readability in the essays he published, and avoiding academic jargon and the philosophical extremes. He disliked stodginess, and encouraged the publication of both critiques and bibliographical studies; among others, he provided a home for over ten years for Marshall Tymn's annual guides to the secondary literature of the genre. For its first thirteen years, until the founding of *Foundation* in 1972 and *Science-Fiction Studies* in 1973, *Extrapolation* was the *only* periodical regularly to feature rigorously examined scholarly articles on fantastic literature. Clareson set the standards for the rest of the field to follow.

In 1970, sensing that the number of academics seriously interested in the study of SF literature had reached a critical level, he founded the Science Fiction Research Association (SFRA), and served as its President and guiding hand for six difficult years, until it was well enough established to continue life on its own. Included in the initial proposal for the organization was a series of annual academic conferences devoted to the study of fantastic fiction, the creation of a lifetime accolade (the Pilgrim Award) to honor career contributions to the study of the literature (an honor he was himself given in 1977), and the publication of the *SFRA Newsletter* (which became the *SFRA Review* in 1992) to provide members with news and reviews of interest.

Clareson's own works included five anthologies of criticism and one of fiction, the first annotated checklist of *SF Criticism* (Kent State, 1972), critical studies on *Frederik Pohl* (Starmont House, 1987) and *Robert Silverberg* (Starmont House, 1983), and *Robert Silverberg: A Primary and Secondary Bibliography* (G. K. Hall, 1983), the compilation of two large microfilm collections on the pulp magazines and early science fiction novels (Greenwood, 1984), a general guide to *Understanding Contemporary American Science Fiction* (University of South Carolina Press, 1990), and two major works on the bibliography and history of fantastic literature: *Science Fiction in America, 1870s-1930s* (Greenwood Press, 1984) and *Some Kind of Paradise: The Emergence of American Science Fiction* (Greenwood Press, 1985). Forthcoming are a major biographical and critical study of *Robert A. Heinlein* and an untitled collection of his essays, both from Borgo Press.

Tom was truly a modest man, he drove like a maniac, he smoked terribly for far too many years, and he was brilliant and fun and knowledgeable and a great conversationalist, a genius whose passion and belief in the study of science-

Xenograffiti, by ROBERT REGINALD

fiction literature legitimatized and made possible the immense blossoming of SF secondary sources during the 1970s and '80s. He was determined to attend the SFRA Conference in Reno between June 16-20th, 1993, and when the airlines refused to allow him to fly with his oxygen tank, he and Alice made the difficult cross-country trip from Ohio to Nevada by car. He was thin and tired, but hadn't lost any of his humor or *élan.* When I embraced him on the morning of the 20th, I knew it was the last time I would see him. He had a difficult journey home, catching a bug that just wouldn't go away. But his passing on July 6, 1993 was totally unexpected, for us and for Alice, for no one expects such a torch ever to dim. *Ave utque vale,* old friend.

MICHAEL L. COOK

Michael Lewis Cook, 58, bibliographer, genealogist, and historian, died suddenly of a heart attack on June 14, 1988, at Evansville, IN. He was born at Evansville on June 28, 1929, and had lived there all his life, working as an insurance agent, office manager, and real estate broker before retiring in 1976 to become a full-time researcher and publisher. He was the author of forty-seven books, including eleven indexes and bibliographies of mystery, pulp, and adventure fiction. His last book, *Mystery, Detective, and Espionage Fiction,* was published by Garland a month after he died, as the first of a three-volume set indexing mystery, adventure, and science fiction pulp magazines. Work had nearly been completed on Volume Two, *Adventure, War, and Sports Fiction,* and that book, together with Volume Three on the science fiction magazines, will be completed by Cook's collaborator, Steve Miller, with help from William G. Contento on the latter.

RICHARD CONDON

Richard Thomas Condon, 81, well-known American novelist, died on Apr. 9, 1996 at Dallas, Texas. He was born on Mar. 18, 1915 at New York, New York, and worked as a

Xenograffiti, by ROBERT REGINALD

publicist for various film companies in New York and Hollywood from 1936-1957. He began writing in the 1940s, selling stories and travel articles to the slick magazines, and having a play, *Men of Distinction*, produced on Broadway in 1953. His first novel, *The Oldest Confession*, appeared in 1958, but it was his next book, *The Manchurian Candidate* (McGraw-Hill, 1959), which dealt with sophisticated brainwashing techniques, that vaulted him into the ranks of the bestsellers. His best-known later work was *Prizzi's Honor*, one of a series of four novels focusing on a fictional Mafia family. In the SF field he produced a number of satirical near-future works, including: *A Talent for Loving; or, The Great Cowboy Race* (McGraw-Hill, 1961), *Winter Kills* (Dial, 1974), *The Star-Spangled Crunch* (Bantam, 1974), *The Whisper of the Axe* (Dial, 1976), *Emperor of America* (Simon & Schuster, 1990), and *The Final Addiction* (St. Martin's, 1991).

PAM CONRAD

Pam Stampf Conrad, 48, died of breast cancer on Jan. 22, 1996 at her home at Rockville Center, Long Island, New York. She was born on June 18, 1947 at New York City, and received a B.A. from the New School for Social Research. Conrad was a well-known children's writer, her first book, *I Don't Live Here!*, being published by Dutton in 1983. She first attained widespread notice with *Prairie Songs* (1985), a young adult western, which won the Spur Award from Western Writers of America and many library accolades. In the SF field her only novel was *Stonewords: A Ghost Story* (Harper & Row, 1990), which won an Edgar Allan Poe Award and a California Young Reader Medal. A sequel, *Zoe Rising*, is scheduled to be published by HarperCollins in June of 1996.

TED DIKTY

Xenograffiti, by ROBERT REGINALD

He was the best man I ever knew. In a business known for its cutthroat deals, back alley politics, and pervasive cynicism, he never lost his innocence, his sense of wonder, his outright joy at being able to spend his life doing exactly what he loved most—publishing and editing—and getting paid for it.

Thaddeus Maxim Eugene Dikty was born on June 16, 1920 at Port Clinton, Ohio. He married writer and fan Julian "Judy" May on January 10, 1953, and they had three children: Alan Sam, David, and Barbara. He became an editor for Shasta Publishers in 1948, and stayed with that firm until its demise in 1957; he later worked as an editor for several other Chicago-area publishing houses before founding FAX Collector's Editions in the early 1970s. He edited the first series of "best of the year" science fiction anthologies with Everett F. Bleiler beginning in 1949, and continuing through 1958. He founded FAX Collector's Editions in 1972 with Darrell C. Richardson to reprint pulp classics, and Starmont House, Inc. in 1976 to publish criticism about science fiction.

Ted believed in the essential goodness of people. He was unfailingly kind and courteous towards friends and strangers alike, a truly "gentle" man, in the older sense of the word. Not a milquetoast nor a cipher, not by any means: I've seen him angry, but never abusive; I've seen him upset at people, but never vindictive. There wasn't a spot of meanness anywhere in that giant soul. He knew publishing backwards and forwards and sideways, but he never let the needs of his business dictate the way he treated people.

Once a week or so I'd give him a call. "Hey, Thaddeus," I'd say, "How's it going?" He'd laugh, and we'd talk business for a few moments, and then get down to the *real* business of schmoozing for as long as we could get away with it. And we'd talk. About life, the universe, about everything. About death. He was ill, seriously ill, on and off for the last two years, mostly with circulatory problems. He didn't want to die, and he certainly didn't want Starmont to die with him. But even though he had felt much better during the last three months, he knew the end was coming. We all did. And he provided as best he could for the future of both his family and his business. Starmont House will continue under his daughter's direction.

A month before his passing I told him I'd be flying up to Seattle in October. It had been two years since our last meeting, and we were greatly looking forward to a few days together. Then the conversation took a strange turn, as we started reminiscing about all the good and awful publishing decisions we had made during our respective careers, each trying to outdo the other in a facetious way with bad examples, and noting that, had we only had the benefit of hindsight, we could have both retired long since. It gave us a good laugh: we knew perfectly well, of course, that retirement was never an option for either of us.

Thaddeus Dikty never made much money in publishing. He wasn't a household name, even in the microcosm of science fiction. He never sought the limelight, and rejected any attempts to be dragged into the public eye. But those who knew the man any length of time came to love him dearly, heart and soul, without exception.

I made my plane reservation for Sunday, Oct. 13th, 1991. Ted kept another appointment, damn him, on the afternoon of Friday, Oct. 11th, sitting at his desk editing a manuscript. It was the way he would have chosen to go: quietly, without fuss, doing the work he loved so well. I think somewhere he's doing it still. Old friend, dear friend, rest in well deserved peace.

WILLIAM K. EVERSON

William Keith Everson, 67, film historian and critic, died of cancer at New York, New York on Apr. 14, 1996. He was born on Apr. 8, 1929 at Yeovil, Somersetshire, England. He came to the U.S. in 1950, where he worked as a publicist, writer, editor, and producer for various film and television companies, and also taught occasional classes at New York University and other schools. Beginning in the 1950s, he amassed one of the largest private collections of classic and obscure films in the world, amounting to over 4,000 motion pictures, which he kept for private viewing in his apartment.

Xenograffiti, by ROBERT REGINALD

He also wrote hundreds of articles and some twenty books on cinema, including *Classics of the Horror Film* (Citadel Press, 1974) and its sequel, *More Classics of the Horror Film* (Citadel Press, 1986).

HERK HARVEY

Harold A. "Herk" Harvey, 71, died on April 3, 1996 at Lawrence, Kansas. He was born in Colorado, and later attended school at the University of Kansas at Lawrence, majoring in theater arts. He joined the staff of Centron Films at Lawrence, and produced over 400 educational and industrial films for them. His only feature film, *Carnival of Souls* (Herts-Lion, 1962), was independently produced and directed by Harvey at Lawrence for less than $100,000. This atmospheric and chilling ghost story starred Candace Hillgoss in the main role, with Harvey himself playing the leader of the dead. The move was never given a proper release in the theaters, but slowly gained a following from periodic showings on late-nite TV and at film festivals, finally achieving cult status in the 1980s and '90s, and earning favorable reviews in *The New Yorker* and other publications.

RYERSON JOHNSON

(Walter) Ryerson "Johnny" Johnson, 93, died on May 24, 1995 in Florida. He was born on October 19, 1901, and became a well-known writer for the pulp magazines, specializing in mystery and western stories. In the SF field he authored three Doc Savage novels during the 1930s under the house name, Kenneth Robeson: *The Fantastic Island* (reprinted by Bantam Books in 1966); *Land of Always-Night* (Bantam, 1966); and *The Motion Menace* (Bantam, 1971). In later life he wrote a number of popular children's books. A collection of his pulp westerns, *Torture Trek and Eleven Other Tales of the Wild West* (Barricade Books), was published just before his death in 1995.

Xenograffiti, by ROBERT REGINALD

DAVID LASSER

David Lasser, 94, died May 5, 1996 at Rancho Bernardo, Calif. He was born on Mar. 20, 1902 at Baltimore, Maryland. After serving in France with the U.S. Army during World War I, he attended M.I.T. and then worked briefly as an engineer in New Jersey. In 1927 he was hired by Hugo Gernsback for Gernsback Publications and Stellar Publishing Corporation, and edited the pulp magazines *Science Wonder Stories* and *Air Wonder Stories* from 1929 (the two titles were combined as *Wonder Stories* in 1930) and *Wonder Stories Quarterly*, also beginning in 1929; he also briefly edited Gernsback's *Scientific Detective Monthly* in 1930. He left Stellar in 1933, but not before writing *The Conquest of Space* (Penguin Press, 1931), the first serious attempt to outline the possibility of real-life exploration of the solar system, including a manned trip to the Moon; the book influenced an entire generation of science fiction writers. To promote his beliefs he helped create the American Interplanetary Society in 1930, which metamorphosed into the American Institute of Aeronautics and Astronautics. In 1935 Lasser founded a Depression-era labor organization, the Workers Alliance of America, but resigned in 1940 when the Communists took over the union; ironically, he was unjustly labeled as a Communist during the Joseph McCarthy era because of his previous association with the group. From 1950-1969 he served with the International Union of Electrical Radio and Machine Workers.

ANDREW LYTLE

Andrew Nelson Lytle, 92, died Dec. 12, 1995 at Monteagle, Tennessee. He was born on Dec. 26, 1902 at Murfreesboro, Tennessee, and graduated from Vanderbilt University in 1925. There he became associated with the Agrarians, a group of writers (among them Robert Penn Warren and John Crowe Ransom) who railed against the effects of technology on modern society, and who advocated a return to a simpler, farm-based way of life. He had a long and distinguished career as an author, lecturer, and teacher of creative writing at the University of Florida and University of the South; his many students included well-known writer Flannery O'Connor. Lytle's first novel, *The Long Night*, was published in 1936. His only fantasy novel was *A Name for Evil* (Bobbs-Merrill, 1947), a psychological ghost story with gothic overtones, which was later reprinted in the omnibus *A Novel, a Novella, and Four Short Stories* (Obolensky, 1958), and separately by Avon Books in the 1970s.

OG MANDINO

Og Mandino, 72, died of an aneurysm on Sept. 3, 1996 at Antrim, NH. Augustine A. Mandino was born on Dec. 12, 1923 at Boston, MA, and briefly attended Bucknell Junior College before entering the Army Air Force as a 1st Lieut. during World War II; he received the Distinguished Flying Cross and Air Medal for his valor. Following the war, he became a successful life insurance salesman and manager, retiring in 1965. He then founded the magazine *Success Unlimited* to promote his motivational ideas. His first book, *A Treasury of Success Unlimited*, was published in 1966, but he was best known for such inspirational classics as *The Greatest Salesman in the World* (1968) and *The Greatest Secret in the World* (1972); his nineteen books sold more than thirty million copies in aggregate. His only venture into SF was the novel *The Christ Commission* (Lippincott & Crowell, 1980), in which a disillusioned 20th-century time traveler returns to the Jerusalem of 36 A.D. to determine for himself the truth behind Christ's resurrection.

ANNETTE PELTZ MCCOMAS

Annette Peltz McComas, 83, died on Oct. 7, 1994 at her home in Oakland, CA. Annette Peltz was born on June 26, 1911 at San Francisco, California, daughter of Alfred and Jennie Peltz. At age five she moved with her family to a small Jewish community in Hutchinson, Kansas, where she lived until 1929. She received her bachelor's degree from the University of California, Berkeley, during the early 1930s, and her master's degree from Cornell University a few years later. She then worked for several years in New York as a stage manager and short story writer, and later taught at UC Berkeley and at a community college at Oakland, California. She married Jesse Francis McComas (later co-editor of *The Magazine of Fantasy & Science Fiction*) in 1943, and had one son who died at the age of thirty-seven; they were divorced in 1961, and he died in 1978. In later years she wrote, directed plays, and traveled extensively until losing much of her sight. She edited the SF anthology, *The Eureka Years: Boucher and McComas's The Magazine of Fantasy and Science Fiction, 1949-54*, for Bantam Books in 1982. She is survived by her grandson, Tony Stoughton, and a great-granddaughter. An autobiography, *Kansas and Me: Memories of a Jewish Childhood*, was published by The Borgo Press in 1995.

CHRISTOPHER MILNE

Christopher Robin Milne, 75, died on Apr. 20, 1996 at London. He was born on Aug. 21, 1920 at London, the son of well-known writer A. A. Milne. In 1924 the elder Milne published a book of light verse called *When We Were Very Young* which was inspired by the antics of his four-year-old son, and soon had produced the classic children's book, *Winnie-the-Pooh* (1926), based upon Christopher's love for a bear of that name at the London zoo. Milne Junior spent the rest of his life trying to live down the fame that *Winnie* and its sequels engendered, finally publishing his own examination of his own life and those of his parents in *The Enchanted Places* (1974), which was followed by two sequels, *The Path Through the Trees* (1979) and *The Hollow in the Hill* (1982).

MAYO MOHS

Mayo Mohs, 62, was killed in an automobile accident at Santa Monica, Calif., on August 22, 1996. The son of Lewis Mohs, former owner of the Los Angeles Lakers basketball team, Mayo Mohs began working as a high school teacher in

Xenograffiti, by ROBERT REGINALD

Los Angeles, while simultaneously pursuing a career as a freelance writer. His submissions to *Time* magazine earned an invitation from that publication to join its staff in 1968 as Religious Editor. Ten years later he transferred to Times Mirror's companion publication, *Discover*. He retired in 1987. His first book, the anthology *Other Worlds, Other Gods: Adventures in Religious Science Fiction* (Doubleday, 1971), reflected his interest in philosophy and theology. In the mid-1970s he also co-authored two phonograph records, *The God Beat* and *Media and the Church*, plus a well-received political biography of the Prince of Wales, *H.R.H.: The Man Who Will Be King* (Arbor House, 1979), written with Tim Heald.

FRANK RILEY

Frank Riley, 80, died on Apr. 24, 1996 at Manhattan Beach, California. His legal name was Frank Wilbert Ryhlick, and he is believed to have been born on June 8, 1915 at Hibbing, Minnesota. He joined the *New York Daily News* in the late 1930s, and published his first book, *Dixie Demagogues* (Vanguard Press), in 1939 under his real name. After service with the U.S. Merchant Marine during World War II, he settled in Manhattan Beach in the late 1940s. He later became travel editor for the *Los Angeles Times*, and regularly contributed articles on traveling to West Coast magazines. He also wrote three novels, among them *They'd Rather Be Right* (Gnome Press, 1957; also published as *The Forever Machine*, Galaxy, 1958), co-authored with Mark Clifton, which won the Hugo Award for Best Science Fiction Novel (for the serialized magazine version) in 1955.

MAY SARTON

May Sarton, 83, died of breast cancer on July 16, 1995 at her home in York, Maine. She was born Eléanore Marie Sarton on Mar. 12, 1912 at Wondelgem, Belgium, and was brought to the U.S. by her parents during World War I. A well-known feminist and lesbian, she penned poetry, novels, chil-

Xenograffiti, by ROBERT REGINALD

dren's books, and (late in life) a series of journals about growing old. Her one work of fantastic literature was the classic cat novel, *The Fur Person* (Rinehart & Co., 1957), which was later reprinted in paper by New American Library.

STIRLING SILLIPHANT

Stirling Dale Silliphant, 78, died on Apr. 26, 1996 at Bangkok, Thailand. He was born on Jan. 16, 1918 at Detroit, Michigan, and received a B.A. in journalism from the University of Southern California in 1938. He worked briefly as a publicist for Walt Disney Studios before entering the U.S. Navy during World War II. After the war, he worked as publicity director for Twentieth Century Fox in New York, quitting his job in 1953 to become a full-time writer. His first novel, *Maracaibo*, appeared two years later. He is best known in the SF field for his screenplays *Village of the Damned* (1960, adapted from the novel *The Midwich Cuckoos*, by John Wyndham), *Charly* (1968, adapted from the novella, "Flowers for Algernon," by Daniel Keyes), *The Poseidon Adventure* (1972, adapted from the novel by Paul Gallico), *The Towering Inferno* (1974, adapted from the novel *The Glass Inferno*, by Thomas N. Scortia and Frank M. Robinson), *The Swarm* (1978, adapted from the novel by Arthur Herzog), and *Circle of Iron* (1979), an original creation. He also wrote the teleplay for the TV miniseries *Space* (1985, adapted from the novel by James A. Michener). He settled in Thailand in 1988.

DAN STREIB

Daniel Thomas Streib, 67, died at his home in San Diego on March 4, 1996. He was born on Nov. 8, 1928 at Rockford, Ill. He received a B.A. from the University of Iowa, and an M.A. from San Diego State University. He served in Korea from 1951-1953, earning the Silver Star, and later worked as a reporter, advertising executive, and high school and college teacher. His first story was published while he was still a teenager, and his first book, *Operation: Countdown*, appeared from the short-lived Powell Books in 1970. He also wrote children's books, historical novels under the name Jonathan Schofield, war novels as J. Farragut Jones, and historical romances under the name Lee Davis Willoughby. He was best known for two men's adventure series published under his own name: a ten-book set featuring Michael Hawk, and an eight-volume series based around a near-future strike group called COUNTER FORCE for Fawcett Gold Medal: *Counter Force* (1983), *The Trident Hijacking* (1983), *Death Shuttle* (1983), *The Karate Killers* (1983), *Terror for Sale* (1984), *Titans Duel* (1984), *The Mind Breakers* (1984), and *The Bloody Rose* (1985).

P. L. TRAVERS

Pamela Lyndon Travers, 96, died on Apr. 23, 1996 at London. She was born Helen Lyndon Goff in 1899 at Maryborough, Australia, and began writing poems and essays while still a teenager. She settled in England in 1924. Her best-known creation was *Mary Poppins*, first published in book form in 1934 (Gerald Howe), which was followed by several sequels, including *Mary Poppins Comes Back* (L. Dickson and Thompson, 1935), *Mary Poppins Opens the Door* (Reynal and Hitchcock, 1943), *Mary Poppins in the Park* (Peter Davies, 1952), and *Mary Poppins in Cherry Tree Lane* (Collins, 1982). The Walt Disney Studios film version of her original book, released in 1964 with Julie Andrews, was enormously successful, but Travers refused to sell the rights to a sequel, saying: "The film lives in its own world, and the books live in theirs. They're not quite the same worlds."

ELLESTON TREVOR

Elleston Trevor, 75, died of cancer on July 21, 1995 at his home in Cave Creek, Arizona. He was born Trevor Dudley-Smith on Feb. 17, 1920 in England, later moved to France, and settled in the United States twenty years ago. Trevor began writing at age twenty while serving in the Royal Air Force during World War II, and became a well-known writer

Xenograffiti, by ROBERT REGINALD

of suspense, espionage, and war stories, particularly under the names Elleston Trevor and Adam Hall. His SF works include: *The Immortal Error* (Swan, 1946), *Forbidden Kingdom* (Lutterworth, 1955), *The Mind of Max Duvine* (Swan, 1960), *The Theta Syndrome* (New English Library, 1977), *The Sibling* (as Adam Hall, Playboy Press, 1979), and *Deathwatch* (Beaufort, 1984). His eighteenth and last Quiller spy novel (as Adam Hall) was completed just before his death.

LEONARD WIBBERLEY

Leonard Patrick O'Connor Wibberley, 68, author of the Grand Fenwick books and a number of juvenile science fiction and fantasy novels, died suddenly on November 22, 1983, in Santa Monica, California, while on the way to an art lesson. He had suffered a major heart attack in 1975, and had been intermittently ill with complications ever since.

Wibberley was born April 9, 1915 at Dublin, Ireland. After World War II he became an American correspondent for the *London Evening News* in New York and Chicago; about the same time, he began writing his first book, *The Lost Harpooner*, which was published in 1947. He moved to Southern California in the early 1950s to take a job with the *Los Angeles Times*, but quit his position in 1954 after finishing *The Mouse That Roared*. *Mouse*, published in 1955 by Little, Brown, established Wibberley as a major writer of whimsical fantasy, and was later made into a popular motion picture starring Peter Sellers. Wibberley followed this early success with four sequels, the last being *The Mouse That Saved the West* (1981); a sixth "Grand Fenwick" novel, started during the Watergate crisis, was never completed.

Wibberley remained a prolific writer until his death, having penned just over a hundred books, some under the pseudonyms Leonard Holton, Patrick O'Connor, and Christopher Webb. Perhaps three-fourths of his output consisted of biographies, adventure stories, and science fiction aimed at the teenage market; but he also wrote adult fantasies, serious historical novels, a popular mystery series of eleven novels featuring a Catholic priest (Father Bredder) under the

Xenograffiti, by ROBERT REGINALD

pen name Leonard Holton, and poignant tales of his native Ireland. In his last years, he returned to his first love, journalism, by writing a series of syndicated newspaper articles on a wide variety of subjects, the last of which appeared just a few days before his death; some of these were collected into the posthumous book, *Shamrocks and Sea Silver and Other Illuminations*, published by Borgo Press in 1992.

He leaves a wife, five surviving children, many friends, and several unpublished books, including two juvenile fairy tales and an adult fantasy novel commissioned by Ballantine Books, but never published by them.

Of my friend, I remember the first time we met, on the occasion of Borgo's republication of *Beware of the Mouse* in 1978. As we sat around a table at Anna's Restaurant in Westwood near the UCLA campus, not knowing quite what to say to each other, this gruff, Santa Claus of a man, with his full white beard and deep, Irish voice, suddenly began to regale us with stories of his life and experiences. We sat there utterly enthralled. Unpretentious, kind, well-mannered, a natural storyteller with a broad sense of humor, Leonard was a gentleman of the old school; his very presence reminded one of simpler times and cherished values. Alas, the years were not kind to Wibberley: during his last decade, physical ailments and falling sales brought about frequent periods of depression and doubt—in his church, his life, even in his own ability as a writer. Between these moments of crisis, his basic good nature would always reassert itself. When I last talked to him, two months ago, he was full of plans for the future, for his recently-completed fairy tales, a new departure for him. We talked again of doing a full-length interview book on his life and career, for which his good friend Robert Nathan had already contributed an introduction (later used as the foreword for *Shamrocks*). The end was mercifully sudden, a fatal heart attack on a Southern California freeway. Those who knew him, personally or through his work, will miss him deeply. Rest in peace, Leonard.

Xenograffiti, by ROBERT REGINALD

ELEANOR CAMERON

Eleanor Cameron, 84, well-known children's book author, died on Oct. 11, 1996 at Monterey, California. She was born Eleanor Frances Butler on Mar. 23, 1912 at Winnipeg, Manitoba, and worked as a clerk and librarian in Los Angeles from 1930-1959. Her first book and only adult novel, *The Unheard Music*, was published by Little, Brown in 1950. But it was with her five-book juvenile science fiction series which featured the strange little man, Tycho Bass, beginning with *The Wonderful Flight to the Mushroom Planet* (Little, Brown, 1954), that she made her mark in the SF field. The "Mush-room Planet" books were highly acclaimed by librarians and readers alike, and one was included in 1979 on Scholastic Book Service's list of all-time "one hundred [juvenile paperback] bestsellers." The sequels included: *Stowaway to the Mushroom Planet* (1956), *Mr. Bass's Planetoid* (1958), *A Mystery for Mr. Bass* (1960), and *Time and Mr. Bass* (1967). Cameron also wrote the juvenile dinosaur novel, *The Terrible Churnadryne* (1959) and its sequel, *The Mysterious Christmas Shell* (1961), the two "Stone Children" fantasies, *The Court of the Stone Children* (Dutton, 1973) and *To the Green Mountains* (1975), and *Beyond Silence* (1980). Her final book, *The Seed and The Vision: On the Writing and Appreciation of Children's Books*, appeared from Dutton in 1993.

WALT BURGESS

Roy Walter "Walt" Burgess, 75, of Medford, died Monday (Feb. 16, 1998) at Providence Medford Medical Center. A private service is planned. Interment will be in the Eagle Point National Cemetery. Memorial contributions may be made to Sacred Heart Catholic Church, 449 S. Ivy St., Medford, OR 97501.

He was born July 4, 1922 in Biggar, Saskatchewan, and moved with his family to Oregon in 1924.

At the onset of World War II, he enlisted in the U.S. Army Air Corps, serving as a fighter pilot. He was awarded the Distinguished Flying Cross and the Air Medal with 14 oak leaf clusters. He also served in the Korean War, and retired with the rank of Major in 1963.

On Oct. 15, 1945 in Spokane, Wash., he married Betty Jane Kapel, who survives.

Mr. Burgess moved to Medford in 1969, where he bought the Royal Crest Motel. Later he was a bus driver and Supervisor of Transportation for the Medford School District before retiring in 1982.

He enjoyed camping and fishing.

Survivors, in addition to his wife, include four sons, Mark, Beaverton; Scott, Philomath; Michael, San Bernardino, Calif., and Stephen, Placentia, Calif.; a brother, Osmer, Cottage Grove; two sisters, Mary Cleland and Margaret Jones, both Portland; and three grandchildren. He was preceded in death by a sister, Eva Richards.

Arrangements: Perl Funeral Services-Siskiyou, Medford.

ADDENDUM NOVEMBER 2003

My father was a good man, an honorable man, an intelligent man, sometimes a hard man. To say that I understood him well during his life would be a lie, for we walked very different paths in this world, almost diametrically opposed. He started with absolutely nothing during the Great Depression, and made a good life for himself and his family. I regret very much indeed that we could never seem to get closer to each other than we did. I hope that he was proud of what he had produced in me, but I was never quite sure of his feelings on that subject—and he could not express them himself. I loved him dearly and miss him tremendously. Even our endless arguments on politics and people and life in general were, in the end, something that I think both of us relished. He died five days after my fiftieth birthday, but I can still feel his presence with every breath I take, with every word I utter. I hope I always will.

Xenograffiti, by ROBERT REGINALD

ART NELSON

Arthur Edward Nelson, 76, died on September 25, 2003 at San Bernardino of a stroke. He had been ill for many years. He was born on June 19, 1927 at St. Paul, Minnesota, the son of Arthur Edwin and Violet (Riley) Nelson. He married (Mary) Katherine Leahy on Jan. 29, 1949 at St. Paul, and they had five children, all of whom survive: Evelyn (Senior), Richard, Julie, Mark, and Michael.

Nelson enlisted in the U.S. Navy in 1944, serving for two years on the hospital ship, U.S.S. Samaritan, staying with that vessel through its decommissioning in 1946. Upon returning home, he obtained a B.A. in history at St. Thomas College, St. Paul, and an M.A. in history and M.A.L.S. at the University of Minnesota.

He came to Los Angeles in 1954, when he took an entry-level position at Loyola University. He accepted a post as bibliographer and cataloger at California State College, Hayward, in 1959, serving there for four years.

This was a time of great expansion in higher education in California, with new campuses being opened at rapid intervals, and Nelson was approached at the beginning of 1963 with an offer to become the founding Library Director of the as yet unnamed state college planned for the Inland Empire. This was the institution that would later become California State University, San Bernardino.

He officially started his new position on April 1, 1963, working out of a warehouse on South Lugo Street in San Bernardino. His initial charge was to build the core collections of the new state colleges then being established at San Bernardino and Dominguez Hills. Two copies were purchased of every book acquired, and then processed and boxed for shipment, with one set destined for each campus. Both colleges opened their doors in the fall of 1965, each with a starting complement of 50,000 volumes.

The Cal State San Bernardino library at first occupied temporary quarters in the south half what is now Sierra Hall, but Nelson and his staff had already begun planning the construction of a massive, six-story building located at the exact center of the new campus. The structure was delayed for a year by weather and other problems, but finally opened in June of 1971.

Nelson served as Library Director at Cal State San Bernardino for exactly twenty-five years, returning to the ranks on April 1, 1988. He officially retired from CSUSB in 1991.

Art Nelson will be remembered for his intelligence, his wit, his energy, and his acumen, but his memory is forever enshrined within the great library that he built for the university.

It was he who picked the initial complement of librarians and staff who helped develop the collection—and he chose wisely. It was he who planned and constructed a beautiful yet utilitarian structure for the library that also anticipated the future needs of the university—and he designed well. But most of all, it was he who understood that the very heart and soul of the university must be comprised of a broadly-based collection of superlative books and serials that would strongly support the curriculum thereof—and he bent all of his strength, all of his energy, towards achieving that goal.

His spirit lives on within the hallowed walls of the University Library that he loved so well. Walk down any aisle, examine any shelf, and his name echoes and rebounds from the richness of the volumes so boldly arrayed there. Generations of students and scholars will forever remain in his debt.

We are all in his debt.

XLV.

AMEN FOR NOW

(December 7, 2003)

"A date that will live in infamy...."
A date that is today almost forgotten, as the veterans who survived the conflagration at Pearl Harbor have themselves gradually faded away.

The truth is, we all fade away sooner or later, and mostly, we're not much remembered thereafter. It doesn't take long. My mentor as a librarian, Art Nelson, died earlier this year, twelve years after he had retired from his position at California State University, San Bernardino. Most of the librarians there only know him as a name. Of the eleven library faculty on our staff, six were hired after he left. In twenty years, no one at Cal State will recall who he was or what he did, or anything at all about the founding Library Director at CSUSB, a man who built the original collection of monographs and journals at the university over a twenty-five-year period and who hired all of the original staff.

Ah, well. That's just the nature of things.

If the study of genealogy has taught me anything, it's that the vast majority of us lose our identities almost completely within a generation of our passing. Very few individuals make any kind of lasting mark in the world. Indeed, very few leave anything behind them to commemorate their lives—good or ill!

Authors delude themselves, of course, into thinking that they're somehow different from the *hoi polloi*, but who remembers or reads the vast majority of the writers who were published professionally during the nineteenth and

Xenograffiti, by ROBERT REGINALD

twentieth centuries? Who *was* Morgan Robertson or T. Earl Hickey or Emile C. Tepperman? Nobodies, today. Be honest with yourselves, folks: you've never even heard of these penmen.

Even bestselling writers are not immune. Jacqueline Susann faded quickly from public view after her sudden death in 1974, and is scarcely mentioned by anyone thirty years later. I had the pleasure of meeting Irving Wallace at his home about a decade before he died; his books today are mostly out-of-print, and his surviving children, well, they're nowhere near as capable as their Old Man.

Is this right? Is it fair? Should not writers or artists or musicians be saved from the Deathman's seemingly universal scythe, which pares all of our withered stalks down to the same, ground-level size?

There are no answers to such questions.

To the extent that a maker of miracles succeeds in putting something of his or her persona into permanent or fixed form—a poem, a story, a play, a painting, a song—and disseminates it into some public forum, he (or she) has succeeded in doing something that 99.9% of the population cannot; and he (or she—or it!) has bought a chance at the golden ring of immortality, to the extent that "immortality" can be defined as an active memory of one's work on earth.

When I set down my precious verbiage in printed form, it has some chance, however small, of being picked up and actually read by someone a century or two hence; and I may thereby have extended my presence into that future, although I myself, of course, won't be there in any personal or real way to affect that outcome.

Of course, there's a real risk that the values that I ascribe to my own work, or the materials that I myself regard most highly among my writings will not be so received by generations yet to come. By all accounts, Conan Doyle had come to detest his best-known creation, Sherlock Holmes, by the end of his long life; but the novels that he valued most highly of his own creations, the historical fictions, plus the serious psychic investigations in fairies and the like that he conducted during his final decade of life, are today held to be minor or even irrelevant to his overall career. He is remem-

Xenograffiti, by ROBERT REGINALD

bered primarily for one character, Sherlock Holmes, and secondarily for his Professor Challenger stories. And he has nothing at all to say about this.

Which is, perhaps, just as it should be.

Readers ultimately choose what they wish to read. Sometimes they're influenced by the scholars or the critics or the teachers, sometimes not. H. Rider Haggard's two classic adventure novels, *King Solomon's Mines* and *She*, are still enjoyed today, although not much taught in our schools; but the remainder of his vast output languishes, perhaps unjustly, in permanent obscurity. Yet even so, he is blessed beyond most of his contemporary brethren, in that *any* of his works are still read at all.

Of all my books, the one most likely to survive the test of time is *The House of the Burgesses*, my family genealogy, which will be passed down and cherished from generation to generation, and disseminated widely on the future equivalent of the internet. It isn't my best work—thus far that accolade (at least in my opinion) must go to *The Dark-Haired Man*—but it touches the lives of tens of thousands, maybe hundreds of thousands, of individuals, in an ever-widening circle that will never end, unless civilization itself should someday fall.

That one volume is my primary contribution to the world of letters. I already know this. The thought is even more humbling than my recent heart attack.

And so I say "Amen for now."

I will write what I am allowed to write in the years I have remaining. I will continue to strive for unobtainable perfection, knowing that it can never be found. I may even produce a third edition someday of the Burgess book.

This series of autobiographical essays which commenced with a look at the history of Borgo Press must now conclude, as I move back into the crafting of "real" fiction.

I feel the juices flowing again. I think I can do this again. I know I can.

To those of you who have borne with me during these reminiscences of my earlier days, bless you all.

And amen for now.

Xenograffiti, by ROBERT REGINALD

BIBLIOGRAPHY

Allard, Yvon. *Paralittératures*. Montréal: La Centrale des Bibliothèques, 1979.
Anderson, Poul. *The Broken Sword*. New York: Abelard-Schuman, 1954.
Annan, Ralph. *The Spider-Men: A Science-Fantasy Adventure*. New York: Vantage Press, 1979.
Anthony, Piers. *Piers Anthony's Hasan*. San Bernardino, CA: The Borgo Press, 1977.
Arnold, Edwin Lester. *The Wonderful Adventures of Phra the Phoenician*. New York: Harper & Bros., 1890.
Ashley, Mike. *The John Spencer Fantasy Publications*. Wallsend, England: Cosmos Literary Agency, 1979.
Atwood, Margaret. *Cat's Eye*. Toronto: McClelland & Stewart, 1988.
Atwood, Margaret. *The Edible Woman*. Toronto: McClelland & Stewart, 1969.
Atwood, Margaret. *The Handmaid's Tale*. Toronto: McClelland & Stewart, 1985.
Atwood, Margaret. *Lady Oracle*. Toronto: McClelland & Stewart, 1976.
Atwood, Margaret. *Surfacing*. Toronto: McClelland & Stewart, 1972.
Bangs, John Kendrick. *A House-Boat on the Styx: Being Some Account of the Divers Doings of the Associated Shades*. New York: Harper & Bros., 1895.
Bangs, John Kendrick. *The Pursuit of the House-Boat: Being Some Further Account of the Divers Doings of the Associated Shades, Under the Leadership of Sherlock Holmes, Esq.* New York: Harper & Bros., 1897.
Barringer, Leslie. *Gerfalcon*. London: William Heinemann, 1927.
Barringer, Leslie. *Joris of the Rock*. London: William Heinemann, 1928.
Barringer, Leslie. *Shy Leopardess*. London: Methuen, 1948.
Bellairs, John. *The Face in the Frost*. New York: Macmillan, 1969.
Blair, Karin. *Meaning in Star Trek*. New York: Warner Books, 1979.
Brand, Kurt. *Blitzkrieg Galactica*. Van Nuys, CA: Master Publications, 1979. Perry Rhodan #129.
Brand, Kurt. *Peril Unlimited*. Van Nuys, CA: Master Publications, 1979. Perry Rhodan #130.

Xenograffiti, by ROBERT REGINALD

Brand, Kurt. *The Sinister Power.* Van Nuys, CA: Master Publications, 1978. Perry Rhodan #124.
Brand, Kurt. *Volunteers for Frago.* Van Nuys, CA: Master Publications, 1978. Perry Rhodan #122.
Bretnor, Reginald, editor. *Modern Science Fiction: Its Meaning and Its Future.* Chicago: Advent:Publishers, 1979.
Bulmer, Kenneth, as Alan Burt Akers. *Golden Scorpio.* New York: DAW Books, 1978.
Campbell, Clive S. *The Day the Sun Came Through.* New York: Vantage Press, 1979.
Caprio, Betsy. *Star Trek: Good News in Modern Images.* Mission, KS: Sheed, Andrews & McMeel, 1978.
Carter, Lin, ed. *Golden Cities, Far.* New York: Ballantine Books, 1970.
Chalker, Jack L., and Mark Owings. *The Science-Fantasy Publishers: A Critical and Bibliographic History.* 3rd ed. Westminster, MD: The Mirage Press Ltd., 1991.
Cirilius, Marcus. *Prehistoric Epic!* New York: Vantage Press, 1978.
Coffman, C. C. *Spacedust One.* New York: Vantage Press, 1979.
Comeau, Alexander de. *Monk's Magic.* London: Methuen, 1931.
Cover, Arthur Byron. *Autumn Angels.* New York: Pyramid Books, 1975.
Cover, Arthur Byron. *An East Wind Coming.* New York: Berkley Books, 1979.
Cover, Arthur Byron. *Planetfall.* New York: Avon Books, 1988.
Cover, Arthur Byron. *The Platypus of Doom and Other Nihilists.* New York: Warner Books, 1976.
Cover, Arthur Byron. *The Sound of Winter.* New York: Pyramid Books, 1976.
Cover, Arthur Byron. *Stationfall.* New York: Avon Books, 1989.
Darlton, Clark. *Atom Fire on Mechanica.* Van Nuys, CA: Master Publications, 1978. Perry Rhodan #121.
Darlton, Clark. *Sentinels of Solitude.* Van Nuys, CA: Master Publications, 1979. Perry Rhodan #127.
Davis, Lindsey. *The Iron Hand of Mars.* London: Hutchinson, 1992.
Davis, Lindsey. *Poseidon's Gold.* London: Century, 1993.
Davis, Lindsey. *Shadows in Bronze.* London: Sidgwick & Jackson, 1990.
Davis, Lindsey. *The Silver Pigs.* London: Sidgwick & Jackson, 1989.
Davis, Lindsey. *Venus in Copper.* London: Hutchinson, 1991.
[De Morgan, John]. *Bess: A Companion to Jess.* New York: Norman L. Munro, 1887.
[De Morgan, John]. *He: A Companion to She: Being a History of the Adventures of J. Theodosius Aristophano on the Island of Rapa Nui in Search of His Immortal Ancestor.* New York: Norman L. Munro, 1887.
[De Morgan, John]. *It: A Wild, Weird History of Marvelous, Miraculous, Phantasmagorical Adventures in Search of He, She, and Jess, and*

Xenograffiti, by ROBERT REGINALD

Leading to the Finding of "IT": A Haggard Conclusion. New York: Norman L. Munro, 1887.
[De Morgan, John]. *King Solomon's Wives.* New York: Norman L. Munro, 1887.
Diamond, Graham. *Dungeons of Kuba.* New York: Playboy Press, 1979.
Diamond, Graham. *Lady of the Haven.* New York: Playboy Press, 1978.
du Maurier, Daphne. *The House on the Strand.* London: Victor Gollancz, 1969.
Fanthorpe, Patricia, and Lionel Fanthorpe. *The Black Lion.* Cardiff, Wales: Greystoke Mobray, 1979.
Fanthorpe, Patricia, and Lionel Fanthorpe. *The Holy Grail Revealed: The Real Secret of Rennes-le-Château.* North Hollywood, CA: Newcastle Publishing Co., 1982.
Fanthorpe, Patricia, and Lionel Fanthorpe. *Rennes-le-Château: Its Mysteries and Secrets.* Middlesex, England: Bellevue Books, 1991; as: *Secrets of Rennes-le-Château.* York Beach, ME: Samuel Weiser, 1992.
Gilman, Charlotte Perkins. *Herland.* New York: Pantheon Books, 1979.
Grebens, G. V. *Ivan Efremov's Theory of Science Fiction.* New York: Vantage Press, 1978.
Haggard, H. Rider. *King Solomon's Mines.* London: Cassell, 1885.
Haggard, H. Rider. *She: A History of Adventure.* London: Longmans, Green, 1887.
Haldane, Charlotte. *Melusine; or, Devil Take Her! A Romantic Novel.* London: Arthur Barker, 1936.
Heron-Allen, Edward, as Christopher Blayre. *The Cheetah Girl.* London: Privately Printed, 1923.
Heron-Allen, Edward, as Christopher Blayre. *The Purple Sapphire and Other Posthumous Papers Selected from the Unofficial Records of the University of Cosmopoli.* London: Philip Allan, 1921.
Heron-Allen, Edward, as Christopher Blayre. *Some Women of the University: Being a Last Selection from the Strange Papers of Christopher Blayre.* London: R. Stockwell, 1934.
Heron-Allen, Edward, as Christopher Blayre. *The Strange Papers of Dr Blayre.* London: Philip Allan, 1932.
Hubin, Allen J. *The Bibliography of Crime Fiction, 1749-1975: Listing All Mystery, Detective, Suspense, Police, and Gothic Fiction in Book Form Published in the English Language.* Del Mar, CA: Publisher's Inc., 1979.
Ingram, Eleanor M. *The Thing from the Lake.* Philadelphia: J. B. Lippincott, 1921.
Isaac, Rondall. *Stories of the Unforeseen.* New York: Vantage Press, 1979. New York: Vantage Press, 1979.
Jenkins, Harry. *An Affair of Survival: A Novel.* New York: Vantage Press, 1979.

Xenograffiti, by ROBERT REGINALD

Kies, Cosette N. *Supernatural Fiction for Teens: More than 1300 Good Paperbacks to Read for Wonderment, Fear, and Fun.* 2nd ed. Englewood, CO: Libraries Unlimited, 1992.
Knowles, Vernon. *Eternity in an Hour: A Study in Childhood.* London: Collins, 1932.
Knowles, Vernon. *Here and Otherwise.* London: Robert Holden, 1926.
Knowles, Vernon. *The Ladder.* London: Mandrake Press, 1929.
Knowles, Vernon. *Silver Nutmegs.* London: Robert Holden, 1927.
Knowles, Vernon. *The Street of Queer Houses and Other Stories.* New York: Boullion-Biggs, 1924.
Knowles, Vernon. *Two and Two Make Five.* London: George Newnes, 1935.
Kurtz, Katherine, and Deborah Turner Harris. *The Adept.* New York: Ace Books, 1991.
Kurtz, Katherine. *The Bastard Prince.* New York: Ballantine Books, 1994.
Kurtz, Katherine. *The Bishop's Heir.* New York: Ballantine Books, 1984.
Kurtz, Katherine. *Camber of Culdi.* New York: Ballantine Books, 1976.
Kurtz, Katherine. *Camber the Heretic.* New York: Ballantine Books, 1981.
Kurtz, Katherine. *Deryni Checkmate.* New York: Ballantine Books, 1972.
Kurtz, Katherine. *Deryni Rising.* New York: Ballantine Books, 1970.
Kurtz, Katherine. *The Harrowing of Gwynedd.* New York: Ballantine Books, 1989.
Kurtz, Katherine. *High Deryni.* New York: Ballantine Books, 1973.
Kurtz, Katherine. *In the Service of the King.* New York: Ace Books, 2003.
Kurtz, Katherine. *King Javan's Year.* New York: Ballantine Books, 1992.
Kurtz, Katherine. *King Kelson's Bride.* New York: Ace Books, 2000.
Kurtz, Katherine. *The King's Justice.* New York: Ballantine Books, 1985.
Kurtz, Katherine. *Lammas Night.* New York: Ballantine Books, 1983.
Kurtz, Katherine. *Saint Camber.* New York: Ballantine Books, 1978.
Kurtz, Katherine. *The Quest for Saint Camber.* New York: Ballantine Books, 1986.
Lang, Andrew. *The Book of Dreams and Ghosts.* London: Longmans, Green, 1897.
[Lang, Andrew, and Walter H. Pollock]. *He.* London: Longmans, Green, 1887.
LeBlanc, Richard. *The Fangs of the Vampire.* New York: Vantage Press, 1979.
Leiber, Fritz. *The Sinful Ones.* New York: Universal Giant, 1953. Bound with: *Bulls, Blood, and Passion,* by David Williams.
Leiber, Fritz. *You're All Alone.* New York: Ace Books, 1972.

Xenograffiti, by ROBERT REGINALD

Macauley, David. *Motel of the Mysteries.* Boston: Houghton Mifflin Co., 1979.
Mahr, Kurt. *The Beasts Below.* Van Nuys, CA: Master Publications, 1979. Perry Rhodan #128.
Mahr, Kurt. *Between the Galaxies.* Van Nuys, CA: Master Publications, 1978. Perry Rhodan #119.
Mahr, Kurt. *Fortress in Time.* Van Nuys, CA: Master Publications, 1978. Perry Rhodan #123.
Marinelli, Jean. *From Blight to Height.* New York: Vantage Press, 1979.
McAllister, Bruce. *Dream Baby.* New York: Tor, 1989.
McAllister, Bruce. *Humanity Prime.* New York: Ace Books, 1971.
Moore, Ward. *Bring the Jubilee.* New York: Farrar, Straus & Young, 1953.
Morris, William. *The Well at the World's End.* Hammersmith, England: The Kelmscott Press, 1896.
Nathan, Robert. *So Love Returns.* New York: Alfred A. Knopf, 1958.
Newbolt, Sir Henry. *Aladore.* Edinburgh: William Blackwood & Sons, 1914.
Nolan, William F. *The Black Mask Murders.* New York: St. Martin's Press, 1994.
Nolan, William F. *Helltracks.* New York: Avon Books, 1991.
Nolan, William F., and George Clayton Johnson. *Logan's Run.* New York: Dial Press, 1967.
Nolan, William F. *Logan's Search.* New York: Bantam Books, 1980.
Nolan, William F. *Logan's World.* New York: Bantam Books, 1977.
Nolan, William F. *Look Out for Space.* New York: International Polygonics, 1985.
Nolan, William F. *The Marble Orchard.* New York: St. Martin's Press, 1996.
Nolan, William F. *Night Shapes.* Baltimore, MD: CD Publications, 1995.
Nolan, William F. *Space for Hire.* New York: Lancer Books, 1971.
Nolan, William F. *Things Beyond Midnight.* Santa Cruz, CA: Scream/Press, 1984.
Nolan, William F. *3 for Space.* Brooklyn, NY: Gryphon Books, 1992.
Norman, John. *Tarnsman of Gor.* New York: Ballantine Books, 1966.
Page, Spider. *Legend in Blue Steel.* New York: Python Books, 1979.
Ragged, Hyder (pseud. of Henry Chartres Biron). *King Solomon's Wives; or, The Phantom Mines.* London: Vizetelly & Co., 1887.
Reaves, Michael. *The Burning Realm.* New York: Baen Books, 1988.
Reaves, Michael, and Byron Preiss. *Dragonworld.* Garden City, NY: Nelson Doubleday, 1979.
Reaves, Michael, and Steve Perry. *Hellstar.* New York: Berkley Books, 1984.
Reaves, Michael. *Night Hunter.* New York: Tor, 1995.
Reaves, Michael. *The Shattered World.* New York: Timescape Books, 1984.

Xenograffiti, by ROBERT REGINALD

Reginald, Robert. *Science Fiction and Fantasy Literature.* Detroit: Gale Research Co., 1979.
Reginald, Robert. *Stella Nova: The Contemporary Science Fiction Authors.* Los Angeles, CA: Unicorn & Son, 1970.
Resnick, Michael. *The Official Price Guide to Comic & Science Fiction Books, Third Edition.* Orlando, FL: House of Collectibles, 1979.
Roberts, Keith. *Pavane.* Garden City, NY: Doubleday & Co., 1968.
Rosenberg, Betty, and Diana Tixier Herald. *Genreflecting: A Guide to Reading Interests in Genre Fiction.* 3rd ed. Englewood, CO: Libraries Unlimited, 1991.
Sabrina. *Witch Bitch*, bound with *Dance of Love*, by Martine. New York: Pleasure Books, 1979.
Saxton, Mark. *Havoc in Islandia.* Boston: Houghton Mifflin Co., 1982.
Scheer, K. H. *The Guns of Everblack.* Van Nuys, CA: Master Publications, 1979. Perry Rhodan #126.
Scherwinsky, Felix. *Der Neologismen in der modernen französischen Science-Fiction.* Meisenheim am Glan, West Germany: Verlag Anton Hain, 1978.
Schlobin, Roger C. *The Literature of Fantasy: A Comprehensive, Annotated Bibliography of Modern Fantasy Literature.* New York: Garland Publishing, 1979.
Schreuders, Piet, translated by Josh Pachter. *Paperbacks, U.S.A.: A Graphic History, 1939-1959.* San Diego, CA: Blue Dolphin Enterprises, 1981. As: *The Book of Paperbacks.* London: Virgin Books, 1981.
Smith, Lynn S. *Space Voyages, 1591-1920: A Bibliography of Works Held in the Library of the University of California, Riverside.* Riverside, CA: Special Collections Dept., University Library, University of California, Riverside, 1979.
Stableford, Brian. *The Angel of Pain.* London: Simon & Schuster, 1991.
Stableford, Brian. *The Carnival of Destruction.* London: Pocket Books, 1993.
Stableford, Brian. *The Empire of Fear.* London: Simon & Schuster, 1988.
Stableford, Brian. *Journey to the Center.* Garden City, NY: Doubleday & Co., 1982.
Stableford, Brian. *The Werewolves of London.* London: Simon & Schuster, 1990.
Stevenson, Noel C. *Genealogical Evidence: A Guide to the Standard of Proof Relating to Pedigrees, Ancestry, Heirship, and Family History.* Laguna Hills, CA: Aegean Park Press, 1979.
Taylor, R. G. *Futura Man: An Orphan in Time.* New York: Vantage Press, 1979.
Trainor, Sandy. *Future Sex.* New York: Pleasure Books, 1979. Cover byline reads Sharon Taylor.
Trainor, Starr. *Pleasure Planet.* New York: Pleasure Books, 1979. Cover byline reads Sharon Taylor.

Xenograffiti, by ROBERT REGINALD

Tymn, Marshall B., Robert H. Boyer, Kenneth J. Zahorski. *Fantasy Literature: A Core Collection and Reference Guide*. New York: R. R. Bowker Co., 1979.
Vinicoff, Eric, and Marcia Martin. *Spacing Dutchman*. Berkeley, CA: Aesir Press, 1978.
Voltz, William. *Killers from Hyperspace*. Van Nuys, CA: Master Publications, 1978. Perry Rhodan #120.
Voltz, William. *Robots, Bombs, and Mutants*. Van Nuys, CA: Master Publications, 1979. Perry Rhodan #125.
Waggoner, Diana. *The Hills of Faraway: A Guide to Fantasy*. New York: Atheneum, 1978.
Watson, Ian, ed. *Pictures at an Exhibition*. Cardiff, Wales: Greystoke Mobray, 1981.
Wisconsin State Historical Society, Madison Library Author-Title Catalog. New York: Greenwood Press, 1974, microfiche.
Wurfel, Clifford. *An Introduction to the J. Lloyd Eaton Collection of Science Fiction and Fantasy*. Riverside, CA: Special Collections Dept., University Library, University of California, Riverside, 1979.
Zebrowski, George. *Beneath the Red Star: Studies on International Science Fiction*. San Bernardino, CA: The Borgo Press, 1996.
Zebrowski, George, and Charles Pellegrino. *The Killing Star*. New York: William Morrow, 1995.
Zebrowski, George. *Macrolife*. New York: Harper & Row, 1979.
Zebrowski, George. *The Omega Point*. New York: Ace Books, 1972.
Zebrowski, George. *The Omega Point Trilogy*. New York: Ace Books, 1983.
Zebrowski, George. *The Stars Will Speak*. New York: Harper & Row, 1985.
Zebrowski, George. *Stranger Suns*. New York: Bantam Books, 1991.
Zebrowski, George. *Sunspacer*. New York: Harper & Row, 1984.

Xenograffiti, by ROBERT REGINALD

INDEX

3 for Space (William F. Nolan), 156
The 500 Hats of Bartholomew Cubbins (Dr. Seuss), 194
A. Merritt (Ronald Foust), 189
"Aalila" (Edward Heron-Allen), 105
Abarbanell, Jacob Ralph, 27
Abbey of Maillezais, 66
Abrash, Merritt, 181
Abstracts of Virginia's Northern Neck Warrants & Surveys (Peggy S. Joyner), 133
"Academic Program at Chicon IV" (Donald M. Hassler), 178
"The Accursed Isle" (Mary Elizabeth Counselman), 171, 183
Ace Books, 91, 198, 202, 256-257
"*Ace G-Man Stories* Bibliography" (Phillip H. Nelson), 189
Ackerman, Forrest J, 256-258
Ackerman, Wendayne, 256-258
Addams, Charles, 112
The Adept (Katherine Kurtz & Deborah Turner Harris), 149
"Adept" series (Katherine Kurtz & Deborah Turner Harris), 149
Adleman, Robert H., 275
The Adolescence of P-1 (Thomas P. Ryan), 181
Advent:Publishers, 262
The Adventure Magazine Index (Richard J. Bleiler), 192
Adventure, War, and Sports Fiction (Michael L. Cook & Steve Miller), 279
"Adventures of the Empire Princess" series (Graham Diamond), 251-252
Aesir Press, 261
An Affair of Survival (Harry Jenkins), 249, 251
Agnew, Spiro Theodore, 275-276
Agrarians (writers group), 284

Agrippa, Cornelius, 21
AIAA—SEE: American Institute of Aeronautics and Astronautics
Aickman, Robert, 186
Air Wonder Stories, 284
Akers, Alan Burt—SEE: Bulmer, Kenneth
Aladore (Henry Newbolt), 95-98
Aldiss, Brian W., 182
Alfred A. Knopf, 80
Alfred Bester (Carolyn Wendell), 176
Alice in Blunderland (John Kendrick Bangs), 108
Allard, Yvon, 245-246
Allen, Steve, 109
"The Alleys of Singapore" (Robert E. Howard), 171
"'Almost Better': Surviving the Plague in Stephen King's *The Stand*" (Mary Pharr), 197
Amadis of Gaul, 242
Amalgamated Children's Encyclopedia (Leslie Barringer), 84-85
Amalgamated Press, 84
Amazing Stories, 13-14
"Amen for Now" (Robert Reginald), 296-298
The American Boys' Book Series Bibliography, 1895-1935 (Alan S. Dikty), 199-200
American Fantasy and Science Fiction: Toward a Bibliography of Works Published in the United States (Marshall B. Tymn), 173
"American Gothic: Joseph Payne Brennan" (Alan Warren), 186
American Institute of Aeronautics and Astronautics, 284
American Interplanetary Society, 284
American Trade Union movement, 244

Xenograffiti, by ROBERT REGINALD

America's Secret Service Ace: The Operator 5 Story (Nick Carr), 179
Amis, Kingsley, 10, 18
"Anatomy of a Phenomenon" (Robert Reginald), 9-18
Anatomy of Wonder (Neil Barron), 274
Anderson, Poul, 16, 239-241
Andrews, Julie, 289
The Angel of Pain (Brian Stableford), 204
Anglican Church, 146
Anima Books (a division of Warner Books), 248
Annan, Ralph, 249, 251
Anne McCaffrey (Mary T. Brizzi), 182
Annie Deane (Robert H. Adleman), 275
The Annotated Guide to Fantastic Adventures (Edward J. Gallagher), 179
The Annotated Guide to Robert E. Howard's Sword & Sorcery (Robert Weinberg), 174
The Annotated Guide to Startling Stories (Leon Gammell), 182
The Annotated Guide to Stephen King: A Primary and Secondary Bibliography of the Works of America's Premier Horror Writer (Michael R. Collings), 182
The Annotated Guide to Unknown & Unknown Worlds (Stefan R. Dziemianowicz), 195
The Annotated Index to The Thrill Book: Complete Indexes to and Descriptions of Everything Published in Street & Smith's The Thrill Book (Richard J. Bleiler), 195
Annual Reviews, Inc., 165
Anthony, Piers, 113-116, 178
ap Hugh, Dafydd, 158
"Approaches to Course Structure: The SF Class" (Marshall B. Tymn), 188
"Arcalaus the Enchanter," 242
Arbor House, 287
Arbur, Rosemarie, 181
Argosy, 196
Aristo, 242
Arkham House, 189-190

Arkham House Companion: Fifty Years of Arkham House: A Bibliographical History and Collector's Price Guide to Arkham House/Mycroft & Moran, Including the Revised and Expanded Horrors and Unpleasantries (Sheldon Jaffery), 189-190
Arno Press, 26-27, 76
Arnold, Edwin, Sir, 117
Arnold, Edwin Lester, 117-120
Arnold, H. F., 190
"Ars Scientia = Ars Poetica" (Rosemarie Arbur), 181
"The Art of Darkness" (Douglas E. Winter), 178
Arthur C. Clarke (Eric S. Rabkin), 174-175
Arthur H. Stockwell, 58
"Arthur Machen: Philosophy and Fiction" (S. T. Joshi), 198
Artur Moewig Verlag, 257
Ashley, Mike, 164, 195, 198, 247
Ashley Books, 249
Asimov, Isaac, 15, 18, 170, 195, 263
Assassin of Gor (John Norman), 71
Associated Press, 251
Astounding Stories, 15
Atheneum, 264
"Atlan" series (ed. Forrest J Ackerman), 257
Atom Fire on Mechanica (Clark Darlton), 256
Aton, James L., 171
Atwood, Margaret, 206-211
Aubrey, Frank, 262
"August Derleth: Myth-Maker" (Robert M. Price), 197
The Autobiography of Methuselah (John Kendrick Bangs), 108
"The Automatic Executioner" (Adolphe de Castro), 197
Autumn Angels (Arthur Byron Cover), 150-151
Avon Books, 266, 285
Bachman, Richard—SEE: King, Stephen
Badger Books, 128-129
Baigent, Michael, 42-49
Baker, G. P., 98, 265
Ballantine, Betty, 71, 242-243
Ballantine Adult Fantasy series, 113, 241

Xenograffiti, by ROBERT REGINALD

Ballantine Books, 70-71, 73, 199, 239, 241, 243, 291
Ballard, J. G., 16-17, 181
Balliol College, Oxford, 21
Bangs, John Kendrick, 107-112
Bantam Books, 266, 283, 286
Baring-Gould, Sabine, 193
"Baring-Gould and the Ghouls: The Influence of *Curious Myths of the Middle Ages* on 'The Rats in the Wall'" (Steven J. Mariconda), 193
Barker, Clive,
Barnes, Ronald, 215
Barr, Marleen S., 178, 183
"The Barricade" (Hugh B. Cave), 186
Barricade Books, 283
Barringer, Leslie, 84-90
Barron, Neil, 164, 273-274
The Bastard Prince (Katherine Kurtz), 147-148
The Battle of Dorking (George Chesney), 24
Baycon (science fiction convention), 162
BBC—SEE: British Broadcasting Corp.
Beagle, Peter, 187
"A Beast Is Born" (W. Wayne Robbins), 185
The Beasts Below (Kurt Mahr), 256
Beasts of Gor (John Norman), 71
Beauchamp, Gordon, 169, 179
Beaufort (publisher), 290
Beaumont, Charles, 154, 156
"Beauty for Sale" (J. O. Quinliven), 185-186
Bedford-Jones, H., 172
Behind the Stars (George Zebrowski), 143
Behrends, Steve, 192-193
Bellairs, John, 99-102
Bellamy, Edward, 24, 253
Beneath the Red Star: Studies on International Science Fiction (George Zebrowski; ed. Pamela Sargent), 143
Benson, A. C., 198
Benson, E. F., 198
Benson, R. H., 198
"Berber Loot" (H. Bedford-Jones), 172
Berghof, Herbert, 276
Bernard of Trèves, 82

Besch, Bibi, 276
Bess, Eric, 170
Bess: A Companion to Jess (John De Morgan), 25-27
Best SF of the Year (ed. Ted Dikty & Everett F. Bleiler), 167, 281
Bester, Alfred, 176
Betancourt, John Gregory, 152
"Between Order and Chaos: The Fiction of Bruce McAllister" (Robert Reginald), 121-124
Between the Galaxies (Kurt Mahr), 256
"Beware of the House: The Nature of Reality in Daphne du Maurier's Fantasy" (Robert Reginald & Mary A. Burgess), 54-57
Beware of the Mouse (Leonard Wibberley), 291
"Beyond Armageddon: Stephen King's *The Stand* and the Post Catastrophic World in Speculative Fiction" (Steven Kagle), 198
The Bibliography of Crime Fiction, 1749-1975: Listing All Mystery, Detective, Suspense, Police, and Gothic Fiction in Book Form Published in the England Language (Allen J. Hubin), 254-255
Bid Time Return (Richard Matheson), 56
The Big Time (Fritz Leiber, Jr.), 16
"The Biggest Horror Fan of Them All" (Don Herron), 180
Biggle, Lloyd, Jr., 188
Bikey the Skycycle and Other Tales of Jimmie (John Kendrick Bangs), 108
"Billy Bob Burnette Buys Books" (Billy Bob Burnette), 178
"Binary First Contact" (Lawrence I. Charters), 182
"The Birds" (Vernon Knowles), 77
Biron, Henry Chartres, Sir, 25-26
Bishop, Zealia Brown, 196
The Bishop's Heir (Katherine Kurtz), 147
Bissell, Whit(ner), 276
"Black Flag" (Talbot Mundy), 172
Black Forbidden Things: Cryptical Secrets from the "Crypt of Cthulhu" (ed. Robert M. Price), 196-197

308

"The Black Gargoyle" (Hugh B. Cave), 186
The Black Lion (R. Lionel & Patricia Fanthorpe), 130
"Black Mask Boys" series (William F. Nolan), 157
The Black Mask Murders (William F. Nolan), 157
Blackstone, William, Sir, 109
Blade Runner (film), 182
Blair, Karin, 247-249
Blassingame, Wyatt, 186, 189
Blayre, Christopher—SEE: Heron-Allen, Edward
Bleiler, Everett F., 25-26, 163-164, 167, 170, 281
Bleiler, Richard J., 192, 195
The Blind Worm (Brian Stableford), 202
Blish, James, 248
Blitzkrieg Galactica (Kurt Brand), 256
Bloch, Robert, 183-184, 186, 191, 193
Blood, Bulls, and Passion (David Williams), 91
Blood Brothers of Gor (John Norman), 71
"Blood Brothers: The Supernatural Fiction of A. C., R. H., & E. F. Benson" (Mike Ashley), 198
"Blood of the Gods" (Robert E. Howard), 173
The Bloody Rose (Dan Streib), 289
Bloomquist, Jane, 178
Blue, Tyson, 191
Blue Dolphin Enterprises, 266
The Blue Fairy Book (Andrew Lang), 22
"The Blue Lenses" (Daphne du Maurier), 54
Boas, Marcus, 173
Bobbs-Merrill, 285
Bodily Harm (Margaret Atwood), 206
Boerem, R., 184
Bogstad, Janice M., 182
Bok, Hannes, 170
"Bomb-Proof Town Tamer" (William R. Cox), 189
Bonibooks, 266
The Book of Dreams and Ghosts (Andrew Lang), 19-22
The Book of Paperbacks—SEE: *Paperbacks, U.S.A.*
Boorman, John, 101

Borgo Press, 187, 199-200, 217-220, 278, 286, 291, 298
Bosch, Hieronymus, 150
Bosky, Bernadette Lynn, 180, 186, 197
Boston, Bruce, 192
Boucher, Anthony, 263, 286
Bowling Green State University Popular Press, 190
"A Boy and His Dog" (Harlan Ellison), 209
Boyer, Robert H., 264-265
Boyno, Edward A., 181
Boys' Book Collector (Alan S. Dikty), 200
Bradbury, Ray, 16, 104, 186, 191
Bradley, Marion Zimmer, 181
Brand, Kurt, 256
"The Breath of Dragons" (Michael Reaves), 125
Brede's Tale (Julian May), 176
Breiding, G. Sutton, 187
Brennan, Joseph Payne, 186-187
Brent, Loring, 172, 195
Bretnor, Reginald, 112, 262-263
Brian Aldiss (Michael R. Collings), 182
"Brian Lumley—Reanimator" (Robert M. Price), 193
Brigg, Peter, 181, 185
Bring the Jubilee (Ward Moore), 28, 34-39
British Broadcasting Corporation, 84
British Museum Catalog, 25
Brizzi, Mary T., 175, 177, 182
"The Broken Statue" (Vernon Knowles), 78
The Broken Sword (Poul Anderson), 239-241
Brooks, Stan, 188
Brooks, Terry, 231
"Brother John" (Keith Roberts), 30-31
Brunner, John, 16
"The Brush of Æons: George Zebrowski's Fictional Universe" (Robert Reginald), 140-144
Bucknell Junior College, 285
Budrys, Algis, 10
Bulletin of the Science Fiction Writers of America, 143
Bulmer, Kenneth, 247
"Burgess, Ann-Marie" (pseud.)—SEE: Gerson, Noel B.

Xenograffiti, by ROBERT REGINALD

Burgess, Betty Jane (Kapel), 293
Burgess, Eva—SEE: Richards, Eva (Burgess)
Burgess, Margaret "Peggy"—SEE: Jones, Margaret "Peggy" (Burgess)
Burgess, Mark E., 293
Burgess, Mary A. (Wickizer), 7-8, 51, 54, 62, 95, 99, 107, 206, 217-220, 232-233, 247-249, 251-254
Burgess, Mary P.—SEE: Cleland, Mary (Burgess)
Burgess, Michael, 293—SEE ALSO: Reginald, Robert
"Burgess, Michael," (pseud.)—SEE: Gerson, Noel B.
Burgess, Osmer R., 293
Burgess, Roy Walter "Walt," 292-293
Burgess, Scott Alan, 293
Burgess, Stephen A., 293
Burgess family, 135, 292-293
Burleson, Donald R., 193
Burnette, Billy Bob, 178
The Burning Realm (Michael Reaves), 125-126
Burroughs, Edgar Rice, 119, 197, 242, 260
Butler, Eleanor Frances—SEE: Cameron, Eleanor
Butler, Octavia, 183-184
Butrick, Merritt, 276
Byrne, Leon, 186
Byrne, Stuart J., 256
Byron, George Gordon, Lord, 20
C. Arthur Pearson, 170
Cal State—SEE: California State University, San Bernardino
California State University, Dominguez Hills, 294
California State University, San Bernardino, 125, 215-216, 224-227, 294-296
California Young Reader Award, 280
Camber of Culdi (Katherine Kurtz), 147
Camber the Heretic (Katherine Kurtz), 147
Cameron, Eleanor, 292
Campbell, Clive S., 249, 251
Campbell, John W., Jr., 15-16, 18, 262-263, 277
Campbell, Ramsey, 178, 186-187, 197

"Canaries in a Gilded Cage: Mental and Marital Decline in *McTeague* and *The Shining*" (Brian Kent), 194
The Canfield Decision (Spiro Agnew), 276
"The Cannibal and the Cop" (Stephen King), 178
Cannon, Peter H., 193
The Canterbury Tales (Geoffrey Chaucer), 96
Caprio, Betsy, 247-249
"Captain of the Corpse Crew" (Harry Lee Fellinge), 189
Captive of Gor (John Norman), 71, 73-74
Carlton Press, 249
The Carnival of Destruction (Brian Stableford), 204
Carnival of Souls (film), 283
Carr, Wooda "Nick," 179, 190-191
Carroll, Jonathan, 180
Carroll, Lewis, 193
Carter, Lin, 193-197, 199, 241-243
"The Carter-Smith 'Collaborations'" (Steve Behrends), 193
"CAS & Diverse Hands" (Steve Behrends), 193
Case, David, 186
"Case, Justin"—SEE: Hugh B. Cave
Casebeer, Ed, 198
A Casebook on The Stand (ed. Tony Magistrale), 197
Cassuto, Leonard, 197
"Casting a Long Shadow" (Melissa Mia Hall & Douglas E. Winter), 178
Cat's Eye (Margaret Atwood), 207
Cavaliers and Pioneers: Abstracts of Virginia Land Patents and Grants: Supplement, Northern Neck Grants No. 1, 1690-1692 (Nell Marion Nugent & Susan Bracey Sheppard), 133
Cave, Hugh B., 186-187, 195
"Cave of the Blue Scorpion" (Loring Brent), 172
"The Cavern" (Manly Wade Wellman), 190
La Centrale des Bibliothèques, 245
Centron Films, 283
Cerasini, Marc A., 185, 193
Chalker, Jack L., 259, 269-271

Chambers, Robert W., 198
"Chamber of Horrors"(Sheldon Jaffery), 186
"Chambers and *The King in Yellow*" (Lee Weinstein), 198
Chandler, Raymond, 157
"Chapel of Mystic Horror" (Seabury Quinn), 171, 183
"Character Gullibility in Weird Fiction; or, Isn't Yuggoth Somewhere in Upstate New York?" (Darrell Schweitzer), 184
"Chariots of the Old One" (Robert M. Price and Charles Garofalo), 197
Charles Williams (Kathleen Spencer), 183
Charly (film), 288
Charnas, Suzy McKee, 183-184
Charters, Lawrence I., 182
Chaucer, Geoffrey, 96
The Checklist of Fantastic Literature (Everett F. Bleiler), 25, 163, 167, 170
The Cheetah Girl (Edward Heron-Allen), 103
"Chelsea Quinn Yarbro" (Kevin E. Proulx), 198-199
Chesney, George, Sir, 24
Chesnoff, Richard Z., 28
Chester, William L., 193
Chicon IV (science fiction convention), 177
"Children of Tomorrow" (Arthur Leo Zagat), 196
Children's Fantasy (Francis J. Molson), 190
"Children's Fantasy and Science Fiction" (Francis J. Molson), 176
Children's Science Fiction" (Francis J. Molson & Susan G. Miles), 188
"The Chimpanzee" (Vernon Knowles), 78
China (travel), 185
"Choice, Sacrifice, Destiny, and Nature in *The Stand*" (Bernadette Lynn Bosky), 197
The Christ Commission (Og Mandino), 285
Christopher Priest (Nicholas Ruddick), 190
"The Chronicles of the Deryni" (Katherine Kurtz), 146-147
Circle of Iron (film), 288

Cirilius, Marcus, 249, 251
Citadel Press, 283
City Beneath the Sea (TV film), 276
"The Clam of Catastrophe" (Arthur Byron Cover), 151
Clareson, Alice, 179
Clareson, Thomas Dean "Tom," 168-169, 176, 178, 184, 277-279
Clarion Workshop, 125
Clark, Beverly Lyon, 193
Clark Ashton Smith (Steve Behrends), 192
"The Clark Ashton Smythos" (Will Murray), 193
Clarke, Arthur C., 174-175, 263
Clarke, Boden—SEE: Reginald, Robert
Classic Comics, 150
Classics of the Horror Film (William K. Everson), 283
Cleland, Mary (Burgess), 293
Clement, Hal, 177
Clifton, Mark, 287
"Clive Barker" (Kevin E. Proulx), 198
Clute, John, 164
Codex Derynianus (Robert Reginald & Katherine Kurtz),
Coffman, C. C., 249-251
Cogell, Elizabeth Cummins, 176
Cohen, Alan, 194
"The Cold Beyond Bearing" (Ronald L. Weston), 178
Coleridge, Samuel Taylor, 105
"The Collapse of Family and Language in Stephen King's *The Shining*" (Alan Cohen), 194
"Collecting Paperbacks" (Piet Schreuders), 267
"Collecting Stephen King" (Darrell Schweitzer), 180
College of Wooster, 277
Collier, John, 112, 186
Collings, Michael R., 169, 178, 180-183, 185, 188, 192
Collins, Max Allan, 218
Collins (publisher), 289
"Colossus of the Radio" (Leslie Ramón), 196
"Comeau's *Magic*" (Robert Reginald), 58-61
Compton, D. G., 122
Conan Doyle, Arthur, 297

311

"Conan" series (Robert E. Howard), 174
"Concerning David Case" (Jeffrey K. Goddin), 186
Condon, Richard Thomas, 279-280
"Conferences and Conventions" (Marshall B. Tymn), 188
Connecticut College for Women, 276
The Conquest of Space (David Lasser), 284
Conrad, Pam Stampf, 280
Contemporary Authors (Gale Research), 163
Contento, William G. "Bill," 164, 279
Cook, Frederick, 172-173
Cook, Michael Lewis, 279
Cook, Robin, 178
Cooper, James Fenimore, 20
"Corfe Gate" (Keith Roberts), 32-33
Cornell University, 286
"The Corpse Maker" (Hugh B. Cave), 186
The Corpse Maker (Hugh B. Cave; ed. Sheldon Jaffery), 186
Cort, Jim, 193, 197
"Cosmic Fear and the Fear of the Lord: Lovecraft's Religious Vision" (Robert M. Price), 197
Cosmos Literary Agency, 247
Coulson, Robert, 180
Counselman, Mary Elizabeth, 171, 183
Counter Force (Dan Streib), 289
"Counterforce" series (Dan Streib), 289
"Country of the Knife" (Robert E. Howard), 173
The Court of the Stone Children (Eleanor Cameron), 292
Cover, Arthur Byron, 150-153
Coward-McCann, 262
Cox, Arthur Jean, 184, 186
Cox, William R., 189
Coye, Lee Brown, 171
Coyne, John, 180
Craig, Brian, 202-205
Crawford, Gary William, 180, 186-187, 198
"Creation Unfinished: Astronomical Realities in the Hainish Fiction of Ursula K. Le Guin" (Thomas P. Dunn), 182

The Creature from the Black Lagoon (film), 276
"Creatures of the Ray" (James L. Aton), 171
Creepshow (film and comic book), 179
"Critical Studies and Reference Works" (Marshall B. Tymn), 176
"Critical Studies in Horror Literature: A Selected, Annotated Bibliography" (Marshall B. Tymn), 180
Cronenberg, David, 179
Crosby Library, 222
Crossley, Robert, 183
Crypt of Cthulhu (magazine), 192-193, 196-197
C.S. Lewis (Brian Murphy), 177
CSUSB—SEE: California State University, San Bernardino
Cthulhu Mythos (H. P. Lovecraft), 64, 184, 193, 197, 199
"The Cthulhu Mythos Fiction of Robert Bloch" (Randall D. Larson), 103
"The Cthulhuers" (John Strysik), 193
Cujo (Stephen King), 180
Cummings, Ray, 171
Curious Myths of the Middle Ages (Sabine Baring-Gould), 193
"Curious Things: The Horror Fiction of Eleanor M. Ingram" (Robert Reginald & Mary A. Burgess), 62-65
Currey, Lloyd W., 164, 259
"The Curse of the Crimson God" (Robert E. Howard), 172
"The Curse of the Khan" (R. Lionel Fanthorpe), 130
Cycle of the Werewolf (Stephen King), 180
"*Cycle of the Werewolf* and the Moral Tradition of Horror" (Randall D. Larson), 180
Dagger Magic (Katherine Kurtz & Deborah Turner Harris), 149
Dahl, Roald, 187
Dahlgren (Samuel R. Delany), 178
D'Ammassa, Don, 180, 186
Dance of Love ("Martine"), 260
"Dance of the Bloodless Ones" (Francis James), 185

Xenograffiti, by ROBERT REGINALD

"Dance of the Spheres: Keith Roberts and the *Pavane* of History" (Robert Reginald), 28-33
Dancer of Gor (John Norman), 71
"Dangerous Tastes: Science and Fiction" (Donald M. Hassler), 181
Dangerous Visions (bookstore), 151
Dann, Jack, 231
Dante, 221, 226
"Dark Genesis: *Watchers & Shadowfires* (Stan Brooks), 188
"The Dark Side of Childhood: *The 500 Hats of Bartholomew Cubbins* and *The Shining*" (Vernon Hyles), 194
"The Dark Side of the American Dream: Dennis Etchison" (Michael E. Stamm), 180
"Dark Streets and Bright Dreams: Rationalism, Technology, and 'Impossible Knowledge' in Stephen King's *The Stand*" (Michael A. Morrison), 197-198
Dark Transformations: Deadly Visions of Change (Michael R. Collings), 192
Darkfall (Dean R. Koontz), 188
The Dark-Haired Man (Robert Reginald), 298
Darkworld Detective (Michael Reaves), 125-126
Darlton, Clark, 256
d'Arras, Jean, 66
Darwinian philosophy, 72
"The Daughter of Erlik Khan" (Robert E. Howard), 171
David Lindsay (Gary K. Wolfe), 177
"David Morrell: Tasting First Blood" (Douglas E. Winter), 179
David Morrell's *The Totem*: The Link Is Control" (Brooks Landon), 179
Davis, Frederick C., 185
Davis, J. Madison, 194
Davis, Lindsey, 212-214
DAW Books, 71, 184-185, 194, 202-203, 247
Day, Bradford M., 163
Day, Nora G., 178
Day, Phyllis J., 178
"The Day the Gorf Took Over" (William F. Nolan), 156
The Day the Sun Came Through (Clive S. Campbell), 249, 251

"The Days of Future Past, or Utopians Lessing and Le Guin Fight Future Nostalgia" (Kathe Davis Finney), 177
De Bolt, Joe, 176
de Camp, L. Sprague, 61, 112, 263
de Castro, Adolphe, 197
de Comeau, Alexander, 58-61
de la Mare, Walter, 198
De Morgan, John, 25-27
"The Dead Wagon" (Greye La Spina), 190
"Dean R. Koontz: A Chronology" (Bill Munster), 188
"Dean R. Koontz: A Brief and Informal Appreciation" (Joe R. Lansdale), 189
"Dean R. Koontz and Stephen King: Style, Invasion, and an Aesthetics of Horror" (Michael R. Collings), 188
"Dean R. Koontz's *Twilight Eyes*: Art and Artifact" (Michael R. Collings), 188
Death of an Adept (Katherine Kurtz and Deborah Turner Harris), 149
The Death Ship (William Clark Russell), 117
Death Shuttle (Dan Streib), 289
Deathwatch (Elleston Trevor), 290
"Definitions of Science Fiction and Fantasy" (Roger C. Schlobin), 176
Delany, Samuel R., 16, 177
Dell Books, 159, 266
"The Demon" (Edward Heron-Allen), 104
"Dennis Etchison: The Unknown Writer" (Karl Edward Wagner), 178-179
Derleth, August, 184, 193, 197-198
"The Derleth Mythos" (Richard L. Tierney), 184
The Deryni Archives (Katherine Kurtz), 145-147
Deryni Checkmate (Katherine Kurtz), 146-147
Deryni Rising (Katherine Kurtz), 145-147
"Deryni" series (Katherine Kurtz), 67, 145-149
"Derynian Dreams: The Fantasy Worlds of Katherine Kurtz" (Robert Reginald), 145-149

313

Xenograffiti, by ROBERT REGINALD

"The Destiny Gorilla" (Robert E. Howard), 171
"The Devil Took Her!: Charlotte Haldane's *Melusine*" (Robert Reginald), 66-69
"The Devil Who Played God" (Theodore Roscoe), 189
The Devil's Brigade (Richard H. Adleman), 275
The Devil's Brigade (film), 275
The Devil's Notebook: Collected Epigrams and Pensées of Clark Ashton Smith (ed. Donald Sidney-Fryer & Don Herron), 192
DeVore, Howard, 176
Di Fate, Vincent, 176
Dial Press, 280
"Dialogue Within the Archetypal Community of *The Stand*" (Ed Casebeer), 198
Diamond, Graham, 251-252
"The Diary of Alonzo Typer" (William Lumley), 197
Dick, Philip K., 16, 28, 177, 182
Dickens, Charles, 105, 107
Dickerson, Mary Jane, 194
Different Seasons (Stephen King), 178
"Different Writers on *Different Seasons*" (Charles L. Grant, David Morrell, Alan Ryan, & Douglas E. Winter), 178
"Digging Up Irem" (Lin Carter), 193
Dikty, Alan Sam, 199-200, 281
Dikty, Barbara, 169, 281
Dikty, David, 281
Dikty, Judy—SEE: May, Julian
Dikty, Thaddeus Maxim Eugene "Ted," 163, 167-201, 280-282
The Dinosaur Trackers—SEE: *Robert Silverberg's Time Tours*
"Directory of Specialty Publishers" (Marshall B. Tymn), 176
Discover (magazine), 287
Discovering Classic Horror Fiction I (ed. Darrell Schweitzer), 198
Discovering H. P. Lovecraft (ed. Darrell Schweitzer), 184
Discovering Modern Horror Fiction (ed. Darrell Schweitzer), 179-180
Discovering Modern Horror Fiction II (ed. Darrell Schweitzer), 186-187
Discovering Stephen King (ed. Darrell Schweitzer), 180-181

"The Disk" (Rondall Isaac), 266
Diskin, Lahna F., 176
Disney Adventures (comic book), 152
"Disturb Not The Dead" (Hugh B. Cave), 186
Dixie Demagogues (Frank W. Ryhlick, i.e., Frank Riley), 287
Do Androids Dream of Electric Sheep? (Philip K. Dick), 182
"Doc Savage" series (Ryerson Johnson et al. as "Kenneth Robeson"), 283
"Doctoral Dissertations in Science Fiction and Fantasy, 1970-1979" (Douglas R. Justus), 176
Don Juan (Lord Byron), 20
Don't Bite the Sun (Tanith Lee), 184
"Don't Look Now" (Daphne du Maurier), 54
"Doom of the House of Duryea" (Earl Pierce, Jr.), 171, 183
Dorrance & Co., 249
Double Trouble: A Bibliographic Chronicle of Ace Mystery Doubles (Sheldon Jaffery), 198
The Mystery Scene Movie Guide (Max Allan Collins), 218
"Double Your Pleasure, Double Your Fun, Schizoid Living for Everyone! On Being a Pseudonym" (Robert Reginald), 235-238
Doubleday, 287
Dover Publications, 22
Down & Dirty (George R. R. Martin), 152
Drabble, Margaret, 191
"Dragon Moon" (Henry Kuttner), 196
Dragons, Elves, and Heroes (ed. Lin Carter), 241
Dragonworld (Michael Reaves & Byron Preiss), 125-126
"Dray Prescot" series (Kenneth Bulmer), 247
Dream Baby (Bruce McAllister), 122-124
The Dream-Quest of Unknown Kadath (H. P. Lovecraft), 197
du Maurier, Daphne, 54-57
Duane, Diane, 127
Dudley-Smith, Trevor—SEE: Trevor, Elleston
Dungeons of Kuba: Adventures of the Empire Princess #2 (Graham Diamond), 251-252

Dunn, Thomas P., 178, 182
Dunsanian tales, 76-77, 197
Dunsany, Lord, 76-77, 106, 184, 197
Dziemianowicz, Stefan R., 195
"The Early Tales: Stephen King and *Startling Mystery Stories*" (Chet Williamson), 180
"The Ears of Donkey Daudette" (Theodore Roscoe), 189
An East Wind Coming (Arthur Byron Cover), 151
Eastern Orthodoxy, 146
Eaton, J. Lloyd, 163, 261-262
Eaton Award—SEE: J. Lloyd Eaton Award
Eaton Collection—SEE: J. Lloyd Eaton Collection
E.C. Comics, 179
Edgar Allan Poe Award, 280
The Edible Woman (Margaret Atwood), 206-207
Edinburgh Academy, 20
E.E. "Doc" Smith (Joe Sanders), 183
Efremov, Ivan, 263
"The Eighth Green Man" (G. G. Pendarves), 190
The Eighth Green Man (and Other Strange Folk) (ed. Robert E. Weinberg), 190
Eisgruber, Frank, Jr., 181
Eldridge, Paul, 119
"Eli Still Goes On" (R. Lionel & Patricia Fanthorpe), 130
Eliot, George Fielding, 190
"The Elixir of Invisibility" (Henry Kuttner), 196
Eller, Jackie, 194
Ellison, Harlan, 16, 209
Emperor of America (Richard Condon), 280
The Empire of Fear (Brian Stableford), 203-204
The Enchanted Places (Christopher Milne), 286
The Enchanted Type-Writer (John Kendrick Bangs), 108
Eng, Steve, 187
Engebretson, David, 182
Enterprise Stardust (ed. Forrest J Ackerman), 256
E. P. Dutton, 58, 280, 292
Equality (Edward Bellamy), 24

"E.R.B. and H.P.L." (William Fulwiler), 197
Erlich, Richard D., 178
Eroticism in Supernatural Literature (Brian Stableford), 202-203
Essays Lovecraftian (Darrell Schweitzer), 181
"Et in Arcadia Ego" (R. Lionel Fanthorpe & Patricia Fanthorpe), 130
Etchison, Dennis, 178-179
Eternity in an Hour (Vernon Knowles), 76
The Eureka Years: Boucher and McComas's The Magazine of Fantasy & Science Fiction (ed. Annette Peltz McComas), 286
Everson, William Keith, 282-283
"The Execution of Lucarno" (Julius Long), 171, 183
Explorers of Gor (John Norman), 71
Exposition Press, 249
Extrapolation (magazine), 277-278
"F. Paul Wilson" (Kevin E. Proulx), 198
Fabian, Stephen E., 168, 171-172, 174-175
Fabian in Color (artwork; Stephen E. Fabian), 175
Fabun, Don, 263
The Face in the Frost (John Bellairs), 99-102
Faces of the Beast (Bruce Boston), 192
"The Faces Outside" (Bruce McAllister), 121-122
"Fafhrd and the Grey Mouser" series (Fritz Leiber, Jr.), 91
"Falco" series (Lindsey Davis), 212-214
Falconer, Lee N.—SEE: May, Julian
"The Fan Movement" (Joe Sanders), 188
"Fane, Bron"—SEE: Fanthorpe, R. Lionel
The Fangs of the Vampire (Richard LeBlanc), 265-266
Famous Fantastic Classics #1 (anon. ed. Robert Weinberg), 171
Famous Fantastic Classics #2 (anon. ed. Robert Weinberg), 172
"Famous Last Words" (Robert M. Price), 197

Xenograffiti, by ROBERT REGINALD

Famous Pulp Classics #1 (anon. ed. Robert Weinberg), 172
Fantastic Adventures (magazine), 179
"The Fantastic Cinema" (Vincent Miranda), 176
"Fantastic Fictions at the Edge and in the Abyss: Genre Definitions and the Contemporary Cross-Genre Novel" (Janice M. Bogstad), 182
The Fantastic Island (Ryerson Johnson as "Kenneth Robeson"), 283
Fantastic Stories (magazine), 113
"The Fantasy and Mystery Bookshop" (Peter H. Cannon), 193
Fantasy Literature: A Core Collection and Reference Guide (Marshall B. Tymn, Robert H. Boyer & Kenneth J. Zahorski), 264-265
Fantasy Literature: A Reader's Guide (Neil Barron), 274
Fantasy Literature for Children and Young Adults: An Annotated Bibliography (Ruth Nadleman Lynn), 273
Fantasy Review, 274
Fanthorpe, Patricia, 40-49, 130
Fanthorpe, R. Lionel, 40-49, 128-130, 159
"Far Below" (Robert Barbour Johnson), 171, 183
Far Below and Other Horrors (ed. Robert Weinberg), 171, 183
Farley, Ralph Milne, 172
Farmer, Philip José, 16, 175
Farrar & Rinehart, 268
Farris, John, 198
"The Fasterfaster Affair" (William F. Nolan), 156
"The Fat Man, the Consulting Detective, and the Seller of Speculations: The Curious World of Arthur Byron Cover" (Robert Reginald), 150-153
"Father Bredder" series (Leonard Wibberley), 290-291
Fawcett Gold Medal, 289
FAX Collector's Editions, 167-201, 281
Fear to the World: Eleven Voices in a Chorus of Horror (Kevin E. Proulx), 198-199
Fearn, John Russell, 247
Fellinge, Harry Lee, 189
"Femmes Fatales? The Women Protagonists in Four Koontz Novels" (Elizabeth Massie), 188-189
Ferreira, Patricia, 194
"A Few Words, a Very Few Words, on Writing" (Robert Reginald), 231-234
Fezandié, Clement, 170
Fighting Slave of Gor (John Norman), 71
The Films of Stephen King (Michael R. Collings), 183
The Final Addiction (Richard Condon), 280
Finney, Jack, 56
Finney, Kathe Davis, 177
Firefly: A Novel of the Far Future (Brian Stableford), 202-205
Fires of Isis (Alexander de Comeau), 58
Fireside Theatre, 152-153
"The First Lewis Theobald" (R. Boerem), 184
Fish, Kay Niman, 251
Fisher, Philip M., Jr., 196
Fitzgerald, Gil, 186
Flash Gordon (Arthur Byron Cover), 152
Flash Gordon (film), 152
"Les Fleurs du Mal" (Brian Stableford), 204-205
Les Fleurs du Mal (Brian Stableford), 204
Flint, Homer Eon, 171
"The Floor Above" (M. L. Humphreys), 190
"Flowers for Algernon" (Daniel Keyes), 288
"Flying Dutchman"—SEE: *The Death Ship*
The Flying Spy: A History of G-8 (Nick Carr), 190
Flynn, T. T., 195
Forbidden Kingdom (Elleston Trevor), 290
Force Fields (Andrew Joron), 184
The Forever Machine—SEE: *They'd Rather Be Right*
"Forgotten Words, Spoken by Forgotten Ancestors" (Douglas E. Winter), 178
Fortress in Time (Kurt Mahr), 256
Foster, David L., 177-178

Foster, Tom, 171
Foundation (magazine), 278
"The Four Faces of the Outsider" (Dirk W. Mosig), 184
"Four Lashes an Hour" (Johnston McCulley), 172
Foust, Ronald, 189
Fowler, Douglas, 187
Frane, Jeff, 175
Frank Herbert (David M. Miller), 175
"Freaking the Mundane: A Sociological Look at Science Fiction Conventions, and Vice Versa" (Phyllis J. Day & Nora G. Day), 178
Frederik Pohl (Thomas D. Clareson), 168, 184, 278
"Free Will and Sexual Choice in *The Stand*" (Anthony Magisrale), 197
Friedell, Egon, 185
Fritz Leiber (Jeff Frane), 175
"From Beyond" (H. P. Lovecraft), 197
From Blight to Height (Jean Marinelli), 265-266
"From Pessimism to Sentimentality: Do Androids Dream of Electric Sheep? Becomes *Blade Runner*" (Philip E. Kaveny), 182
"From the Pulps to the Classroom: The Strange Journey of Science Fiction" (James Gunn), 176
Fryer, Donald Sidney—SEE: Sidney-Fryer, Donald
"Full Fathom Five: The Supernatural Fiction of William Hope Hodgson" (Alan Warren), 198
Fulwiler, William, 197
Fungi from Yuggoth (H. P. Lovecraft), 197
The Fur Person (May Sarton), 288
Futura Man: An Orphan in Time (R. G. Taylor), 265
Future and Fantastic Worlds: A Bibliographical Retrospective of DAW Books (1972-1987) (Sheldon Jaffery), 185
Future Sex (Sharon Taylor as "Sandy Trainor"), 260
Futurefall (Arthur Byron Cover), 152
Futuristic Science Stories, 128
"The G-Man Years" (Don Hutchison), 189
Galaxy (magazine), 16, 287
Gale Group, 8

Gale Research Co., 163
Gallagher, Edward J., 179
Gallico, Paul,
Gammell, Leon, 182
Gangland's Doom: The Shadow of the Pulps (Frank Eisgruber, Jr.), 181
Gardner, Craig Shaw, 179
Gardner, Erle Stanley, 157
Garland Publishing Co., 264, 273, 279
Garofalo, Charles, 197
A Gazeteer of the Hyborian World of Conan, Including Also the World of Kull and an Ethnogeographical Dictionary of the Principal Peoples of the Era, with Reference to The Starmont Map of the Hyborian World (Julian May as "Lee N. Falconer"), 174
Geisel, Theodore Seuss—SEE: Seuss, Dr.
Gene Wolfe (Joan Gordon), 183
Genealogical Evidence (Noel C. Stevenson), 44
Genealogical Publishing Co., 133
"Genesis of the Cthulhu Mythos" (George Wetzel), 184
Genreflecting: A Guide to Reading Interests in Genre Fiction (Betty Rosenberg & Diana Tixier Herald), 273-274
Gentlemen of Hades (Frederic Arnold Kummer), 112
"George R. R. Martin" (Kevin E. Proulx), 198
Gerald Howe, 289
Gerfalcon (Leslie Barringer), 84-90
Gernsback, Hugo, 14, 284
Gernsback Publications, 284
Gerrold, David, 181
Gerson, Noel B., 235-236
"The Ghost and the Skeleton" (Wyatt Blassingame), 189
Ghosts I Have Met and Some Others (John Kendrick Bangs), 108
Gibson, William, 199
Gilliland, Alexis A., 191
Gilman, Charlotte Perkins, 252-253
G.K. Hall, 278
Glasby, John, 128
The Glass Inferno (Thomas N. Scortia & Frank M. Robinson), 288
Gnome Press, 287
The God Beat (Mayo Mohs), 287

Goddin, Jeffrey K., 186
Goff, Helen Lyndon—SEE: Travers, P. L.
Gold, H. L., 16
Golden, Bruce, 215
Golden Cities, Far (ed. Lin Carter), 241-243
Golden Scorpio (Kenneth Bulmer as "Alan Burt Akers"), 247
"Gol-Goroth, a Forgotten Old One" (Robert M. Price), 193
"The Gong of Transportation" (Vernon Knowles), 77
Gonzaga University, 162, 222
"Good and Evil in Stephen King's *The Shining*" (Burton Hatlen), 194
"Gopa" (C. C. Coffman), 250-251
"Gor" series (John Norman), 70-75
Gordon, Joan, 169, 175, 183
"Gory Interludes: John Norman and the Ennui of Sexual Fantasy" (Robert Reginald), 70-75
Goya y Lucientes, Francisco José de, 194
Grand Army War Songs (various), 185
"Grand Fenwick" stories (Leonard Wibberley), 290
Grant, Charles L., 178, 186
A Grave Must Be Deep (Theodore Roscoe), 190
Gray, Gertrude E., 133
Gray, Russell, 195
"The Gray Death" (Loual B. Sugarman), 190
The Great Cowboy Race—SEE: *A Talent for Loving*
The Greatest Salesman in the World (Og Mandino), 285
The Greatest Secret in the World (Og Mandino), 285
Grebens, G. V., 263
Greenwood Press, 278
"Greenwood" tales (G. P. Baker), 98
Griffith, George, 119, 170
"The Grim Imperative of Michael Shea" (Arthur Jean Cox), 186
Guardsman of Gor (John Norman), 71
"Guest-Room in Hell" (Leon Byrne), 186
Gunn, James E., 176
The Guns of Everblack (K. H. Scheer), 256

"H. Russell Wakefield: The Man Who Believed in Ghosts" (Ben P. Indick), 198
Hagen, Ordean, 254-255
Haggard, Henry Rider, Sir, 13-14, 22-27, 298
"Hainish" fiction (Ursula K. Le Guin), 182
Hal Clement (Donald M. Hassler), 177
Hala, James, 194
Haldane, Charlotte, 66-69
Haldane, J. B. S., 66
Haldeman, Joe, 175
Haldeman-Julius publications, 266
Hall, Adam—SEE: Trevor, Elleston
Hall, Hal W., 164
Hall, Melissa Mia, 178
Hamlet (William Shakespeare), 110-111
Hammett, Dashiell, 157
The Handmaid's Tale (Margaret Atwood), 207-211
Harbottle, Philip, 247
"Harlan Ellison's Use of the Narrator's Voice" (Joseph F. Patrouch, Jr.), 178
Harper & Bros., 170
Harper & Row, 280
HarperCollins, 280
Harper's Monthly, 108
Harper's Weekly, 108
Harris, Deborah Turner, 149
The Harrowing of Gwynedd (Katherine Kurtz), 147-148
Harvey, Harold A. "Herk," 283
"Has Success Spoiled Stephen King?" (Alan Warren), 180
Hasan (Piers Anthony), 113-116
Hassler, Donald M., 169, 177, 181-182, 195
Hatlen, Burton, 178, 194
The Haven (Graham Diamond), 251-252
Havoc in Islandia (Mark Saxton), 267-268
"Hawk of the Hills" (Robert E. Howard), 171
He: A Companion to She, Being a History of the Adventures of J. Theodosius Aristophano on the Island of Rapa Nui in Search of His Immortal Ancestor (John De Morgan), 25-27

Xenograffiti, by ROBERT REGINALD

He (Andrew Lang & Walter H. Pollock), 25-27
Heald, Tim, 287
Heard, Gerald, 263
Heaven and Hell and the Megas Factor (Robert Nathan), 80
Heinlein, Robert A., 15-16, 278
"The Heirs of Saint Camber" (Katherine Kurtz), 147-148
"Held Over By Popular Demand: David Cronenberg" (Richard Meyers), 179
Heldreth, Leonard G., 180
Hellstar (Michael Reaves & Steve Perry), 126
Helltracks (William F. Nolan), 156
Hemingway, Ernest, 156
"Henry Kuttner's Cthulhu Mythos Fiction: An Overview" (Shawn Ramsey), 193
Herald, Diana Tixier, 273-274
Herbert, Frank, 175
Herbert, James, 186
Here and Otherwise (Vernon Knowles), 76-79
Herland (Charlotte Perkins Gilman), 252-254
Heron-Allen, Edward, 103-106
"Herr Yama from Yokohama" (Day Keene), 189
Herron, Don, 180, 192
Herts-Lion (film producer), 283
Herzog, Arthur, 288
H.G. Wells (Robert Crossley), 183
Hickey, Bill, 276
Hickey, T. Earl, 297
High Deryni (Katherine Kurtz), 146-147
Hillgoss, Candace, 283
The Hills of Faraway: A Guide to Fantasy (Diana Waggoner), 264-265
"His Brother's Keeper" (George Fielding Eliot), 190
"The Histories of King Kelson" (Katherine Kurtz), 147-148
"History as Horror: Chelsea Quinn Yarbro" (Gil Fitzgerald), 186
A History of G-8—SEE: *The Flying Spy*
Hodgson, William Hope, 198
Hoffman, Charles E., 185, 193
Holden, William, 275

The Hollow in the Hill (Christopher Milne), 286
Holton, Leonard—SEE: Wibberley, Leonard
Holy Blood, Holy Grail (Michael Baigent, Richard Leigh, & Henry Lincoln), 42-49
The Holy Grail Revealed: The Real Secret of Rennes-le-Château (R. Lionel & Patricia Fanthorpe), 40-49, 130
Holy Matrimony (film), 276
Homer, 20-21
Hoover, J. Edgar, 189
"Horror and the Limits of Violence: A Forum of Interviews" (ed. Douglas E. Winter), 179
"The Horror at His Heels" (Wyatt Blassingame), 186
Horror Literature: A Reader's Guide (Neil Barron), 273-274
The Horror of It All: Encrusted Gems from the "Crypt of Cthulhu" (ed. Robert M. Price), 192-193
Horrors and Unpleasantries (Sheldon Jaffery), 190
Houghton Mifflin, 255, 267
"The Hound" (H. P. Lovecraft), 193
"'The Hound'—A Dead Dog!" (Steven J. Mariconda), 193
House of Collectibles, 258
"The House of Evil" (Hugh B. Cave), 186
The House of the Burgesses (Michael R. Burgess), 298
"The House of the Worm" (Mearle Prout), 190
The House on the Strand (Daphne du Maurier), 54-57
"The House on the Way to Hell" (Edward Heron-Allen), 105
A House-Boat on the Styx (John Kendrick Bangs), 108-112
"House-Boat" stories (John Kendrick Bangs), 107-112
Howard, Robert E., 168, 171-174, 183, 185, 252
H.P. Lovecraft (S. T. Joshi), 177
"H.P. Lovecraft: A Basic Reading List" (Darrell Schweitzer), 184
"H.P. Lovecraft and Pseudomathematics" (Robert Weinberg), 184

Xenograffiti, by ROBERT REGINALD

H.P. Lovecraft and the Cthulhu Mythos (Robert M. Price), 192
"H.P. Lovecraft and *The Dream-Quest of Unknown Kadath*" (S. T. Joshi), 196-197
H.P. Lovecraft: The Decline of the West (S. T. Joshi), 192
"H.P. Lovecraft's *Fungi from Yuggoth*" (David E. Schultz), 197
H.R.H.: The Man Who Will Be King (Mayo Mohs & Tim Heald), 287
Huber, Gusti, 276
Hubin, Allen J., 254-255
"The Hubris of Science" Wells' Time Traveller" (Merritt Abrash), 181
Hugo Award, 16, 205, 287
Humanity Prime (Bruce McAllister), 122-124
Humphreys, M. L., 190
"The Hunger and Ecstasy of Vampires" (Brian Stableford), 204
Hunters of Gor (John Norman), 71, 73-74
Hutchison, Don, 189, 195
"Hyborean" world—SEE: *The Hyborian World of Conan*
The Hyborian World of Conan: Being Here Newly Researched and Embellished for the Information and Edification of the Faithful, and Including All Locales Set Forth in the Immortal Saga, As Well As in Divers Works of a Comical Nature, and in Certain Incunabula Attributed to the Master, Robert E. Howard (Julian May as "Juliana ux. Thaddei Maximi fecit"), *map*, 174
"Hyder Ragged"—SEE: Biron, Henry Chartres, Sir
Hyles, Vernon, 194
I Don't Live Here! (Pat Conrad), 280
I Found Cleopatra (Thomas P. Kelley), 172
"I, the Vampire" (Henry Kuttner), 196
"I Think the Government Stinks!: Stephen King's *Stand* on Politics" (Douglas Keesey), 197
"I Want My Cake! Thoughts on *Creepshow* and E.C. Comics" (Douglas E. Winter), 179
I Was a Teenage Frankenstein (film), 276

I Was a Teenage Werewolf (film), 276
IAFA—SEE: International Association for the Fantastic in the Arts
If Israel Lost the War (Richard Z. Chesnoff, Edward Klein, & Robert Littell), 28
If the South Had Won the Civil War (MacKinlay Kantor), 28
Ikenberry, Dennis, 215
Iliad (Homer), 20-21
Illustrated London News, 118
The Immortal Error (Elleston Trevor), 290
"In High Society" (Robert E. Howard), 171
In the Center of the Galaxy (ed. Forrest J Ackerman), 257
"In the Classroom: Teaching Tools" (Marshall B. Tymn), 188
"In the Dragon's Lair" (Hugh B. Cave as "Justin Case"), 195
"In the Midst of Life" (Richard Laymon), 188
In the Service of the King (Katherine Kurtz), 148
The Incredible Adventures of Dennis Dorgan (Robert E. Howard), 171
Index to the Science-Fantasy Publishers (Jack L. Chalker & Mark Owings), 259
Indick, Ben P., 180, 184, 186, 198
Inferno (Dante), 221, 226
Ingram, Eleanor M., 62-65
International Association for the Fantastic in the Arts, 274
International Science Fiction Yearbook, 274
International Union of Electrical Radio and Machine Workers, 284
"Interview with Dean R. Koontz" (Bill Munster), 188
"Introduction: Ooze from the Muse" (Robert Reginald), 7-8
An Introduction to the J. Lloyd Eaton Collection of Science Fiction and Fantasy (Clifford Wurfel), 261-262
Invasion of the Body Snatchers (film), 276
I.O. Evans Studies in the Philosophy and Criticism of Literature, 187
Ira Levin (Douglas Fowler), 187

The Iron Hand of Mars (Lindsey Davis), 214
Irving, Washington, 107, 112
Isaac, Rondall, 265-266
Isaac Asimov (Donald M. Hassler), 170, 195
Isaac Asimov's Robot City: Prodigy (Arthur Byron Cover), 152
Islandia (Austin Tappan Wright), 267-269
"The Isle of Wonders," 242
The Islar (Mark Saxton), 268
It: A Wild, Weird History of Marvelous, Miraculous, Phantasmagorical Adventures in Search of He, She, and Jess, and Leading to the Finding of "It": A Haggard Conclusion (John De Morgan), 25-27
It's Raining Corpses in Chinatown (ed. Don Hutchison), 195
"It's Raining Corpses in Chinatown" (Russell Gray), 195
"It's Up To You" (J. Edgar Hoover), 189
Ivan Efremov's Theory of Science Fiction (G. V. Grebens), 263
J. Lloyd Eaton Award, 170, 195
J. Lloyd Eaton Collection, 163, 261-262
Jack and the Check-Book (John Kendrick Bangs), 108
Jack London (Gorman Beauchamp), 179
"Jack's Nightmare at the Overlook: The American Dream Inverted" (Patricia Ferreira), 194
Jackson, Shirley, 179
Jacob, Piers Anthony—SEE: Anthony, Piers
"The Jade Joss" (T. T. Flynn), 195
"The Jade Monkey" (Robert E. Howard), 171
Jaffery, Sheldon, 169-170, 185-186, 189-190, 196, 198
JAI Press, 165
James, Francis, 185
James, Henry, 107
"James Herbert: Notes Toward a Reappraisal" (Ramsey Campbell), 186
James Tiptree, Jr. (Mark Siegel), 181
Jantsang, Tani, 193
Jean II, King of France, 66

Jenkins, Harry, 249
"Jenny Among the Zeebs" (William F. Nolan), 156
Jess (H. Rider Haggard), 27
Jesus Christ, 46-47
"Jewels of Fantasy: The Dunsanian Pastiches of Vernon Knowles" (Robert Reginald), 76-79
J.G. Ballard (Peter Brigg), 181
"J.N. Williamson" (Kevin E. Proulx), 198
Joan D. Vinge—SEE: *Suzy McKee Charnas*
Joan of Arc (history; Andrew Lang), 21
Joe Haldeman (Joan Gordon), 175
"Joe R. Lansdale" (Kevin E. Proulx), 198
"John Coyne: The Craftsman and the Monsters" (A. J. Montesi), 180
"John Farris" (Kevin E. Proulx), 198
John R. Commons Collection, 244
John Spencer & Co., 128-129, 247
The John Spencer Fantasy Publications (Mike Ashley), 247
Johns, Jorun, 215
Johnson, George Clayton, 154-155
Johnson, Robert Barbour, 171
Johnson, Samuel, 109
Johnson, (Walter) Ryerson "Johnny," 283
"Jonathan Carroll: Galen to Vienna to the World" (Edna Stumpf), 180
"Jones, J. Farragut"—SEE: Streib, Dan
Jones, Margaret "Peggy" (Burgess), 293
Jones, Robert Kenneth, 172, 190
"Jorgas" (Robert Nelson), 190
Joris of the Rock (Leslie Barringer), 84-90
Joron, Andrew, 184
Joshi, S. T., 169, 177, 184, 192-193, 196-198
Journal of the International Association for the Fantastic in the Arts, 274
Journey to the Center (Brian Stableford), 203
Joyner, Peggy S., 133
"J.R.R. Tolkien (David Stevens & Carol D. Stevens), 199

321

Xenograffiti, by ROBERT REGINALD

Le Juif errant [*The Wandering Jew*] (Eugène Sue), 117—SEE ALSO: *The Wandering Jew*
"Juliana ux. Thaddei Maximi fecit"— SEE: May, Julian
Jundis, Orvy, 173
Jungian psychology, 248
Justus, Douglas R., 176
Kabala, 99, 101
The Kabala of Numbers ("Sepharial" [William Gorn Old]), 99
Kagle, Steven, 198
Kafka, Franz, 194
Kajira of Gor (John Norman), 71
Kaleidoscope Books, 259
"Kalem, F. Gumby"—SEE: Robert M. Price
Kaluta, Michael William, 171-172
Kansas and Me: Memories of a Jewish Childhood (Annette Peltz McComas), 286
Kantor, MacKinlay, 28
Kapel, Betty Jane—SEE: Burgess, Betty Jane (Kapel)
The Karate Killers (Dan Streib), 289
"Karl Edward Wagner and the Haunted Hills (and Kudzu)" (Darrell Schweitzer), 180
Katselas, Milton, 276
Katydid & Other Critters (Robert Reginald), 237
Kaveny, Philip E., 182
Kay the Left-Handed (Leslie Barringer), 84
Keene, Day, 189
"Keeping Pace with the Master" (David B. Silva), 188
Keesey, Douglas, 197
Kelley, Thomas P., 172
Kent, Brian, 194, 197
Kent State University (Press), 277-278
Kerman, Judith B., 182
Kethley, T. William, Jr., 131-139
Keyes, Daniel, 288
"The Kid and the Cutthroats" (Theodore Roscoe), 189
Kies, Cosette N., 272-273
Killers from Hyperspace (William Voltz), 256
The Killing Star (George Zebrowski & Charles Pellegrino), 143

King, Stephen, 164, 177-178, 180-183, 185, 188, 191, 194, 197-198, 231
"King Cobra" (Sidney Hershel Small), 195
King George County, Virginia—SEE: Stafford County, Virginia
The King in Yellow (Robert W. Chambers), 198
King Javan's Year (Katherine Kurtz), 147-148
King Kelson's Bride (Katherine Kurtz), 148
King of the Dead (Frank Aubrey), 262
King Solomon's Children: Some Parodies of H. Rider Haggard (ed. Robert Reginald & Douglas Menville), 26-27
King Solomon's Mines (H. Rider Haggard), 23-24, 298
King Solomon's Wives; or, The Phantom Mines ("Hyder Ragged" *i.e.*, Henry Chartres Biron), 25-26
King Solomon's Wives (John De Morgan), 25-26
King Solomon's Treasures (John De Morgan), 25
The King's Justice (Katherine Kurtz), 147
Kinnaird, John, 183
Kioga of the Wilderness (William L. Chester), 193
Kiplinger, Christina, 186
Kirk, Russell, 180
Kittredge, Mary, 179-180
Klein, Edward, 28
Klein, T. E. D., 186
"A Knight of the Round Table" (Robert E. Howard), 171
Know Ye Not Agincourt (Leslie Barringer), 84
Knowles, Vernon, 76-79, 106
"KO'd at the OK Corral; or, The Perils of Pullulating Pseudonymity" (Robert Reginald), 228-230, 233
Koontz, Dean R., 188
"Kubla Khan" (Samuel Taylor Coleridge), 105
Kubrick, Stanley, 194
"Kubrick's or King's—Whose *Shining* Is It?" (James Smith), 184
"Kubrick's *The Shining*: The Specters and the Critics" (James Hala), 194

Kummer, Frederic Arnold, 112
Kurt Vonnegut (Donald E. Morse), 199
Kurtz, Katherine, 69, 145-149
Kuttner, Henry, 193, 196
L. Dickson and Thompson, 289
La Spina, Greye, 190
The Ladder (Vernon Knowles), 76, 78-79
Ladies of Hades (Frederic Arnold Kummer), 112
"The Lady Margaret" (Keith Roberts), 29
Lady of the Haven: Adventures of the Empire Princess (Graham Diamond), 251-252
Lady Oracle (Margaret Atwood), 207
Lammas Night (Katherine Kurtz), 149
Lancer Books, 235
"Lances of Tartary" (Malcolm Wheeler-Nicholson), 172
Land of Always-Night (Ryerson Johnson as "Kenneth Robeson"), 283
Landon, Brooks, 179, 188
Lane, Ann, 253
"The Landscape of Sin: The Ghost Stories of J. Sheridan Le Fanu" (Gary William Crawford), 198
Lang, Andrew, 19-22, 25-27
Lang, Jan Sellar, 20
Lang, John, 20
Lang, Leonora Alleyne, 21
Lange, John—SEE: Norman, John
"Languid Dreams: Andrew Lang and *The Book of Dreams and Ghosts*" (Robert Reginald), 19-22
Lansdale, Joe R., 189
Larson, Randall D., 169, 180, 183, 186, 191, 193
Lasser, David, 284
The Last Days of the Edge of the World (Brian Stableford), 202
"Laughing Like Hell: Brian Stableford's World of Agony" (Robert Reginald & Brian Craig), 202-205
Law, Richard, 177, 183
Laymon, Richard, 188
Le Guin, Ursula K., 182
Leahy, Katherine—SEE: Nelson, Katherine "Kathy" (Leahy)
LeBlanc, Richard, 265-266
Lee, Robert E., 37
Lee, Tanith, 184

Le Fanu, J. Sheridan, 198
Legend in Blue Steel (Spider Page), 158
"The Legend of Sleepy Hollow" (Washington Irving), 107
"The Legends of Camber of Culdi" (Katherine Kurtz), 147
Leialoha, Stephen E., 173
Leiber, Fritz, Jr., 16, 91-94, 175, 184, 186
Leigh, Richard, 42-49
Lem, Stanislaw, 194
Leroux, Gaston, 273
Lessing, Doris, 177
Levin, Barry R., 259
Levin, Ira, 187
Lewis, C. S., 177
Lewis Carroll (Beverly Lyon Clark), 193
Libraries Unlimited, 272-273
Library of Congress, 25
Lieut. Gullivar Jones: His Vacation (Edwin Lester Arnold), 119
"The Life of Death: Robert Nathan and the Necessity of Love" (Robert Reginald), 80-83
"The Light of Other Days" (Bob Shaw), 105
Lighter Than a Feather (David Westheimer), 28
"Limericks from Yuggoth" (Lin Carter), 197
Lin Carter: A Look Behind His Imaginary Worlds (Robert M. Price), 195-196
Lincoln, Henry, 42-49
Lindsay, David, 177
Lippincott & Crowell, 285
"Literary Awards in Science Fiction" (Howard DeVore), 176
"A Literary Copernicus" (Fritz Leiber, Jr.), 184
The Literature of Fantasy: A Comprehensive, Annotated Bibliography of Modern Fantasy Literature (Roger C. Schlobin), 264-265
Littell, Robert, 28
Little, Brown Co., 290, 292
Lobdell, Jared, 181
The Lodge of the Lynx (Katherine Kurtz & Deborah Turner Harris), 149

Xenograffiti, by ROBERT REGINALD

"Logan" series (William F. Nolan), 155-156
Logan's Run (William F. Nolan & George Clayton Johnson), 155-156
Logan's Search (William F. Nolan), 155-156
Logan's World (William F. Nolan), 155-156
London, Jack, 179
London Daily Telegraph, 117
London Evening News, 290
Long, Julius, 171, 183
The Long Night (Andrew Lytle), 285
Longmans, Green, 26
Look Out for Space (William F. Nolan), 156
Looking Backward, 2000-1887 (Edward Bellamy), 24, 253
Lord, Mindret, 171, 183
"Lords and Ladies" (Keith Roberts), 31
"Lords of Sorandor" (Katherine Kurtz), 145
Los Angeles Lakers, 286
Los Angeles Times, 287, 290
The Lost Harpooner (Leonard Wibberley), 290
The Lost Valley of Iskander (Robert E. Howard), 171
"The Lost Valley of Iskander" (Robert E. Howard), 171
Lovecraft, H. P., 62, 64-65, 177, 180, 184, 192-193, 196-197, 199
Lovecraft: A Look Behind the Cthulhu Mythos: The Background of a Myth That Has Captured a Generation (Lin Carter), 199
"Lovecraft and Lord Dunsany" (Darrell Schweitzer), 184
"Lovecraft As I Seem to Remember Him" (Robert M. Price as "F. Gumby Kalem"), 193
"'Lovecraftianity' and the Pagan Revival" (Robert M. Price), 197
"Lovecraft's Ghouls" (Will Murray), 193
"Lovecraft's Ladies" (Ben P. Indick), 184
"Lovecraft's Letters to Santa Claus: An Introduction" (Robert M. Price), 193
"Lovecraft's New York Exile" (David E. Schultz), 197
"Lovecraft's Revisions: How Much of Them did He Write?" (S. T. Joshi), 192
"The Loved Dead" (H. P. Lovecraft), 193
Loyola University, 294
Lumley, Brian, 193
Lumley, William, 197
Lupoff, Richard A., 173
The Lure of Adventure (Robert Kenneth Jones), 190
Lusignan, Geoffroy de, 66
Lutterworth, 290
Lynn, Ruth Nadleman, 273
Lytle, Andrew Nelson, 284-285
Ma (Jacob Ralph Abarbanell), 27
Macaulay, David, 255-256
Machen, Arthur, 198
Macrolife (George Zebrowski), 141-142
Madigan, Mark, 194
Madison (Wisconsin) Library, 244-245
The Magazine of Fantasy & Science Fiction, 286
"Magician" (C. C. Coffman), 250-251
Magicians of Gor (John Norman), 71
Magistrale, Anthony "Tony," 169, 191, 194, 197
Magsino, Frank, 173
Mahr, Kurt, 256
"Mail-Call of Cthulhu," 197
"Mainstream Horror in *Whispers* and *Phantoms*" (D. W. Taylor), 188
Malamud, Bernard, 180
"The Man Dog and Maine" (Burton Hatlen), 178
Man in a Cage (Brian Stableford), 202
The Man in the High Castle (Philip K. Dick), 28
"The Man in the Moon" (Homer Eon Flint), 171
"The Man Who Killed the Jew" (Edward Heron-Allen), 105-106
The Manchurian Candidate (Richard Condon), 280
"The Mandarin Ruby" (Robert E. Howard), 171
Mandino, Augustine A. "Og," 285
"Mano Pantea" (Edward Heron-Allen), 104

Xenograffiti, by ROBERT REGINALD

Manor Books, 260
Man's World (Charlotte Haldane), 66
The Many Facets of Stephen King (Michael R. Collings), 181
"Many Years Ago, When We All Lived in the Forest" (Charles L. Grant), 178
The Many-Colored Land (Julian May), 176
Maracaibo (Stirling Silliphant), 288
Marauders of Gor (John Norman), 71
The Marble Orchard (William F. Nolan), 157
"Margaret Atwood: The Young Woman in Agony" (Robert Reginald & Mary A. Burgess), 206-211
Margaret Drabble: Symbolic Moralist (Nora Foster Stovel), 191
Mariconda, Steven J., 193
Marinelli, Jean, 265-266
Marion Zimmer Bradley (Rosemarie Arbur), 181
"Mars" romance novels (Edgar Rice Burroughs, *et al.*), 119
Martin, George R. R., 152
Martin, Marcia, 261
"Martine" (pseud.), 260-261
Mary Poppins (P. L. Travers), 289
Mary Poppins (film), 289
Mary Poppins Comes Back (P. L. Travers), 289
Mary Poppins In Cherry Tree Lane (P. L. Travers), 289
Mary Poppins in the Park (P. L. Travers), 289
Mary Poppins Opens the Door (P. L. Travers), 289
Mary Shelley (Allene Stuart Phy), 187
"The Mask" (Vernon Knowles), 77
"The 'Masked Author Strikes Again': Writing and Dying in Stephen King's *The Shining*" (Mary Jane Dickerson), 194
"The Masque of the Red Death" (Edgar Allan Poe), 194
"Masquerade" (Mearle Prout), 171, 183
Massachusetts Institute of Technology (M.I.T.), 284
Massie, Elizabeth, 188-189
Master Publications, 256-257

"Masterpieces of Modern Fantasy: An Annotated Core List" (Roger C. Schlobin), 176
"The Mathematics in Science Fiction: Of Measure Zero" (Edward A. Boyno), 181
Matheson, Richard, 56, 154
Matheson, Richard Christian, 198
"A Matter of Choice: Stephen King's *Cujo* and Malamud's *The Natural*" (Debra Stump), 180
May, Julian, 168, 174, 176, 281
McAfee, Ward, 215
McAleer, John J., 164
McAllister, Bruce, 121-124
McCaffrey, Anne, 182
McCarthy, Joseph, 284
"McCarthy" era, 284
McComas, Annette Peltz, 285-286
McComas, Jesse Francis, 286
McCulley, Johnston, 172
McDowell, Michael, 186
McGhan, Harlan, 176
McGraw-Hill, 280
McMillan, William, 178
McTeague (Frank Norris), 194
Meaning in Star Trek (Karin Blair), 247-249
"Measuring the Marigolds: The Fall and Rise of Borgo Press" (Robert Reginald), 217-220
Media and the Church (Mayo Mohs), 287
Mellott, Constance M., 181-182
Melusine; or, Devil Take Her! (Charlotte Haldane), 66-69
Men of Distinction (play; Richard Condon), 280
Menville, Douglas A., 26
Mercenaries of Gor (John Norman), 71
"Merovingian Dreams: The Neustrian Fantasies of Leslie Barringer" (Robert Reginald), 84-90
Merril, Judith, 10, 16-17
Merritt, A., 189
Merton College, Oxford, 21
Meschkow, Sanford Z., 180
"The Metalinguistic Racial Grammar of Bellona: Ethnicity, Language and Meaning in Samuel R. Delany's *Dahlgren*" (Marleen Barr), 178

325

"The Metamorphosis" (Franz Kafka), 194
Methuen, 58
Meyers, Richard, 179
"Michael Hawk" series (Dan Streib), 289
"Michael McDowell and the Haunted South" (Michael E. Stamm), 186
Michener, James A., 288
Middleton, Richard, 198
The Midwich Cuckoos (John Wyndham), 288
Midwood Books, 235
"Mildew from Shaggai" (Robert M. Price), 197
Miles, Susan G., 188
Milford Award, 170
Milford Series: Popular Writers of Today, 168, 199
Miller, David M., 175
Miller, Steve, 279
Milne, A. A., 286
Milne, Christopher Robin, 286
The Mind Breakers (Dan Streib), 289
The Mind of Max Duvine (Elleston Trevor), 290
Mirage Press, 269, 271
Miranda, Vincent, 176
"The Mirror That Remembered" (Edward Heron-Allen), 105
"Mistress of the Blood-Drinkers" (Ralston Shields), 185
M.I.T.—SEE: Massachusetts Institute of Technology
Mitarachi, Sylvia Wright, 268
Modern Language Association, 277
Modern Science Fiction: Its Meaning and Its Future (Reginald Bretnor), 262-263
"A Modest Proposal" (Robert Reginald), 158-161
Mohs, Lewis, 286
Mohs, Mayo, 286-287
"The Mole Men Want Your Eyes" (Frederick C. Davis), 185
Molson, Francis J., 176, 188, 190
Monarch Books, 235
Monet, Lireve, 190
"Monkey See, Monkey Do" (Theodore Roscoe), 189
Monk's Magic (Alexander de Comeau), 58-61

"The Monster of Gruesome Grange" (R. Lionel & Patricia Fanthorpe), 130
The Monster of the Lagoon (George F. Worts), 196
Monterey, California, 292
Montesi, A. J., 180
Monty Python, 152
The Moon Metal (Garrett P. Serviss), 170
"Moon-Watcher, Man, and Star Child: *2001* as Paradigm" (Richard D. Erlich), 178
Moore, Rosalie, 263
Moore, Ward, 28, 34-39
"Moral/Immoral: The Fictional Universe of Michael Reaves" (Robert Reginald), 125-127
The Moral Voyages of Stephen King (Anthony Magistrale), 191
More Classics of the Horror Film (William K. Everson), 283
Morgan, Bassett, 190
Morrell, David, 178-179
Morris, William, 95, 98, 241-244, 253
Morrison, Michael R., 188, 197-198
Morrow, W. C., 198
Morse, Donald E., 199
"Mortimer Gray's History of Death" (Brian Stableford), 204-205
Mosig, Dirk W., 184
Moskowitz, Sam, 10-11, 198
Motel of the Mysteries (David Macaulay), 255-256
The Motion Menace (Ryerson Johnson as "Kenneth Robeson"), 283
"The Mound" (H. P. Lovecraft & Zealia Brown Bishop), 196
The Mouse That Roared (Leonard Wibberley), 290
The Mouse That Roared (film), 290
"Mouse That Roared" series (Leonard Wibberley), 290
The Mouse That Saved the West (Leonard Wibberley), 290
Moving the Mountain (Charlotte Perkins Gilman), 253
Mr. Bass's Planetoid (Eleanor Cameron), 292
Mr. Bonaparte of Corsica (John Kendrick Bangs), 108
Mr. Morton's Subtler, and Other Romances (John De Morgan), 26

Xenograffiti, by ROBERT REGINALD

Mr. Münchausen (John Kendrick Bangs), 108
Much Darker Days (John De Morgan), 26
Mundy, Talbot, 172
Munro, H. H.—SEE: "Saki"
Munster, Bill, 188
Murphy, Brian, 177
Murray, Will, 193, 197
"Mushroom Planet" series (Eleanor Cameron), 292
Mustazza, Leonard, 194, 197
"A Mutation of a Science Fiction Writer" (Stan Brooks), 188
"My Pupil—The Idiot!" (Hugh B. Cave), 186
Mycroft & Moran, 189-190
The Mysterious Christmas Shell (Eleanor Cameron), 292
Mystery, Detective, and Espionage Fiction (Michael L. Cook & Steve Miller), 279
A Mystery for Mr. Bass (Eleanor Cameron), 292
The Mystery of Edwin Drood (Charles Dickens), 105
"Naked Lady" (Mindret Lord), 171, 183
Naked to the Sun: Dark Visions of Apocalypse (Michael R. Collings), 181
A Name for Evil (Andrew Lytle), 285
"Narcissism and Romance in McCaffrey's *Restoree*" (Mary T. Brizzi), 177
Nathan, Robert, 56, 76, 79-83, 106, 256, 291
National Endowment of the Arts (NEA), 123
National Union Catalog, 163
The Natural (Bernard Malamud), 180
NEA—SEE: National Endowment of the Arts
"Neb" (Robert Reginald), 50-53
Nebula Award, 159-160
"The *Necronomicon*: The Origin of a Spoof" (Colin Wilson), 197
Nelson, Arthur Edward "Art," 294-296
Nelson, Arthur Edwin, 294
Nelson, Julie, 294
Nelson, (Mary) Katherine "Kathy" (Leahy), 294
Nelson, Mark, 294

Nelson, Michael, 294
Nelson, Phillip H., 189
Nelson, Richard, 294
Nelson, Robert, 171, 183, 190
Nelson, Violet (Riley), 294
Der Neologismen in der modernen französischen Science-Fiction (Felix Scherwinsky), 263-264
"Neustrian Cycle" series (Leslie Barringer), 84-90
New American Library, 288
New English Library, 290
New School for Social Research, 280
New Waggings of Old Tales (John Kendrick Bangs & Frank D. Sherman as "Two Wags"), 108
New Wave, 10, 16-18
New York Daily News, 287
New York University, 282
The New Yorker, 283
Newbolt, Henry, Sir, 95-98
Newcastle Publishing Co., 84
News from Nowhere (William Morris), 253
Newsletter of the Conference on Science-Fiction of the Modern Language Association—SEE: *Extrapolation*
Nicholls, Peter, 164
Night Hunter (Michael Reaves), 127
Night Shapes (William F. Nolan), 156
"The Night Wire" (H. F. Arnold), 190
Nino, Alex, 173
Nolan, William F., 154-157
Nomads of Gor (John Norman), 71, 74
Norden, Eric, 28
Norman, John (*i.e.*, John Lange), 70-75
Norman L. Munro, 26-27
"Norn" (Lireve Monet), 190
Norris, Frank, 194
"The North and South of Horror" (Alan Ryan), 178
Norton, Andre, 259
"Notes on an Entity" (Robert Bloch), 184
A Novel, a Novella, and Four Short Stories (Andrew Lytle), 285
Nugent, Nell Marion, 133
"Obed and Obadiah Marsh" (Robert M. Price & Tani Jantsang), 193
Obolensky, 285
Occidental College, 224

327

Xenograffiti, by ROBERT REGINALD

O'Connor, Flannery, 285
"O'Connor, Patrick"—SEE: Wibberley, Leonard
Octavia Butler—SEE: *Suzy McKee Charnas*
"The Octopus of Hongkong" (Loring Brent), 195
Odyssey (Homer), 20-21
The Official Price Guide to Comic & Science Fiction Books (Michael Resnick), 258-260
The Official Guide to Comic Books (House of Collectibles), 258
Official Guide to the Fantastics—SEE: *The Official Price Guide to Fantastic Literature*
The Official Price Guide to Fantastic Literature (House of Collectibles), 258-259
Olaf Stapledon (John Kinnaird), 183
Old, Walter Gorn (*i.e.*, Sepharial), 99
The Oldest Confession (Richard Condon), 280
Oliver, Chad, 154
"Oliver Onions: The Man at the Edge" (Mike Ashley), 198
Olsen, Lance, 199
Olympian Nights (John Kendrick Bangs), 108
The Omega Point (George Zebrowski), 140-141
The Omega Point Trilogy (George Zebrowski), 140-141
"On Be(com)ing a Librarian" (Robert Reginald), 221-227
"On the Edge: The Ghost Stories of Walter de la Mare" (Gary William Crawford), 198
"On 'The Loved Dead'" (David E. Schultz), 193
On Writing (Stephen King), 231
"Once, Out of Nature: The Topiary" (Michael N. Stanton), 194
"Once Upon a Time: An Introduction to *The Holy Grail Revealed: The Real Secret of Rennes-le-Château*, by Patricia and Lionel Fanthorpe" (Robert Reginald), 40-49
"One Is One and All Alone: Fritz Leiber's Solipsistic Fantasy" (Robert Reginald), 91-94
Onions, Oliver, 198

Operation: Countdown (Dan Streib), 288-289
The Operator 5 Story—SEE: *America's Secret Service Ace*
"'Orders from the House': Kubrick's *The Shining* and Kafka's 'The Metamorphosis'" (Mark Madigan), 194
"The Origin of Lovecraft's 'Black Magic' Quote" (David E. Schultz), 192
Orlando Furioso (Ariosto), 242
"The Other Side of Magic: A Few Remarks About Shirley Jackson" (Mary Kittredge), 179
Other Worlds, Other Gods: Adventures in Religious Science Fiction (ed. Mayo Mohs), 287
Ourland (Charlotte Perkins Gilman), 253
"Out of the Deep" (Robert E. Howard), 171, 183
"Out of the Silence" (Garret Smith), 196
Outlaw of Gor (John Norman), 71
"Outstanding Science Fiction Books: 1927-1979" (Joe De Bolt), 176
Over the Plum-Pudding (John Kendrick Bangs), 108
"Overview of American Paperback Publishers" (Piet Schreuders), 267
Owings, Mark, 259, 269-271
Pa (Jacob Ralph Abarbanell), 27
Pachter, Josh, 266
Page, Spider, 258
"The Palace of Illusions," 242
"Paladorean Idylls: Sir Henry Newbolt's *Aladore*" (Robert Reginald & Mary A. Burgess), 95-98
Pantheon Books, 252
"Papap's Planet" (William F. Nolan), 156
Paper Chase (Mark Saxton), 268
Paperbacks, U.S.A.: A Graphic History, 1939-1959 (Piet Schreuders), 266-267
Paralittératures (Yvon Allard), 245-246
Parente, Audrey, 186-187, 199
The Path Through the Trees (Christopher Milne), 286
Patrouch, Joseph F., Jr., 177-178

Xenograffiti, by ROBERT REGINALD

Patterns of the Fantastic: Academic Programming at Chicon IV (ed. Donald M. Hassler), 177-178
Patterns of the Fantastic II: [Academic Programming at ConStellation] (ed. Donald M. Hassler), 181-182
Pavane (Keith Roberts), 28-33
Pellegrino, Charles, 143
Peltz, Alfred, 285
Peltz, Annette—SEE: McComas, Annette Peltz
Peltz, Jennie, 285
Pendarves, G. G., 171, 183, 190
Penguin Press, 284
Pennsylvania State (Penn), 277
Perfecting Visions (George Zebrowski), 143
Peril Unlimited (Kurt Brand), 256
Perry, Ralph R., 195
Perry, Steve, 126-127
"Perry Rhodan" series (various), 256-258
Peter Beagle (Kenneth J. Zahorski), 187
Peter Davies, 289
"Peter Straub: From Academe to Shadowland" (Bernadette Bosky), 186
Phantom of the Opera (Gaston Leroux), 273
Phantoms (Dean R. Koontz), 188
Pharr, Mary, 197
Philip Allan, 103
Philip José Farmer (Mary T. Brizzi), 175
Philip K. Dick (Hazel Pierce), 177
Phoenix Renewed: The Survival and Mutation of Utopian Thought in North American Science Fiction (Hoda M. Zaki), 187
Phra the Phoenician—SEE: *The Wonderful Adventures of Phra the Phoenician*
Phy, Allene Stuart, 187
Pickle the Spy (Andrew Lang), 21
Pictures at an Exhibition (ed. Ian Watson), 130
Pierce, Earl, Jr., 171, 183
Pierce, Hazel, 177
Piercy, Marge, 177
Piers Anthony (Michael R. Collings), 178

Pilgrim Award, 162-166, 278
"Pilgrim Award Acceptance Speech" (Robert Reginald), 162-166
Planetfall (Arthur Byron Cover), 152
The Platypus of Doom and Other Nihilists (Arthur Byron Cover), 151
Playboy Press, 251-252, 276, 290
Players of Gor (John Norman), 71
"Playing Journalist" (Robert E. Howard), 171
"Playing Santa Claus" (Robert E. Howard), 171
Pleasure Books, 260
Pleasure Planet (Sharon Taylor as "Starr Trainor"), 260
Pocket Books, 91, 266
Poe, Edgar Allan, 194
"The Poetics of the Unconscious: The 'Strange Stories' of Robert Aickman" (Gary William Crawford), 186
"Poetry of Darkness: The Horror Fiction of Fritz Leiber" (Michael E. Stamm), 186
Pohl, Frederik, 107, 168, 175, 184, 278
Pollock, Walter H., 25-27
"The Pool" (Donald R. Burleson), 193
Popular Library, 266
Popular Publications, 196
Portfolio (*artwork*; Stephen E. Fabian), 174
Portrait of Jenny (Robert Nathan), 56, 80
The Poseidon Adventure (Paul Gallico), 288
The Poseidon Adventure (film), 288
Poseidon's Gold (Lindsey Davis), 214
Powell Books, 289
"The 'Power of Blackness' in *The Stand*" (Leonard Cassuto), 197
Powers, Tim, 188
Prairie Songs (Pat Conrad), 280
Pratt, Fletcher, 61, 112, 263
Prehistoric Epic! ("Marcus Cirilius"), 249, 251
"Prehuman Language in Lovecraft" (Will Murray), 197
Preiss, Byron, 125-126
"The Presence of Things Unseen" (Jack Sullivan), 178
Price, Robert M., 169, 180, 192-193, 195-197

329

Xenograffiti, by ROBERT REGINALD

Priest, Christopher, 190
Priest-Kings of Gor (John Norman), 71, 74
"Private Eye: A Semiotic Comparison of the Film *Blade Runner* and the Book *Do Androids Dream of Electric Sheep?*" (Judith B. Kerman), 182
Prizzi's Honor (Richard Condon), 280
Prodigy—SEE: *Isaac Asimov's Robot City*
"Professor Challenger" stories (Arthur Conan Doyle), 298
"Prospero Updated: The Fantasy of John Bellairs" (Robert Reginald & Mary A. Burgess), 99-102
Proulx, Kevin E., 198-199
Prout, Mearle, 171, 183, 190
"The Pseudo-Intellectual in Weird Fiction" (Robert M. Price), 197
Psychic Killer (film), 276
Publisher's Inc., 254
"The Publishing of Science Fiction" (Anthony Boucher), 263
Puck (magazine), 108
The Pulp Magazine Index (Leonard A. Robbins), 187, 191, 194, 196
Pulp Man's Odyssey: The Hugh B. Cave Story (Audrey Parente), 187
Pulpmaster: The Theodore Roscoe Story (Audrey Parente), 199
"The Purple Sapphire" (Edward Heron-Allen), 104
The Purple Sapphire and Other Posthumous Papers (Edward Heron-Allen as "Christopher Blayre"), 103-106
The Pursuit of the House-Boat: Being Some Further Account of the Divers Doings of the Associated Shades, Under the Leadership of Sherlock Holmes (John Kendrick Bangs), 108-112
Pygmalion (George Bernard Shaw), 276
Python Books, 258
The Quest for Saint Camber (Katherine Kurtz), 147
"Quietly Soaring: Peter Tremayne" (Christina Kiplinger), 186
"Quiller" spy novels (Elleston Trevor), 290
Quinliven, J. O., 186

Quinn, Seabury, 171, 183
R. Stockwell, 103
Rabkin, Eric S., 174-175
The Radio Flyers (Ralph Milne Farley), 172
Radio Times (magazine), 84
Raiders of Gor (John Norman), 71
"Rainbow" fairy tale series (Andrew Lang), 21-22
Raleigh, Walter, Sir, 109
Ramón, Leslie, 196
Ramsey Campbell (Gary William Crawford), 187
"Ramsey Campbell" (Kevin E. Proulx), 198
"Ramsey Campbell: An Appreciation" (T. E. D. Klein), 186
"Ramsey Campbell: No Light Ahead" (Jack Sullivan), 178
Ramsey, Shawn, 193
Randall, William R., 195
"Randolph Carter, Warlord of Mars" (Robert M. Price), 197
Ransom, John Crowe, 284
"The Rats in the Wall" (H. P. Lovecraft), 193
Ray Bradbury (William F. Touponce), 191
"Reading Lists in Science Fiction" (Marshall B. Tymn), 188
"The Real World and the Dream World in Lovecraft" (S. T. Joshi), 192
Reaves, (J.) Michael, 125-127
Rebecca (Daphne du Maurier), 54
The Rebellious Heroine (John Kendrick Bangs), 108
"The Recent Fantasies of Manly Wade Wellman" (Robert Coulson), 180
"Reconstructing *De Vermis Mysteriis*" (Robert M. Price), 193
"The Red Death's Sway: Setting and Character in Poe's 'The Masque of the Red Death' and King's *The Shining*" (Leonard Mustazza), 194
Red Twilight; World's End: Two Classic Novels from Argosy (Harl Vincent & Victor Rousseau), 196
"The Redrum of Time: A Meditation on Francisco Goya's 'Saturn Devouring His Children' and Stephen King's *The Shining*" (Greg Weller), 194

Xenograffiti, by ROBERT REGINALD

Reesman, Jeanne Campbell, 194
Reginald, Robert, 7-8, 26, 50-53, 162-166, 215-238, 296-298
"Reginald" stories ("Saki"), 236
René, King of Burgundy, 85
Renegades of Gor (John Norman), 71
Rennes-le-Château: Its Mysterious Secrets (R. Lionel & Patricia Fanthorpe), 130
"Repaying Service with Pain: the Role of God in *The Stand*" (Leonard Mustazza), 197
"A Requiem for Starmont House and FAX Collector's Editions, 1972-1993: A History and Bibliography" (Robert Reginald), 167-201
Resnick, Michael, 258-260
"Resources for Teaching Science Fiction" (Marshall B. Tymn), 176
Restoree (Anne McCaffrey), 177
"The Resurrected Enemy" ("Bron Fane" [R. Lionel Fanthorpe]), 129
The Return of Skull-Face (Robert E. Howard & Richard A. Lupoff), 173
The Return of the Time Machine (Egon Friedell), 185
"Return to Death" (J. Wesley Rosenquest), 171, 183
Rex Stout: A Biography (John J. McAleer), 164
Reynal and Hitchcock, 289
Reynolds, Mack, 24
"Richard Christian Matheson" (Kevin E. Proulx), 198
"Richard Middleton: Beauty, Sadness, and Terror" (Darrell Schweitzer), 198
Richards, Eva (Burgess), 293
Richardson, Darrell C., 167-168, 170-171, 281
Richardson, Dean, 170
"The Ringer of the Doorbell" (Jim Cort), 197
Riley, Frank, 287
Riley, Violet—SEE: Nelson, Violet (Riley)
Rinehart & Co., 288
"The River and the Road" (Vernon Knowles), 77-78
Roald Dahl (Alan Warren), 187
"Roald Dahl: Nasty, Nasty" (Alan Warren), 180

Robbins, Leonard A., 187, 191, 194, 196
Robbins, W. Wayne, 185
Robert Bloch (Randall D. Larson), 183
The Robert Bloch Companion (Randall D. Larson), 191
Robert E. Howard (Marc A. Cerasini & Charles E. Hoffman), 185
Robert Silverberg (Thomas D. Clareson), 178, 278
Robert Silverberg: A Primary and Secondary Bibliography (Thomas D. Clareson), 278
Robert Silverberg's Time Tours: The Dinosaur Trackers (Arthur Byron Cover, Tim Sullivan & John Gregory Betancourt as "Thomas Shadwell"), 152
Roberts, Keith, 28-33
Robertson, Morgan, 297
Robeson, Kenneth (house pseud.), 283
Robinson, Frank M., 288
Robots, Bombs, and Mutants (William Voltz), 256
Roddenberry, Gene, 249
Roger Zelazny (Carl B. Yoke), 175
Rogers, Whitney Louise, 219
Rogue of Gor (John Norman), 71
Roscoe, Theodore, 172, 188-191, 199
The Rose in Splendour (Leslie Barringer), 84
Rosenberg, Betty, 273-274
Rosenquest, J. Wesley, 171, 183
Rousseau, Victor, 196
R.R. Bowker Co., 254, 264, 273
Ruddick, Nicholas, 190
Rule Britannia (Daphne du Maurier), 54
Rush, James, 16
Russell, Ray, 154
Russell, William Clark, 117
"Russell Kirk: Ghost Master of Mecosta" (Don Herron), 180
"Rustlings and Slitherings in the Shadows" (Alan Ryan), 178
Rutgers University, 275
Ryan, Alan, 178
Ryan, Thomas P., 181
Ryhlick, Frank Wilbert—SEE: Riley, Frank
Saberhagen, Fred, 180

331

Xenograffiti, by ROBERT REGINALD

"Saberhagen's New Dracula: The Vampire As Hero" (Neal Wilgus), 180
"Sabrina" (pseud.), 260-261
"A Sacrifice to Science" (Adolphe de Castro), 197
Sagan, Carl, 143
Saint Camber (Katherine Kurtz), 147
"Saki" (pseud. of H. H. Munro), 236
Salvaggio, Ruth, 183
"Sam Space" series (William F. Nolan), 156
"Sam Spade" pastiches, 156
Samuel R. Delany (Jane Branham Weedman), 177
San Diego State University, 288
Sanders, Joe, 183, 188
"The Sandman Will Still Be There" (Alan Ryan), 178
Sapphires (Vernon Knowles), 76
"Sardonic Fantasistes: John Collier" (Ben P. Indick), 186
Sargent, Pamela, 143
Sarton, May (Eléanore Marie), 287-288
"Saturn Devouring His Children" (painting by Francisco Goya), 194
Savages of Gor (John Norman), 71, 74
Saxton, Mark, 267-269
Scheer, K. H., 256
Scherwinsky, Felix, 263-264
Schlobin, Roger C., 168, 176, 178-179, 264-265
"Schofield, Jonathan"—SEE: Streib, Dan
Scholastic Book Services, 292
Schreuders, Piet, 266-267
Schubert, Franz, 105
Schultz, David E., 192-193, 197
Schweitzer, Darrell, 169, 179-181, 184, 186-189, 198
Science Fiction: A Teacher's Guide and Resource Book (ed. Marshall B. Tymn), 187-188
"Science Fiction and Fantasy and the Academic Enterprise" (Donald M. Hassler), 177
"Science Fiction and Fantasy Collections in U.S. and Canadian Libraries" (Elizabeth Cummins Cogell), 176
Science Fiction and Fantasy Literature (Robert Reginald), 163
"Science Fiction and Fantasy Periodicals" (Marshall B. Tymn), 176
Science Fiction and Fantasy Research Index (Hal W. Hall), 164
Science Fiction and Fantasy Writers of America, Inc., 158-161
"Science Fiction Art: Some Contemporary Illustrators" (Vincent Di Fate), 176
Science Fiction Book Review Index (Hal W. Hall), 164
"Science Fiction Fandom/A History of an Unusual Hobby" (Joe Siclari), 176
Science Fiction in America, 1870s-1930s: An Annotated Bibliography of Primary Sources (Thomas D. Clareson), 277-278
"Science Fiction in the Movies" (Brooks Landon), 188
"Science Fiction Organizations and Societies" (Marshall B. Tymn), 176
"Science Fiction Periodicals" (Joe Sanders & Marshall B. Tymn), 188
Science Fiction Quarterly, 277
The Science Fiction Reference Book: A Comprehensive Handbook and Guide to the History, Literature, Scholarship, and Related Activities of the Science Fiction and Fantasy Fields (ed. Marshall B. Tymn), 175-176
Science Fiction Research Association, 160, 162-166, 274, 278
Science Fiction Review, 274
"Science Fiction Theater the Moebius Way" (Jane Bloomquist & William McMillan), 178
"Science Fiction Women: Victims, Rebels, Heroes" (Richard Law), 177
Science Wonder Stories, 284
The Science-Fantasy Publishers: A Critical and Bibliographic History (Jack L. Chalker & Mark Owings), 269-271
Science-Fiction Studies, 274, 278
Scientific Detective Monthly, 284
Scientific Romance in Britain, 1890-1910 (Brian Stableford), 202
Scortia, Thomas N., 288

Scott, J. E., 25
Scott, Walter, Sir, 20
"The Seance" (R. Lionel Fanthorpe as "Bron Fane"), 129
Seaside Library, 26
"Secret of the Earth Star" (Henry Kuttner), 196
Secret of the Earth Star and Others (Henry Kuttner, ed. Sheldon Jaffery), 196
The Seed and the Vision: On the Writing and Appreciation of Children's Books (Eleanor Cameron), 292
"Selected Obituaries" (Robert Reginald), 275-295
"Selected Reviews" (Robert Reginald), 239-275
"Self-Parody in Lovecraft's Revisions" (Will Murray), 197
Sellers, Peter, 290
Sentinels of Solitude (Clark Darlton), 256
"Sepharial"—SEE: Old, Walter Gorn
Serviss, Garrett P., 170
A Set of Chinese Boxes (Vernon Knowles), 78-79
Seuss, Dr., i.e., Theodore Seuss Geisel, 194
Seven Days in May (film), 276
"*Seven Men*" (Theodore Roscoe), 188
SF Criticism (Thomas D. Clareson), 278
SFRA—SEE: Science Fiction Research Association
SFRA Conference, Reno, 279
SFRA Newsletter—SEE: *SFRA Review*
SFRA Review, 274, 278
SFWA—SEE: Science Fiction and Fantasy Writers of America, Inc.
SFWA Forum, 158
"The Shadow over Derleth" (Paul Spencer), 198
Shadowfires—SEE: *Watchers*
Shadowings: The Reader's Guide to Horror Fiction, 1981-1982 (ed. Douglas E. Winter), 178-179
Shadows in Bronze (Lindsey Davis), 213-214
"Shadwell, Thomas" (i.e., Arthur Byron Cover, Tim Sullivan & John Gregory Betancourt), 152

Shakespeare, William, 100, 109-110, 129, 194
"Shakespeare in 58 Chapters: *The Shining* as Classical Tragedy" (Anthony Magistrale), 194
Shamrocks and Sea Silver and Other Illuminations (Leonard Wibberley), 291
Shanghai Year: A Westerner's Life in the New China (Peter Brigg), 185
"Shards from Shaggai" (Robert M. Price), 197
Shasta Publishers, 167, 170, 281
The Shattered Goddess (Darrell Schweitzer), 188
The Shattered World (Michael Reaves), 125-126
Shaw, Bob, 105
Shaw, George Bernard, 276
She (H. Rider Haggard), 23, 298
Shea, Michael, 186
Sheed, Andrews & McMeel, 247
Shelley, Mary Wollstonecraft, 187
Sheppard, Susan Bracey, 133
"Sherlock Holmes" series/pastiches (Arthur Conan Doyle and others), 109, 151, 297-298
Sherman, Frank D., 108
Shetler, Charles, 245
Shields, Ralston, 185
The Shining (Stephen King), 180, 194
The Shining (film), 194
The Shining Reader (ed. Anthony Magistrale), 194
"The Shop in the Off Street" (Vernon Knowles), 78
"A Short History of Science Fiction" (Marshall B. Tymn), 188
Shorter Works of Stephen King (Michael R. Collings), 182
The Shudder Pulps: A History of the Weird Menace Pulps of the 1930s (Robert Kenneth Jones), 172
Shy Leopardess (Leslie Barringer), 84-90
Shylock Holmes: His Posthumous Memoirs (John Kendrick Bangs), 108-109
The Sibling (Elleston Trevor as "Adam Hall"), 290
Siclari, Joe, 176
Sidney-Fryer, Donald, 192
Siegel, Mark, 181

Xenograffiti, by ROBERT REGINALD

"The Signaller" (Keith Roberts), 29-30
Silliphant, Stirling Dale, 288
Silva, David B., 188
Silver Nutmegs (Vernon Knowles), 76-79
The Silver Pigs (Lindsey Davis), 213
Silverberg, Robert, 16, 152, 178, 278
Simon & Schuster, 203, 280
The Sinful Ones—SEE: *You're All Alone*
The Sinister Power (Kurt Brand), 256
The Skin of Our Teeth (Thornton Wilder), 181
Sketch (magazine), 25
"Skylark" series (E. E. "Doc" Smith), 15
Slave Girl of Gor (John Norman), 71
"Slicing Away at Suburbia: The Fantastic Fiction of William F. Nolan" (Robert Reginald), 154-157
"The Slitherer from the Tomb" (Lin Carter), 197
Small, Sidney Herschel, 195
"Small World" (William F. Nolan), 154-155
Smith, Clark Ashton, 192-193
Smith, E. E. "Doc," 15, 183
Smith, Garret, 196
Smith, James, 194
Smith, Lynn S., 261-262
Smith, Thorne, 112
"Smith, Trevor Dudley"—SEE: Trevor, Elleston
"The Snow Girl" (Ray Cummings), 171
So Love Returns (Robert Nathan), 56, 80-83
"The Social Science Fiction of Robin Cook" (Thom Dunn), 178
"Solar Pons Meets Cthulhu" (S. T. Joshi), 193
"Solar Pons" stories (August Derleth), 193
Some Kind of Paradise: The Emergence of American Science Fiction (Thomas D. Clareson), 278
"Some Thoughts on Lovecraft" (Arthur Jean Cox), 184
Some Women of the University: Being a Last Selection from the Strange Papers of Christopher Blayre (Edward Heron-Allen), 103-106

Sometimes the Magic Works (Terry Brooks), 231
Son of the White Wolf (Robert E. Howard), 173
"Son of the White Wolf" (Robert E. Howard), 173
The Sound of Winter (Arthur Byron Cover), 151-152
"The Sources for 'From Beyond'" (S. T. Joshi), 197
Soylent Green (film), 276
Space (James A. Michener), 288
Space (TV), 288
Space for Hire (William F. Nolan), 156
Space Voyages, 1591-1920: A Bibliography of Works Held in the Library of the University of California, Riverside (Lynn S. Smith), 261-262
Spacedust One (C. C. Coffman), 249-251
Spacing Dutchman (Eric Vinicoff & Marcia Martin), 261
Sparacio, Ruth, 137
Sparacio, Sam, 137
Spencer, Kathleen, 183
Spencer, Paul, 198
The Spider-Men: A Science-Fantasy Adventure (Ralph Annan), 249, 251
Spur Award, 280
St. Andrews University (Scotland), 20
St. Martin's Press, 280
St. Nicholas (magazine), 170
St. Thomas College, 294
Stableford, Brian, 203-205
Stafford County, Virginia, 131-139
"The Stafford Connection: An Introduction to *Stafford County, Virginia Tithables, 1723-1790*, by John Vogt and T. William Kethley, Jr." (Robert Reginald), 131-139
Stafford County, Virginia Tithables, 1723-1790 (John Vogt & T. William Kethley, Jr.), 131-139
"The Stagnant Death" (H. Bedford-Jones), 172
Stamm, Michael E., 110-111, 186
The Stand (Stephen King),
"*The Stand*: Science Fiction into Fantasy" (Michael R. Collings), 180

334

Stanislaw Lem (J. Madison Davis), 194
Stanton, Michael N., 194
Stapledon, Olaf, 83, 140, 183
Star Trek (original TV series), 247-249, 259
Star Trek II: The Wrath of Khan (film), 276
Star Trek: Good News in Modern Images (Betsy Caprio), 247-249
Star Trek: The Next Generation (TV), 127
Stationfall (Arthur Byron Cover), 152
Starblaze Editions, 188
Starmont Contemporary Writers, 187, 191, 200
Starmont Facsimile Fiction, 189-191, 196, 201
Starmont Hardcover Collection, 184-185, 193-194, 201
Starmont House, Inc., 167-201, 278, 281-282
Starmont Magazine Indexes, 187, 191-192, 194, 196
Starmont Popular Culture Studies/Series, 189, 185-187, 189, 191-192, 195, 198-199, 201
Starmont Popular Fiction, 183, 188-190, 201
Starmont Pulp and Dime Novel Studies, 179, 181, 190, 201
Starmont Reader's Guides, 168, 174-179, 181-187, 189-195, 199, 201, 278
Starmont Reference Guides, 169, 179, 182, 185, 187, 195, 201
Starmont Studies in Literary Criticism, 169, 177-188, 191-192, 194-196, 198, 201
The Stars Will Speak (George Zebrowski), 143
Starship (magazine), 274
Starship Troopers (Robert A. Heinlein), 16
The Star-Spangled Crunch (Richard Condon), 280
Startling Mystery Stories, 180
Startling Stories, 182
"The Statement of Lin Carter" (Robert M. Price), 193
Stella Nova (Robert Reginald), 162-163
Stellar Publishing Corp., 284

Stephen King (Douglas E. Winter), 177
"Stephen King: A Bibliography" (Marshall B. Tymn), 180
"Stephen King and His Readers: A Dirty, Compelling Romance" (Brian Kent), 197
"Stephen King and Peter Straub: Fear and Friendship" (Bernadette Bosky), 180
"Stephen King and the Lovecraft Mythos" (Robert M. Price), 180
"Stephen King and the Tradition of American Naturalism in *The Shining*" (Jeanne Campbell Reesman), 194
"Stephen King as an Epic Writer" (Ben P. Indick), 180
Stephen King as Richard Bachman (Michael R. Collings), 182
"Stephen King in Context" (Joseph F. Patrouch, Jr.), 177
The Stephen King Phenomenon (Michael R. Collings), 185
"Stephen King with a Twist: The E.C. Influence" (Debra Stump), 180
"Stephen King's American Gothic" (Gary William Crawford), 180
"Steve Rasnic Tem" (Kevin E. Proulx), 198
Stevens, Carol D., 199
Stevens, David, 199
Stevenson, Noel C., 44
Stevenson, Robert Louis, 22-23, 107
"A Stitch in Time: Free Will in Ward Moore's *Bring the Jubilee*" (Robert Reginald), 34-39
"Stone Children" series (Eleanor Cameron), 292
Stonewords: A Ghost Story (Pat Conrad), 280
Stories of the Unforeseen (Rondall Isaac), 265-266
"Story-Writing" (H. P. Lovecraft), 184
Stoughton, Tony, 286
Stovel, Nora Foster, 191
Stowaway to the Mushroom Planet (Eleanor Cameron), 292
"The Strange Case of Robert Ervin Howard" (Charles Hoffman & Marc A. Cerasini), 193

Xenograffiti, by ROBERT REGINALD

"Strange Lessons: Edward Heron-Allen's Cosmopoli Tales" (Robert Reginald), 103-106
"Strange Manuscript Found in the Vermont Woods" (Lin Carter), 193
The Strange Papers of Dr Blayre (Edward Heron-Allen), 103-106
Stranger in a Strange Land (Robert A. Heinlein), 16
Stranger Suns (George Zebrowski), 142
Straub, Peter, 180, 186
Street & Smith, 25, 195
The Street of Queer Houses and Other Stories (Vernon Knowles), 76-79
"Street of Shadows" (TV; Michael Reaves), 127
Streib, Daniel Thomas "Dan," 288-289
Strysik, John, 193
Stump, Debra, 180
Stumpf, Edna, 180
Sturgeon, Theodore, 15, 176
"Styx Tryx: The Humorous Fantasies of John Kendrick Bangs" (Robert Reginald & Mary A. Burgess), 107-112
"The Subtle Terrors of Charles L. Grant" (Don D'Ammassa), 186
Success Unlimited (magazine), 285
Sudden Fear: The Horror and Dark Suspense Fiction of Dean R. Koontz (ed. Bill Munster), 188-189
Sue, Eugène, 117, 119, 188
Sugarman, Loual B., 190
"The Suicide Squad and the Murder Bund" (Emile C. Tepperman), 189
Sullivan, Jack, 178
Sullivan, Tim, 152
The Super Feds: A Facsimile Selection of Dynamic G-Men Stories from the 1930s (ed. Don Hutchison), 189
Supernatural Fiction for Teens: More than 1300 Good Paperbacks to Read for Wonderment, Fear, and Fun (Cosette N. Kies), 272-273
Supernatural Stories, 128-130
Surfacing (Margaret Atwood), 206-207
Sunspacer (George Zebrowski), 143
The Sunspacers Trilogy (George Zebrowski), 143
Susann, Jacqueline, 297
Sutherland, Duke of, 20
Suzy McKee Charnas, Octavia Butler, Joan D. Vinge (Marleen S. Barr, Ruth Salvaggio, Richard Law), 183-184
Swan (publisher), 290
The Swarm (Arthur Herzog), 288
The Swarm (film), 288
Swords of Shahrazar (Robert E. Howard), 172
Swigart, Leslie Kay, 164
"Synopses of Stephen King's Fiction" (Sanford Z. Meschkow), 180
T Tauri (Associated Student Body, CSUSB), 215-216
A Talent for Loving; or, The Great Cowboy Race (Richard Condon), 280
"Tales of Childhood and the Grave: Ray Bradbury's Horror Fiction" (Darrell Schweitzer), 186
Target Earth (film), 276
Tarnsman of Gor (John Norman), 70-71, 74
Taylor, D. W., 188
Taylor, R. G., 265
Taylor, Sharon, 260
"Teacher-Preacher: R. Lionel Fanthorpe and the Literature of Abundity" (Robert Reginald), 128-130
"A Teacher's Reference Shelf" (Marshall B. Tymn), 188
"Teaching Science Fiction as Current Events" (Lloyd Biggle, Jr.), 188
"T.E.D. Klein" (Robert M. Price),
Tem, Steve Rasnic, 198
The Tempest (William Shakespeare), 100
The Templar Treasure (Katherine Kurtz & Deborah Turner Harris), 149
Temple University, 275
"Tentacles in Dreamland: Cthulhu Mythos Elements in the Dunsanian Stories" (Will Murray), 197
Tepperman, Emile C., 189, 297
The Terrible Churnadryne (Eleanor Cameron), 292
Terror for Sale (Dan Streib), 289

Xenograffiti, by ROBERT REGINALD

"Textual Problems in Lovecraft" (S. T. Joshi), 184
"Theobald, Lewis"—SEE: Lovecraft, H. P.
Theodore Sturgeon (Lahna F. Diskin), 176
The Theta Syndrome (Elleston Trevor), 290
"'They' Live! The Parodies of H. Rider Haggard" (Robert Reginald), 23-27
They: Three Parodies of H. Rider Haggard's She (ed. Robert Reginald & Douglas Menville), 26
They'd Rather Be Right (Frank Riley & Mark Clifton), 287
The Thing from the Lake (Eleanor M. Ingram), 62-65
"The Thing from the Swamp" (Hugh B. Cave), 186
"Thing of Darkness" (G. G. Pendarves), 171, 183
"The Thing That Smelt" (Edward Heron-Allen), 104
Things Beyond Midnight (William F. Nolan), 156
"Things That Go Bump in the Movies" (Craig Shaw Gardner), 179
The Third Millennium (Brian Stableford), 203
"Thirty Years, 1965/66-1995/96: An Introduction to *T Tauri*" (Robert Reginald), 215-216
Thomas Nelson & Sons, 84
"Thornton Wilder as Fantasist and the Science-Fiction Antiparadigm: The Evidence of *The Skin of Our Teeth*" (Jared Lobdell), 181
The Thousand and One Nights (myth), 113, 115
"A Thousand Nights in Serendip: Piers Anthony's *Hasan*" (Robert Reginald), 113-116
"Three by Bachman" (Don D'Ammassa), 180
"Three Faces of Evil: The Monsters of *Whispers*, *Phantoms*, and *Darkfall*" (Michael A. Morrison), 188
"Three Poets of Horror: Tierney, Breiding, and Brennan" (Steve Eng), 186-187
The Thrill Book, 195

Through the Earth (Clement Fezandié), 170
Tierney, Richard L., 184, 187
Time (magazine), 287
Time and Again (Jack Finney), 56
Time and Mr. Bass (Eleanor Cameron), 292
The Time Machine (H. G. Wells), 181, 204
The Time Machine (film and TV), 276
The Time Tunnel (TV), 276
Times Mirror, 287
Tiptree, James, Jr., 181
Titans Duel (Dan Streib), 289
T-K Graphics, 181
"T.M. Wright" (Kevin E. Proulx), 198
To Challenge Chaos (Brian Stableford), 202
To the Green Mountains (Eleanor Cameron), 292
Tolkien, J. R. R., 113, 199
"Tomorrow" (Arthur Leo Zagat), 171
"Tongman's Bargain" (William R. Randall), 195
Toppleton's Client; or, A Spirit in Exile (John Kendrick Bangs), 108
Torture Trek and Eleven Other Tales of the Wild West (Ryerson Johnson), 283
The Totem (David Morrell), 179
Toughest in the Legion (Theodore Roscoe, ed. Sheldon Jaffery), 189
"Toughest in the Legion" (Theodore Roscoe), 189
Touponce, William F., 191
"Toward a History of Science Fiction" (Thomas D. Clareson), 175-176
"The Tower from Yuggoth" (Ramsey Campbell), 197
The Towering Inferno (film), 288
"Trainor, Sandy or Starr"—SEE: Taylor, Sharon
"The Transition of Colin Wilson" (Charles Hoffman & Marc A. Cerasini), 193
Travers, P. L., 289
"The Treasure of Shaibar Khan" (Robert E. Howard), 172
"The Treasures of Tartary" (Robert E. Howard), 172
A Treasury of Success Unlimited (Og Mandino), 285
Tremayne, Peter, 186

337

Xenograffiti, by ROBERT REGINALD

Trevor, Elleston, 289-290
Tribesmen of Gor (John Norman), 71
The Trident Hijacking (Dan Streib), 289
"The True History of the Tcho-Tcho People" (Robert M. Price & Tani Jantsang), 193
Tuck, Donald H., 164
"A Turbot at a Time: The Mystery Novels of Lindsey Davis" (Robert Reginald), 212-214
"The Turkish Menace" (Robert E. Howard), 171
Twayne U.S. Authors Series, 168
Twentieth Century Fox, 288
"Twilight" series (various), 272
Twilight Eyes (Dean R. Koontz), 188
The Twilight Zone (TV), 127
Two and Two Make Five (Vernon Knowles), 76-79
The Two Kingdoms (Mark Saxton), 268
"Two Views of the Sentient Computer: Gerrold's *When HARLIE Was One* and Ryan's *The Adolescence of P-1*" (Constance M. Mellott), 181-182
"Two Wags"—SEE: Bangs, John Kendrick & Sherman, Frank D.
"Tycho Bass" series—SEE: "Mushroom Planet" series
Tymn, Marshall B., 169, 173, 175-176, 180, 187-188, 264-265, 277
"The Ultimate Horror: The Dead Child in Stephen King's Stories and Novels" (Leonard G. Heldreth), 180
The Ultimate Solution (Eric Norden), 28
"The Uncanny Power of Edwin Cobalt" (Henry Kuttner), 196
"Under the Green Star" (Lin Carter), 194-194
"Under the Tomb" (Robert Nelson), 171, 183
"Under Your Spell" (Henry Kuttner), 196
Understanding Contemporary American Science Fiction (Thomas D. Clareson), 278
"Uneasy Lies the Head" (Theodore Roscoe), 172

Unfinished Symphony (Franz Schubert), 105
The Unheard Music (Eleanor Cameron), 292
University of Baltimore, 275
University of California, Berkeley, 285-286
University of California, Los Angeles (UCLA), 291
University of California, Riverside (UCR), 163, 262
"University of Cosmopoli" tales (Edward Heron-Allen), 103-106
University of Florida, 285
University of Iowa, 288
University of Kansas at Lawrence, 283
University of Maryland, 275
University of Minnesota, 294
University of Reading, 202
University of South Carolina Press, 278
University of Southern California (USC), 223-224, 227, 288
University of the South, 285
Unknown (Worlds), 91, 195
The Unseen King (Tyson Blue), 191
Urania's Daughters: A Checklist of Women Science-Fiction Writers, 1692-1982 (Roger C. Schlobin), 179
"Urban Gothic: The Fiction of Ramsey Campbell" (Gary William Crawford), 180
Vagabonds of Gor (John Norman), 71
"Val Stearman (La Noire)" series ("Bron Fane" [R. Lionel Fanthorpe]), 129
Valdar the Oft-Born: A Saga of Seven Ages (George Griffith), 119, 170
van Vogt, A. E., 15
Vanderbilt University, 284
Vandegrift, George, 185
Vanguard Press, 287
"vanity" publishing, 249-251, 265-266
Vantage Press, 249, 263, 265
Varney the Vampyre; or, The Feast of Blood; a Romance (unknown), 262
Venus in Copper (Lindsey Davis), 214
Verlag Anton Hain, 263
Verne, Jules, 13-14
Viereck, George Sylvester, 119

Xenograffiti, by ROBERT REGINALD

Village of the Damned (film), 288
Villani, Jim, 177
Vincent, Harl, 196
Vinge, Joan, 183-184
Vinicoff, Eric, 261
Virgin Books, 266
Virginia, history of, 131-139
Virginia Northern Neck Land Grants, 1694-1742 (Gertrude E. Gray), 133
Virginia State Archives, 137
Virginia State Library, 133
"Vivo, Ergo Sum: The Problem of Immortality in Edwin Lester Arnold's *Phra the Phoenician*" (Robert Reginald), 117-120
E. Vizetelly, 25
Vizetelly & Co., 26
Vogt, John, 131-139
"The Voice Says Die!" (Edward S. Williams), 189
Voltz, William, 256
"The Volume Out of Print" (Jim Cort), 193
Volunteers for Frago (Kurt Brand), 256
Vonnegut, Kurt, 199
"W.C. Morrow: Forgotten Master of Horror—First Phase" (Sam Moskowitz), 198
Waggoner, Diana, 264-265
Wagner, Karl Edward, 179
Wahrman, Sig, 256
Wakefield, H. Russell, 198
The Walking Shadow (Brian Stableford), 202
Wallace, Irving, 297
Walt Disney Studios, 288-289
The Waltzing Wizard: Cartoons (Alexis A. Gilliland), 191
The Wandering Jew (George Sylvester Viereck & Paul Eldridge), 119—SEE ALSO: *Le Juif errant*
Warner Books, 247
Warren, Alan, 180, 186-187, 198
Warren, Robert Penn, 173, 284
Watson, Ian, 130
Watchers & Shadowfires (Dean R. Koontz), 188
"The Water Sculptor" (George Zebrowski), 140
The Water-Ghost and Others (John Kendrick Bangs), 108

We Are All Legends (Darrell Schweitzer), 189
The Weans (Robert Nathan), 256
Webb, Christopher—SEE: Wibberley, Leonard
Weedman, Jane Branham, 177
Weinbaum, Stanley G., 15
Weinberg, Robert, 168, 171-174, 179, 181, 183-184, 190
Weinstein, Lee, 198
Weird Tales, 65, 173
The Weird Tales Story (Robert Weinberg), 173
The Weirds: A Facsimile Selection of Fiction from the Era of the Shudder Pulps (ed. Sheldon Jaffery), 185-186
Welch, Raquel, 252
"The Welcome" (C. C. Coffman), 250-251
The Well at the World's End (William Morris), 243-244
Weller, Greg, 194
Wellman, Manly Wade, 190
Wells, H. G., 13-14, 181, 183, 204
Wendell, Carolyn, 176
"Wendy Torrance, One of King's Women: A Typology of King's Female Characters" (Jackie Eller), 194
The Werewolves of London (Brian Stableford), 204
The Western Pulp Hero: An Investigation into the Psyche of an American Legend (Nick Carr), 191
Western Writers of America (WWA), 280
Westheimer, David, 28
Weston, Ronald L., 178
Wetzel, George, 184
"What Hath Me?" (Henry Kuttner), 196
"What Makes Him So Scary?" (Ben Indick), 180
Wheeler-Nicholson, Malcolm, 172
When HARLIE Was One (David Gerrold), 181
"When the Stars Are Right" (Richard L. Tierney), 184
When We Were Very Young (A. A. Milne), 286

Xenograffiti, by ROBERT REGINALD

"Where None (No One) Have Gone Before" (TV; Michael Reaves & Diane Duane), 127
The Whisper of the Axe (Richard Condon), 280
Whispers (Dean R. Koontz), 188
"Whispersoft and Shadowfast" (Roger C. Schlobin), 178
White, Edward, 215
"The White Boat" (Keith Roberts), 31-32
"White Mother of Shadows" (George Vandegrift), 185
Who Done It? (Ordean Hagen), 254-255
"Who Wrote 'The Mound'?" (S. T. Joshi), 196
"Who's Who in Cover Art" (Piet Schreuders), 266-267
Wibberley, Leonard (Patrick O'Connor), 290-291
"Wild Card" novels (George R. R. Martin), 152
Wilde, Oscar, 204
Wilder, Thornton, 181
Wildside Press, 219
Wilgus, Neal, 180
William Gibson (Lance Olsen), 199
Williams, Charles, 183
Williams, David, 91
Williams, Edward S., 189
Williamson, Chet, 180
Williamson, J. N., 198
"Willoughby, Lee Davis"—SEE: Streib, Dan
Wilson, Colin, 193, 197
Wilson, Donald, 262
Wilson, F. Paul, 198
Wilson, Gahan, 112
"Winner Takes All" (C. C. Coffman), 250-251
Winnie-the-Pooh (A. A. Milne), 286
Winnipeg, Manitoba, 292
Winter, Douglas E., 177-179
Winter Kills (Richard Condon), 280
Wisconsin State Historical Society, Madison Library, *Author-Title Catalog*, 244-245
Witch Bitch ("Sabrina"), 260
Wolfe, Gary K., 169, 177
Wolfe, Gene, 183
"The Wolf-Woman" (Bassett Morgan), 190
Wollheim, Donald A., 3, 71, 202
"The Woman Science Fiction Writer and the Non-Heroic Male Protagonist" (Jim Villani), 177
"Woman on the Edge of Narrative: Language in Marge Piercy's Utopia" (David L. Foster), 177
Wonder Stories (*Quarterly*), 284
The Wonderful Adventures of Phra the Phoenician (Edwin Lester Arnold), 117-120
The Wonderful Flight to the Mushroom Planet (Eleanor Cameron), 292
Workers Alliance of America, 284
World Publishing Co., 275
"World Without Air" (Henry Kuttner), 196
The World's Desire (Andrew Lang & H. Rider Haggard), 22
World's End—SEE: *Red Twilight*
"Worlds Within Worlds" (Philip M. Fisher, Jr.), 196
Worlds Within Worlds: Four Classic Argosy Tales of Science Fiction (various), 196
"Worlds Without End" (R. Lionel Fanthorpe), 128
Worts, George F., 196
"The Writing Awards" (Harlan McGhan), 176
Wright, Austin Tappan, 20, 267-269
Wright, Sylvia—SEE: Mitarachi, Sylvia Wright
Wright, T. M., 198
"The Wrong Move" (Ralph R. Perry), 195
Wurfel, Clifford, 261-262
WWA—SEE: Western Writers of America
Wylie, Philip, 263
Wyndham, John, 288
"Xanth" series (Piers Anthony), 115
Yarbro, Chelsea Quinn, 186
"The Year in Review" (1981-1982), 179
"The Yellow Cobra" (Robert E. Howard), 171
"Yellow Shadows" (Don Hutchison), 195
The Yellow Wallpaper (Charlotte Perkins Gilman), 253
Yoke, Carl B., 175

Xenograffiti, by ROBERT REGINALD

Young Blood (Brian Stableford), 204
Young Magicians (ed. Lin Carter), 241
You're All Alone (Fritz Leiber, Jr.), 91-94
"Yours Truly, Robert Bloch" (Randall D. Larson), 186
Z Is for Zombie (Theodore Roscoe), 191
Zagat, Arthur Leo, 171, 196
Zahorski, Kenneth J., 169, 187, 264-265
Zaki, Hoda M., 169, 187
Zardoz (film), 101
Zebrowski, George, 140-144, 231
Zelazny, Roger, 16, 175
Zoe Rising (Pat Conrad), 280

www.ingramcontent.com/pod-product-compliance
Ingram Content Group UK Ltd.
Pitfield, Milton Keynes, MK11 3LW, UK
UKHW041422180426
11947UKWH00007B/240